THE NEXUS

International Terrorism and Drug Trafficking from Afghanistan

THE NEXUS

International Terrorism and Drug Trafficking from Afghanistan

FRANK SHANTY

PENTAGON PRESS

The Nexus: International Terrorism and Drug Trafficking from Afghanistan
by **Frank Shanty**

First Indian Edition 2012

ISBN 978-81-8274-623-7

First published by ABC-CLIO, LLC, 130 Cremona Drive, P.O. Box 1911, Santa Barbara, California 93116-1911. This edition published in arrangement.

Published in India by

PENTAGON PRESS
206, Peacock Lane, Shahpur Jat
New Delhi-110049
Phones: 011-64706243, 26491568
Telefax: 011-26490600
email: rajan@pentagonpress.in
website: www.pentagonpress.in

Printed at **Chaman Enterprises**, 1603, Pataudi House,
Darya Ganj, New Delhi - 110 002.

Never be Diverted from the Truth by What You Would Like to Believe.

Statement from an unknown source provided
by my father, Dr. Frank Shanty

Contents

Preface

This book examines criminal drug traffickers and international terrorist networks in Afghanistan from 1979 to 2006, to ascertain whether sufficient evidence exists to substantiate claims of an operational nexus between international criminal drug traffickers and international terrorist networks in Afghanistan. Data on significant factors affecting the opium trade, terrorism, and nexus issues was collected through 2006.[1]

The research strategy was single-case study utilizing embedded units of analysis. Data sources included historical and contemporary documents, articles, reports, and interviews with knowledgeable individuals. A recurrent theme in the literature was the lack of "open source" empirical data relative to specific international drug/terror group alliances in Afghanistan. Claims supporting a nexus were often based on anecdotal reports which lacked specific detail and corroborating information.

The epistemological basis of this research is "critical intersubjectivity."[2] To establish the epistemological validity of the findings the methodological process of data triangulation (Yin, 2003, pp. 97–99)[3] was utilized to provide a systematic intersubjective verification to the analytical process. The analytical strategies relied on "theoretical propositions" and the use of "rival explanations" as described by Yin (1994, 1998, and 2003). The initial propositions provided the framework for building an explanation of the case.

This study takes a critically intersubjective perspective in that it involved the examination of conflicting and differing views of many individuals with various backgrounds, experiences, beliefs, and motivations.[4] Combining critical intersubjectivity[5] (Fay, 1996; Heron and Reason 1997 and 1997a) and data triangulation (Yin, 2003) provide a systematic and holistic evaluation and analysis of the data; a more focused and apt method for scrutinizing and verifying information.

Therefore, through a process of interconnectability this study attempted to provide a comprehensive and objective understanding of the purported relationship between Afghan opium trade actors and international terrorists who have operated or perpetrated terrorist activity from Afghanistan. My conclusions and findings were based on a multiplicity of data sources, various methods of data collection, many conflicting perspectives, and required cross-validation of the data extracted from these sources.[6]

This study examined three distinct phenomena. First, the existence, characteristics, and behavior of international terrorists operating from Afghanistan, specifically the evolution and ascendancy of Al Qaeda, and the Taliban, and the nature of their relationship. Second, Afghanistan's opium trade was examined relative to specific actor involvement. Third, allegations of a linkage between terrorists in Afghanistan and international drug criminals were examined.

An initial search for relevant topic-related material was conducted in an attempt to summarize the current state of knowledge relative to the purported drug trafficking-terrorist nexus in Afghanistan. An emphasis was placed on the central or major findings of the works, key positions taken by knowledgeable sources, conclusions drawn, and relevant methodological issues. The literature search attempted to encompass all relevant issues and to access the current thinking on this subject. From this background of information additional insights were obtained and new questions generated. Data sources included books, monographs, scholarly articles, news reports, and government documents, including U.S. Congressional transcripts and interviews with subject/area experts.

The terms empirical, circumstantial, and anecdotal evidence as defined in chapter 1 are utilized in this study to provide the author's assessment of the data used in reviewed reports and obtained in interviews as evidence of the existence or lack of existence of linkage between international drug traffickers, particularly drugs from Afghanistan, and terrorist networks with global reach.

Additionally, a review of the current state of knowledge aided in the preparation of specific relevant questions which formed the basis for addressing the propositions cited in chapter 1 (Cooper, 1984; cited in Yin, 2003, p. 9) and underlined specific information which needed to be collected, examined, and triangulated. The crime-terror nexus in general is a fairly recent international security concern. Receiving the most attention regarding the alleged links between terrorism and crime is in the area of illicit narcotics. However, specific detail within this realm is scant at best and "derived from relatively few cases" (Schmid, 2004, p. 44).[7] Consequently, this phenomenon is an emergent area of inquiry.

The study's design and data collection techniques were guided by the availability of credible sources given the limited and problematic range of material available on activity which, by its very nature, is organizationally covert and operationally secretive: namely drug trafficking and terrorism. Conversely, information regarding underworld or otherwise surreptitious activity that is available needs to be subjected to a rigorous evaluation regarding the credibility of the providing source.

The primary objective of this work was to determine if specific terrorists/ extremist groups based in or operating from Afghanistan are deriving revenue from the opium trade or are aligned operationally with international drug trafficking networks.

During the course of this study it was necessary to utilize mainstream as well as non-mainstream media sources and to seek out reports that were reliable, detailed, and preferably investigative in scope.[8] The reliability and subsequent utilization of a given report was based on the in-country experience of the author, the news outlet delivering the story, and whether the information added credible input to this study. This is a particularly tough problem to negotiate considering the various and often competing perspectives of various credible persons and source material and further highlights the need for a rigorous triangulation of data from documentary as well as interviewed sources and cross-triangulation between both.

Moreover, many news reports are merely restatements of previously published articles by various journalists through different media outlets. Conversely, there have been several investigative reports that provided compelling information regarding linkages between certain terrorist entities and the opium trade in Afghanistan. While not carrying the weight of direct evidentiary data, information from these reports, when examined holistically with other credible and triangulated source material, can provide a compelling reason to believe that various state and non-state actors are involved in relationships with drug trade entrepreneurs.[9]

In most research when investigating areas of activity where present knowledge is limited due to a lack of prior empirical efforts the analyst is often compelled to make judgments[10] based on insufficient data. Personal judgments become more relevant to the overall analysis when the subject matter itself or the event under investigation is rather murky and concomitantly there is not a lot of sufficiently reliable and factual-based information from which to draw valid conclusions. The drug-terrorism controversy in Afghanistan involves many unknowns. The primary area which contributes to our lack of understanding is the paucity of detailed information regarding the organizational and operational aspects of Afghanistan's opium trade and the specific roles of and relations between various individuals and networks involved in this growing enterprise. In the absence of a clear understanding of the nature of these relationships it becomes very difficult to formulate sound judgments. Indeed, in order to advance an enterprise (e.g., the Afghan opium trade) of this magnitude there must be present a somewhat coherent and organized criminal infrastructure involving many individuals whose reach extends beyond the borders of Afghanistan.

Additionally, information that is available is often subject to varying interpretations. Knowledge which is derived from primarily qualitative information will often rely on an in-depth look at a problem from a variety of viewpoints. It may also require a reformulation or a breaking down of the original problem in order to gain an adequate understanding of its component parts. Such an examination may reveal insights that were not initially considered. Finally, assessments and conclusions which are drawn from any detailed study of a particular phenomenon often involve a certain amount of empirically-based fact, personal judgment, and conjecture.[11]

Acknowledgments

This research was personally challenging and demanding and represents the combined input of many country, regional and topic specific experts. First, I would like to thank God for giving me this opportunity.

During the course of this research many individuals assisted me and therefore deserve my deepest gratitude. My father, Dr. Frank Shanty, who provided ongoing technical support, reviewed much of the manuscript, and provided extensive feedback. My wife, Melanie, and my children Christina, Jason, Melissa, and Joshua provided overwhelming patience, moral support, and encouragement for the entire project. Without Melanie this effort could not have succeeded.

I would like to express my sincere gratitude to my doctoral thesis advisor Dr. David Lundberg, School of International Studies, Division of Education, Arts and Social Sciences, for providing consistent guidance, methodological insights, and wise feedback. I would also like to extend a heartfelt thanks to my associate advisor Dr. Shamsul Khan, School of International Studies, Division of Education, Arts and Social Sciences, for his advice, support, and encouragement throughout the entire project, especially during the critical ethics prospectus application/approval phase. I also thank the University of South Australia for giving me this opportunity and for staff support during the entire process.

I thank all those who contributed as respondents to my interviews and other inquiries during the course of this research.

A number of people deserve special acknowledgment: my sister Kathy Amrein and her husband Jerry, who provided moral support during and following the critical period when our father passed, my brother Mark, his wife Liza, and Dr. Richard Shanty and his wife Joyce whose unselfishness and courage helped provide me with the opportunity to see this effort to completion. I also acknowledge four very good friends: Mac Caldwell, Tom Sweitzer, Msgr. Michael Schleupner, and Ralph Carrick, a man who was more a brother than a friend, who passed away during the course of this study. They have always been there and provided an understanding ear and sound advice. Special acknowledgments go to Dr. Alex Schmid, former head of the United Nations Office on Drugs and Crime and current director of the Terrorism Research Initiative, for his ongoing support during the updating process, Professor Rohan Gunaratna, head of the International Centre for Political Violence and Terrorism Research, Singapore, for providing updated factual information, and to my neighbor and friend Gus Brown, J.D., who provided critical insights into the various types of evidence.

A special debt of gratitude goes to my young friend, Ryan Jacoby. Ryan is a computer genius; if there was a computer-related-technical problem Ryan was there, usually within the hour.

I also thank the staff at Praeger Security International for the opportunity to publish this manuscript, and a special thanks to Steve Catalano, senior editor, for providing valuable assistance in the preparation and presentation of this work.

Finally, I dedicate this work to my father, Dr. Frank Shanty, who passed away on June 1, 2008, after a long battle with cancer, and my mother, Rita Shanty, who is struggling with Alzheimer's disease. They were always there as parents, friends, and mentors. I owe them a profound debt of gratitude that I will never be able to repay.

CHAPTER 1

Afghanistan: Introduction, Research Questions, Terms, and Concepts

INTRODUCTION

This book examines the specific issue of whether or not there is a nexus (link or point of convergence) between international opium and heroin trafficking and terrorist networks[1] operating in or from Afghanistan. Since 9/11 many public officials and others have made definitive statements concerning an alleged nexus between criminal narcotics trafficking and terrorist networks in Afghanistan. This issue needs to be addressed because Afghanistan may be particularly vulnerable to the development of such a nexus, for the following reasons:

1. Over the past thirty years Afghanistan became the principal worldwide producer/supplier of opium and its derivative heroin. During this period of time Afghanistan's percentage of worldwide opium production increased to about 93 percent in 2007.[2]
2. Afghanistan's essentially contested or ineffectual national government during this period probably made that country easily accessible for internationally active terrorist groups, such as Al Qaeda, Hezb-i-Islami (HIG), the Islamic Movement of Uzbekistan (IMU),[3] and for international criminals seeking large quantities of opium/heroin for illegal international markets.[4]
3. The economy of the country was decimated by the 10-year Soviet-Afghan war.[5] During and following this conflict the cultivation of opium provided the impoverished peasant farmers a means to support their families and provided the various feuding factions a funding source for weaponry and other war materiel (Goodson, 2001, pp. 97–104).[6]
4. The ascendancy of the Taliban movement[7] in 1996 and their subsequent links to the Al Qaeda organization may have further facilitated the activities of this group.[8]

5. The current insurgency, which conducts terrorist operations against Western targets, Afghan civilians, and International Security Assistance Forces (ISAF),[9] is supported, in part, by funds generated from Afghanistan's opium trade.

Throughout the 1990s the Southwest Asian drug trade evolved into an enterprise which spanned national as well as international borders. It has been and continues to be a destabilizing factor in the development of Afghanistan and a grave regional and international security challenge. Although the opium poppy has been an agricultural commodity in Afghanistan for many years it was not a regionally destabilizing issue prior to the mid- to late 1970s; its cultivation was limited to local use and regional markets (McCoy, 2003, p. 466). In fact, until 1989, Pakistan was supplying upwards of 70 percent of the world's heroin supply (Rashid, 2001f, p. 120), funneling an estimated $8 billion annually into Pakistan's economy (McCoy, 2003, p. 23). While opium has been cultivated in Afghanistan for hundreds of years, Afghan opium cultivation's rise to global prominence has only spanned the past three decades (Ward and Byrd, 2004, p. 2). Opium cultivation has been increasing steadily since the early 1980s as covert alliances and conditions on the ground have encouraged the cultivation, production, and trafficking of opiates (McCoy, 2003, pp. 15–16).[10] Since the 1980s, Afghanistan's opium trade has dominated that country's political, economic, and social fabric.

The alleged relationship between terrorist networks and international drug traffickers, operating from Afghanistan and neighboring countries, has been the subject of much political debate and controversy. Although some anecdotal and circumstantial evidence suggests that a linkage between drug traffickers and international terrorists may exist in Afghanistan, the question is whether a convincing case based on sound empirical data[11] can be made regarding a nexus or linkage between Afghan-based terrorists and national or internationally-based drug traffickers.

This study has three aspects. First, Afghanistan's opium trade and the trafficking component will be examined relative to specific actor involvement. Open-source historical and contemporary documentary material and conversations with a number of informed individuals portrays a dynamic and complex picture regarding the actors and relationships that presently comprise the narcotics trade in Afghanistan.

Second, the characteristics and behavior of international terrorists operating from Afghanistan will be examined. The evolving relationship between the Taliban, whose goals were initially national, and Al Qaeda, which has remained globally focused, will be examined. This book will study the evolution and rise of Al Qaeda and the Taliban. These two organizations have been among the primary actors in Afghanistan's violent recent past. Since the early 1990s, Al Qaeda has morphed into a decentralized global movement which is sustained by and continues to attract would-be Islamist jihadists through the global reach of its ideology. The Taliban has also undergone a gradual but profound transmutation during their ascendancy period (i.e., 1996–1999).

This study will also provide evidence that the Taliban militia as it existed prior to October 2001 began a very subtle ideological shift under the tutelage of Osama bin Laden beginning in 1997 and since then has further undergone a process of radicalization that has transformed the movement into a much more dangerous force. Furthermore, this study will address the transformation and expansion of Al Qaeda into an international jihadist movement with global reach. The proper classification of various non-state terrorist actors in Afghanistan, particularly the Taliban and Al Qaeda, is central to the examination of the drug traffickers/terrorists nexus problem. Therefore, defining exactly what constitutes a terrorist act will be addressed.

Third, this study will examine whether a nexus, linkage, or relationship between terrorists in Afghanistan and national and/or international drug criminals can be established with open-source data. Since the events of September 11, 2001, and the subsequent occupation of Afghanistan by U.S. and coalition forces, key U.S. congressional leaders, United Nations (UN) representatives, and other international figures have made definitive statements claiming a clear link between the Afghan opium/heroin trade and Afghanistan-based terrorist networks. These statements will be examined to determine if there is an evidentiary basis to support these claims. Data acquired during this research process were compiled into categories listed and defined in the "Range of Evidentiary Data" section of this chapter.

PROBLEM STATEMENT AND RESEARCH QUESTIONS

Statements have been made by respected and influential sources that an operational nexus exists between criminal traffickers in drugs originating from Afghanistan and global terrorist networks, specifically Al Qaeda. If true, this would constitute a major international problem. These statements provided varying qualities of anecdotal, circumstantial, and/or empirical evidence to support the claims that a linkage between international drug traffickers and terrorists exists in Afghanistan.

The central focus question guiding this study is: Does corroborated direct testimony[12] and/or compelling circumstantial evidence substantiate claims that an operational nexus exists between criminal opium and heroin drug traffickers and international terrorist networks operating in or from Afghanistan? In order to address this question this study examines how international drug trafficking networks and terrorist organizations operate in Afghanistan. This research sought to uncover likely points of convergence between transnational drug organizations/networks and international terrorism and to ascertain whether solid evidence of linkages exist between these two entities. If convincing links exist then efforts to disrupt the activities of transnational drug cartels could have a detrimental impact on what may be a major revenue producing source available to insurgents and terrorist entities in Afghanistan.

Interrupting any such linkages may also reduce the scope for trafficking of arms and other illegal commodities, including nuclear, biological, chemical, and radiological (NBCR) weapons and materiel. This study will argue that an indirect relationship exists between drug trade actors and terrorists in Afghanistan. Furthermore, this symbiotic relationship is driven by opportunity based on territorial control, and shared operational and logistical considerations.

At the outset of this work, 12 subsets of topic-specific questions were formulated to establish boundaries around the central focus question, guide the systematic data collection strategy, and incorporate the theoretical framework discussed below.[13] Although the central focus question directing this study was the possible connection between international criminal drug traffickers, particularly of drugs originating from Afghanistan, and international terrorist networks with global reach, these ancillary questions are subsumed within the primary research focus. These questions embraced the principal issues of the investigation (Sarantakos, 1993, p. 262) and embodied a framework which facilitated a focused approach to data collection and analysis. The research questions cited below also provided a guideline for exploring various possibilities and points of view, and formed the basis for establishing the set of propositions listed in the following section. These descriptive and explanatory questions[14] also served as a guide for interviewee selection. The 12 subsets of subquestions which identify the issues related to the central focus question addressed in the study are listed as follows:

Afghan opium and heroin trafficking:

1. Which group(s) or individuals control opium and heroin drug production in Afghanistan? Who are the primary players in opium and heroin trafficking from Afghanistan? How are the proceeds from opium and heroin trafficking dispersed?
2. What factors have contributed to the massive growth of opium and heroin drug trafficking in Afghanistan? Are international opium and heroin drug trafficking criminal groups active inside Afghanistan?

Afghan insurgency and terrorism:

3. Is there a connection between the insurgent escalation in Afghanistan and the boom in opium crops, specifically in Helmand Province?

4. How have non-state actors,[15] including local and regional warlords and drug barons, contributed to the violence and political instability that has been such a major factor in Afghanistan's turbulent history? Who benefits from this political instability?
5. What is the nature of the Taliban movement? Have they committed acts which meet the definition of international terrorism as used in this study? Are Taliban activities and objectives confined solely to Afghanistan or do they harbor regional or international ambitions? Should the Taliban movement be classified as an international terrorist group?
6. How has the Al Qaeda-Taliban relationship evolved? What is the present nature of the Al Qaeda-Taliban relationship? Are Al Qaeda forces currently operating in Afghanistan? Are other terrorist entities a part of the current insurgency?

Afghan drug trafficking/terrorist nexus:

7. What or whose agenda is served by promulgating the existence of a drug trafficking/terrorist nexus?
8. What if any evidence is cited that backs up the claims in open source literature that terrorist groups operating in Afghanistan are directly or indirectly involved in the opium trade?
9. If a drug trafficking/terrorist nexus exists, which groups are involved and what is the extent and nature of this involvement?
10. Is there a connection between local and regional warlords and drug barons and Afghan terror networks? Is opium and heroin revenue being channeled to local and regional warlords and Afghan terror networks? If so, under what circumstances is this occurring?
11. If a drug trafficking/terrorist nexus exists, is it a result of the lack of government control/law enforcement endemic to conflict zones?
12. If a relationship between drug criminals and terrorists in Afghanistan does exists, is it an ongoing operational alliance (providing other areas of opportunity such as smuggling arms or other commodities) or sporadic (borne of convenience and opportunity)?

In addressing the central focus question of this study and the 12 subsets of related research questions, the scope of this work is limited primarily to open source materials published before August 1, 2010 in English or English translations.

STUDY PROPOSITIONS

During the examination of primary sources of anecdotal, circumstantial, or empirical evidence upon which allegedly definitive published statements claiming an Afghan drugs/terrorism nexus were based, the following theoretical and epistemological propositions were used. These propositions guided and instructed the data collection protocol and directed the analytical component of the study:[16]

- Increasing opium/heroin production in Afghanistan is likely to be connected with the lack of available and comparable economic activities for landowners and rural workers and the increasing influence and power of local and regional warlords.
- The scope of effective government and policing in Afghanistan is likely to be adversely affected by the legacy of protracted past and continuing conflict, corruption induced by the opium/heroin trade, and by the influence of regional warlords within the government structure.
- Islamist terrorist organizations that have distinct entities with their own operational command and support structures may cooperate tactically based on a shared ideological commitment to global Islamist jihad against non-Muslims or Muslim targets that do not espouse the same ideological objectives.
- Any organization in Afghanistan that has undertaken past and/or present violent acts against noncombatants in accordance with the definition of terrorism used in this study should be designated as a Foreign Terrorist Organization (FTO).
- Whether or not they actually cooperate, Afghan heroin drug traffickers and Islamist terrorist organizations have common interests in weak government and policing, and active smuggling networks that can evade or corrupt government control and taxation to move a variety of people and materiel.
- The protracted presence of foreign forces in Afghanistan, civilian casualties arising from their activities, and government corruption generates increasing political support for, or tolerance of, Islamist terrorist organizations. Foreign forces and the Government of Afghanistan (GoA) need to provide increasing tangible benefits to the Afghan population to offset or overcome negative valuations of their presence if they are to promote the legitimacy of the Afghan government.
- Statements claiming a direct link between terrorists and the opium/heroin trade in Afghanistan may be based on speculation, hearsay, and conjecture, and may serve a politically-motivated agenda, influenced by the events of 9/11. This possibility should arouse skepticism about such claims.
- The continued expansion of the opium trade before 1996 and substantial increase in production after October 2001 provides circumstantial evidence against either the Taliban or Al Qaeda controlling the opium trade in Afghanistan.
- Correlations between patterns of increasing opium/heroin production and increasing insurgent/terrorist activity in a region provide circumstantial evidence of the possibility of a nexus. Establishing the actual existence of a nexus requires corroborated direct testimony and/or a far more compelling pattern of circumstantial evidence.[17]
- In the context of this study, corroborated direct testimony constitutes substantial empirical evidence. Corroboration of testimony evidence is based on the technique of "triangulation."[18] The epistemological basis of the acceptance of corroborated direct testimony as empirical evidence is Fay's formulation of "critical intersubjectivity," as opposed to objectivism or relativism.[19]

Furthermore, the above cited propositions provided a theoretical and epistemological framework for this case study analysis of a possible drug/terrorism nexus in Afghanistan. Yin (2003, p. 22) notes that, "each proposition directs attention to something that should be examined within the scope of study." In this study, that directing function is primarily performed by the central focus question (and the 12 subsets of related research questions defined above). The statements, testimony and literature cited in chapters 2–4 represents some of the current thinking relative to the general issue of a nexus between drugs and terrorism in Afghanistan, and provides a credible source for generating additional insightful questions. Furthermore, this information was triangulated with other documentary and interview source data to determine if the above cited propositions are indeed valid.

Finally, the findings generated in this study are specific to Afghanistan. Therefore, inferences drawn from this study should not be generalized to the issue of a drugs-terrorism nexus in other contexts, although it may provide useful heuristic leads for such inquiries. In this way, "analytical generalizations" may be made by using the evidence of specific case studies to compare, validate, and expand upon each study's theoretical propositions.[20]

RESEARCH APPROACH

As previously stated, the approach selected for this research was a case study design.[21] Bernstein and others emphasize the central importance of case study analysis in politics and international relations, although their advocacy of scenario analysis is not relevant to this particular study.[22] Yin (2004, p. 3) states that, "The case study method is best applied when research addresses descriptive or explanatory questions and aims to produce a first-hand understanding of people and events." He further argues that the case study is a holistic research strategy, which addresses all aspects of the research process from design through analysis (Yin, 2003, p. 14). Reasons for this selection are as follows:

> The case study is preferred in examining contemporary events, but when the relevant behaviors cannot be manipulated . . . the case study's unique strength is its ability to deal with a variety of evidence—documents, artifacts, interviews, and observations-beyond what might be available in a conventional historical study (Yin 2003, pp. 7–8).

The relationship between drug traffickers and terrorists in Afghanistan still requires systematic analysis relative to the propositions described above. Afghanistan has experienced three decades of continuous war and there are acute difficulties inherent in conducting research on such a volatile environment. The inherent secrecy of these two sets of "dark networks"[23] operating throughout Afghanistan, and of a possible nexus between them, makes data collection very difficult. Many attempts at researching Afghanistan have been hindered by this lack of reliable quantitative data.[24]

Although many influential people within both the public and private sector claim that a nexus between drugs and terrorists exists in Afghanistan, during the initial search of relevant topic-specific literature no systematic studies were found that established a drug/terrorism nexus in Afghanistan substantiated by reliable empirical data. Primarily due to the complexities posed by the secrecy of the actors being investigated and the limited empirical data on either drug trafficking or terrorism in Afghanistan, and the quantitative data[25] relative to specific terrorist events, a case study design using a mixed-methods (qualitative and quantitative) approach to the collection of data was selected. This approach utilizes historical and contemporary documentary material as well as interviews with knowledgeable people, many with in-country field experience.

The objective was to examine directly drug-trafficking and terrorism in Afghanistan, as a basis for testing the assertions made by those advocating a case for a nexus or, in the case of an alternative argument, those believing that such a nexus does not exist. Due to the ever-changing political landscape in Afghanistan, the collapse of the Taliban regime, the dispersal of Al Qaeda and the senior leadership of the Taliban into the north-west regions of Pakistan, and the alleged impact of opium on political and military events following the October 7, 2001, invasion, certain portions of this study were broken down into pre- and post-9/11 time frames.

RANGE OF EVIDENTIARY DATA: EMPIRICAL, CIRCUMSTANTIAL, AND ANECDOTAL

Empirical or Direct Evidence

This study will attempt to locate empirical, circumstantial, and anecdotal data which links internationally-based drug traffickers to terrorists in Afghanistan. For the purpose of this study the following definitions will apply:

> Direct evidence is clear evidence of a fact, happening or thing that requires no additional thought to prove its existence, as opposed to circumstantial evidence. Direct evidence may consist of a witness' testimony who saw acts done or heard words spoken that relate directly to an issue in dispute. It is not introduced for the purpose of having inferences drawn from it, but rather is to be considered on its face (U.S. Legal, n.d.).[26]

An eyewitness account or observation of an event is an example of empirical or direct evidence. However, there are problems associated with the above U.S. "legal" definition, which embodies a rather naïve "objectivism" (Fay, 1996, pp. 199–204). Consistent with judicial practice, corroboration by others who witnessed the same phenomena and reported the same event or outcomes may lend further credibility to this type of evidence or cause further confusion. For example, two individuals could witness the same event and offer different interpretations of their observations. In his treatise *Metaphysics*, Aristotle made the following statement relative to truth:

> . . . truth is not what appears exists, but that what appears exists for him to whom it appears . . . for things do not appear either the same to all men or always the same to the same man, but often have contrary appearances at the same time.[27]

Therefore, this type of evidence must be examined and scrutinized since such accounts are often recorded differently by different people. A sound epistemology requires a "triangulation" approach to assessing corroboration that embodies the principles of "critical intersubjectivity," that are analogous with determination of contested issues based on evidence by a court.[28]

Circumstantial Evidence

Circumstantial evidence is derived from events or facts[29] that, standing alone, seem unrelated. The evidence becomes more credible when these facts are linked thus enabling one to draw a certain conclusion from these linked facts through inference.

> Circumstantial evidence is indirect evidence which creates an inference from which a main fact may be inferred . . . When circumstantial evidence is cumulative, the weakness of such circumstantial evidence is strengthened (U.S. Legal, n.d.).

One piece of circumstantial evidence may not indicate culpability; however several pieces of circumstantial evidence properly vetted, triangulated with other data, and pointing to the same conclusion may indicate guilt in a U.S. court of law or, as applied in this study, a link between individuals or groups. Circumstantial evidence can be compelling. In other words, so powerful that a reasonable person is led to draw a certain conclusion based on the weight of all the evidence when considered together. Circumstantial evidence becomes more incriminating or valid when direct or empirical evidence is present. However, many legal cases have been won based on circumstantial evidence alone. An example of circumstantial evidence was the confiscation, by U.S. and coalition forces, of large quantities of opium gum from a known Al Qaeda hideout in the mountains of Afghanistan.[30]

Anecdotal Evidence

An anecdote by definition is a story or narrative. For the purposes of this study an anecdote is defined as a "short personal account of an incident or event"[31] recorded by one or more individuals. Assessing the reliability of anecdotal data presents similar problems with respect to credibility as empirical and circumstantial evidence. Anecdotal as well as empirical information is often based on memory. Furthermore, anecdotes are often secondhand accounts; therefore it is difficult to draw conclusions since memory recollection and secondary accounts have a tendency to be reshaped by ongoing experiences, thoughts, attitudes, and personal biases. Goldman (1999, pp. 123–124) notes that:

> A reporter's competence is his ability to detect and retain the kind of event or fact in question. This ability rests on some combination of perceptual, inferential, and memorial skills . . . Psychological studies indicate that memory for an event can be distorted by post-event occurrences, including fantasized scenarios or verbal promptings by others as to what might have happened.[32]

Because anecdotal evidence is subjective, as are all observations, it becomes more credible when triangulated with other reports addressing the same event or incident.

ASSESSING MULTIDIMENSIONAL ARGUMENTS

All three types of evidence ultimately involve the perceptions and interpretations of the originator of the information (Goldman, 1999, pp. 123–124). Perceptions and interpretations are subjective, i.e., they are based on how an event is viewed or internalized and are therefore specific to each individual. Lebow (2007, p. 18) notes that, "Social understanding is inherently subjective." Perceptions are also based on the importance attributed to an event as it is initially experienced at the time the event was observed. Over time these convictions or beliefs once held may become influenced by totally unrelated factors, thereby skewing the original conviction and rendering the anecdote a subjective opinion and not based on corroborating information.

Thus, regardless of evidence "type," if the information provided insights into the drug-terror nexus it was assessed during the data collection process; its reliability and credibility determined through the process of triangulation.[33] This includes arguments that corroborate, rival, or challenge the original propositions.[34] Triangulation of multiple sources of evidence allows for the convergence and validation of evidentiary data and builds a more accurate and convincing argument for drawing conclusions; one that is supported by evidence which has been carefully reviewed.

Furthermore, triangulation of multiple data sources strengthens the findings and can uncover errors and omissions in the analytical process (Kaplan and Duchon, 1988, pp. 575, 582).

All three types of evidence collected through multiple data sources can be strengthened by converging lines of inquiry (Yin, 2003, p. 98) through the process of cross-validation. Therefore, the findings and conclusions ultimately reached are not based on a single source of information but rather multiple viewpoints which coalesce to build a persuasive and compelling case. In fact, much of the evidence provided in this study is anecdotal and circumstantial. Nevertheless, properly triangulated circumstantial and anecdotal evidence can come together to form a comprehensive picture of the various issues and relational patterns under investigation. As noted by Denzin and Lincoln (2005, p. 5), "The use of multiple methods, or triangulation, reflects an attempt to secure an in-depth understanding of the phenomenon in question." This view is supported by Jick (1979, p. 603) in a discussion on mixed-methods triangulation when he argues that, "Triangulation . . . can be something other than scaling, reliability, and convergent validation. It can also capture a more complete, *holistic*, and contextual portrayal of the unit(s) under study."[35]

Moreover, this approach is necessary given the limited empirical work undertaken to date and the volume of personal anecdotes in much of the existing literature. The evaluation and weight given to each type of evidence is an interpretive process in that it is subjective and based on the investigator's judgment.[36] Fay (1996, p. 214) argues that, "evidence does not always speak with such clarity that it supports only one conclusion."[37] Biases and limitations, intrinsic in all methods, are controlled by utilizing a variety of methods and sources for data acquisition including questionnaires and interview data.

Thus, the arguments made in this book will be supported by all three types of evidence, if available through open-source channels, and be based on the author's interpretation of this evidence. The evidence will address the theoretical propositions and incorporate major rival explanations and opinions relative to the primary issue being examined. Additionally, opinions of experts (e.g., Rashid, Gunaratna, et al.) will be weighed according to their experience and established credibility. According to Goldman (1999, p. 126), "If a speaker is found to be reliable enough, at least within a specified domain, the hearer is thenceforth justified in trusting her [his] utterances in that domain on subsequent occasions." Furthermore, this study will provide conclusions based on a reasonable and logical interpretation of the data. All source material will be documented as in-text referencing, endnotes, and in the bibliography.

Critical to an objective investigation of this problem are clear and concise definitions of terms and concepts as they have been used in this study. It should be noted that at this time no universally agreed upon definition exists as to what constitutes a terrorist act, what is meant by the term narcoterrorism, and whether the use of this term adds anything substantial to the political debate concerning a nexus. However, for the purpose of this study, definitions proposed by others were reviewed, and working definitions for these terms were selected. These definitions were consistently applied throughout this work and are provided in the following section.

DEFINITIONS OF KEY TERMS AND CONCEPTS

Terrorism

The term *terrorism* was first introduced during the French Revolution (1789–1794). Hoffman (1998, p. 15) states:

> In contrast to its contemporary usage, at that time terrorism had a decidedly positive connotation. The system or *regime de la terreur* of 1793–1794—from which the English word came—was adopted as a means to establish order during the transient anarchical period of turmoil and upheaval that followed the uprisings of 1789, as it has followed in the wake of many other revolutions. Hence . . . the *regime de la terreur* was an instrument of governance wielded by the recently established revolutionary state.

Since that time the meaning and usage of the word has changed "to accommodate the political vernacular and discourse of each successive era" (Hoffman, p. 28).[38] Since the early 1970s the United Nations (UN) has been attempting without success to define the phenomena.[39]

At this writing there is still no international political consensus even though there have been thirteen multilateral and seven regional conventions which have addressed various aspects of the problem. The UN is continuing work on achieving global agreement on a definition of the term. In 2005, a draft sought to have world leaders agree "that the targeting and deliberate killing of civilians and noncombatants cannot be justified or legitimized by any cause or grievance." The 2005 draft also sought agreement that any such action "to intimidate a population or to compel a government or an international organization to carry out or to abstain from any act cannot be justified on any ground and constitutes an act of terrorism" (Associated Press, July 23, 2005). Unfortunately, the debate continues, essentially because "the desire to carve out exceptions" still remains an obstacle to a universal definition (Gaer, 2005). Indeed, even among United States (US) federal agencies (e.g., State and Defense Departments and the Justice Department's Federal Bureau of Investigation) there is no clear consensus.

The RAND Corporation, a public policy research firm, has served as a forerunner in the field of terrorism studies. Their numerous reports and monographs have focused on many issues relative to the terrorism problem.

They are also known for their annual terrorist incident reports; in a joint effort with the Memorial Institute for the Prevention of Terrorism (MIPT) reports of these incidents have been entered into a publicly accessible database.[40] Incidents from 1968 to the present are recorded in this data file. The RAND definition of terrorism is:

> . . . violence, or the threat of violence, calculated to create an atmosphere of fear and alarm. These acts are designed to coerce others into actions they would not otherwise undertake, or refrain from actions they desired to take.[41]

The U.S. Department of State has adopted the following terms[42] from Title 22 of the U.S. Code, Section 2656f (d): "the term 'terrorism' means premeditated, politically motivated violence perpetrated against noncombatant targets by subnational groups or clandestine agents usually intended to influence an audience" (U.S. Department of State, 2005a, p. 1).[43] Alex Schmid, (Former Officer-in-Charge of the Terrorism Prevention Branch of the United Nations (UN) Office on Drugs and Crime) defined terrorism as follows:

> Terrorism is an anxiety-inspiring method of repeated violent action, employed by (semi-) clandestine individual, group or state actors, for idiosyncratic, criminal or political reasons, whereby—in contrast to assassination—the direct targets of violence are not the main targets. The immediate human victims of violence are generally chosen randomly (targets of opportunity) or selectively (representative or symbolic targets) from a target population, and serve as message generators. Threat- and violence-based communication processes between terrorist (organization), (imperiled) victims, and main targets are used to manipulate the main target audience(s), turning it into a target of terror, a target of demands, or a target of attention, depending on whether intimidation, coercion, or propaganda is primarily sought (Schmid and Jongman, 1988, p. 28).

Schmid and Jongman examined 109 definitions of terrorism and listed the most important elements common to each definition. The top three elements or words which appeared in over 50 percent of the examined definitions were: violence (force), political, and fear (terror emphasized).[44] Although the above cited definition has received wide acceptance by many in the international academic community it has not achieved the global consensus, which would need to be established, prior to the development of a "comprehensive convention outlawing international terrorism" (Gaer, 2005). The well-worn refrain about the equivalence between terrorists and freedom fighters in the contemporary literature on terrorism is indicative of the problem of trying to define the concept.

Apparently, two of the problems associated with the establishment of an international consensus are the issues of state terrorism and national liberation movements. These issues, which focus primarily on Third World conflicts, have created a chasm within the international community. The argument here comes down to the proverbial "one man's terrorist is another man's freedom fighter."[45]

The Foreign Ministers of the Organization of Islamic Conference (OIC) at the extraordinary session held at Kuala Lumpur in April 2002 were unable to reach a consensus on how terrorism or a terrorist act should be defined. The delegates to this conference had a problem distinguishing between acts of terrorism and similar acts performed in the course of what was regarded as a legitimate struggle:

> We reject any attempt to link Islam and Muslims to terrorism as terrorism has no association with any religion, civilization or nationality;
>
> We reiterate that preventive action taken to combat terrorism should not result in ethnic or religious profiling or the targeting of a particular community;
>
> We unequivocally condemn acts of international terrorism in all its forms and manifestations, including state terrorism, irrespective of motives, perpetrators and victims as terrorism poses a serious threat to international peace and security and is a grave violation of human rights;
>
> We reiterate the principled position under international law and the Charter of the United Nations of the legitimacy of resistance to foreign aggression and the struggle of peoples under colonial or alien domination and foreign occupation for national liberation and self-determination. In this context, we underline the urgency for an internationally agreed definition of terrorism, which differentiates such legitimate struggles from acts of terrorism (The Islamic Conference of Foreign Ministers on Terrorism, April 1–3, 2002).

The central issue that prevented the OIC ministers from agreeing to a formal legal definition was enumerated by the host of the conference, then Malaysian Prime Minister Dr. Mahathir bin Mohamad, in his opening remarks regarding OIC support for Palestinians in the Arab-Israeli dispute. It appears that the axiom, "one man's terrorist is another man's freedom fighter,"[46] has up until this point in time prevented a universal definition of an international problem. As with any issue which impacts international security it is crucial to be assiduous in defining terms, particularly those which affect responses to the object defined.

A sound working definition of terrorism should avoid attempts at interpreting motivations. The focus here needs to be on the "act" itself regardless of intentions.[47] In the political context of an ongoing insurgency, such as Afghanistan, it is very difficult to isolate specific actor responsibility and even more difficult to assess various motivations which may spawn a given incident of violence across time and place. As illustrated in chapter 5, acts committed against unknown perpetrators against non-combatant foreign entities are defined as acts of international terrorism regardless of the causal agent(s)[48] (Shanty and Picquet, 2000, pp. 6–7; 2004, pp. 8–9).

The working definition of terrorism cited below focuses on the observable behavior of the activity and will be used throughout this study:

> Terrorism is pre-meditated violence, or the threat of violence against non-combatant targets by governments, sub-national or clandestine agents calculated to create an atmosphere of fear and alarm to bring about political or social change or to coerce a government, the civilian population or any segment thereof (Shanty and Picquet, 2000, p. 6; 2004, pp. 7–8).

In this context terrorism is defined in terms of the tactics employed by the perpetrators against non-combatants, including civilians and military personnel who, at the time of the incident, were unarmed or not on duty or in a peacekeeping role.[49]

Terrorist Group

The term terrorist group is taken from Title 22 of the United States Code, Section 2656f (d) and modified to address incidents described below. Therefore, for the purpose of this study the term terrorist group is defined as "any group practicing, or that has significant subgroups that practice, [domestic or] international terrorism."[50]

International, Domestic, and State Terrorism

For the purpose of this study international terrorism is defined as:

> Terrorism involving citizens of more than one country. This includes incidents in which terrorists go abroad to do their violence or they select victims or targets within their own country that have connections to a foreign state (e.g., diplomats, foreign business persons, offices or other facilities of foreign corporations) or create international incidents by attacking resident or transitory foreigners (e.g., visitors, airline passengers, personnel and equipment). It also includes all incidents wherein foreigners become victims of terrorist acts, regardless of whether they were the principal target of the attack or just persons in the wrong place at the wrong time (Shanty and Picquet, 2000 p. 6; 2004 pp. 7–8).[51]

Domestic terrorism is violence perpetrated "by terrorists within their own country against their own nationals"; state terrorism is violence perpetrated "by governments against their own citizens"[52] (Shanty and Picquet, 2000, p. 6; 2004, pp. 7–8).

Islamist Extremism

For the purpose of this study the term Islamist extremism was taken from *Al-Qaeda: The Many Faces of an Islamist Extremist Threat*, a report issued by the U.S. House Permanent Select Committee on Intelligence in June 2006. The report states that:

> Islamist extremism refers to the political philosophy that says that, in order to defend a carefully defined vision of Islam and protect pious Muslims around the world, one has to impose, essentially, a 7th century political structure over the people of the Islamic world, and that this political structure must be implemented by violent Jihad, or Holy War (U.S. House of Representatives 2006, p. 5).[53]

Additionally, for the purposes of this study the terms Islamist militant groups and Islamist extremists are interchangeable.

Organized Crime: Transnational Organized Crime, Organized Crime Group, and Structured Group

Definitions of organized crime vary depending upon the specific laws of individual states and jurisdictions. In this study organized crime[54] is defined as: an illegal business enterprise comprising two or more individuals which has as its sole purpose the generation of profit.[55] The term transnational organized crime, which includes drug trafficking, will be defined as:

> . . . a crime or series of crimes that are conducted by a group of two or more people that crosses at least one national border. A transnational organized crime group is self-perpetuating and characterized by a hierarchical structure, a willingness to use force or the fear of force, and the use of bribery and/or corruption in the pursuit of illicit profit and/or power (Moran, 2007, p. 47).

The following two definitions were taken from the UN Convention on Transnational Organized Crime (2000). For the purpose of this study an organized crime group is:

> . . . a structured group of three or more persons, existing for a period of time and acting in concert with the aim of committing one or more serious crimes or offences established in accordance with this Convention, in order to obtain, directly or indirectly, a financial or other material benefit. A *structured group* is a group that is not randomly formed for the immediate commission of an offence and that does not need to have formally defined roles for its members, continuity of its membership or a developed structure (United Nations Convention Against Transnational Crime, 2000, Article 2a and 2c).[56]

Narcoterrorism

Since the 1980s scholars and researchers have often used the term narcoterrorism to describe the linkage between drug traffickers and terrorists.[57]

Following the events of September 11, 2001, the topic of narcoterrorism has received much attention in the media, among various government officials, researchers, and the academic community. While both international terrorism and the international drug trade are threats to global security very little empirical attention has been paid to the convergence of these two distinct threats to international security. Hence, research in this area has not kept pace with the changing global political landscape since the end of the Cold War.

The broad and controversial topic of narcoterrorism has been studied and discussed among public officials and a few independent researchers both in the United States and abroad. Moreover, several books and scholarly articles have been published on the subject. Rachel Ehrenfeld (1990, 2003) and Loretta Napoleoni (2003) have studied the subject extensively and have each written books on the topic.[58] Criminologist Rachel Ehrenfeld defines narcoterrorism as "the use of drug trafficking to advance the objectives of certain governments and terrorist organizations" (Ehrenfeld, 1990, p. xiii). How terrorist organizations generate revenue has been a subject that has created a great deal of controversy and political debate. In a book which details the financing of terrorist organizations, economist and journalist Loretta Napoleoni (2003, p. 229) defines narcoterrorism as the "use of terror tactics by the narco-traffickers and drug lords to protect their illegal businesses. It also describes the alliance between drug lords and armed organisations. Both have interest in destabilising governments and breaking down the established social order." While there are various definitions for the term, in the post 9/11 world a consensus is growing among certain government officials as well as the general public that the term narcoterrorism somehow ties the three-decade-old war on drugs to the present day war on terrorism.

The term narcoterrorism itself originated in Latin America in the early 1980s and was applied to such groups as Sendero Luminosa (Shining Path) in Peru and the Revolutionary Armed Forces of Colombia (FARC) in Colombia. These groups were utilizing the illicit drug trade to finance their insurgent campaigns.[59]

The concept of narcoterrorism has been used as a propaganda tool by various governments and agencies within governments seeking to influence public debate in order to gain support for measures and policies designed to fight the illicit trade in narcotic drugs. Many believe that such was the case during the Reagan administration in the 1980s. The ongoing debate on the current war on terrorism has also been impacted by the alleged connection between Afghanistan's drug trade and terrorist organizations operating in that country. Linking a publicly identified terrorist group to the illicit trade in narcotics projects a "public enemy no. 1" image in the minds of many politicians as well as ordinary citizens. This further enhances public support, unifies a target audience, and engenders compliance among rival political factions.

While the term may invoke a sense of outrage among the public and serve to legitimize the actions taken by governments, many scholars and students of the subject believe that it does not adequately advance the understanding of either the drug or terrorism issues.

The extent to which terrorist/extremist groups' based/operating in Afghanistan are dependent upon the drug trade for financing their operations is a central issue in this study. It has been alleged that Afghanistan's Taliban militia have in the past and are currently deriving revenue from the opium/heroin trade by imposing a tax on producers (peasant farmers), traders, and traffickers.[60] It has also been alleged that the Taliban may also be involved in protecting conversion labs, drug shipments, and other hands-on activities relative to the opium trade.[61] Furthermore, the involvement of terrorist groups with global reach (e.g., Al Qaeda) in either the cultivation, production, transportation, or protection aspects of this enterprise is a central issue in this study.

There are a number of definitions of narcoterrorism that are currently in use, for example the U.S. Department of Defense (DoD) defines the term as:

> . . . terrorism conducted to further the aims of drug traffickers. It may include assassinations, extortion, hijackings, bombings, and kidnappings directed against judges, prosecutors, elected officials, or law enforcement agents, and general disruption of a legitimate government to divert attention from drug operations (DoD, 2004, p. 355).[62]

In testimony before the U.S. Senate Judiciary Committee, Subcommittee on Technology, Terrorism, and Government Information, Asa Hutchinson, former administrator of the U.S. Drug Enforcement Administration (DEA), defined narcoterrorism:

> . . . as a subset of terrorism, in which, terrorist groups or associated individuals, participate directly or indirectly in the cultivation, manufacture, transportation, or distribution of controlled substances and the monies derived from these activities . . . narco-terrorism may be characterized by the participation of groups or associated individuals in taxing, providing security for, or otherwise aiding or abetting drug trafficking endeavors in an effort to further, or fund, terrorist activities (Hutchinson, 2002, p.10).[63]

For the purposes of this study the term narcoterrorism implies a direct or indirect financial benefit accrued to terrorist/extremist groups based in or operating from Afghanistan by their involvement in any aspect of the opium trade.[64] Additionally, the term applies to any Afghan state or public official who is deriving revenue from this activity knowingly undermining the authority of the central government in Kabul and/or is channeling a portion of this revenue to insurgent/terrorist groups in order to support subversive elements. While the connection between drugs and terror has been well documented in various countries in the Western Hemisphere, most notably, Colombia, Peru, and the tri-border region of Paraguay, Argentina, and Brazil, much less is known of the organizational and operational dynamics of the drug trade in Afghanistan, the world's leading producer of opium and its derivative, morphine base/heroin.

Drug Trafficking

As used throughout this study, drug trafficking is the illegal transport of an internationally banned or controlled substance (e.g., opium, morphine, heroin). Controlled substances include plant-based as well as synthetic substances and may also include certain precursor agents as defined by the International Narcotics Control Board (INCB) such as acetic anhydride, a chemical agent used in the production of heroin (INCB, 2005, p. 79).[65]

Drug trafficking also involves the producing agent (i.e., one who cultivates or produces the product, e.g., raw opium), the middleman or trader who purchases the product from the farmer or producer (this person may also further refine or chemically alter the original substance for sale to persons or organizations, e.g., traffickers, smugglers), or other criminal elements responsible for transporting the product into designated consumer countries or regions.[66]

CONCLUSION

This chapter defined the central problem which this study addresses and specified a subset of 12 related issues, in the form of specific questions which need to be examined in order to properly address the principal research question. The theoretical and epistemological propositions relate to the central focus question of this study (and the 12 subsets of related research questions). This chapter cited and defined various types of evidence and key terms and concepts used throughout this book.

The opium problem and terrorism in Afghanistan tended to be addressed independently prior to the 1998 African embassy bombings. Following the events of 9/11 purported linkages between these two entities became a major topic of debate. A close examination of the opium problem reveals that a dynamic set of factors (e.g., social, political, economic, and geographic) spanning three decades have stimulated opium production in Afghanistan. However, prior to addressing the nexus issue an examination of both the Afghan drug trafficking problem and terrorism in Afghanistan needs to be undertaken.

CHAPTER 2

Afghanistan's Opium Problem

HISTORY AND DYNAMICS OF THE OPIUM TRADE IN AFGHANISTAN

Opium has been cultivated in the Golden Crescent[1] of Southwest Asia "since at least the sixteenth century" (Booth, 1996, p 251).[2] In Afghanistan, evidence suggests that it has been a part of the agricultural landscape for at least 200 years; however, its cultivation prior to the 1970s was limited.[3] Historically, the Southeast Asian region encompassing the mountainous areas of Myanmar (Burma), Laos, and Thailand, referred to as the Golden Triangle, have been a major opium producer supplying the demand of the world's addicts as well as recreational users:

> Research by the U.S. Bureau of Narcotics showed that by the late 1950s Southeast Asia's Golden Triangle region was harvesting approximately 700 tons of raw opium, or about 50% of the world's total illicit production . . . starting as a drug-deficient region reliant on imports in the 1930s, Southeast Asia became self-sufficient in opium during the 1950s and would by the 1980s emerge as the world's main heroin supplier (McCoy, 2003, p. 128).

However, political and military events in Southwest Asia, a severe drought (1978–1980) in the Southeast Asian producing countries, and law enforcement efforts, which slashed opium output in Turkey, spurred production in Afghanistan and Pakistan. Haq (1996, p. 948) argues that an additional factor accounted for a disruption in the flow of opium from the Golden Triangle and therefore precipitated a surge in Golden Crescent opium output. This occurred in the mid-1970s with the collapse of the governments of Laos and Vietnam.[4] Less than 400 tons of opium was produced in the Golden Triangle during the 1979–1980 harvesting seasons. During this same period, "heroin from Afghanistan and Pakistan captured 60% of the U.S. market . . ." (McCoy, 2003, p. 464).

With cultivation of opium in other producing areas throughout Asia (i.e., the Golden Triangle) diminishing and the demand for the product increasing in the West and in neighboring countries opium was the ideal crop that had the potential to provide the quickest and most profitable return for farmers and itinerant laborers. Afghanistan has always been an agrarian society but had not been heretofore dependent upon the opium poppy as a sole means of livelihood.

The regional surge in heroin production in South Asia had its origin in Pakistan, which was producing about 800 metric tons a year during the 1980s. According to Ahmed Rashid,[5] a prominent journalist and Afghanistan-Central Asian scholar, Pakistan was supplying "70 per cent of the world's supply of heroin until 1989" (Rashid, 2000, p. 120). By comparison, McCoy (2003, p. 23) concludes that, "By 1988, Pakistan's heroin industry was grossing an estimated $8 billion annually, half the size of the legal economy . . ."[6] However, in 2002, the United Nations Office for Drug Control and Crime Prevention (UNODCCP)[7] reported that at the beginning of this decade Pakistan's opium cultivation had decreased significantly:

> . . . from 9,400 hectares in 1992 to some 230 hectares in the 2000–2001 season. This was the result of the government's determination to eliminate opium poppy and to launch sizeable alternative development projects largely funded by the international community (UNODCCP, 2002a, p. 5).

Rashid's and McCoy's conclusions in 2000 and 2003, respectively, are in general agreement with the findings of a much earlier work by Lamour and Lamberti. In 1974 they wrote,

> Afghanistan and northern Pakistan represent a source of opium as yet virtually untapped by European traffickers whose supplies came from Turkey until poppy cultivation was banned there in 1972. . . . The political conditions in their opium producing areas make these places an ideal refuge where racketeers from Europe could go about their business untroubled by the international law enforcement agencies" (Lamour and Lamberti, 1974, p. 177).[8]

Based on these assessments it is reasonable to conclude that while opium has been cultivated in Afghanistan for hundreds of years its rise over the past three decades has been, for the most part, a by-product of nearly thirty years of turmoil and war in Afghanistan.[9]

In 1978, prior to the Soviet invasion, the Noor Mohammad Taraki (1978–1979) government in Kabul sought to implement measures aimed at extinguishing the drug trade which was supporting and financing various emerging insurgent factions. At that time total opium yield in

Afghanistan was relatively low at around 300 tons per year.[10] This met with much resistance:

> As early as the spring of 1979, before Washington committed to the rebels, press accounts revealed their financial dependence on drugs. U.S. narcotics experts reported in 1980 that Afghan guerrillas were fighting "on a schedule determined in part by opium poppy planting and harvest seasons." The DEA predicted, quite rightly, that Afghanistan and its neighbors "could become pre-eminent in the U.S. and Western European market in the 1980s" (Marshall, 1991, p. 48).[11]

International press reports during this period confirm the fact that opium began to take on a wider significance in the region than at any preceding period. In fact, according to Peter Bensinger, then head of the U.S. DEA, "at the end of 1978, only 17 percent of the heroin in the United States originated in the Golden Crescent . . . At the end of 1979, Bensinger 'guesstimated,' the amount of Golden Crescent heroin reaching the States had doubled to 35 percent of the total." Bensinger also said that, "his agency has found evidence of heroin processing labs in Pakistan for the first time, though the great majority of the opium from the Golden Crescent is converted into heroin . . . in labs in Turkey" (Babcock and Kotkin, 1980, p. A8). Bensinger's fears were apparently justified because four years later the *New York Times* reported that Pakistani suppliers were responsible for 80 percent of the heroin entering the East Coast of the United States (Vinocur, 1984, p. A2).

Two principal geopolitical factors can be attributed to this surge in opium cultivation and heroin production: the Soviet-Afghan war (1979–1989) which facilitated a spike in the trade, and at least the refusal or inability of the two leading sponsors of the resistance, Pakistan and the United States, to implement strategies to curtail this growing threat.[12]

Additionally, the return of the Ayatollah Khomeini to head the government of Iran in February 1979 and the revolution in that country by Islamic fundamentalists sparked an initial increase in that country's opium production. The political and social turmoil in Iran during this period made it very difficult for law enforcement and interdiction agencies to police and prevent the cultivation of opium (McCoy, 2003, p. 471). Nevertheless, by the end of 1980 Iranian officials had succeeded in eradicating its opium fields.[13] However, the demand remained high so consequently the drug problem remained.[14] With diminished Iranian domestic supplies Afghanistan and Pakistan provided alternative sources of supply.

As Pakistan's opium cultivation decreased in the latter 1990s Afghanistan became Iran's primary supplier. This situation currently exists despite ongoing intensive efforts on the part of the Iranian government to prevent the flow of opiates from crossing their border (UNODCCP, 2002a, pp. 4–5). In fact according to a report released in 2001 by the Iranian government

100 percent of all imported opiates enter the country by way of Pakistan, from Afghanistan (UNODC, 2003a, pp. 35–36). Given the political landscape during this period there is ample justification for concluding "that a radically transformed international market" for Afghan opium was emerging in the late 1970s to the early 1980s (Haq, 1996, p. 949). Prior to 1979 heroin was not a problem in Pakistan. However, political unrest in Afghanistan and Iran drove millions of refugees into that country. Many of these people had been involved in various aspects of the opium trade. This factor and the introduction of the Hadd Ordinance, which spawned the drug mafia, provided the catalyst to transform and expand the opium/heroin market (Shafiq and Shah et al., 2006, p. 94).[15]

Moreover, Afghans have historically been involved in the smuggling of various commodities, and the Afghan terrain is conducive to this type of enterprise. These factors created conditions that would not only encourage but ensure that illegal drug activity would flourish. Afghan opiates would soon feed the ever rising demand in Europe and the United States. Booth (1996, p. 291) notes, "the 1980s saw an unprecedented explosion of addiction across the Western world and especially in the USA where drugs had created an extensive, often alluring and sometimes attractive, subculture." According to Mathea Falco, then assistant secretary of state for International Narcotics Matters, the Golden Crescent countries of Iran, Pakistan, and Afghanistan together combined to produce a record opium crop of 1,500 tons in 1979. This was triple the amount produced in the Golden Triangle area which encompasses the mountain regions of Myanmar (Burma), Laos, and Thailand (Falco, 1980, p. A19).

OPIUM IN THE SOVIET-AFGHAN WAR (1979–1989)

Following the 1979 invasion and occupation of Afghanistan by Soviet forces, the United States, Pakistan, Saudi Arabia, China, and others began funneling huge sums of money, weaponry, and other supplies to various mujahideen (holy warriors) factions hand-picked by Pakistan's Directorate for Inter-Services Intelligence (ISI). Throughout the ten-year conflict ISI served as the lead agency coordinating the logistical efforts on behalf of the Afghan resistance.[16]

McCoy (2003, p. 465) argues that:

> Although the drug pandemic of the 1980s had complex causes, the growth in global heroin supply, could be traced, in large part, to two key aspects of U.S. policy—the failure of DEA prohibition in the war on drugs and CIA protection for drug lord allies in its covert wars.[17]

In other words, the United States and its allies were totally committed to driving Soviet forces out of Afghanistan. The prevailing view was to create a military situation similar to what the United States experienced in Vietnam; if the "war on drugs" had to be superseded by this effort then so be it.

From an economic perspective the Soviet invasion's impact on the Afghan economy was catastrophic. Between five and six million people were displaced. Many of these people sought refuge in Pakistan and Iran and others sought refuge in safer parts of Afghanistan. This left many rural areas unpopulated and farmland untended. Since Afghanistan's economy is agriculturally-based it wasn't long before the remaining population began to experience severe food shortages and a drastic decline in basic services, i.e., energy, medical care, sanitation, and other essentials. Moreover, much of the widespread Soviet carpet bombing destroyed critical irrigation networks and only hastened Afghanistan's economic collapse.[18]

A study conducted by the U.S. Defense Intelligence Agency (DIA, 1983, p. iv) concluded:

> The effect of the Soviet occupation of Afghanistan has been catastrophic for the development of the Afghan economy. The evidence suggests a serious decline in the gross national product (GNP) and the abandonment of many Soviet-aided industrial projects which had been completed or were under construction in 1979. . . . With its agricultural base adversely affected by war and collectivization, the country has also become a net food importer after being a net exporter in previous years. In addition, Soviet involvement in Afghanistan has lessened the prospects for beneficial Western economic involvement through both trade and aid transactions.

Not only was Afghanistan embroiled in a vicious battle with Soviet forces, but Iran and Pakistan's Northwest Frontier Province (NWFP)[19] were also experiencing political unrest. Consequently, because of this regional turmoil the drug trade was proliferating unhampered and opium production in the Golden Crescent began to escalate.[20]

It is important to note that the primary resistance to the Soviet invasion came from Afghan nationals. The non-Afghans or Afghan-Arabs (mujahideen), as they refer to themselves, were never a very significant factor in the outcome of the war.[21] However, from this group of mostly foreign combatants would merge a global proliferation of Islamic extremism which would be nurtured in the rugged and mountainous Afghan terrain. The movement which was spawned by the 1979 Iranian revolution[22] and the Soviet-Afghan War[23] will be examined in more detail in chapter 5. These two factors which are credited with the transformation and proliferation of the opium trade also spawned the rise of jihadist militant groups. According to Gunaratna (2002, p. 3):

> Two momentous events in 1979—the Islamic Revolution in Iran and the Soviet invasion of Afghanistan—marked the rise of a new wave of Islamists movements which toppled the Shah of Iran and eventually drove

the Soviet Union from Afghanistan. And it was the enduring impact of the Iranian Revolution and the defeat of communism which precipitated the creation of over one hundred contemporary Islamist movements in the Middle East, Asia, Africa, the Caucasus, the Balkans, and also in Western Europe.

The sudden surge in opium cultivation in Afghanistan during the 1980s was primarily borne out of necessity (Walia, 2006; Calvani, 2008, p. 3). Much of the Afghan infrastructure had been destroyed by Soviet combat operations and opium provided the ideal crop to feed poor farmers and their families. While opium did provide Afghan and insurgent forces a financial means to conduct offensive operations it also caused problems among Soviet troops, many of whom turned to abusing heroin, a derivative of the crop.

In the early 1980s, Brian Freemantle, an investigative reporter and novelist, conducted a study of the global drug trade and published his findings in a book titled, *The Fix: Inside the World Drug Trade*. His research received the support of the Reagan White House and many U.S. and foreign law enforcement and drug interdiction agencies. During the course of his research the author interviewed numerous Eastern-bloc officials. Some of these people had been to Kabul and had intimate knowledge regarding the severity of this problem:

> From discussions with "Soviet defectors and clandestine contact with the mujahideen, the guerrillas who oppose the Russian occupation, there is evidence that the Afghan fighters are fully exploiting their opium and marijuana crops. They have so successfully cultivated a drug habit among Soviet soldiers that Moscow . . . has in some cases cut to nine months the period their military personnel are stationed in Afghanistan in an effort to reduce addiction" (Freemantle, 1986, pp. 179–180).[24]

A 1988 report prepared for the U.S. Army by Alexander Alexiev of the RAND Corporation substantiates the claims made by Freemantle. The report titled, *Inside the Soviet Army in Afghanistan*, confirms that the use of drugs by Soviet soldiers in Afghanistan was widespread. The drugs most widely abused were hashish, marijuana, opium, and heroin. The author validates the findings of Freemantle when he states that, "the need to procure drugs on a regular basis for those who have become habituated is also said to be the driving force behind the widespread theft and pilferage of military property, including weapons and ammunition, taking place in Afghanistan" (Alexiev, 1988, p. 51). Tanner (2002, p. 263) also notes that a major problem which confronted the Soviet military was "a noticeable drop in morale among their troops, most clearly represented by widespread drug use."

In *Unholy Wars: Afghanistan, America and International Terrorism,* John Cooley discusses the operational significance of Afghanistan's opium trade. In a fundamental sense:

> . . . the CIA and its allies, in order to help finance the proxy U.S.-Soviet war, tolerated the rise of the biggest drug empires ever seen east of the giant Colombian cocaine cartels. While the U.S. Drug Enforcement Administration (DEA) and other agencies were spending billions of dollars to stem the tidal wave of narcotics from South Asia, the CIA and its allies were turning a blind eye or actively encouraging it (Cooley, 2002, p. 107).

The drug trade is a complex phenomenon and many internal and external forces contributed and indeed promoted the rise in opium cultivation and production in Afghanistan during the 1980s. Opium poppy was and continues to be capable of generating huge revenues; consequently the trade was promulgated by various insurgent groups and public officials in an effort to sustain the war effort. Moreover, ordinary peasants engaged in the trade in order to purchase food and other necessities for themselves and their families, and various criminal groups, exploiting the chaos, were looking to make a profit (Haq, 1996, p. 951).

Rebel involvement in the trade was a closely held secret during the war. Officials in Islamabad as well as Washington knew of the increasing role that opium was playing in the war but never addressed the problem until they were in the final throes of the conflict. In 1986, Arthur Bonner, a reporter for the *New York Times*, spent several weeks traveling through the major opium producing provinces in southern Afghanistan. He reported that according to Afghan commanders the harvesting of opium was critical to the overall success of their campaign against Soviet forces. Bonner states in his article that, "the rebels, encountered here and elsewhere on a 1,000-mile journey through three southern Afghan provinces admitted they are involved in opium cultivation. The war, the rebels said, created its own economic and moral imperatives; they said the opium harvest was crucial to their survival and their continued efforts to oust the Communists" (Bonner, 1986, p. A1).

In this same report a young rebel commander spoke of dealers coming from Iran willing to buy their farmers' opium. In addition to providing cash for the insurgency the money pays for food and other family necessities.[25] A Pakistani narcotics control officer said that opium was currently being produced in "12 of the country's 29 provinces" (Bonner, 1986, p. A1).

Other works indicate that there were many players involved in the drug trade during the 1980s. Booth (1996, p. 289) cites rebel involvement in the trade and also implicates the Pakistani military and Inter-Services Intelligence (ISI) Directorate:

> Opium arrived at border posts where it was bought by Pakistani refiners of whom there were about 150 operating in 1986 in the Khyber district of

> the North-West Frontier Province, protected by the provincial governor. Pakistani military vehicles frequently transported opium made immune to police search by ISI passes.

Booth (1996, p. 289) asserts that although the CIA was aware that some of the rebel commanders were indeed involved in the drug business they [CIA] did not want to jeopardize the battle against communism by interfering in an enterprise which served to generate much needed revenue for the anti-Soviet forces they were supporting. Haq (1996, p. 945) takes this argument one step further and notes that, "CIA intervention provided the political protection and logistics linkage that joined Afghanistan's poppy fields, through Pakistan's land mass, to heroin markets in Europe and America."[26]

Detailed information relative to the opium situation in Afghanistan during the occupation is scant given the reluctance of many of the major Western media outlets to report on this phenomenon and the ongoing conflict made data collection very difficult. However, there is ample justification from information that is available that opium cultivation during the 1980s increased throughout the country. Evidence also suggests that as opium cultivation increased during this period its conversion into heroin inside Afghanistan also began. As Goodson notes, "the cultivation of opium poppies has increased tremendously since the beginning of the Afghan war, and local processing of heroin is entirely a post-1980 phenomenon" (Goodson, 2001, p. 101).

When the last Soviet forces withdrew from Afghanistan in February 1989 conflict between the Soviet-backed Najibullah regime in Kabul and opposition forces continued. Since 1979 Afghanistan has experienced a continual cycle of conflict, state collapse, social and political upheaval, and a war economy which is heavily reliant on the opium trade. Since 1979 "Afghanistan's opium production increased more than 15-fold" (UNODC, 2003a, p. 5).[27] This escalation can be attributed to a number of factors: extreme poverty, the lack of alternative livelihoods, infrastructure decimation, and thirty years of political turmoil.[28]

In three decades of conflict in Afghanistan there has been very little empirical research undertaken inside that country.[29] Due to the lack of credible national data, ongoing security concerns, and the distrust of foreigners, inherent among Afghans, it has been very difficult to compile meaningful data. This is especially true of the period 1980–1989. What we do know is that throughout the 1980s, opium cultivation and the heroin trade played a vital role in the successful Afghan and foreign resistance to Soviet occupation forces. According to the U.S. Drug Enforcement Agency (DEA) and State Department officials, "heroin production in Afghanistan, slowed greatly by the Soviet military intervention and subsequent fighting, has increased steadily since late 1984" (Cullen, 1987, p. 1). Drugs and arms were transited oftentimes via the same supply routes. Drugs trafficked through Pakistan traversed the same logistical channels as arms and other war materiel.

The Helmand River Valley is located in southwestern Afghanistan. Historically, this area has provided a large percentage of Afghanistan's total opium output.[30] It has been alleged that during the Soviet-Afghan war various leaders of the Afghan resistance employed intermediaries, "including other mujaheddin factions such as the radical Hezb-i-Islami (HIG) party, and some Pakistan military officials to coordinate the guerrillas' arms supplies." These intermediaries were active in Afghanistan as well as Pakistan with Peshawar serving as the nucleus for mujahideen smuggling operations (Haq, 1996, p. 951).

As the Soviet offensive began to lose steam many local commanders sought financial gain through the opium trade, thus allowing many of them to become self-sufficient and powerful warlords "increasingly independent of the external donors and local society" (Rubin, 1995, p. 117).

Following the Soviet-Afghan conflict large numbers of refugees began returning to their homeland from refugee camps in Iran and Pakistan. The pre-war economy and industrial base, though not particularly strong prior to the war, was now destroyed. Returning refugees came home to a country that was plagued by lawlessness, continued violence, and poverty. With much of the agricultural infrastructure destroyed or riddled with land mines many returning refugees and those who decided to stay were confronted with very limited viable alternatives. Moreover, following the downfall of the Soviet-backed government in 1992 a state of civil war erupted as fighting between rival insurgent factions intensified.[31] By the time the Taliban emerged in 1994 fighting had spread to all major cities. Much of Afghanistan's pre-1980 economic infrastructure had been destroyed by fifteen years of war. Many parts of the country were "'uninhabitable." Major implications of this reality were a complete destruction of Afghanistan's economic, social, and political institutions.[32]

An economy based on the production and cultivation of opium began to take shape in the waning years of the war. In 1986 the number of hectares allocated for opium poppy cultivation was approximately 29,000. In 2005 that number jumped to 104,000, an increase of approximately 260 percent.[33] This surge in opium did not abate following the end of the Soviet occupation.

TALIBAN OPIUM BAN AND U.S. INVASION

The instability and lack of governance brought on by the Soviet-Afghan war helped to insure that Afghanistan would become one of the world's major opium producers. In his best-selling book, *Ghost Wars,* author and then managing editor of the *Washington Post,* Steven Coll provided the following appraisal of the magnitude of the opium problem as it existed in Afghanistan in the early 1990s:

> From fertile Helmand in the south to the gorge valleys of the northeast, Afghanistan flowered each spring with one of the world's largest crops of opium poppies. Untroubled by government, and funded by smugglers and organized crime networks rooted in Pakistan, Afghan poppy farmers supplied heroin labs nestled in cities and along the lawless Afghanistan-Pakistan border. By 1992 hundreds of tons of refined heroin flowed from these labs east through Karachi's port or north through the new overland routes of the Russian mafia, destined for European cities (Coll, 2004, p. 233).[34]

During the Taliban ban in 2000 most of the country's opium production occurred in Northern Alliance-held territory, specifically Badakhshan province, where production soared "by 158 percent from 2000–2001" (Cornell, 2006, p. 44).[35] However, the ban spawned a significant decline in opium poppy cultivation in areas where the Taliban had political and military control.[36]

Although the Taliban's ban on opium cultivation appears to have had a considerable amount of success, the trafficking of opium and its derivatives continued (Davids, 2002, p. 32) and the Taliban was able to draw a considerable amount of tax revenue from those engaged in trafficking the product.[37] Moreover, the Taliban did not appear to interfere or challenge those engaged in the processing of opium.[38]

Following the U.S.-led coalition attack and occupation of Afghanistan, opium poppy cultivation would eventually spread throughout the country, reaching unprecedented levels and provide various insurgent factions, warlords, and corrupt government officials with financial and political capital.[39]

After the fall of the Taliban in November 2001, farmers seized the opportunity to plant opium poppy since there was no central governing authority which could restrict or inhibit their agricultural efforts and warlords were reestablishing control over territory once occupied by Taliban forces.[40] Goodhand (2003, p. 8) points out that there was no real incentive for warlord cooperation with the newly formed government in Kabul. He states, "Afghanistan is reverting to the pattern of governance of the early 1990s."[41]

Land allocated for poppy cultivation has increased dramatically since the Taliban fell from power.[42] This reflects two realities. First, it reflects opium's importance to the Afghan economy, and secondly, it affirms the fact that the political climate and ongoing turmoil which has existed since the Taliban's demise has fostered an environment conducive to an expansion of the drug trade, even though the central government in Kabul issued a decree in January 2002 outlawing it. It also seems that those engaged in this trade find the status quo economically desirable, and the continued lawlessness and ongoing conflict provides drug merchants with the necessary cover and protection to expand their control over the major poppy growing regions. In 2004, opium poppy was being grown in all of Afghanistan's 34 provinces (UNODC, 2005c, pp. 10 and 39).[43]

In the absence of viable alternative livelihoods, opium cultivation has served and continues to serve as a survival mechanism for many of Afghanistan's rural poor.[44] Opium provides the rural farmer with a high value, non-perishable, "cash crop" that is in large demand with established markets. Moreover, farmers are often paid in advance against future harvest yield and, although labor intensive, it is easy to transport.[45] According to Ward and Byrd (2004, pp. 26–27):

> In 2003 the average gross income per hectare from opium cultivation exceeded that of wheat, the main alternative crop, by as much as 27 times . . . In some parts of the country where poppy cultivation is concentrated wage rates of as much as US$11–12 per day for opium harvesting work have been reported, five times the market wage rate for rural unskilled labor. At the processing and trafficking level high margins in an otherwise dismal economy have driven keen interest.[46]

The *salaam* arrangement, noted briefly above, provides farmers with a system whereby they receive credit and advanced payment on their future opium harvest.[47] While this practice of extending what amounts to informal credit provides some advantages to the farmer and his family, it often works to the farmer's disadvantage.[48]

Many of these opium dependent individuals/families remain in a continual cycle of debt, often owing large sums of money to landlords who make no allowances if the farmer cannot deliver. Additionally, many of these people have to depend entirely upon foreign assistance for food.[49] From a national security perspective, continued reliance on opium poppy has a negative and counterproductive impact on the state as a whole—impacting the state's ability to govern effectively and provide needed goods and services to its citizens. Additionally, it drains state, regional, and global resources due to the efforts and capital expenditures necessary to combat it.

Thus the drug industry creates a self-perpetuating environment which is constantly expanding and promoting the interests of often violent and self-serving non-state actors and corrupt government officials.

A pattern of narcotics and conflict has persisted in Afghanistan since the early days of the Soviet occupation and continued through the turbulent civil war years, the Taliban ascendancy period,[50] through the present "war on terrorism." Opium cultivation in Afghanistan has played a major role in each conflict. Moreover, this ongoing trade has primarily benefited violent non-state actors. Research conducted by Svante Cornell of the Central Asia-Caucasus Institute supports this notion. According to Cornell:

> The growth of a narcotics industry in a conflict zone is likely to disproportionably benefit the non-state actor (typically the weaker actor) in financial terms. This enables it to pay fighters, acquire weapons and, potentially, even buy legitimacy with the local population (Cornell, 2005, p. 754).

The tumultuous Afghan environment has been equally beneficial to other non-state actors such as organized criminals, drug traffickers, and provides a safe haven for terrorist groups.

The Afghan drug trade continues to proliferate and further entrench itself into the Afghan economy. In fact, the expansion of opium poppy cultivation in the provinces has surged since the Taliban were ousted in December 2001.[51]

In 2004, opium was being cultivated in what are now 34 Afghan provinces and approximately 2.3 million people were involved in its cultivation. This represents about "10% of the total population in Afghanistan or 12–14% of the rural population" (UNODC, 2005c, p. 179). These findings suggest that a very close nexus exists between rural poverty in Afghanistan and the cultivation, production, and processing of opium. Furthermore, two additional assessments can be made. First, for a majority of the 2.3 million people involved in opium crop production, the opium poppy has become a critical component in the ability of these people to sustain even a most rudimentary type of existence. Secondly, the opium trade in Afghanistan is resilient. It has been able to develop and prosper despite bans on cultivation and ongoing conflict. Indeed, the ongoing turmoil within the country has been a facilitating factor in the proliferation and expansion of the trade. Taking opium out of the Afghan equation will take a monumental effort on the part of the Afghan government and international community. Given the current undeveloped state of Afghanistan's infrastructure, the lack of a strong central government with national reach, laws that are enforceable, alternative livelihoods for the millions of people who rely on opium for their existence, and agricultural and industrial reconstruction efforts on the part of the international community, the prospects for resolving the opium problem in Afghanistan look bleak.

Today Afghanistan's opium output continues to play a leading role in that country's inability to achieve political, economic, and social stability. Attempts at eradication and crop substitution have to date not been successful and the United States, its NATO allies, and the current Afghan government have been unable to formulate viable strategies to deal with this growing problem. Moreover, opium crop eradication has increased the Taliban's political capital with those whose livelihoods are dependent on the crop.[52]

PROCESSING LABORATORIES INSIDE AFGHANISTAN

In addition to the post-9/11 surge in cultivation, laboratories that convert raw opium to morphine base and heroin have also increased dramatically throughout the border areas of Afghanistan (Townsend, 2005, pp. 14–18):

> In early 2004 the Tajik Drug Control Agency estimated that there were 80 Afghan processing laboratories along the border, essentially functioning as export-oriented factories . . . With secure supplies of precursor chemicals it is beneficial for traffickers to process the opium within Afghanistan . . . detection and closure of processing laboratories is less likely in Afghanistan (Townsend, 2005, pp. 16–17).[53]

Townsend also notes that Afghanistan's processing capabilities have increased significantly during the recent conflict.[54] In this regard the United Nations Office on Drugs and Crime (UNODC) reported in October 2002 that, "while Afghanistan has been a major opium producing country for the last two decades, Afghan heroin manufacture is a rather new phenomenon" (UNODCCP, 2002a, p. 6).[55] A more detailed analysis of this trend is provided in a 2004 report compiled by the United Nations Office on Drugs and Crime:

> There is clear evidence of heroin production in Afghanistan. Afghan authorities dismantled 120 'fixed laboratories' and 30 "movable laboratories" in 2003, mainly in Helmand, Nangarhar (notably in Shanwar district) and in Badakshan. Additional raids also took place in 2004. Laboratories are often located rather close to the border areas. . . . Analyzing reported seizures from Afghanistan and neighbouring countries (Pakistan, Iran and the countries of Central Asia) 77% of the seizures (expressed in opium equivalents) were already in the form of heroin and morphine in 2003, and only 23% in the form of opium (UNODC, 2004a, p. 105).

Mark McDonald, an investigative journalist and former Moscow Bureau Chief for Knight Ridder newspapers, spent time on the Afghan-Tajik border during this current conflict. He interviewed many border guards and from these discussions he reached the same conclusion as Townsend (2005) relative to Afghanistan's opium processing capabilities. McDonald reported that:

> . . . the number of processing facilities in Afghanistan has exploded over the last year. The trade and huge sums of money involved threaten to undermine vulnerable border-states such as Tajikistan (McDonald, 2004a, p. A01).

McDonald also interviewed Avaz Yuldashov of the Tajikistan Drug Control Agency. During the course of their discussion Yuldashov stated:

> There is absolutely no threat to the laboratories inside Afghanistan . . . our intelligence shows there are 400 labs making heroin there, and 80 of them are situated right along our border. Some of them even work outside in the open air (McDonald, 2004a, p. A01).

Stemming the flow of narcotics through the porous Tajik-Afghan border is extremely difficult given the terrain, the length of the border, and the endless supply of potential couriers willing to sacrifice arrest and imprisonment for the prospect of making a quick profit (Townsend, 2005, pp. 62–63).

The above cited United Nations report further identifies the area extending from Faizabad to Kunduz (northern Afghanistan) where laboratories of various sizes have been set up to manufacture heroin. UNODCCP points out that the labs are usually run by families and are limited in size to thwart interference by coalition forces and/or law enforcement officials. These small labs are generally capable of producing a daily heroin output of between 5–10 kilograms (Townsend, 2005, p. 22).[56] This trend is also evident in the south. In December 2007, the Associated Press reported that in Musa Qala, a district in northern Helmand province, and then a Taliban stronghold, 50–70 conversion labs were processing opium that was cultivated in northern Helmand. These labs, depending upon production capacity, employed between 15–60 Afghans (Khan, 2007).[57]

Converting raw opium into heroin prior to sending it across national borders has a dual benefit of increasing its market value and providing a measure of security for traffickers since transporting heroin takes less space (one-tenth the weight of opium) and is easier to conceal (Ward and Byrd, 2004, p. 41). It is estimated that approximately 60 percent of the opium produced in Afghanistan is converted to morphine/heroin prior to export.[58]

TRANSIT ROUTES: COUNTRIES THAT SERVE AS TRADITIONAL DRUG SMUGGLING ROUTES

Since the early 1990s through the present, Afghanistan's opium, much of which is processed/converted into heroin in the border regions prior to leaving the country, has been the major source of supply to markets in Europe and Russia. Increasing amounts of Afghan opiates also provide a steady flow of drugs to satisfy the internal demands in Afghanistan and neighboring countries (Iran, Pakistan, Central Asian Republics). Local and regional consumption in these countries has steadily increased over the years, especially in the post-Soviet era.[59] While this determines how much Afghan opiates leaving the country stay in the region to feed area addicts, the majority of opiates smuggled out of Afghanistan are destined for Western Europe.

Opiates from Afghanistan exit the country through all six neighboring state borders.[60] The major opium cultivation areas "are situated near exit routes from Afghanistan and close to major population centers in the neighboring country" (Raghavan, 2005).

Narcotics interdiction agencies and border control personnel determine the locations of various narcotic transit routes primarily through seizure data, which historically accounts for only a small percentage (5–10) of the total amount trafficked. The location of heroin processing laboratories, usually situated close to national borders, is also a pretty good indicator of the proximity of main trafficking routes. Since the end of the Cold War, the Central Asian Republics have served as a conduit for much of the opium and heroin smuggled out of Afghanistan.[61]

Since Afghanistan is a land-locked country, drugs have historically exited Afghanistan through two primary routes. One route passes through northern Pakistan, primarily through the Khyber PakhtunKhwa,[62] and in the southern provinces the opium/heroin transits into Pakistan primarily through Helmand: "drug traffickers use the vast deserts of, and the numerous caravan routes across Baluchistan, Pakistan and Seistan via Baluchistan, Iran" (Center for Geopolitical Drug Studies, 2002a, p. 6). Peshawar, provincial capital of the NWFP,[63] is a major narcotics transit hub.[64] Quetta, capital of Balochistan province in Pakistan, is another international trafficking hub, as is Karachi, a densely populated city is the capital of Sindh province and the largest city in Pakistan.[65]

According to Raghavan (2005) "some of the important drug barons are based out of Peshawar and Quetta." As stated above, the second route enters Pakistan through the southern provinces of Afghanistan, primarily through Helmand and Kandahar, two of the country's main opium poppy cultivation provinces.

Historically, Iran has served as a major conduit for Afghan opiates despite the possible imposition of the death penalty if caught. "The drugs enter Iran mainly at Zahedan, Zabol and Torbat-e Jam and, then, either reach the port of Bandar Abbas or travel on to Turkey via Kerman, Ispahan and Tabriz. At Meshed, the opiates may be transported to either Turkmenistan or Tehran." Since Iran is a major opiate consumer, the capital Tehran serves as an international transportation hub for further transfer to European and Turkish markets (Center for Geopolitical Drug Studies, 2002b, p. 6).

Since the late 1970s Iran has been responsible for a large percentage of regional drug seizures. A briefing paper prepared by the U.S. Government Accountability Office (GAO) for the U.S. Senate Caucus on International Narcotics Control cited that, "despite Iran's efforts to curtail heroin smuggling, its border with Afghanistan remains a major transshipment point for Afghanistan opium/heroin." They further state that, "this is a result of established routes, numerous caves for storage, and the history of trafficking drugs through Iran" (U.S. GAO, 2000). While Iran and also Turkey have historically been used as major transportation hubs, increased law enforcement efforts have made smuggling through these countries more risky and consequently less desirable.

Iran, for example, has built a "system of channels, concrete dam constructions, sentry points and observation towers, as well as a road alongside the entire eastern border . . . the country regularly deploys 30,000 law enforcement personnel to guard this border" (Olcott and Udalova, 2000, p. 8.). It has been reported that since the 1979 Iranian Revolution over 3,000 Iranian security force personnel have been killed while attempting to intercept drug shipments coming across the Iranian border with Afghanistan (Reuters, November 10, 2006). Although still a major concern, these efforts by the Iranians have been successful in stopping large shipments of opiates from entering their country. According to UN figures, Iran confiscates approximately 250 tons of Afghan opiates each year. This, according to the UNODC accounts for about 90 percent of all global seizures of opium and 10 percent of all worldwide heroin seizures (Dinmore, 2002, p. 10). This, in part, has made the Central Asian states a very desirable alternative for traffickers.

The collapse of the USSR led to the relaxation of trade barriers, and more porous borders. Consequently, three of the five Central Asian states: Tajikistan, Turkmenistan, and Uzbekistan, have seen a considerable amount of Afghan opiates enter their country:

> Afghan and Central Asian traffickers smuggle heroin along the Silk Route into Russia, the Baltic States, Poland, Ukraine, the Czech Republic and other parts of Europe. Tajikistan, Uzbekistan, Kyrgyzstan, Kazakhstan and Turkmenistan are vital transit countries, with an estimated 24% of Afghan heroin smuggled along this route (INTERPOL, 2005).[66]

Additionally, the northeastern Afghan province of Badakhshan, which borders Tajikistan has become a major opium cultivation and production center which, according to Chouvy (2003), "puts more pressure on Central Asia as a main drug trafficking route." Tajikistan's terrain, which makes it difficult to patrol, its long border with Afghanistan, and the 1992–1997 civil war were additional factors that contributed to the country becoming a major conduit for Afghan opiates (ICG, 2001, pp. 2 and 5).

While it is very difficult to determine the total volume of opiates trafficked through Central Asia in a given year, one fact is clear: as the demand for opiates in Central Asian states increases, the volume of trafficking through these states also increases.[67] According to Swanstrom (2003):

> The Central Asian states have increased their heroin interception by 50 percent in the past few years. The high increase in the number of seizures

> only exemplifies that the actual trade has increased . . . The increase in the drug trade can be seen in that the price of heroin and other drugs has been relatively constant in Central Asia and China but demand in consumption countries has increased. This indicates that production has increased, and more drugs are smuggled across the region.[68]

Similar findings were cited in the, *U.S. International Narcotics Control Strategy Report*[69] issued in March 2001 and a report, *Current/Planned Activities in Central Asia: Illicit Drugs Situation in the Central Asian States and the Response to It by UNDCP*, issued in September of the same year by the United Nations Drug Control Program (UNDCP). The UNDCP report is based on information provided by INTERPOL and the World Customs Organization. Both reports suggest that, "in 1999–2000, seizures of opiates were made in Europe that were unequivocally identified to have been smuggled through Central Asia" (Redo, 2004, pp. 100 and 131, notes 15 and 16).

The Central Asian states of Tajikistan, Turkmenistan, and Uzbekistan are ideal points of transit. The governments are weak, the borders are porous, and since the collapse of the Soviet Union border security has been lax. Additionally, corruption of border guards, public officials, and the lack of well-trained and armed national drug enforcement agencies contribute to the problem.[70]

While drugs are still transited through China, today trafficking through the country is primarily destined for Xianjing province and does not constitute a significant amount.[71] China's terrain is also a factor which curtails the amount of Afghan opium that crosses the Chinese-Indian border (Townsend, 2005, p. 32). Furthermore, opiates entering China from Afghanistan are, as Townsend notes, "theoretically in competition with those of networks distributing from eastern China" (Townsend, 2005, p. 70). Nevertheless, if production trends continue as they have been traffickers may be forced to source their product from Afghan suppliers (Townsend, 2005, p. 74). Drug smugglers using the northern routes "cross into Pakistan's 'tribal belt' especially in the NWFP, via myriad mountain passes, such as the famed Khyber Pass . . . Dorah, Tochi and Gomal . . ." (Center for Geopolitical Drug Studies, 2001, p.6).[72]

East Africa also serves as a drug transit route for Afghan opiates. Much of the drug traffic passing through this region supplies neighboring consumer countries as well as North American markets (INTERPOL, 2005).

Additionally, annual heroin production in Afghanistan requires approximately 13,000 tons of precursor agent (UNODC, 2010d, p 247). The primary precursor chemical used in heroin production is acetic anhydride. This important chemical is usually obtained by diverting legally manufactured shipments from source countries (i.e., India, China) and smuggling them through the same channels to various heroin processing laboratories inside Afghanistan and/or Pakistan. Acetic anhydride is also produced in the Central Asian states of Kazakhstan, Turkmenistan, and Uzbekistan (ICG, 2001, p. 7). Diverting legal consignments of acetic anhydride is more cost effective than trying to mass-produce the chemical and does not require detailed processing and production knowledge.[73]

While efforts are continuing to address Afghanistan's problems relative to public safety and security, it will be some time before appropriate laws are established and are able to be adequately enforced at the local, provincial, and national levels. Until this happens it appears that the drug problem, which is contributing to state instability and a myriad of other difficulties, will continue to be a major factor in Afghanistan's ability to evolve into a functioning, self-sustaining entity. As Ward and Byrd (2004, pp. 4 and 22) note, "In the absence of effective law enforcement and of a working judicial and penal system, drug trafficking and processing have been virtually unchecked in the past." Until these problems are addressed it is highly likely that the opium problem in Afghanistan will continue to expand, further aggravate tensions in Southwest and Central Asia, and provide the bulk of the global supply of illicit opiates.

AFGHANISTAN'S OPIUM TRADE: THREAT TO REGIONAL SECURITY

The cultivation and production of opium in Afghanistan poses many political, social, and economic challenges for Asia as well as the entire international community.[74] Nowhere is this more evident than in the Central Asian states.[75] According to Rashid (2001f, p. 120):

> Central Asia was the hardest hit by the explosion in Afghan heroin. The Russian mafia, with ties to Afghanistan established during the Soviet occupation, used their networks to move heroin through Central Asia, Russia, the Baltics and into Europe. Tajikistan and Kyrgyzstan developed important opium routes and became significant opium producers themselves.[76]

Central Asia became an international security concern when the Soviet Union dissolved in 1991 and, following the events of 9/11, important players in the global battle against terrorism. These states which had previously relied upon the former superpower for economic, social, and political cohesion were now coming to grips with their national identity and the problems inherent in an evolving nation-state entity: unemployment levels rose, goods and services were drastically curtailed, and non-state actors intensified their ongoing struggle of exerting their influence throughout the region.[77]

Williams (2003, p. 83) argues that Central Asia is an innate conduit for Afghan opiates en route to European and Russian markets.[78] Indeed, the opium problem has created a number of security challenges for the countries which border Afghanistan.[79] The republics of Central Asia have been infiltrated with Afghan opium and this has caused many social, political, and economic problems as criminal groups are exerting an increasing amount of influence on the already weak political apparatus of the Central Asian states (Lubin, 2001, Parts 1, 2, and 3). The director of the Tajik drug control agency, General Rustam Nazarov, stated that in 2002 his agency confiscated over six tons of drugs of which three tons were heroin. Furthermore, he added that along the northern provinces of Afghanistan bordering his country there were approximately "50 mini-laboratories" processing heroin that would eventually find its way into Tajikistan and other "Central Asia regions" (*Financial Times*, January 20, 2003).

In essence, the large sums of money available to those at the higher end of the drug "food chain" can literally buy influence, a voice at the policy table, and fuel corruption among public officials.[80] Hence, Afghanistan's opium industry not only undermines its own reconstruction efforts, but the ongoing instability within the country, fueled in part by the continued expansion of the illicit drug trade, reaches across national borders promoting corruption within all levels of government (Roston, 2002, pp. 23–26). The ramifications of this are far-reaching as efforts to build stable institutions, capable of providing meaningful employment to the populace, are undermined; concomitantly prohibiting any positive economic impact of potential foreign investors. This inability to build sound economic infrastructures, coupled with the lucrative profits to be made in the illicit drug sector, also fosters corruption within the region's individual law enforcement and state security apparatus particularly along main smuggling routes from the source country to the "destination market" (UNODC, 2010d, p. 248).

On the problem of corruption and weak states, Cornell and Swanstrom (2006, p. 16) point out that the drug trade stymies economic development and this process tends to "keep weak states weak and poor populations poor." The weaker the state becomes the easier it is to engage in activities such as drug production which further undermines the state's legitimacy. Furthermore, these authors make the following significant point: The corrupt political environment acts as a magnet and breeding ground for organized crime and, with "key individuals" within the government becoming involved in the drugs trade, it becomes very difficult to reverse the trend.[81]

Media reports and research conducted by internationally renowned public policy institutes indicate that members of various law enforcement agencies, those charged with providing domestic security and border protection, often become willing or unwilling participants in the movement of opiates. For example, "there have been many allegations that troops on the Tajik-Afghan border engage in the drug trade and some confirmation of this came in April and May 2004 when, in separate incidents, the

Tajik Drug Control Agency arrested two members of the Russian border guard service" (Townsend, 2005, p. 68). Russia has been involved in Tajikistan since their intervention in the Tajik Civil War (1992–1997). Russian intervention in the former Soviet states of Central Asia has been under the guise of protecting the 10 percent minority of "ethnic Russians" from Islamic militancy. "Russian border guards also have been stationed along the Tajik-Afghan border to defend 'the southern border of the Commonwealth of Independent States,' although the CIS has ceased to exist in almost every other way" (Dunn, 1993, p. 55).[82]

Tajik border officials have also been known to ignore or knowingly allow drug shipments to enter the country even if they themselves were not profiting from the traffic. As cited above, a report issued by the International Crisis Group (ICG) points to the dangers inherent at border crossings especially when large shipments of drugs are involved. The fear is that confiscation of a drug shipment, especially a "major shipment," would not only jeopardize the well-being of the individual who seized the drugs but his family as well (ICG, 2001, p. 15).

Furthermore, this report cites a July 2001 interview conducted by the ICG with Sharif Zhuraev, procurator general for the Tajikistan customs department. During this exchange Zhuraev revealed that the number of customs officials involved, to some degree, in the drug trade may be as high as 50 percent. The report also cites the arrest, in Osh, Kyrgyzstan, of the director of the drug enforcement administration and several of his employees for their involvement in illegal drug activity (ICG, 2001, pp. 8–9).[83]

For years there has been speculation that the Russian military has been involved in transporting opiates into Russia (Williams, 2003, pp. 85–86). In an interview published on May 29, 2001, in *Moskovskie Novosti*, a Moscow weekly newspaper, a former Russian intelligence official, Anton Surikov, claimed that, "'Russian military planes, helicopters and trains transported large quantities of Afghan opiates from the Tajik capital, Dushanbe.'" During the interview Surikov discussed the specifics of his allegations:

> You can come to an arrangement [with custom officials] so that the search of military transport planes remains purely formal. The same goes for train convoys carrying military cargo [to Russia from Tajikistan] (Peuch, 2001).[84]

In this respect a January 2001 report in the *Times of Central Asia* cites charges brought against members of Russia's 201st Mechanized Infantry Division.[85] Twelve members of this unit, which was based in Tajikistan, were arrested in Moscow attempting to transport eight kilograms of drugs of which three kilograms was heroin (Manayev, 2001).[86]

With huge quantities of opiates transiting Central Asian borders, local populations are taking an active part in the trade due to a lack of viable economic opportunities in their home country and the amount of money that can be made relative to licit employment. It is estimated that the Central Asian drug trade generates approximately $14 billion (U.S.) and "involves several million people" (Manayev, 2000). Additionally, as previously mentioned, the addict population throughout Central Asia is increasing dramatically. It is estimated that more than half of the opium transported through the Central Asian states stays in the region to feed an expanding addict population (*Asia Today*, April 26, 2002).

This puts a strain on already compromised economies and public health infrastructures as many of these addicts administer these drugs intravenously and engage in the practice of needle-sharing which increases incidence of drug-related disease, particularly HIV/AIDS. Given this fact Swanstrom (n.d., p. 11), in a discussion on "drug related effects on the security dimension: human security," points out that there is a direct correlation between diseases such as hepatitis, HIV/AIDS, other STDs, and drug trafficking routes. Additionally, the International Crisis Group (ICG) points out that prior to the collapse of the Soviet Union, heroin addiction and HIV/AIDS in the Central Asian states was almost non-existent (ICG, 2001, p. 1).

The Central Asian countries with their weak central governments also create an environment conducive for insurgent, criminal, and terrorist groups. Many young people feeling alienated and, with not much chance for upward mobility, are often drawn to these groups with promises of a better life and a sense of purpose and identity. Upon joining such organizations these individuals often feel that they have become part of a movement for change, i.e., an opportunity to correct past and present injustices, albeit real or perceived, forced upon them by a political system under which they felt alienated, ignored, and out of control. In effect, by aligning themselves to these organizations, they feel that they have become part of something larger than themselves; that they are serving the common and greater good.

With money generated from illicit activity, primarily the drug trade, these non-state groups are able to exert control over local populations and pose a direct threat to established regimes due to their ability to recruit people and purchase weapons, thereby increasing their threat to national governments and regional security (Cornell, 2005c, p. 754).

Moreover, Pakistan's efforts to control Afghan opiates from penetrating their borders have not brought much success. Low-level government corruption, the lawless territory of the Federally Administered Tribal Areas (FATA),[87] and the Khyber PakhtunKhwa, has made narcotics enforcement extremely difficult. These areas have traditionally been known to provide support, shelter, and protection to drug traffickers, terrorists, and insurgent groups, including the Taliban and Al Qaeda. In addressing Pakistan's drug issue, the 2003 U.S. State Department's, *International Narcotics Control Strategy Report* (INCSR), stated:

> U.S. officials have "no evidence" that any senior government officials were involved with the narcotics trade or drug money laundering, although the report also stated that narcotics remained a source of "persistent corruption" among lower level officials (Blanchard, 2006, p. 22).

However, in testimony before the U.S. House of Representatives International Relations Committee, U.S. ambassador to Pakistan, Wendy Chamberlain, when asked what role the Pakistan intelligence agency played in the narcotics trade responded by saying, ". . . the role of Pakistan's Inter-Services Intelligence Directorate (ISI) in the heroin trade from 1997–2003 had been 'substantial'" (Blanchard, 2006, p. 22). The subject of Pakistani involvement in Afghanistan's drug trade will be explored in more detail in chapter 6.

CONCLUSION

The drug industry in Afghanistan has been a major problem since the late 1970s.[88] The Soviet invasion in December 1979 and occupation throughout the 1980s exacerbated this problem. Afghanistan's opium industry is a complex, multifaceted activity which has a profound detrimental impact on the process of state building and impedes the current reconstruction process of the international community. The opium trade in Afghanistan breeds indigenous and regional corruption as it thwarts drug enforcement and control efforts. Afghanistan's drug trade is, for the most part, decentralized with many people involved in various stages of the process. This makes it somewhat competitive, often creating conflict between and among opposing interests.

The drug trade is also adaptable and can adjust very well to outside influences. This can be seen in the myriad of trafficking routes and the establishment of mobile laboratories which convert raw opium into morphine/heroin, thereby increasing its value prior to transport. The problem is so pervasive and the profits are so great that attempts to suppress the trade are usually met with violence. Unfortunately, the central government in Kabul is presently ill-equipped to deal with this ongoing and expanding threat.

The following chapter will examine the statements and testimony of both U.S. congressional leaders and national and international subject and area experts regarding the narcotics trade emanating from Afghanistan. This chapter will also address and examine law enforcement efforts to find a causal connection between Al Qaeda and other extremist groups' terrorist operations and the expanding drug trade in Afghanistan. Since the events of September 11, 2001, and the subsequent occupation of Afghanistan by U.S. and coalition forces, key U.S. congressional leaders, United Nations representatives, and other international figures have made definitive claims, counterclaims, and accusations regarding the purported drug/terror nexus in Afghanistan. It is clear that the continued growth and expansion of Afghanistan's $2.8 billion annual drug economy is driven primarily by the various agendas and ambitions of specific national and internationally-based individuals and groups.

CHAPTER 3

Drugs-Terror Nexus in Afghanistan: Claims, Counterclaims, and Accusations

OPIUM, THE TALIBAN, AL QAEDA ET AL. STATE OF KNOWLEDGE: PRE-INVASION

In a May 7, 1998, congressional debate on the Intelligence Authorization Act for fiscal year 1999 held in the U.S. House of Representatives, Congressman John Conyers (D-Michigan) inserted into the official hearing record a list titled, "A Tangled Web: A History of CIA Complicity in Drug International Trafficking." A part of that list contained the following reference to Afghanistan in the period leading up to and including the Soviet-Afghan war:

> APRIL 1978
>
> Soviet-backed coup in Afghanistan sets stage for explosive growth in Southwest Asian heroin trade. New Marxist regime undertakes vigorous anti-narcotics campaign aimed at suppressing poppy production, triggering a revolt by semi-autonomous tribal groups that traditionally raised opium for export. The CIA-supported rebel Mujahedeen begins expanding production to finance their insurgency. Between 1982 and 1989, during which time the CIA ships billions of dollars in weapons and other aid to guerrilla forces, annual opium production in Afghanistan increases to about 800 tons from 250 tons. By 1986, the State Department admits that Afghanistan is probably the world's largest producer of opium for export and the poppy source for a majority of the Southwest Asian heroin found in the United States. U.S. officials, however, fail to take action to curb production. Their silence not only serves to maintain public support for the Mujahedeen, it also smooths relations with Pakistan, whose leaders, deeply implicated in the heroin trade, help channel CIA support to the Afghan rebels (Conyers, 1998, pp. H2955–H2956).[1]

The above reference is a synopsis of the genesis of the expansion of opium poppy cultivation in Afghanistan.

On December 13, 2000, a hearing was conducted by the U.S. House of Representatives Committee on the Judiciary, Subcommittee on Crime. Frank J. Cilluffo, Deputy Director of the Global Organized Crime Program and Director of the Counterterrorism Task Force for the Center for Strategic and International Studies provided the following testimony,[2] taken from the hearing transcript[3] regarding the Taliban's involvement in the Afghan opium trade:

> The Taliban gets funding from taxing all aspects of the drug trade. Opium harvests are taxed at around 12 percent. Then the heroin manufacturing labs are taxed at $70 per kilogram of heroin. In the final stage, the Taliban gives transporters a permit for $250 per kilo of heroin to carry for presentation to Taliban checkpoints throughout the country. The Observatoire Geopolitique des Drogues (OGD) estimates that this adds up to $75 million per year in taxes for the Taliban (Cillufo, 2000, p. 73).[4]

Indeed, as noted in chapter 2 during their reign (1996–2001) the Taliban derived some income from taxing the trade (as they did other commodities) but were not involved in production or trafficking.[5] The *International Narcotics Control Strategy Report 2000* (INCSR), issued on March 1, 2001, by the U.S. Department of State noted that during the ban both the Taliban and Northern Alliance allowed opium to be traded and trafficked through their respective areas of control.[6] Additionally, during the ban most of the opium grown in Afghanistan was in areas controlled by the Northern Alliance (U.S. Department of State, 2001, pp. VII–3).

While it has been established that the Taliban benefited financially from the opium trade, Al Qaeda involvement is tougher to prove. On October 5, 1998, the *Washington Post* reported that "credible reports" from various U.S. intelligence agencies indicate that members of Al Qaeda may be involved in the protection of narcotics shipments and "may have traded guns for drugs on a small scale". These reports also indicate that there is no firm evidence linking Osama bin Laden directly to the opium trade (Farah and Constable, 1998, p. A15).

Following the events of 9/11, terrorism became this country's number one international security concern. Hence, the U.S. government began to tackle the terrorism problem with a more hands-on approach than had previously been employed. In addition to military, law enforcement, intelligence gathering, and diplomatic strategies, efforts were made to track the sources of terrorist financing; a "follow the money" approach was adopted. As part of the U.S. government's overall strategy to understand the sources of terrorist financing and therefore be able to more appropriately address the terrorist threat, a study was conducted to examine potential and alleged sources of Al Qaeda's financing. This study was conducted by the National Commission on Terrorist Attacks Upon the United States staff members. In the report which followed this investigation the CIA, based on intelligence reporting in April 2001, characterized the then existing state of knowledge relative to Al Qaeda's financial network and support structures:

> Usama Bin Ladin's financial assets are difficult to track because he uses a wide variety of mechanisms to move and raise money [;] . . . he capitalizes on a large, difficult-to-identify network with few long-lasting nodes for penetration. It is difficult to determine with any degree of accuracy what percentage of each node contributes to his overall financial position. Gaps in our understanding contribute to the difficulty we have in pursuing the Bin Ladin financial target. We presently do not have the reporting to determine how much of Bin Ladin's personal wealth he has used or continues to use in financing his organization; we are unable to estimate with confidence the value of his assets and net worth; and we do not know the level of financial support he draws from his family and other donors sympathetic to his cause (Roth, Greenburg, and Wille, 2004, p. 18).[7]

The U.S. government investigative body examining these issues concluded that due to the lack of intelligence capabilities in this area it is not possible to determine with any degree of certainty how Al Qaeda is financed or how the organization moves or spends its funds.[8]

In the period leading up to the U.S.-led invasion of Afghanistan numerous reports alleging a direct link between Osama bin Laden and the opium/heroin trade in Afghanistan surfaced. Many of these reports were generated by the national and international media, various national and international intelligence agencies, and unconfirmed information acquired through informants. Jason Burke, author of *Al Qaeda: Casting a Shadow of Terror*, and chief reporter for the *Observer* (London) provides an interesting account of the October 4, 2001, intelligence dossier prepared by the British government and "presented to the press." This report cited a direct link between Al Qaeda and the Afghan heroin trade. According to Burke (2003, p. 19) the dossier stated that, "[Al Qaeda] activity includes substantial exploitation of the illegal drugs trade from Afghanistan and claimed that bin Laden's 'drug stockpiles' were protected by the Taliban." Burke further notes that:

> There has never been any evidence that bin Laden has ever been involved in narcotics production, and everyone involved in the trade in Pakistan, Afghanistan and elsewhere, from farmers through to the United Nations experts monitoring drugs production, denies the allegation . . . The British intelligence specialists must have known that the dossier they gave to the prime minister to reveal to parliament and the British public to justify

> involvement in a major conflict included demonstrably false material but felt the war in Afghanistan needed to be fought and the public needed to be convinced of it. Painting bin Laden as profiting from the heroin trade served the same purpose as atrocity stories about the Germans in the First World War (Burke, 2003, p.19).

Burke also states that in 1998 he received faulty intelligence relative to Osama bin Laden and his purported involvement in the drug trade (Burke, 2003, p.252, Endnote 19).[9]

The illicit drug industry in Afghanistan generates between $2.7 to $3 billion (US) per year. Numerous actors are involved in various aspects of this highly profitable enterprise. U.S. congressional hearings have been held since the events of September 11, 2001, in an attempt to gain a firm understanding of the narcotics problem in Afghanistan and how it relates to the terrorism issue in that country. These hearings have produced a variety of viewpoints relative to the drugs-terrorism issue. The following section will address some of the key statements and accusations that have been made by various government officials, non-governmental experts, journalists, and others with direct knowledge of this expanding problem.

THE DRUG-TERROR NEXUS IN AFGHANISTAN: CLAIMS MADE BY U.S. AND INTERNATIONAL OFFICIALS POST 9/11

This section provides a detailed look at some of the most relevant statements made by various government officials and others regarding the drug-terror nexus in Afghanistan.[10] A careful analysis of the transcripts from these proceedings provides a very disturbing and disparate picture of the state of existing knowledge within the U.S. government with regards to the Afghan drug trade and the involvement of various state and non-state entities.[11] The following statements/testimony gleaned from the above-mentioned transcripts have been provided verbatim by this author in order to highlight what is believed to be the most significant and relevant information.

Shortly after the 9/11 attacks, national and international political discourse regarding drugs and terrorism focused on Southwest Asia, specifically Afghanistan and the Taliban regime which had provided safe haven for Osama bin Laden's Al Qaeda network and a number of other radical groups. Public and political debate, spawned in large part by the U.S. and foreign news media, established an immediate connection between the poppy fields in Afghanistan and the terrorists operating from that country.

Numerous press reports alleging a drug-terror nexus surfaced in the period post-9/11. The underlying rationale was terrorists need money to establish a base of operation, move people and material, train future global Islamists (holy warriors), and provide a source of revenue to finance operations. With state sponsorship on the wane these groups are continually looking for alternative sources of revenue.[12] Afghanistan, a global leader in opium poppy cultivation, was well suited to meet the financial needs of not only the Taliban but other Afghan-based extremists groups. While this study will touch upon several of these groups, this section is devoted primarily to statements and allegations regarding the alleged relationship between the Taliban, Al Qaeda, and illicit drugs.

One of the first public debates to address the issue of terrorism and drugs in Afghanistan was conducted on October 3, 2001, in the U.S. House of Representatives approximately three weeks after the terrorist attacks of September 11. The hearing was held before the Subcommittee on Criminal Justice, Drug Policy and Human Resources of the Committee on Government Reform. The focus of the debate was the "Drug Trade and the Terror Network." In his opening remarks, Committee Chairman Mark Souder (R-Indiana) stated:

> The Afghan drug trade has given direct financial support for the Taliban regime to harbor international terrorists and at least indirectly assisted Usama bin Laden and the al-Qaeda terrorist network to grievously attack the United States of America.
>
> The Taliban have controlled as much as 96 percent of the opium growing area in Afghanistan, and have consistently collected a 10 percent so-called 'religious tax' on the narcotics trade, despite the fact that drugs are against traditional Islamic law. Reports also suggest that the Taliban have actively participated in the drug trade by controlling trafficking groups within Afghanistan. Their total drug revenue could be more than $50 million per year (Souder 2001, p. 1).[13]

During the same hearing Asa Hutchinson, of the Drug Enforcement Administration, delivered what would be the first of many such statements as the newly appointed head of the DEA:

> . . . the DEA has no corroborated, direct evidence to confirm that Bin Laden is involved in the drug trade, the relationship between the Taliban and Bin Laden is believed to have flourished, in large part due to the Taliban's substantial reliance on the opium trade as a source of organizational revenue. In fact, the very sanctuary enjoyed by Bin Laden is based on the existence and control of the Taliban, whose modest economy is dependent upon opium. This connection defines the deadly symbiotic relationship between the illegal drug trade and international terrorism.
>
> In reference to the Taliban, DEA possesses substantial source information indicating ties between the drug trade and the Taliban. Acting as the de facto government of Afghanistan, the Taliban taxes and directly benefits from all aspects of the opium trade. DEA intelligence reveals that taxation is institutionalized. It is even institutionalized to the point that the Taliban provides receipts for collected revenues . . . (Hutchinson, 2001, p. 13).[14]

Interestingly, on March 13, 2002, Asa Hutchinson gave testimony before the U.S. Senate, Committee on the Judiciary, Subcommittee on Technology, Terrorism, and Government Information. This hearing titled, *Narco–Terror: The Worldwide Connection Between Drugs And Terrorism,* focused on the connection between terrorism and the global trade in illicit narcotics. During his opening statement Hutchinson, while noting that no direct evidence is available which links Osama bin Laden to the drug trade, did acknowledge that, "multi-source information," received by the DEA reveals "that Bin Laden has been involved in the financing and facilitation of heroin trafficking activities" (Hutchinson, 2002b, p.10).[15] Furthermore, during this same hearing Senator Jon Kyl (R-Arizona), as part of his opening statement, made the following comment regarding Osama bin Laden's purported links to the Afghan drug trade:

> . . . we might not know the full extent of Bin Laden's narco-terror connections—what we do know, however, is that he provided protection to heroin processing labs, was a part owner in numerous labs, part owner of one load shipped to the U.S., and tried to develop a stronger strain of heroin in order to addict more people here (Kyl, 2002, p.5).

Moreover, in reference to the Taliban's involvement in the opium trade Hutchinson, in a speech given on April 2, 2002, at the Heritage Foundation Institute for International Studies, a public policy research institute stated that the Taliban not only taxed the trade but, "in some instances," were involved in the trafficking aspects (Hutchinson, 2002a).[16]

On May 20, 2003, a hearing was held before the U.S. Senate, Committee on the Judiciary. The proceedings were devoted entirely to the subject of narcoterrorism and included testimony from some of this country's leading authorities on terrorism and the drugs trade. According to this author this hearing was one of the most insightful debates regarding the general topic of terrorism and drugs that have been conducted by a governmental body since 9/11.[17]

Prior to 9/11 the subject of narcoterrorism was largely relegated to the Andean countries, specifically, Colombia, Bolivia, and Peru. Drug trafficking in support of international terrorism emanating from Southwest Asia was not an overriding law enforcement or national security concern. According to the hearing transcript, Steven Casteel, assistant administrator for intelligence for the DEA, stated that prior to 9/11 law enforcement viewed these two criminal activities as "separate issues." After the events of 9/11 Casteel noted that, ". . . these two criminal activities are virtually intertwined." He further stated that, "For DEA, investigating the link between drugs and terrorism has taken on renewed importance" (Casteel, 2003, p. 7). As part of his opening statement Chairman Orrin Hatch (R-Utah) cited two specific FBI/DEA investigations and subsequent arrests of individuals alleged to have been providing funds/weapons to support Afghanistan-based terrorists:

> In San Diego, California, in November 2002, two Pakistani nationals and one United States citizen were charged with attempting to exchange 600 kilograms of heroin and 5 metric tons of hashish for cash and four anti-aircraft missiles to supply to the Taliban and Al-Qaeda associates.
>
> Recently, in April 2003, the FBI and DEA disrupted a major Afghanistan–Pakistani heroin smuggling operation with the arrest of 16 individuals, in which heroin was being shipped to the United States, profits from the sale of heroin were laundered through Afghan and Pakistani-owned businesses in the United States, and then sent back to finance terrorists (Hatch 2003, p. 3).[18]

During this hearing three witnesses with extensive knowledge in this area provided prepared statements and testimony: Dr. Rensselaer W. Lee,[19] the president of Global Advisory Services, a firm which advises various government agencies on transnational crime and narcotics located in Alexandria, Virginia; Larry Johnson,[20] Managing Director of Berg Associates, a company that provides risk consultancy and threat assessment for international businesses, located in Washington, D.C.; and Raphael Perl,[21] an analyst with the nonpartisan, Congressional Research Service (CRS).

During direct questioning by then Senator Joseph Biden (D-Delaware), and speaking specifically to the alleged drug-terror nexus in Afghanistan and who exactly controls the opium trade in that country, Dr. Lee stated that he attributes opium production in Afghanistan to "political groups and forces" and "warlords." Concerning Al Qaeda and Taliban involvement Dr. Lee noted:

> There is not a situation that I could see that you describe in which the remnants of Al-Qaeda are systematically extracting revenues from parts of the opium trade somewhere in the country. In fact, my impression has always been that even under the Taliban, the Taliban was successful in taxing the opium crop, but they were far less successful in actually being able to extract money from these clannish tribal trafficking groups that have quite a lot of power and weapons to back up this power (Lee, 2003, p. 39).

Dr. Lee also confirmed that much of Al Qaeda's financing had come from donations.[22] Conversely, while acknowledging that recent efforts at curtailing terrorist financing may have led Al Qaeda to seek revenue from the drug trade, he was noncommittal on this point (Lee, 2003, p. 39). He also voiced concern over the lack of credible intelligence regarding the alleged nexus (Lee, 2003, p. 43).[23]

Throughout the proceeding Senator Biden made several relevant comments regarding the testimony the Committee was receiving. His most germane statement relative to the focus of this chapter is as follows:

> What bothers me about your collective testimony, not any of you individually, is everybody knows that is for sure one of the revenue streams for the Taliban, particularly in the Pashtun area, and in turn Al–Qaeda, although we don't know for certain. None of you know enough to tell me. The intelligence community doesn't know enough to tell me. We don't know even what we don't know. . . . I have not seen a shred of evidence yet, although I don't doubt it—I mean, intuitively it would seem that it is happening—whether or not the funding, these billions of dollars that are made, or the hundreds of millions that are made, is going into the pockets of terrorist organizations now who have as their number one enemy the United States of America (Biden 2003, pp. 24 and 40).[24]

While the hearing focused on the topic of narcotics and its tie to some of the world's major terrorist organizations, it is clear by the direction and specificity of the questions being asked that members of the committee had as their primary focus Afghan-based groups and specifically, Al Qaeda and/or other like-minded groups with global reach.

Raphael Perl, international affairs specialist with the Congressional Research Service, provided an alternative view on the relationship between certain terrorist groups and the drugs trade. Based on his examination and understanding of the problem, Mr. Perl believes that rather than groups with entirely different objectives or raison d'être merging into a single operating entity, ample justification exists to support the view that the activities involved in the illicit trafficking of narcotics may have been adopted by certain terrorist groups as a means of garnering revenue and may be used to spawn new networks and expand the reach of existing ones (Perl, 2003, pp. 40–41).

This hearing did not generate a significant and quantifiable answer to the central issue of the proceeding, i.e., do Islamic fundamentalist groups, specifically Al Qaeda, derive funding or are in any way affiliated with the drug trade in Afghanistan? This question was presented to Steven McCraw, the Federal Bureau of Investigation's assistant director of intelligence, by Senator Joseph Biden and committee chairman, Orrin Hatch.[25] Mr. McCraw responded in part by saying:

> The FBI has not tracked the amount of money Islamic fundamentalist groups such as al Qaeda . . . have derived from drug production and trafficking, and has little corroborated information to offer. . . . The link between the funding of terrorist groups and the illegal drugs trade is, however, supported by anecdotal evidence (McCraw, 2003, p. 45).

Although this hearing provided a wealth of useful albeit general information relative to the drug trade and possible terrorist involvement, it did not produce anything in the way of empirical data which could link Afghan-based terrorist groups to the drug trafficking apparatus operating in Afghanistan.

U.S. CONGRESSIONAL INVESTIGATION, REPORTS, AND ADDITIONAL STATEMENTS BY LEADING EXPERTS AND PUBLIC OFFICIALS

According to a report (Roth, Greenburg, and Wille, 2004) which accompanied the final report issued by the National Commission on Terrorist Attacks Upon the United States, a congressional body established to investigate the events which led up to the attacks on 9/11, Al Qaeda has been accused of involvement in numerous illegal funding enterprises, very little of which can be substantiated. This report further notes that while some Al Qaeda operatives may garner revenue from the drug trade, the 9/11 commission has not received any credible information that its senior operatives were or are involved, nor does it constitute an important revenue source for their organization. The report further notes that, prior to 9/11, the Taliban did derive substantial revenue from the trade. The report makes the following important point:

> . . . there is compelling evidence the Al Qaeda leadership does not like or trust those who today control the drug trade in Southwest Asia, and has encouraged its members not to get involved. . . . In addition to the lack of affirmative evidence, there are substantial reasons to believe that Al Qaeda has no role in drug trafficking: Al Qaeda members are geographically hemmed in and are unable to travel as the narcotics business demands. Trafficking would unnecessarily expose Al Qaeda operatives to risks of detection or arrest. Moreover, established traffickers have no reason to involve Al Qaeda in their lucrative businesses; associating with the world's most hunted men would attract unwanted attention to their activities and exponentially increase the resources devoted to catching them. Furthermore, Al Qaeda neither controls territory nor brings needed skills and therefore has no leverage to break into the sector (Roth, Greenburg, and Wille, 2004, p. 23).[26]

The information that went into this investigative report was provided in part by Doug Wankel, Director, Office of Drug Control, U.S. Embassy in Afghanistan on March 15, 2004, and garnered from interviews with captured Al Qaeda operatives. The commission further acknowledged that although there have been reports citing Al Qaeda involvement in various aspects of the Afghan drug trade, these reports cannot be substantiated (National Commission on Terrorist Attacks Upon the United States 2004, p. 499).

In *Al Qaeda: Global Network on Terror*, renowned author and expert on the Al Qaeda network, Rohan Gunaratna states that there is no "hard evidence" which ties Osama bin Laden or Al Qaeda to the Afghan narcotics trade. He also states that the Taliban profited "substantially" from the cultivation and trafficking of narcotics (Gunaratna, 2002, p. 61). This view is also shared by Pierre Arnaud-Chouvy, internationally renowned expert on illicit drugs and drug trafficking. In an article titled, "Narco-Terrorism in Afghanistan," Dr. Chouvy, cites two statements made by public officials regarding the alleged drug-terror nexus and provides his views on direct Al Qaeda involvement in the Afghan drug trade:

> That some drug money plays a significant role in the ongoing Afghan conflict—even by "being used directly against the Afghan government and the international forces"—is obvious but no novelty in recent Afghan history. Although the head of Afghanistan's Counter Narcotics Directorate estimates that the Taliban and its allies derived more than $150 million from drugs in 2003, hard evidence linking al-Qaida directly to the drug economy is still scarce, most investigators say (Chouvy, 2004, p. 8).[27]

Moreover, in a statement issued before a U.S. congressional hearing on April 1, 2004, Assistant Secretary of State for Narcotics and Law Enforcement Affairs, Robert Charles said, "opium is a source of literally billions of dollars to extremists and criminal groups . . . cutting down the opium supply is central to establishing a secure and stable democracy as well as winning the global war on terrorism" (Charles, 2004a, pp. 14–18). Referencing a chart he had with him, Secretary Charles noted that it "shows the potential relationship of Afghan opium to some of these terrorist and extremist groups" (Charles, 2004a).[28]

Two months prior to Secretary Charles's statement before Congress, Karen P. Tandy, then administrator of the U.S. Drug Enforcement Administration (DEA), testified in a hearing before the U.S. House of Representatives Committee on International Relations (Tandy, 2004a, pp. 17–21). A portion of Administrator Tandy's opening statement addressed the purported links between terrorism and the drug trade in Afghanistan.[29] Concerning this alleged linkage Ms. Tandy stated:

> At this time, we do not have evidence capable of sustaining an indictment of direct links between terrorism and narcotics trafficking groups within Afghanistan. To the extent that allegations have been raised based on more than speculation, they generally come from single sources. Clear corroborating evidence of such sources has been difficult to obtain, in part because many traditional investigative techniques cannot be used within the country for reasons I have previously explained.

> Raw intelligence and uncorroborated confidential sources continue to indicate possible relationships between drug traffic and terrorist groups within Afghanistan (Tandy, 2004a, pp. 20–21).[30]

One of the most detailed insights regarding Afghanistan's narcotics industry came from Thomas W. O'Connell, Assistant Secretary of Defense for Special Operations and Low–Intensity Conflict, U.S. Department of Defense. A portion of his prepared statement focused on the fragmented nature of the narcotics and terrorist threat in Afghanistan and details the multidimensional nature of the threat and the complexities involved in ascertaining specific linkages:

> . . . the problem of narcotics and terrorism in Afghanistan is different from the problem in Latin America. In Afghanistan, the illegal narcotics industry is comparatively fragmented, with numerous organizations and smuggling networks involved in the trade. In addition, the extremist and terrorist elements in Afghanistan, which also are fragmented—including the Taliban remnants, al Qa'ida operatives and leaders, and other extremist groups, like Gulbuddin Hekmatyar's Hizb-i-Islami—do not, by themselves, control narcotics networks. So in Afghanistan, the problem, as we see it, is neither a cartel that is also a terrorist organization; nor is it a terrorist insurgency that controls the narcotics industry in a particular region. Rather, the problem is more diffuse, consisting of different kinds of linkages and cooperative arrangements between disparate trafficking elements, extremist groups, and, sometimes, local leaders and militia commanders (O'Connell, 2004, p. 24).[31]

As noted above, the statements made by DEA Administrator Asa Hutchinson (2002, p. 10) and Republican Senator Jon Kyl (2002, p. 5) six months after the 2001 terrorist attacks on U.S. soil stand in stark contrast to the 2004 statements of Secretary Charles and DEA Administrator Tandy who reiterated the same position in June 2006 in testimony before the U.S. House of Representatives Armed Services Committee.[32]

AL QAEDA, THE TALIBAN, AND OPIUM: DIVERSITY OF VIEWPOINTS

This diversity of viewpoints is troubling considering that this issue has had such a profound political impact in this country as well as abroad and militarily as ISAF continues to battle a growing and violent insurgency in Afghanistan. In recognition of the fact that the two statements cited above [Hutchinson and Kyl] were made five months after the U.S.-led invasion, one could see the strategic value in terms of energizing public opinion to support future policies and actions which in effect tie the decades-old war on drugs to the present war on terrorism.

Perhaps one of the leading proponents of an Al Qaeda-drug nexus is Congressman Mark Kirk (R-Illinois).[33] Representative Kirk is a member of the U.S. House of Representatives Appropriations Foreign Operations Subcommittee. Representative Kirk embarked on a fact-finding mission to Afghanistan in January 2004.[34] His itinerary included meetings with officials from the United States, Britain, Pakistan, and Afghanistan, and discussions on the growing Afghan drug problem. On January 21, 2004, upon returning from Afghanistan, Congressman Kirk issued the following statement before the U.S. House of Representatives:

> I just returned from Pakistan's frontier where Osama bin Laden is likely hiding. We describe bin Laden as a terrorist. While that label applies, I think we can be more accurate. He has become a narco-terrorist. During my mission, I learned that bin Laden's source of donated funds has been reduced. In response, bin Laden has become one of Pakistan's top heroin dealers. Kandahar trafficker Haji Bashir Noorzai provides 1,000 kilograms of heroin each month to bin Laden's organization. That provides Al Qaeda with $24 million a year to fund his attacks against the West. If we are to catch bin Laden and to wrap up his organization, we must attack his new source of income, heroin . . . There are at least three major drug trafficking organizations now operating in Afghanistan, all with links to Pakistan: The Taliban, the HIG and bin Laden's Al Qaeda (Kirk, 2004b, pp. H62–H63).[35]

On February 12, 2004, three weeks after delivering the above, Rep. Kirk issued a prepared statement before the U.S. House of Representatives, Committee on International Relations (Kirk, 2004a, pp. 11–12). His comments provided source information and other detail regarding the illegal narcotics trade and its possible ties to the Taliban militia and Al Qaeda terror network including allegations that prior to the July 2000 ban Mullah Muhammad Omar had stockpiled 300 tons of heroin (Kirk, 2004a, pp. 9–10).[36]

These statements are representative of the confusion and uncertainty which has surrounded this issue prior to and certainly after the events of September 11, 2001. When Representative Kirk noted in his February 12, 2004, congressional statement that Osama bin Laden's organization is "reaping $28 million a year in illicit heroin sales," it is clear, that this "28 million"[37] figure was derived from an unconfirmed source (i.e., that Afghan drug kingpin "Haji Bashir Noorzai reportedly provides 2,000 kilograms of heroin every 8 weeks to bin Laden lieutenants in Pakistan") and was based on the U.S. dollar value that heroin was selling for in Pakistan. There was no mention in his statement before Congress of who precisely provided this information.[38]

Equally disturbing is the fact that the lead agency for drug control in this country, the U.S. Drug Enforcement Agency (DEA), has declined to take such a definitive position regarding Al Qaeda's alleged role in the Afghan drug trade.[39]

Furthermore, the statements made by Representative Kirk, while in line with the position taken by Col. Alexander Kondratiyev and Major Avaz Yuldashov (Maitra, 2005) both having served on the Afghan-Tajik border as members of the Tajikistan Drug Control Agency (DCA), contradict the findings of Blanchard (2004, 2005, 2006, and 2007a) cited below who also interviewed U.S. officials in Kabul in January 2005; one year after Representative Kirk's trip.

Likewise, with regard to Haji Bashir Noorzai, he was convicted in New York on September 23, 2008, for conspiring to move $50 million worth of heroin into various countries, including the United States. He was subsequently sentenced to life imprisonment on April 30, 2009.[40]

Additionally, there seems to be a disconnect between former Assistant Secretary of State Robert Charles's statement issued before a U.S. congressional hearing on April 1, 2004, and the views expressed by Rep. Mark Kirk. This is especially noteworthy considering the fact that Mr. Charles's testimony was taken just three months after the Kirk fact-finding mission. These fundamentally conflicting statements are also incompatible with the testimony, "At this time, we do not have evidence capable of sustaining an indictment of direct links between terrorism and narcotics trafficking groups within Afghanistan," given to the U.S. House Committee on International Relations in February 2004, by U.S. DEA Administrator, Karen Tandy, one month after the above mentioned trip to Afghanistan by Rep. Kirk.

Furthermore, the above statement provided by Administrator Tandy seems to reflect the views of the Congressional Research Service (CRS), a public policy "think tank" providing nonpartisan research for the legislative branch of the U.S. government. In *Afghanistan: Narcotics and U.S. Policy*, a report prepared by the CRS, author Christopher M. Blanchard (2005, pp. 17–18; 2006, p. 16; 2007, p. 16) outlines the major conclusion drawn from interviews with U.S. officials in Kabul:

> According to U. S. officials senior Al Qaeda leaders considered and subsequently rejected the idea of becoming directly involved in managing and profiting from Afghan narcotics. Ideological considerations and fear of increased vulnerability to intelligence and law enforcement reportedly were the predominant factors in their decision.

The above cited December 2007 CRS report is the third update to the initial December 2004 version. The first report was issued on December 7, 2004.[41] Speculation also exists on the precise role the Taliban played in the opium trade during their ascendancy and tenure (1994–2001). There have been many allegations that the opium trade was the primary source of funding in their efforts to defeat the Northern Alliance. Others, such as Rohan Gunaratna, believed that the Taliban benefited quite substantially from the trade but were not instrumental in controlling or facilitating it.[42]

It now appears that since at least 2005 Taliban involvement has become more "hands-on." As noted above, Taliban involvement has now expanded to manufacturing and trafficking.

According to Braun (2009, p. 3), the DEA by 2009 had "unmistakably determined," that Taliban drug activities included "managing and operating major clandestine laboratories, drug cache sites, and poppy bazaars." It is important to note that according to Braun's testimony the DEA, prior to 2003, had not been engaged in Afghanistan since "being forced from the country by the Soviet Union's invasion in 1979."

Based on the above statements and testimony Taliban involvement in the drug trade is clear. Certainly, their involvement in the protection aspect of the trade has been established. However, this author notes that a recurrent theme throughout the above cited proceedings is that many of those in support of an Al Qaeda-drug nexus have made statements on the basis that their allegations have previously been confirmed and therefore are statements of pre-determined fact.

MAJOR THEMES

Testimony, Statements, and Accusations: Fact-based or Politically Motivated?

The lack of supporting and corroborative information in the above transcripts and the range of opinions regarding the drugs-terror problem in Afghanistan seem to support the view that the statements and testimony cited above do not provide evidence that a nexus exists nor do they provide evidence that it does not exist. Moreover, many claims have been couched in very indistinct language and failed to include the premises which supported their statements.[43]

Furthermore, opening statements by various witnesses often did not hold up to questioning by committee members. This is evidenced by the frustration exhibited by Sen. Joseph Biden (D-Delaware) during the aforementioned hearing conducted by the Committee on the Judiciary of the U. S Senate on May 20, 2003.

A noticeable pattern in the statements and testimony is that the more time that had elapsed between the events of 9/11 and the above cited congressional statements and testimony the less focus was placed on Al Qaeda and their purported links to the drug trade. For example, Congressman Mark Souder's most recent comments on September 13, 2006, before the U.S. House of Representatives focused more on Taliban involvement and provincial-level corruption.[44]

Additionally, as previously mentioned, the statements made by DEA Administrator Asa Hutchinson and Senator Jon Kyl, in March 2002, stand in stark contrast to those made by Assistant Secretary of State Robert

Charles and then current head of the U.S. DEA, Karen Tandy, in 2004 and 2006. Moreover, some of the information provided by the media and comments made by public officials from uncorroborated sources has often been used to promote the view that there is a direct link between drug traffickers and international terrorists in Afghanistan (Burke, 2003, pp. 19–20 and 252). What factors, political or otherwise, have entered into this unwavering support of a nexus and the attempt by some to further demonize Osama bin Laden as a narcotics trafficker? One press report cited a comment by Representative Mark Kirk that, "bin Laden is one of the world's largest heroin dealers" (Taylor, 2004, p. A03; Scarborough, 2004b, p. A07). As noted earlier, on February 12, 2004, Rep. Kirk expanded on this allegation in a prepared statement before the U.S. House of Representatives Committee on International Relations.[45]

Bias and political considerations are additional factors that should be considered when evaluating the veracity of various statements and testimony. Drug trafficking is big business. Fighting drugs is also big business that involves many federal, state, and local agencies and therefore large amounts of state and federal money. Drug abuse also poses a lethal threat to society, especially our young population. This is a powerful political incentive. For example what impact, if any, does the drug problem in a given legislator's state/district have on their public position relative to the purported drug-terror nexus in Afghanistan? Furthermore is the war on drugs being tied to the war on terrorism in order to obtain or increase funding or obtain public approval for various policy initiatives (Thomas and Thomas, 2004)? On March 2, 2004, Congressman Mark Souder (R-Indiana) and former chairman of the House Government Reform Subcommittee on Criminal Justice, Drug Policy and Human Resources stated, "While Europe is the primary destination for Afghan heroin today, we suspect that 7 to 10 percent of the illegal crop ultimately reaches the streets of our congressional districts" (Souder, 2004, p. H729).[46]

This concern is real and needs to be addressed. However, there may be a certain amount of political pressure on officials especially in districts with a high incidence of drug usage.[47]

Another recurrent theme in the statements made by congressional leaders, and expert witnesses who provided testimony, is the broad range of opinions offered in each hearing. An examination of various statements made by several of the participants raises some questions as to the overall state of understanding regarding the Taliban militia and its relationship to other extremist groups, i.e., Al Qaeda.

The Taliban-Al Qaeda relationship was different prior to 9/11. Some of the statements made suggest that the Taliban's opium income enabled it to provide safe haven to Osama bin Laden and his ilk. However credible sources reveal the opposite. As noted by Gunaratna (2002, p. 40) shortly after arriving from Sudan Osama bin Laden helped support the Taliban in terms of money, construction projects, and providing guerrilla fighters from Al Qaeda's elite 055 Brigade in an effort to help the Taliban in their armed struggle with the Northern Alliance.[48]

After the U.S.-led invasion, Al Qaeda and the Taliban were forced to take up residence in Pakistan's autonomous tribal areas. Al Qaeda changed from a territorial-based terrorist group with international reach and objectives to a fragmented, cellular, ideology-based movement able to recruit volunteers to its cause without having a central command structure. Although evidence suggests that both groups are ideologically similar and presently cooperate on matters that are mutually beneficial, such as the expulsion of foreign forces from Afghanistan, it has not been established that they are operating as a single entity. On the contrary, all indications are that their ultimate objectives are entirely different. Al Qaeda's focus is global, having established operational cells in at least 60 countries, while the Taliban's objectives appear to be confined to Afghanistan and possibly Pakistan.

Causal Connection through Investigative and Legal Protocols

Since the events of 9/11, the U.S. Drug Enforcement Agency's (DEA) views and investigative efforts relative to criminal vs. terrorist acts was expressed by Steven Casteel (2003, p. 7), assistant administrator for intelligence for the DEA. If indeed they have applied their resources [post-9/11] in this area of "renewed importance" as Mr. Casteel suggests, the open source literature does not indicate that evidentiary information has been discovered to support or refute the drug-terror nexus claims in Afghanistan. As alluded to above, the trend in the presentation of these nexus claims seems to be that the closer to the 9/11 events the more positive and profound these statements are regarding the nexus, whereas as time moves forward one would think that the evidence which spawned the statements would be strengthened by additional evidence. It appears that the opposite has happened, especially considering the aforementioned statement by Mr. Casteel. The initial statements and conclusions made by some members of these agencies immediately following the events of 9/11 appear to have been weakened as time progresses rather than strengthened by continued investigations.

One can thus assume that if updated information relative to the drug-terror nexus in Afghanistan has indeed been uncovered, it would be available in the open sources—given the importance attached to this issue and the heightened public awareness as a result of selective ad campaigns and media reports which have tied the drugs trade to terrorism and more specifically to groups based in Afghanistan. Secondly, if such information does exist, it must be in the classified literature.[49]

Without having direct access to this type of information, the focus needs to turn to observed organizational behavior, e.g., have policies, actions, or the priorities of those responsible for public safety taken on a heightened significance? In other words, has there been an enhancement of efforts by lead government agencies in general, and specifically the DEA, to ascertain whether such relationships exist? Has the government activated efforts, either politically or militarily, which would indicate that they have knowledge of a nexus even though it is not published? Testimony and media accounts indicate that the drug problem in Afghanistan appears to have worsened since the invasion. Indeed, the aforementioned testimony and statements especially by "expert witnesses" leads one to believe that such a conclusion is valid. Furthermore, regarding Al Qaeda it appears the organization has become more fluid and in fact poses a far greater threat to regional and global security than it had prior to the events of 9/11; and as has been noted previously, all indications point to a continuous and alarming expansion of the opium trade in Afghanistan.

The statement by Karen Tandy on February 12, 2004, that, "Raw intelligence and uncorroborated confidential sources continue to indicate possible relationships between drug traffic and terrorist groups within Afghanistan"[50] and the Congressional Research Service reports (Blanchard, 2004, 2005, 2006, 2007) clearly indicate that a direct relationship between Osama bin Laden and/or his Al Qaeda organization and international drug traffickers lacks solid evidentiary support. However, Al Qaeda may have benefitted from the trade indirectly from their affiliation with the Taliban regime.[51] Additionally, evidence does support a finding that the Taliban, upon their ascendancy, did develop a symbiotic relationship with opium and heroin traffickers within Afghanistan. This position is supported by a *U.S. News & World Report* special investigative report published in the December 5, 2005, issue.[52] In the article titled, "Paying for Terror," the authors discuss the issue of terrorists' involvement in organized criminal activity.[53] Speaking about Al Qaeda's possible involvement in the Afghan drug trade the authors provide the following assessment based on interviews with counterterrorism officials and Al Qaeda detainees:

> Al Qaeda's leadership . . . has proved more wary about jumping into the drug trade . . . Osama bin Laden and his remaining lieutenants have steered clear of the largest horde of criminal wealth in years: the exploding Afghan heroin trade. Press reports of bin Laden's involvement in the drug trade are flat wrong, say counterterrorism officials. Long ago, al Qaeda strategists reasoned that drug trafficking would expose them to possible detection, captives have told U.S. investigators. They also don't trust many of the big drug barons, intelligence officials say, and have encouraged their members not to get involved with them (Kaplan, Fang, and Sangwan, 2005, p. 47).

Regarding the rank-and-file members of Al Qaeda, since the U.S.-led invasion elements of the group may have splintered off and therefore not under direct control of the top leadership based in Pakistan's tribal areas.

These rogue members would be free to pursue their own agendas be it criminal, political, or both and to join forces with criminal elements or other extremists groups including the Taliban.

Congressional statements and testimony by some of the legislators/witnesses and various reports by the national media appear to understate and oversimplify the complexities and dynamics of the narcotics trade in Afghanistan.[54] The statement which labels Osama bin Laden a drug trafficker has not been substantiated, at least in the open source literature. The numerous hearings and statements examined in this chapter have not established the existence of empirically-based evidence that Osama bin Laden or Al Qaeda's top leadership is directly involved in the Afghan drug trade.

In reference to the ships seized by the U.S. Navy in the Persian Gulf, some government officials—specifically Congressman Mark Souder (R-Indiana) and Congressman Mark Kirk (R-Illinois)—made statements relative to these seizures which could lead some to believe that these incidents support the nexus assertion in regard to Al Qaeda.[55]

It should be emphasized that initial press reports citing these seizures in the Persian Gulf also referred to the transfer of 10 individuals to Bagram Air Base in Parvan province, Afghanistan, for questioning. On December 30, 2003, the *Washington Post* reported:

> Ten men captured recently aboard boats carrying drugs in the Persian Gulf area have been taken for questioning to a U.S. prison in Afghanistan, a U.S. defense official said yesterday. They are held on Bagram Air Base north of the Afghan capital of Kabul and are being questioned about suspected connections to Osama bin Laden's al Qaeda terrorist network, the official said, speaking on the condition of anonymity (*Washington Post*, 2003, p. A04).

An article which appeared in the *New York Times* on December 20, 2003, cites a written statement issued by the U.S. Navy as stating that, "An initial investigation uncovered clear ties between the smuggling operation and Al Qaeda" (Shanker, 2003, p. A3).[56] Additionally, CNN reported that, "U.S. military officials would not describe the evidence leading them to conclude the links to al Qaeda" (Starr and Courson, 2003). Interestingly, this author was not able to obtain any follow-up information regarding these seizures or the subsequent arrest of the 10 suspects.[57]

Furthermore, in an e-mail communication with journalist David Osler (January 30, 2007) of *Lloyd's List*, a British maritime publication, this author was informed that he [Osler] has "not previously heard claims of AQ [Al Qaeda] being deeply involved in the narcotics trade." However, he does acknowledge in an article titled, "Investigators closing in on bin Laden vessels," that "Associates of Osama bin Laden have built up a fleet of around two dozen ships in recent years, primarily to facilitate the smuggling of high quality heroin and hashish from Afghanistan to the West"(Osler, 2001, p. 1).[58]

The arrest and subsequent trial, conviction, and sentencing in New York of Haji Bashir Noorzai were viewed by some as a link between Afghan opium, Al Qaeda, and the Taliban. According to the U.S. attorney and the specific indictment in question no link to Al Qaeda was mentioned, although the indictment does state that, "the defendant, was closely aligned with the Taliban in Afghanistan" (United States District Court, Southern District of New York, 2005a, p. 3). As recorded in previous testimony, Rep. Kirk (R-Illinois) stated that Haji Bashir Noorzai was providing Osama bin Laden with 1,000 kilograms of heroin per month. According to Kirk the value in Pakistan for 1 kilogram of heroin is $2,000 (US). During questioning by the Defense Intelligence Agency (DIA) and the Federal Bureau of Investigation (FBI) in April 2004 Haji Bashir Noorzai dispelled the notion that Al Qaeda was involved in the drug trade. Referring to Haji Bashir Noorzai in an article published in *TIME* magazine, author Bill Powell states:

> In early April 2004, he traveled to Dubai to meet with two Americans at a JW Marriott hotel. One identified himself as "Mike," from the Defense Intelligence Agency (DIA), the other "Brian," from the FBI. That day, as they would three more times over the next five months, they spent hours grilling Noorzai, trying to find out what he knew about several subjects, including, as Noorzai puts it, "the powder business." According to transcripts TIME has reviewed, the agents were occasionally frustrated by the talks. They pressed Noorzai on how much drug money went to finance al Qaeda. "None," Noorzai replied. "But the entire world says the opposite," Mike responded. Noorzai stood his ground: "I do not believe it."
>
> A friend who had accompanied Noorzai to the meetings interjected, "You should tell them whatever you know. They want to know how much you know. Do you understand?" Noorzai replied, "I am telling them as much as I know, but I'm not going to say something baseless" (Powell, 2007, p.10).[59]

Concerning the 2002 arrest of three men in Hong Kong who were trying to purchase weapons and Stinger missiles in exchange for drugs, a direct link was cited by some, but statements made by the suspects were inconclusive. They initially stated that the weapons were for the Taliban. When pressed on possible Al Qaeda involvement, they said that the Taliban and Al Qaeda were the same.[60]

Another press report revealed that, "An indictment in the United States said the suspects themselves mentioned the al-Qaeda link" (Wong, 2002).[61] The statement by the suspects may suggest that these two groups [Al Qaeda, Taliban] have continued to maintain their mutually beneficial relationship which existed prior to October 2001 by forming an operational alliance since the invasion. Although Al Qaeda does not field an army as such, they have in the past provided fighters to the Taliban, and press reports indicate that Al Qaeda operatives are part of the ongoing Afghan insurgency.[62] According to the Associated Press, "Insurgents of the former ruling Taliban regime and al-Qaida have launched repeated attacks in the lawless south and east of the country in the past year, despite the efforts of 11,000 U.S.-led coalition forces to hunt them down" (Khan, 2004).

Complexities in Ascertaining Linkages

According to much of the testimony, it appears that in the regions/countries which were the focus of many of these hearings drug cultivation, insurgency, terrorism, and organized crime coexists. In areas such as these it is often very difficult to separate and assign culpability to a specific group or set of actors. This is not an uncommon phenomenon given the lack of government control endemic in areas experiencing ongoing conflict, the complex relationships, and the huge profits involved in the illicit narcotics trade.

Perhaps the most striking information against the existence of a nexus came from a report issued by the National Commission on Terrorist Attacks upon the United States. As previously noted, in addressing the question of Al Qaeda involvement in the Afghan drug trade, the report stated in effect that after a careful review of all "relevant intelligence," there is no basis to conclude that Al Qaeda was a major player in the Afghan opium trade "or relied on it as an important source of revenue either before or after 9/11" (Roth, Greenburg, and Wille, 2004, p. 19).

CONCLUSION

Following the events of September 11, 2001, and the U.S.-led invasion which took place the following month, speculations and accusations have emerged among many government and non-governmental officials that prior to 9/11 the Taliban (and Al Qaeda) were the primary culprits behind the heroin trade in Afghanistan, and were therefore deriving substantial revenue from the trade, which in turn provided safe haven and financial and logistical support for Al Qaeda and other foreign terrorist entities.

While evidence does suggest Taliban involvement in the drug trade, this was more or less inherited; the problem was there when the Taliban arrived. However, the Taliban did capitalize on it. Also, if you look at the universe of terrorism and the universe of drugs you will find that in regions of the world where drug production is high (Colombia, Myanmar, Afghanistan) there is also a high incidence of terror/insurgent related activity, and for that matter criminal activity in general. Indeed the possibility exists that those making the definitive statements alleging a nexus and those that deny that such a nexus exists are basing their judgments on entirely different perceptions on what constitutes international terrorism and what constitutes an insurgency. This author acknowledges that the ongoing wars in Iraq and Afghanistan have demonstrated that the line separating these two activities is becoming increasingly blurred.

Today, Afghanistan is experiencing an expanding insurgency; it is composed of many factions and is coordinated and well financed. Its potential for lethality and destruction far exceeds the notion that those charged with combating it are merely engaged in trying to eliminate a bunch of terrorists who are doing little more than creating havoc throughout the eastern and southern provinces. Evidence reveals that this insurgency is made up of various local and foreign factions and further suggests that these entities may be deriving a substantial income from the opium poppy produced in these and other provinces. This income stream may provide a source of funds which allows the insurgency to expand by providing new fighters and advanced munitions and armament.

Although some anecdotal and circumstantial evidence has surfaced which tends to support the theory that a linkage between drug traffickers and international terrorists exists in that country, historical and contemporary documentary sources and conversations with a number of informed individuals paints a much more dynamic and complex picture regarding the actors and relationships that are presently engaged in the narcotics trade in Afghanistan. Moreover, a careful examination of published government transcripts suggests that various insurgent factions, district and provincial power brokers, public officials, terrorists, and international drug traffickers operating from Afghanistan may all play a role in this multi-billion-dollar enterprise.

Chapter 4 will examine the ground situation in Afghanistan and discuss the points cited in this chapter in more detail. Chapter 4 will also examine specific state and non-state actors,[63] including the Taliban, Al Qaeda, the Haqqani network, Hezb-i-Islami (HIG), and other entities which comprise the insurgency.

CHAPTER 4

The Taliban, Al Qaeda, and the Afghan Insurgency

THE TALIBAN MILITIA (1994–2001)

Following the Soviet-Afghan war (1989) and the defeat of the Soviet backed regime in Kabul (1992), a civil war broke out between competing mujahideen[1] factions for control of Afghanistan.[2] Many Taliban members were refugees who escaped into Pakistan at the time of the Soviet invasion or subsequently during the war. Therefore, when they began their ascendancy in Kandahar most of them were young and had spent a majority of their lives in Pakistani refugee camps, primarily in Baluchistan and the Northwest Frontier provinces, and had received training in madrassahs (religious schools).[3]

Many of these schools came into existence during the 10-year Soviet-Afghan war, and many of them received financial support from Pakistan and Saudi Arabia (Stern, 2000, pp. 118–119).[4] Saudi Arabia provided funding to the madrassahs[5] as well as the Taliban. Pakistan viewed the Taliban movement as a means to acquire "strategic depth"[6] in the region, including any armed conflict with India, and provided arms, manpower, and other support to further Taliban efforts to secure Afghanistan.

According to Rashid (2001f, p. 29), by December 1994 the Taliban had approximately 12,000 Afghan and Pakistani religious students among their ranks, and by 1996 they had captured Kabul and had full or partial control of most of the country's provinces. It is estimated that by 2001 the Taliban was in control of approximately 90 percent of the country. The opposing factions led by former commander Ahmad Shah Massoud controlled several provinces in the northeastern part of the country, which included the opium producing Badakshan province and the militarily significant Panjshir valley. Massoud's forces prevented the Taliban from controlling the entire country. Trained in the madrassas in Pakistan under the direction of Jamiat Ulema-e-Islam (JUI), a Pakistani political party, each Talib studied

Islamic law and the Koran and were heavily influenced by the teachings of the JUI which offered these young refugees an ultra-conservative brand of Islam (Rashid, 1999, p. 74; Rashid, 2001f, p. 23).[7] The Taliban follow a strict fundamentalist Sunni view of the Koran and sharia (Islamic law) that is influenced by the Deobandi tradition, (apart from its attitude about jihad).[8]

REPRESSIVE POLICIES

The Taliban and their leader Mullah Mohammad Omar,[9] a veteran of the 10-year war with the Soviets, were initially welcomed by a war-weary people who were fed up with the brutality of competing warlords and the state of anarchy that swept the country. However, the Taliban's welcome was short-lived. The Taliban sought to restore order, disarm the population, and institute a repressive and backward regime. The Taliban instituted the Ministry for the Protection of Virtue and Prevention of Vice, essentially a religious police force. The Taliban enforced, often brutally, a strict interpretation of Islamic law that was contrary to Afghan tribal customs and traditions that had "prevailed for centuries," and also discriminated against non-Pashtun Muslims (Rashid, 1999, p. 24). The Taliban outlawed all forms of entertainment including the Internet, music, and television. Criminal acts were dealt with harshly. Depending upon the offense, the offender had to endure stoning, amputation, or death by beheading or shooting. The punishment for theft usually involved the loss of a limb, and if caught in the act of adultery or homosexuality the death sentence was imposed. Public executions were common. Men were required to grow beards and maintain them at a certain length. Women were required to wear a burka, forbidden to go to school or be out in public without a male relative, and banned from most employment.[10]

Despite their conquest and control of a large portion of the country, the Taliban did very little to improve the war-ravaged infrastructure or provide for the basic needs of the people (Rashid, 2001f, p. 126). The primary economic activity during their reign centered on the smuggling of licit consumer goods and taxing the cultivation, production, and trafficking of opium and its derivatives (Rashid, 2001f, p. 124). Due to their extreme interpretation of Islam and their horrific record of human rights abuses they only received diplomatic recognition as the governing authority in Afghanistan from three countries: Saudi Arabia, Pakistan, and the United Arab Emirates (UAE), the financial hub of the Middle East (Farah, 2002). Ultimately, the Taliban failed to consolidate and unify the country and, due in part to their brutality and harsh policies, they alienated large numbers of Afghans. According to Magnus and Naby (2002, p. 196):

> . . . the main threat to the political stability created under the Taliban came from an exaggerated reliance on Islamic homogeneity as a source of unity. This reliance on Islam was meant to unify a time-honored principle

within Islamic history; and for the Taliban, insistence upon it came from a self-righteousness that governed their actions on several political fronts.

Jalali (2001) takes a broader and more critical view of the Taliban's failure to achieve a functioning and viable government:

> The Taliban's extensive links to Pakistan (especially to the Inter-Services Intelligence [ISI] and Deobandi religious schools ["madrassas"]), to foreign extremist networks, and to wanted terrorists, along with its condoning of massive drug production and its poor human rights record, resulted in international isolation of the movement. Taliban imposition of far-reaching social restrictions and economic failure also caused increasing domestic disapproval.

Following the terrorist attacks on September 11, 2001, the countries that provided initial and ongoing support and recognition to the Taliban severed relations with them. Prior to the October invasion the U.S. government requested that the Taliban turn Osama bin Laden over to U.S. authorities to stand trial. This request was denied. At this poin. they became virtually isolated, although support from Pakistan's ethnic Pashtuns remained—especially in the Federally Administered Tribal Areas (FATA) and among members of Pakistan's Inter-Service Intelligence Agency (ISI) and armed forces (Associated Press, September 3, 2003b).

EVOLUTION OF THE AL QAEDA MOVEMENT IN AFGHANISTAN

Towards the end of the Soviet occupation many members of the Afghan-Arab alumni (mujahideen),[11] evolved into Al Qaeda (the base).[12] Primarily through the efforts of Osama bin Laden, this newly formed network of Afghan "freedom fighters" was formed to continue the jihad (holy war) struggle throughout various countries by mujahideen nationals who participated in the Soviet-Afghan war. From this band of Afghan-Arab war veterans al Qaeda would evolve into a global threat.

The 2003 edition of the *Encyclopedia of World Terrorism* defines Al Qaeda as:

> An ideologically motivated, sophisticated and decentralized global terrorist network headed by its founder and emir (prince), Osama bin Laden. Al Qaeda is a loose association of semi-autonomous cells located in dozens of countries throughout the world. . . . In addition to coordinating its own attacks the organization acts as an umbrella group by financing, training and providing logistical support to a number of other radical groups including groups based in Algeria, Egypt, Ethiopia, the Russian republic of Chechnya,

> Libya, the Philippines, Sudan, Syria and Yemen. The primary goals of the organization are to topple pro-Western Arab governments (e.g., Egypt and Saudi Arabia), drive Americans and American influence from all Muslim lands, destroy the state of Israel and unite all Muslims into a single purified Islamic nation. The group has been suspected of or responsible for numerous high profile attacks over the past decade.[13]

Osama bin Laden, the organization's principal sponsor and "driving force" viewed the Soviet defeat in Afghanistan as follows:

> Those who carried out the jihad in Afghanistan did more than was expected of them because with very meager capacities they destroyed the largest military force (the Soviet Army) and in so doing removed from our minds this notion of stronger nations. We believe that America is weaker than Russia (Spyer, 2004, p. 30).

Thus, this victory over a militarily superior force in the mountains of Afghanistan would not only serve as a catalyst to expand Osama bin Laden's strategic focus but would also enable him to increase his organizational depth through a concerted propaganda and recruitment campaign thus enhancing his group's destructive capability. This organizational expansion was to be accomplished through an alignment with other like-minded, equally dangerous individuals and terrorist organizations that today comprise an international web of terror[14] whose sole raison d'eêtre is jihad on a global scale—an asymmetric battle between the forces of "true Islam," the West, and corrupt, secular Arab states. Today this fight is being waged against individuals, nation-states, and ideologies which directly threaten the core tenets of Islam and seek to subjugate the world's Muslim population as viewed through the eyes of extremist factions such as Al Qaeda, Hezb-i-Islami (HIG),[15] the Taliban, and other Islamist militant groups.[16]

Former British Foreign Secretary, Robin Cook (2005, p. 24), noted that Saudi Arabia and the West had underestimated Osama bin Laden when they provided his recruits with funding and armaments. The West, according to Cook, did not envision Osama bin Laden as a potential future enemy of the United States.

The former British foreign secretary's assessment may be an oversimplification of the facts. Osama bin Laden's primary contribution to the Afghan resistance during the Soviet occupation was his considerable wealth. While some CIA and Saudi money may have found its way to Osama bin Laden's coffers, he used his own personal finances to recruit and care for the thousands of volunteers who descended upon Afghanistan with dreams of joining the jihad. He also used his talents and wealth gained through his father's lucrative construction business to build underground storage facilities (arms depots), roads, and living quarters for the mujahideen, among other things. There is no evidence that Osama bin Laden was recruited by or was directly funded by the CIA.

Although Osama bin Laden attributes the Soviet defeat to the efforts of the "Afghan Arabs," this also appears to be an overstatement. Milt Bearden was based in Pakistan from 1986–1989 as the CIA officer in charge of coordinating the covert action program in support of the Afghan resistance to the Soviet invasion and occupation. Bearden (2001, pp. 17–30) dispels a myth which has been perpetuated by Osama bin Laden and others since the Soviet defeat in 1989. Bearden, who is supported by Rubin,[17] claims:

> Over the ten years of war as many as 25,000 Arabs may have passed through Pakistan and Afghanistan. At one time the CIA considered having volunteer Arab legions take part in the war, but the idea was scrapped as unwise and unworkable. Despite what has often been written, the CIA never recruited, trained, or otherwise used the Arab volunteers who arrived in Pakistan. The idea that the Afghans somehow needed fighters from outside their culture was deeply flawed and ignored basic historical and cultural facts. The Arabs who did travel to Afghanistan from Peshawar were generally considered nuisances by mujahideen commanders, some of whom viewed them as only slightly less bothersome than the Soviets. As fundraisers, however, the Arabs from the Persian Gulf played a positive, often critical role in the background of the war (Bearden 2001, p. 24).[18]

Osama bin Laden's personal fortune has been estimated as high as US $300 million. However, according to Roth, Greenburg, and Wille (2004, p. 20) this information also appears to be a "myth"[19] and "probably originated from rumors in the Saudi business community." Heir to a Saudi construction magnate, Osama bin Laden was angry with the royal family for its decision to base American forces (infidels) on Saudi territory prior to the first Gulf War; he became infuriated when the war ended and American forces remained in the country. In regard to the stationing of U.S. troops on Saudi soil, Osama bin Laden spoke out publicly against the Saudi government and was subsequently exiled from Saudi Arabia. According to Rashid:

> In 1992 he [bin Laden] had a fiery meeting with Interior Minister Prince Naif whom he called a traitor to Islam. Naif complained to King Fahd and bin Laden was declared persona non grata (Rashid, 2001f, p. 133).

Some media reports cited that, "he [bin Laden] was asked by the Saudi government to return, but he refused, so they withdrew his citizenship, cancelled his passport and froze his assets (Shahzad, 2001).

AL QAEDA, THE AFGHAN ARABS AND THE TALIBAN

In 1992, Osama bin Laden and hundreds of his fellow "Afghan Arabs" took up residence in Sudan.[20] In Sudan, Osama bin Laden formed an alliance with Hassan al Turabi, leader of the governing National Islamic Front. According to the National Commission on Terrorist Attacks upon the United States (2004, p. 57), while based in Sudan Osama bin Laden:

> . . . set up a large and complex set of intertwined business and terrorist enterprises. In time the former would encompass numerous companies and a global network of bank accounts and nongovernmental institutions . . . al Qaeda finance officers and top operatives used their positions in bin Laden's businesses to acquire weapons, explosives, and technical equipment for terrorist purposes.

Additional insight into Al Qaeda operations while based in Sudan was provided by Jamal Ahmed Al-Fadl,[21] Osama bin Laden's paymaster and one of the initial members of Al Qaeda. As a founding member and trusted high ranking official within the organization Al-Fadl, who was with Osama bin Laden in Sudan, was involved in several of his Sudan-based businesses. This relationship eventually soured when Al-Fadl was forced to leave Sudan in 1996 after he failed to pay back $110,000 which he had embezzled from several of Osama bin Laden's companies. He traveled to several different countries before ending up in a U.S. embassy visa line in an undisclosed location (Weiser, 2001, p. A1). Al-Fadl was eventually placed in the U.S. Witness Protection Program under FBI protection and was the prosecution's star witness in the trial of *United States of America v Usama bin Laden et al.*, which convened in February 2001.

Four individuals that the U.S. government alleged took part in the 1998 African embassy bombings were put on trial. According to the trial transcript (United States District Court, Southern District of New York, 2001a, pp. 158–535)[22] Al-Fadl provided information relative to Al Qaeda's organizational structure and his own involvement in Osama bin Laden's attempt to purchase enriched uranium. Al-Fadl also provided details concerning Osama bin Laden's Sudanese-based companies, the purpose of which bin Laden had defined as: "our agenda is bigger than business. We [are] not going to make business here, but we need to help the government and the government help our group, and this is our purpose" (United States District Court, Southern District of New York, 2001a, pp. 352–353). Al- Fadl's testimony also disclosed Osama bin Laden's early efforts to form a global coalition of like-minded groups.[23]

Al-Fadl's testimony also revealed that there was often friction and contention within the group. These disagreements centered on finances, salaries, and overall group objectives relative to the jihad and how it was to be advanced (United States District Court, Southern District of

New York, 2001a, pp. 348–411; pp. 158–346 and pp. 411–535). Indeed, this rift in group objectives caused some members of the organization to sever ties with Osama bin Laden.

In 1996, under financial and diplomatic pressure from the U.S. and Saudi governments, Osama bin Laden was expelled from Sudan and returned to Afghanistan where he eventually formed a symbiotic relationship with Taliban emir Mullah Mohammad Omar who provided him and his associates safe haven as "guests." At first Osama bin Laden was welcomed, "like a holy man," (Coll, 2004, p. 325) to Jalalabad by his Afghan associates in the anti-Soviet jihad, but bin Laden did not arrive in a Taliban-controlled area, because he "did not have a comfortable enough relationship with the Taliban's isolated, severe, mysterious leadership group to place himself and his family under their control" (Coll, 2004, pp. 327–328). This would change in 1997 when Osama bin Laden moved to Kandahar.

THE RADICALIZATION OF THE TALIBAN

In 1996, upon the arrival of Osama bin Laden and his entourage of "Afghan Arabs," the Taliban was a political-military force whose objective was the conquest and subsequent control of the entire country (Coll, 2004, p. 328). It was also in 1996 that Osama bin Laden, based in Afghanistan, issued a fatwa (religious proclamation) calling upon all Muslims to attack Americans. The 9/11 Commission Report points out that operationally Al Qaeda had changed its modus operandi upon returning to Afghanistan. From operating as a mere facilitator of global terrorist operations by serving as a logistical conduit for allied groups, the organization was now taking a more hands-on approach.[24]

Interestingly, until the arrival of Osama bin Laden, the Taliban were not particularly anti-West in their views. In fact they were void of a foreign policy and had made many attempts to achieve global recognition and a seat at the UN. According to Rashid (2001f, p. 139) this changed in 1997 as "Bin Laden's worldview began to dominate the thinking of senior Taliban leaders."

According to Rashid (2001c), "bin Laden introduced Omar to the wider world of Islamic radicalism by flattering him and calling him the Emir, or leader, of the whole Muslim world, who had created the purest Islamic state in the world."[25]

The relationship between Al Qaeda and the Taliban was indeed mutually benefiting. The Taliban received funding, manpower, and access to Osama bin Laden's international connections. Al Qaeda had the protection of the Taliban, and an operational base from which they could recruit and train future jihadists, launch attacks against the West, and continue to transform and expand their organization into a global phenomenon.

The United States on many occasions tried to persuade the Taliban leadership to surrender Osama bin Laden for the 1998 attacks on two U.S. embassies in Africa. The request fell on deaf ears. The UN imposed sanctions on the Taliban in 1999 and 2000 for harboring Osama bin Laden, maintaining terrorist training facilities, human rights abuses, and their involvement in the opium trade.[26] The imposition of sanctions had little effect.

In October 2003, the *Terrorism Monitor*[27] reported that in April 2003—shortly after the start of the Iraq war and a renewed Taliban offensive in Afghanistan, Taliban leader Mullah Muhammad Omar issued a declaration in Nangarhar province which called on Muslims to rise up and resist the West. According to Dr. Victor Korgun, a terrorism analyst for the Jamestown Foundation, "the text of the declaration revealed a certain relationship" (Korgun, 2003, p. 7).

Peter Bergen also acknowledged close Al Qaeda-Taliban ties in an interview with CNN's Anderson Cooper on September 27, 2006.[28]

The strength of their relationship was reinforced in July 2007 in an interview that took place between an unnamed Pakistani journalist and Mansoor Dadullah, former Taliban commander and leader in Helmand, the main opium producing province in Afghanistan.[29] This interview illustrates the evolving nature of the movement and the gradual ideological shift that the Taliban has been undergoing since Osama bin Laden took up residence in Afghanistan in May 1996 and began developing a relationship with Mullah Muhammad Omar in Kandahar in September of that year. The statements by this top Taliban commander exemplify a more radicalized and global focused movement. The questions were supplied by Urs Gehriger of *Weltwoche*,[30] a weekly Swiss magazine, and Sami Yousafzai, a correspondent for *Newsweek* magazine. During the interview Dadullah stated that although the Taliban are an independent entity they are closely allied with Al Qaeda and share his vision of a "global struggle." He also confirmed the presence of many foreign fighters, some of whom carry out suicide attacks against coalition forces and the Afghan government (Gehriger and Yousafzai, 2007).[31]

Finally, the Associated Press (AP) reported on September 20, 2007, that a video had been released and was made available on several extremist Web sites.[32] As reported by AP, the contents included political statements made by Mansoor Dadullah during a meeting with Al Qaeda's leader in Afghanistan, Mustafa Abu al-Yazeed.[33] In the aforementioned video Mansoor clarified the tightening of the ideological bonds between the Taliban and Al Qaeda in the following statement: "We shall target the infidels in Afghanistan and outside Afghanistan: inside all the infidel countries oppressing the Muslims" (AP, 2007b).

The political tone of the above statements indicates that they could have been issued by bin Laden or his deputy Ayman al Zawahiri. Additionally al-Yazeed confirmed the bonds between the two organizations by stating that the relationship between the two groups was becoming stronger (AP, 2007b). It should be emphasized that al-Yazeed's input on this video confirms the general thinking among NATO/ISAF and Afghan officials that Al Qaeda is directly involved in insurgent efforts to dislodge foreign forces from Afghanistan. Furthermore, the aforementioned interview and the above cited Associated Press report convey a larger objective, i.e., to spread jihad to neighboring countries and beyond.

It is important to note that the pan-Islamic views espoused above had their genesis in Afghanistan in 1997 when Osama bin Laden began forming a relationship with Mullah Muhammad Omar and other high-ranking Taliban officials. Not only did this relationship spawn an extremist foreign policy but, with Taliban consent, Afghanistan became a training center and refuge for international Islamist militants.[34]

It is this relationship nurtured and influenced by Osama bin Laden that would ultimately revolutionize the Taliban and ideologically unite them and other foreign Islamists under Al Qaeda's vision of global jihad.[35]

FACTIONS INVOLVED IN THE INSURGENCY IN AFGHANISTAN

In the 1980s, the Central Intelligence Agency (CIA) published a pamphlet on insurgency.[36] The pamphlet titled, *Guide to the Analysis of Insurgency*, provided a definition of insurgencies that has been used by scholars as well as practitioners. This definition states:

> Insurgency is a protracted political-military activity directed toward completely or partially controlling the resources of a country through the use of irregular military forces and illegal political organizations. Insurgent activity—including guerrilla warfare, terrorism, and political mobilization, for example, propaganda, recruitment, front and covert party organization, and international activity—is designed to weaken government control and legitimacy while increasing insurgent control and legitimacy. The common denominator of most insurgent groups is their desire to control a particular area. This objective differentiates insurgent groups from purely terrorist organizations, whose objectives do not include the creation of an alternative government capable of controlling a given area or country (Central Intelligence Agency, n.d., p. 2).[37]

It appears that the above definition would apply to the Taliban and allied factions based in Afghanistan and Pakistan's tribal areas. Based on the Taliban's ultimate objectives as expressed in the declarations of Mullah Muhammad Omar and Mansoor Dadullah of driving the "infidels" from the country, regaining power, and becoming the central governing authority in Afghanistan and Al Qaeda's goal, as expressed by Osama bin Laden and his deputy Ayman al-Zawahiri, of ultimately establishing an Islamic caliphate throughout the wider Middle East, it seems that the aspirations of both groups do indeed coincide and include control over a country [Afghanistan] and perhaps ultimately Central Asia, the Middle East/ Persian Gulf, as well as Pakistan. It is clear that although Al Qaeda and the Taliban are separate entities, they seem to have merged together in an ideological sense.[38]

The Taliban insurgency is comprised of various extremist elements including the original Afghan Taliban, Hezb-i-Islami,[39] the Haqqani network,[40] some Al Qaeda operatives[41] and other Afghan and Pakistani-based foreign jihadists.

Gulbuddin Hekmatyar, leader of the fundamentalist group, Hezb-i-Islami (HIG), was the most ruthless of Afghanistan's warlords, who led one of seven resistance factions fighting the Soviets. He was a favorite of Pakistan's ISI because he recruited the "most radical, anti-Western transnational Islamists fighting in the jihad—including bin Laden and other Arabs who arrived as volunteers" (Coll, 2004, p. 119).[42] Subsequently he received a large portion of U.S. and Saudi Arabia funding channeled through the ISI during the 10-year war (Harrison, 1990, p. A11). He is also a known drug trafficker. As funding for the mujahideen began to diminish at the end of the war, Hekmatyar and his men became involved in the drug trade. He fell out of favor with Pakistan when the Taliban entered the fray in 1994. He is also known for his savage attacks on Kabul during the civil war between rival resistance factions which followed the Soviet defeat. Most recently he has aligned himself with the Taliban and Al Qaeda (Wiseman, 2006). According to Chouvy (2004, p. 8):

> Hekmatyar's involvement in the illegal drug economy really started only after 1989, when the United States stopped funding him and others . . . he remains consistent in waging a war against governments he does not recognize, be they Soviet-backed or U.S.-backed. He also may well have increased his participation in the drug economy.[43]

While the various insurgent formations (cited above) may have different short-term agendas and conduct operations in various locations throughout Afghanistan, they do cooperate with each other.[44] All factions support the removal of foreign forces from Afghanistan, the overthrow of the present Kabul government, and the establishment of a fundamentalist Islamic state. According to Seth Jones of the RAND Corporation, who visited Afghanistan as recently as December 2006:

> The insurgency is believed to comprise a diverse fusion of actors, primarily Taliban fighters and former Mujahedeen—the Hizb-I Islami Gulbuddin (HiG)—who battled Soviet invaders in the 1980s. The movement has also begun to attract support from the international realm, including Al Qaeda,

> Pakistani Islamic militants, and foreign jihadists who are notorious for employing extreme tactics in places such as Iraq, Chechnya, and Israel. . . . foreign contingents make up the insurgency's most lethal and effective elements. Foreign militants are committed to fighting the enemy twenty-four hours a day; Taliban fighters, on the other hand, include ordinary Afghan citizens who might participate in the insurgency one day, and the next day resume their jobs as farmers (Hsu and Cole 2006).[45]

It is clear from numerous press reports, statements by U.S., NATO/ ISAF officials. and leading authorities on the subject that members of these groups are responsible for the growing insurgency: "The Taliban has deepened its alliance with warlord Gulbuddin Hekmatyar and his fundamentalist, anti-Western Hizb-i-Islami Party, which remains potent in eastern Afghanistan . . ." (Zabriskie, 2003). Moreover, as noted by Rashid (2001c), Al Qaeda may be assisting the Taliban by providing manpower for various operations (Zabriskie, 2003; Gunaratna, 2002, p. 40). Similar assistance was provided by Osama bin Laden in Taliban efforts against the Northern Alliance prior to 9/11.

On May 12, 2004, Mark L. Schneider, senior vice president of the International Crisis Group (ICG), gave testimony before the U.S. Senate Foreign Relations Committee. According to the hearing transcript Mr. Schneider spoke of the reconstitution of Taliban and Al Qaeda forces and the threat that posed to coalition forces, the fledgling Afghan government in Kabul, and international efforts at reconstruction. He also provided some insight into the growing narcotics problem and the consequences of failure in this area relative to the present insurgency:

> . . . the capacity of Taliban and al-Qaeda today to maintain a deadly insurgency across the south and southwest of the country appears to be increasing. Within Afghanistan, there has also been an unwillingness to take on the hard work of disarming and demobilizing regional warlords and militias, despite its crucial linkage to political stability and to controlling the drug trade. . . . Al-Qaeda and Taliban attacks on UN, NGOs and Afghan government officials have nearly doubled over the past four months compared to last year (Schneider, 2004).

According to a September 2006 report issued by the United Nations General Assembly[46] the insurgency is run from "five Taliban command and control centres," which operate extensively from "safe havens" outside of Afghanistan:

> They include a Taliban command active in Afghanistan's north-eastern provinces, an eastern command and a southern command as well as separate fronts established by two Taliban allies, the veteran warlords Gulbuddin Hekmatyar and Jalaluddin Haqqani. . . . "The leadership relies heavily on cross-border fighters, many of whom are Afghans

> drawn from nearby refugee camps and radical seminaries in Pakistan," the UN report says. "They are trained and paid to serve as medium-level commanders, leading operations inside Afghanistan and are able to retreat back to safe havens outside the country," it adds. The report also states: "The foot soldiers of the insurgency are Afghans recruited within Afghanistan" (Rashid, 2006a, p. 14).[47]

Although not heretofore mentioned by NATO/ISAF military officials, members of Jamiat ul-Ansar, formerly known as Harakat ul-Mujahedin (HUM), are also involved in the ongoing insurgency. On May 31, 2004, an Australian journalist, Rory Callinan,[48] reported a Taliban attack on an Afghan-based humanitarian organization in Kandahar province. Two charity workers and a police officer were killed in the attack. At a roadblock established to apprehend the perpetrators, 12 men were taken into custody. According to Callinan, "What they found revealed the connection between Afghanistan's billion-dollar drug trade and the Taliban fighters and terrorists." The twelve men taken into custody confessed to the slayings in Kandahar's Panjwai district and revealed that, "they had been working as opium harvesters." One of the suspects further stated that he had received prior training from the Pakistan-based organization, Jamiat ul-Ansar and "he had traveled to Afghanistan to, 'kill Americans'" (Callinan, 2004).

As mentioned previously numerous factions have been subsumed under the name Taliban. In a report published by the *New York Times*, the suspect cited above was found to have in his possession a Jamiat ul-Ansar membership card and a list containing the phone numbers of top officials in the organization. The report further stated that during an interview attended by several guards, the suspect—in an attempt to win his release or avoid a prison sentence—revealed that he was originally recruited by Jamiat ul-Ansar and subsequently trained in a camp near Islamabad before being dispatched to Afghanistan. He also said that the organization had "high-level support from within the establishment" (Gall and Rohde, 2004, p. A1). The suspect was ultimately charged with "taking part in a terrorist attack" (Mir, n.d.) and was subsequently found guilty of the murders. He received a 20-year prison term handed down by a judge in Kabul (Gall and Rohde, 2004, p. A1).

Jamiat ul-Ansar is designated a foreign terrorist organization (FTO) by the Australian and U.S. governments (1997). The group is primarily based in Pakistan and conduct operations against Indian forces and civilians in Kashmir.[49] They were also involved in operations against Soviet forces in the decade-long Soviet-Afghan war, and maintained operational training camps in eastern Afghanistan prior to the U.S.-led coalition attack in October 2001. Jamiat ul-Ansar has known ties to Al Qaeda; the former leader of the group, Fazlur Rehman Khalil, signed the initial Osama bin Laden fatwa in 1998 (U.S. Department of State, 2000, p. 102). Since then the group had received funding and training from Al Qaeda in Afghanistan. Jamiat ul-Ansar has been responsible for numerous international terrorist attacks including the 1999 hijacking of an Indian commercial airliner and the abduction and murder of U.S. citizen and *Wall Street Journal* investigative reporter Daniel Pearl in 2002 (SITE Institute, 2004; Government of Australia, 2002; United States Department of State, 2006b).

The above account does not implicate Al Qaeda nor Osama bin Laden in a direct way to the opium/drug trade. However, it adds substance to the allegation that members of the insurgency, who have strong ties to Al Qaeda, are receiving financial support from the lucrative opium trade at various stages of the process.

It appears that insurgent forces, especially in the southern provinces, are exploiting the trade to further their long-term objectives. The above account also supports the view by ICG's Mark Schneider, RAND's Seth Jones, and other individuals who provided first-hand information, that the insurgency includes foreign jihadists who are entering Afghanistan from points in Pakistan.

In May 2009, U.S. Army General Stanley McChrystal became the new commander of U.S. and NATO forces (ISAF) in Afghanistan. Shortly after taking command, General McChrystal issued a report on the ground situation in Afghanistan. This report dated August 20, 2009, was submitted to U.S. Secretary of Defense Robert M. Gates and would set the stage for a major reversal in military strategy as well as new initiatives relative to the civilian component in that country. The report outlines McChrystal's "initial assessment"[50] relative to the ongoing insurgency, Afghan government corruption, the current state of Afghan security forces, and provides his vision for a successful outcome to this eight-year-old conflict. The report calls for major operational changes and views the insurgency as having gained the momentum which needed to be reversed within one year (McChrystal, 2009, p. 1–2). The report notes:

> Most insurgent fighters are Afghans. They are directed by a small number of Afghan senior leaders based in Pakistan that work through an alternative political infrastructure in Afghanistan. They are aided by foreign fighters, elements of some intelligence agencies, and international funding, resources, and training. Foreign fighters provide materiel, expertise, and ideological commitment (McChrystal 2009, pp. 2–5).

Moreover, according to McChrystal, the factions creating the greatest challenges to peace and stability in Afghanistan are: the Quetta Shura Council (QST) headed by Mullah Muhammad Omar and based in Quetta, Pakistan.[51] This group comprises the Afghan Taliban and according to McChrystal is the primary threat to the ISAF mission in Afghanistan (McChrystal 2009, pp. 2–6). The second group, the Haqqani network

(HQN), is based on both sides of the Afghan-Pakistani border and may be the most lethal of the insurgent factions.[52] They are allied with Al Qaeda and other foreign jihadists, and have been responsible for numerous attacks against ISAF and civilian and foreign-based targets in Afghanistan. The third group cited by McChrystal, Hezb-i-Islami Gulbuddin (HIG), discussed in some detail above, is based primarily in three Afghan provinces: "Nangarhar, Nuristan, and Kunar as well as Pakistan . . ." McChrystal notes that each group is independent but "often achieving significant unity of purpose and even some unity of effort . . ." (McChrystal 2009, pp. 2–6).[53]

The new strategy of the ISAF is centered on providing security for the Afghan people, eliminating corruption, targeting drug traffickers,[54] and installing governing structures which can provide much needed services to the people of this war-ravaged country.

MILITIAS, TRAFFICKERS, AND CRIMINALS

Other non-state groups[55] operating in Afghanistan are also contributing to the violence and undermining efforts by the national government and NATO/ISAF forces to achieve stability and the rule of law. An article in the *Christian Science Monitor* on October 14, 2003, provided a brief summation of the current conflict and the problems being encountered by U.S., Afghan, and NATO forces, particularly in the southern provinces:

> Afghanistan remains a land controlled by private armies, militias, and armed gangs, each with its own ethnic power base and ambition to get a piece of the national pie. Efforts to demobilize, disarm, and reintegrate militia fighters—numbered at 600,000 by the Defense Ministry—have been studied and planned, but have yet to actually begin. The reason is twofold: America still needs many of these armed groups to maintain security and fight Al Qaeda; and Afghanistan has yet to figure out how to reintegrate a generation of men who have known no other job than war (Baldauf, 2003, p. 7).

During his May 12, 2004, testimony, cited above, Mark Schneider stated that illegally armed groups, i.e., allied "local commanders" as well as "political opponents" of President Karzai provide protection and transportation services to drug traffickers, thereby enriching themselves by imposing taxes on drug shipments (Schneider, 2004).

With respect to Schneider's comments regarding regional warlords[56] and militias, the Afghan National Development Strategy (ANDS) estimates that there are approximately 1,800 illegally armed groups (IAGs) in Afghanistan comprising over 125,000 individuals.[57] These IAGs are responsible for much of the present instability and therefore pose a direct threat to the Kabul government. According to a report issued by the government of Afghanistan (2006, p. 121)[58] these IAGs are heavily involved in various types of illegal activity including human rights violations as well as drug and human trafficking.

Drug traffickers and criminals operate throughout the country but particularly in the heavy poppy growing areas in the south of the country, e.g., Helmand and Kandahar provinces.[59] In his opening statement before the U.S. House of Representatives Armed Services Committee on June 28, 2006, Lt. Gen. Karl Eikenberry, then the commander of the Combined Forces Command in Afghanistan, shared the following information relative to the various factions operating in the country and the problems they are posing for U.S. and allied forces:

> . . . Afghanistan remains the target of terrorist groups, drug traffickers and a determined criminal element. Not all violence can be attributed to the Taliban or al-Qaeda, as narco-trafficking, tribal conflicts and land disputes also continue to challenge the overall security environment. The enemy we face is not particularly strong, but the institutions of the Afghan State remain relatively weak.[60]

It is important to remember that during the past 30 years Afghanistan has been at war with invading forces or fighting amongst each other. Consequently, throughout this period the "war economy" became linked to the expanding criminal economy in order to generate sufficient revenue to sustain this period of protracted conflict (UNODC, 2006, p. 189). Criminal activity, specifically the trafficking in drugs, became increasingly stronger throughout this period. Today this criminally-driven economy and the corruption that accompanies it are primary factors, which embolden and strengthen the insurgency and curtails efforts at reform and reconstruction.[61]

CONCLUSION

Many allegations regarding the alleged terror-drug nexus in Afghanistan and more specifically the Al Qaeda-drugs nexus stem from post-9/11 international media reports promulgating that the Taliban and Al Qaeda organizations are one and the same. Hence, a perception began to form of a single Taliban-al Qaeda monolithic entity. While both groups seem to be evolving into a unified force, they are at this point in time separate entities. The history of the Al Qaeda organization suggests that upon returning to Afghanistan from Sudan in 1996, Al Qaeda was one of the Taliban's primary sponsors both financially and by providing manpower (al Qaeda's 055 Brigade) in the latter's military efforts against the Northern Alliance.

This author maintains that since the October 2001 invasion, the Taliban and Al Qaeda have morphed into a more fluid and decentralized force. Though they continue to be autonomous and operate independently, they have coalesced ideologically. This in turn impacts countermeasures and policies designed to combat the growing threat that they collectively both represent. Al Qaeda has consistently employed terrorism in an overall strategy against the West, primarily the United States, and secular Arab governments. Osama bin Laden's core objectives have been specifically enumerated through the media, fatwas,[62] and have been made known through trial testimony and interrogation proceedings of various captured members. Additionally, based on numerous media accounts, other reporting entities, and the information provided in this chapter illegally armed groups (IAGs), criminals, and drug traffickers are also contributing to the growing instability and violence throughout the country, specifically in Helmand and Kandahar, the primary opium producing provinces.

Concerning Jamiat ul-Ansar, it has previously been established that members of this group, a U.S. Department of State designated foreign terrorist organization (FTO), which operates primarily in Kashmir, has ties to Al Qaeda. Furthermore, members of this group have been operating in Afghanistan and have conducted strikes against government workers and a humanitarian agency (Callinan, 2004). Subsequent statements made by Jamiat ul-Ansar members revealed that they were involved in the harvesting of opium.

Chapter 5 will examine specific terrorist incidents throughout Afghanistan since the U.S.-led invasion in October 2001, the ascension and transmutation of the Taliban movement, and provide evidence that the Taliban militia as it existed prior to October 2001 began a very subtle ideological shift under the tutelage of Osama bin Laden beginning in 1997. Since then it has further morphed into an entirely different and more dangerous force. In this regard chapter 5 will also examine the term terrorism as applied to the Taliban.

Furthermore, chapter 5 will address the evolution and rise of Al Qaeda following the Soviet withdrawal in 1989, the expansion of this network into an international Islamist movement with global reach, and the evolving relationship between the Taliban and Al Qaeda. Chapter 5 will conclude with a brief examination of the evolving global threat posed by radical Islamists based in Southwest Asia.

CHAPTER 5

International Terrorism in Afghanistan

MAJOR TERRORIST FORMATIONS IN AFGHANISTAN[1]

Of the major terrorist groups currently involved in the ongoing conflict in Afghanistan which have been or are currently based in that country the IMU, the Taliban, Al Qaeda, HIG, and the Haqqani network have perpetrated terrorist attacks against foreign entities either within Afghanistan or beyond its borders. An examination of the MIPT/RAND terrorist incident database reveals that, beginning in 1989—the initial date Al Qaeda[2] was formed, and subsequently the IMU (1999) and the Taliban (1994), through December 31, 2004, these three groups were responsible for 46 attacks which have been designated as international terrorism.

Al Qaeda was first designated a Foreign Terrorist Organization (FTO) in 1999. Between 1989 and December 31, 2004, Al Qaeda perpetrated 23 attacks against foreign targets, and has been credited with attacks in 12 countries including Afghanistan. Ten of these incidents were directed against Saudi Arabia. There were three Al Qaeda attacks in Afghanistan (classified as domestic). Additionally, Al Qaeda's splinter groups, i.e., Al Qaeda in the Arabian Peninsula, were responsible for three attacks; Al Qaeda Organization in the Islamic Maghreb, one attack; and the Al Qaeda Organization in the Land of the Two Rivers, two attacks. Sixteen attacks occurred after the U.S.-led invasion in October 2001, and were carried out in countries other than Afghanistan. Of the six attacks attributed to the Al Qaeda factions cited above, one occurred in 2003, five in 2004.

From January 2005 to August 2007 Al Qaeda (core) did not record an international attack, however, during this period the Al Qaeda Organization in the Islamic Maghreb is credited with five attacks; the Al Qaeda Organization in the Land of the Two Rivers, 25 attacks; and two groups which had not appeared in the prior assessment, the Al Qaeda Organization in

Palestine and Abu Mus'ab al- Zarqawi, were each credited with one attack, the latter having attacked a diplomatic target (U.S. embassy) in Syria on September 12, 2006.

The Taliban is not named on either the Foreign Terrorist Organizations (FTO) or Other Terrorist Organizations (OTO) list, nor are they listed on the Terrorist Exclusion List (TEL).[3] Persons associated with organizations on this list are excluded from entering the United States. Furthermore, they are not designated by Australia, Canada, or the European Union (EU). They are so designated by Russia. However, the Taliban and their commander, Mullah Muhammad Omar, are on the U.S. Treasury Department's "Specially Designated Global Terrorist (SDGT)" list[4] (U.S. Department of the Treasury, 2001a, pp. 53, 73, and 100).

According to the MIPT/RAND database, the Taliban have been cited as perpetrators in 104 attacks between November 1994 and December 31, 2004, 22 of which were carried out against international targets, one attack—an airline hijacking—was perpetrated against India.[5] Between January 1, 2005, and May 1, 2007 (the latest date that data was available), the Taliban are credited with 314 attacks (domestic and international) of which MIPT/RAND cites 36 as international; eight of these attacks occurred in Pakistan. The Taliban have attacked foreign consulates and kidnapped and killed foreign nationals in Afghanistan. On August 30, 2006, the Taliban killed two persons in Pakistan. One of the victims was an Afghan cleric, the other a private Afghan citizen accused by the Taliban of "being a spy for Afghanistan." The Taliban have also been responsible for the kidnapping of 23 South Korean missionaries, killing two before releasing 21 captives in August 2007. This incident took place on June 19, 2007 (Harden, 2007, p. A17).

The Islamic Movement of Uzbekistan (IMU) is a Central Asian-based terrorist group, formed in the Ferghana Valley[6] in the late 1990s to counter the repressive policies of the Islam Karimov (Uzbekistan) regime towards Muslims following the break-up of the Soviet Union. The overall objective of the group was to overthrow the Karimov regime and install a Taliban-like Islamic government. Due to the political and economic policies of the Karimov regime Juma Namangani, co-founder of the group, was able to draw a large following.[7]

The IMU has been identified as a hybrid (terrorist and criminal) organization by Mutschke (2000), Makarenko (2002), Napoleoni (2003),[8] and "an amalgam of personal vendetta, Islamism, drugs, geopolitics, and terrorism," by Baran, Starr, and Cornell (2006, p. 49). The group has attacked targets in Kyrgyzstan, Tajikistan, and Uzbekistan, and was designated a FTO by the U.S. Department of State in 2000. Prior to 9/11 they operated from bases in northern Afghanistan and Tajikistan and have maintained links to Al Qaeda prior to and following the events of 9/11.[9] The organization "is on several countries' lists of terrorist organizations and on the UN's list of organizations associated with the Taliban, Al Qaeda, and Osama bin Laden" (Rotar, 2007).

According to Rashid, the IMU received aid from the Taliban (Rashid, 2001d, and Rashid, 1999, pp. 22–35 at p. 30) and funding from Osama bin Laden (Rashid 2000), Saudi Arabia's Uzbek diaspora, and wealthy Arab patrons.[10] Revenue was also generated by the Afghan drug trade. Rashid (2001d) claims that the IMU was involved in the smuggling of heroin through Central Asia into Russia and Europe.[11] Following the U.S.-led invasion of Afghanistan, the IMU fought against coalition forces in the early stages of the war, with some reports claiming that IMU remnants were allied with anti-coalition forces.[12] Other reports claimed that the IMU suffered severe casualties during the bombing phase of "Operation Enduring Freedom" including the killing of the group's military leader, Juma Namangani. Speculation also exists that remnants of the movement fled with Taliban forces to Pakistan's Federally Administered Tribal Areas (FATA) and are currently based there.[13]

However, Rashid does not see evidence of an IMU revival (Saidazimova, 2006). According to the MIPT/RAND Terrorist Incident Database, the IMU[14] has not been responsible for a terrorist attack inside Afghanistan during the present insurgency. The current strength of the group is presently unknown however anecdotal information reveals that its current leader, Tahir Yuldeshev is in Pakistan's tribal region. Additionally, some members of this group are purportedly playing an active role in the ongoing insurgency.

The MIPT/RAND database credits the IMU with a total of six attacks, one of which was perpetrated against an international target. Although not cited in the MIPT/RAND database the IMU was responsible for the kidnapping of four American citizens in August 2000 (U.S. Department of State, 2001, pp. 35, 37, and 112), four Japanese geologists in August 1999 (U.S. Department of State, 2000, pp. 26, 28, and 85), and 13 Kyrgyzstanis in August 1999 (U.S. Department of State, 2000, pp. 28 and 120). The only attack credited to the IMU since the U.S.-led invasion was an attack against a government target in Tajikistan on June 12, 2005. MIPT/RAND cites this attack as domestic. There have been no attacks orchestrated by the IMU in Afghanistan since the start of offensive operations on October 7, 2001.

Hezb-i-Islami (HIG) is an Afghan-based group formed in the mid-1970s and currently part of the present Afghan insurgency. HIG is not listed as a foreign terrorist organization (FTO) however, they are cited on the U.S. Department of State's list of "Other Terrorist Organizations" (OTO), organizations of relevance in the war on terrorism. HIG's leader, Gulbuddin Hekmatyar, was designated a global terrorist by the U.S. Department of State in February 2003 (U.S. Department of State, 2003b). The group has perpetrated three attacks against targets inside Afghanistan since October 2001. One of these attacks targeted Chinese workers in the city of

Kunduz and was jointly carried out with the Taliban. Eleven persons were killed and four were injured (Gall and French, 2004, p. A13).[15] The Taliban denied involvement in this attack (Habibzai, 2004, p. A14). There were no incidents defined as international terrorism perpetrated by Hezb-i-Islami (HIG) from the period January 1, 2005, through May 1, 2007 (date of the last recorded data).[16]

As discussed in chapter 4, among the insurgent formations the Haqqani network (HQN) is perhaps the most dangerous. The organization is led by Siraj Haqqani, son of Taliban commander Jalaluddin Haqqani,[17] a major recipient of U.S. aid during the 10-year Soviet-Afghan war.[18] They operate from both sides of the Afghan-Pakistani border and have conducted deadly attacks against military and civilian targets, primarily in Afghanistan's eastern provinces, but have also staged operations in the north and south of the country. The HQN was responsible for the January 2008 attack on the Serena hotel[19] in Kabul which killed seven people, including three foreign nationals, and the attempted assassination of Afghan President Hamid Karzai in April 2008. HQN is allied with the Taliban and Al Qaeda. They run madrasas and terrorist training camps in North and South Waziristan, have embraced martyrdom operations (suicide attacks), and recruit and provide protection to foreign fighters, including Al Qaeda.[20]

TERRORIST ATTACKS BY AFGHAN-BASED GROUPS SINCE THE U.S.-LED INVASION

The number of terrorist attacks (domestic and international) has increased dramatically since September 2002. Many of these attacks have occurred in the southern and eastern provinces of the country, where Taliban, Hezb-i-Islami (HIG), and remnants of Al Qaeda have been particularly strong. Moreover, Helmand province—a Taliban stronghold in the south, and Nangarhar in the east, are the two main poppy-producing provinces.[21] Additionally, it was in these two provinces that United Kingdom anti-narcotic forces began their opium poppy eradication campaign in April 2002 (ECO-DCCU, 2004). Indeed, terrorists and/or criminals have infiltrated and increased the number of attacks not only in the southern and eastern provinces since the latter part of 2002, but throughout the rest of the country as well.[22]

These attacks may be designed to further an insurgency, create conditions which facilitate the trafficking of narcotics, or a combination of the two. Nonetheless, for the purposes of this discussion motivations are irrelevant. While in the case of the Taliban it can be argued that their objectives are entirely military (i.e., driving foreign forces out of Afghanistan) or criminal (i.e., to thwart government and coalition efforts at eradication of opium poppy thereby insuring or protecting a present and future revenue source), these acts have a political and social component; they generate fear in an effort to coerce the civilian population and further the political objective of reestablishing a central government in Kabul. This point is justified by the coercive and intimidating tactics they have used against the targeted population and their choice of victims primarily in the southern provinces, specifically Helmand.

As noted by the UN Security Council (UNSC) in Resolution 1456: "any acts of terrorism are criminal and unjustifiable, regardless of their motivation, whenever and by whomsoever committed and are to be unequivocally condemned, especially when they indiscriminately target or injure civilians" (UNSC, 2003, p. 2).

Furthermore, if the target of the attack happened to be an international agency, foreign national, or had any affiliation with a foreign-based organization (e.g., operations designed to thwart reconstruction or humanitarian aid projects) either by design or if collateral damage occurred to a foreign entity as a direct result of this action, then by definition that group has engaged in an act of international terrorism.

WHAT THE EVIDENCE REVEALS

On March 21, 1994, Charles Norchi, the executive director for the International League for Human Rights wrote an Op-Ed piece for the *New York Times*. In this article he discussed the ongoing deterioration and violence in Afghanistan:

> Five years after the last Russian troops left, there is still war in Afghanistan . . . For the first time, Afghanistan is becoming fertile ground for the breeding and export of militant Islamic fundamentalism. It is the ideology of a desperate people, and the seeds of desperation are taking root. With the virtual breakdown of law and order, radical fundamentalist training camps have been flourishing.

Norchi concluded this piece with a somewhat prophetic statement:

> Afghans are victims of the games superpowers once played: Their war was once our war, and collectively we bear responsibility. If something is not done to stop the killing, Afghanistan will only produce refugees, radical fundamentalists and terrorists. Then surely, some day, Afghanistan will again be our war (Norchi, 1994, p. A17).

From October 7, 2001, the date of the American-led invasion of Afghanistan, to February 2, 2007,[23] there were 940 terrorist attacks in Afghanistan. Of those 940 incidents, 132 were classified as international terrorist attacks.[24]

Of these 132 incidents, when the perpetrator was known, 39 attacks were attributed to the Taliban militia. One of these attacks was jointly conducted by the Taliban and Hezb-i-Islami (HIG). The perpetrator(s) for the balance of the attacks (92) cited as international were unknown. There were 808 attacks in Afghanistan during the period cited above that were listed in the database as domestic, i.e., "incidents perpetrated by local nationals against a purely domestic target" (MIPT, 2005).

Of these 808 incidents of domestic terrorism, the Taliban were credited with 304. There were 494 attacks where the perpetrator was unknown. Two attacks each were attributed to Al Qaeda, Hezb-i-Islami (HIG), and Jaish ul-Muslimeen. Hezb-e Azadi-ye Afghanistan, Mujahideen Message, and Saif-ul-Muslimeen are credited with one attack each and one attack was perpetrated jointly by the Taliban and Al Qaeda. Finally, of the 940 terrorist incidents (domestic and international) recorded by MIPT's Terrorism Database as having occurred in the above cited time frame the perpetrators of 586 or 62.3 percent of these attacks were unknown.

This lends credibility to the statement by Lt. Gen. Karl Eikenberry that much of the violence throughout the country is perpetrated by individuals and/or groups other than the Taliban or Al Qaeda and whose agenda is the continued maintenance of insecurity and conflict.[25] This is not meant to imply that some of the perpetrator "unknown" attacks were not Taliban et al. related, but is only meant to suggest that in an environment where there is an ongoing insurgency, various extremist factions, criminal groups, and a tremendous amount of opium being cultivated and subsequently processed into heroin, there are also other forces at work for which a state of instability is not only desirable but necessary.[26]

The U.S. Department of State does not list the Taliban as an international terrorist group. However, according to their definition: "international terrorism means terrorism involving citizens or the territory of more than one country," many of these incidents in which the Taliban were cited as perpetrators are correctly labeled as international in scope by MIPT/RAND. Many of these "international incidents," as acknowledged by RAND in the MIPT Terrorism Knowledge Base, fit both the U.S. Department of State's definition of international terrorism and the definition used throughout this study. Furthermore, numerous incidents cited in the database fulfill the criteria of all three elements of this definition. An examination of the MIPT/RAND database reveals that the Taliban perpetrated six attacks prior to October 7, 2001 that fall within this category (two in 1995, two in 1996, one in 1999, and one in 2001).[27]

In summary, the occurrence of terrorist acts in Afghanistan since the beginning of the current conflict has been high, with the Taliban playing a principal role—including the perpetration of incidents classified as international wherein Taliban terrorists have conducted attacks against foreign targets in both Afghanistan and Pakistan.

THE TALIBAN: TERRORISTS OR INSURGENTS?

According to the definition cited in chapter 4, insurgent activities may include terrorism[28] which is "designed to weaken government control and legitimacy while increasing insurgent control and legitimacy" (Central Intelligence Agency, n.d.).[29]

In the above definition, terrorism is subsumed under insurgency as activity which promotes or furthers the objectives of the insurgents. That may be true, however, in a theater of conflict as complex as Afghanistan, trying to determine the precise objectives of a multitude of violent non-state groups is difficult and, for the purposes of classifying a specific act as terrorism, it is an unnecessary exercise. The activities of both insurgents and terrorists are designed to achieve some form of political objective and both employ fear tactics to influence local and broader-based populations.

With respect to the Taliban these "fear tactics" include attacks on international aid agencies, other non-governmental organizations (NGOs), and Afghan and foreign nationals. Moreover, ample evidence exists—including the pronouncements of senior Taliban members that their primary political and military objective is to ultimately return to power. Therefore, Taliban et al. efforts to achieve this goal have included actions designed to win the "hearts and minds" (by carrot or stick) of the rural population. Once broad-based support is established, international coalition efforts against insurgent forces becomes much more difficult. Winning mass support is a necessary component in waging a successful insurgency.[30]

Indeed, throughout history other insurgencies have used terrorist type attacks aimed at noncombatants for the purpose of acquiring territory and to broaden and expand their operational base. However, in respect to the situation which currently exists in Afghanistan, it is extremely difficult, if not impossible, to isolate acts of domestic and international terrorism from insurgent or criminal activity that may or may not be viewed by some scholars, government officials, and others as terrorism. For example, this dilemma is made more complicated by the fact that many of the previously cited attacks in which the perpetrator could not be identified may very well have been carried out by criminal groups whose objective is to sabotage government opium eradication efforts and/or implementation of alternative livelihood strategies, thereby maintaining control over the population and the opium trade.[31]

Nevertheless, attacks targeting international civilians or property that have been attributed to the Taliban or for which responsibility was claimed by the Taliban fall under the designation of international terrorism. Furthermore, some of these attacks, classified as international in scope, may have been carried out by criminal elements allied with insurgent/terrorist factions or by Pakistan-based insurgent forces. On September 21, 2006, General James Jones, the Supreme Allied Commander for NATO in Afghanistan, told a U.S. Senate hearing that the Taliban leadership was based in Quetta, Pakistan (Rubin, B. R., 2006).[32] Moreover, if elements of the Taliban and affiliated groups are presently based in Pakistan as General Jones and others suggest, then their attacks against civilian targets and foreign interests in Afghanistan as represented by the above examples meet the criteria to be defined as acts of international terrorism.

There is ample evidence to support the fact that the Taliban, while conducting insurgent operations in Afghanistan—especially in the southern and eastern provinces, have used terrorist tactics as part of their operational modus operandi.[33] Moreover, following the October 7, 2001, invasion the Taliban has selected Afghan-based non-combatant international targets for attack; this tactic of targeting foreign entities has increased exponentially since 2002.[34] Furthermore, it has been shown that the Taliban insurgency is allied with other militant factions or individuals who have been so designated, e.g. Al Qaeda, Jamiat ul-Ansar, Gulbuddin Hekmatyar, and the IMU.

The problem regarding proper classification of the Taliban does not reside with the definition used throughout this study but rather the application of the definition to a group whose actions are defined by the elements that comprise the definition. Irrespective of the fact that the U.S. Department of State chooses not to apply their rigorous definition to the Taliban, based on Taliban actions against international targets prior to and following the U.S.-led invasion, this author concludes that the Taliban is a foreign terrorist organization as well as an insurgent force allied with Al Qaeda and other Islamist militants in Afghanistan and in Pakistan's tribal areas. Therefore, the terror-drug nexus claims may very well be applied to the Taliban.

This study finds that the actions of the Taliban do have political relevance; these actions against international targets are intended to influence a broader audience. The actions of the Taliban, in addition to enhancing the insurgency, creating an environment conducive for the drug trade, and disrupting efforts at reconstruction, have been able to impact a much wider audience i.e., the populations of Western countries engaged in counterinsurgency operations and other support functions in Afghanistan, as well as the coercion and intimidation of the Afghan population.

In summary, terrorist attacks by the Taliban, Al Qaeda and other anti-government forces may be a by-product of the insurgent campaign; however, these attacks are also designed to influence a wider target audience i.e., the citizens of the states represented in the coalition as well as elements within the world's Muslim population from which they draw various levels of support and new recruits to their cause.[35]

DEFINITIONAL DILEMMA

The beginning of wisdom is the definition of terms.

Socrates (469–399 BCE)

As discussed in chapter 1, a global consensus on the definition of terrorism and exactly what constitutes a terrorist act has yet to be achieved; the U.N. and international community have wrestled with this problem for years. The definitional issue has existed, not just in the United States but throughout the world, since statistical data on terrorist events began to be compiled in 1968 (Mickolus, 1980). Furthermore, the lack of a uniform and internationally accepted definition of terrorism poses methodological and analytical problems; in the wake of 9/11 this problem has taken on an added urgency.

Based on events in Afghanistan following the U.S.-led attack, it can be argued that this definitional problem may very well be applied to Al Qaeda and, as discussed in the previous section, the Taliban. In the case of post-9/11 Al Qaeda: What exactly is Al Qaeda? Is it still an organization that was spawned in the waning years of the Soviet-Afghan war and eventually evolved into a terrorist organization with international reach, or have circumstances dictated that to ensure its survival it had to adapt to the situation in Afghanistan and the loss of its safe haven and some of its senior leadership? Moreover, has the organization further evolved into a global jihadist movement of like-minded Islamists? This global association could now be more appropriately characterized as a highly fluid, more dangerous, ideologically-driven terrorist-insurgent group with national, regional, and, according to some of their political statements, global ambitions.

These are important questions. If we expand our definition as suggested by Bergen (2003) and Rabasa (2006) in the following section and support their views regarding the evolving post-9/11 nature of Al Qaeda, then we have to consider the possibility that in the larger universe of Islamic radicalism the ideology of Al Qaeda transcends the importance of any specific group. As stated in a report issued by the U.S. House of Representatives Permanent Select Committee on Intelligence (2006, p. 17), "some terrorists increasingly are tied to the ideology rather than the group. These individuals are willing to support terrorist attacks that support their particular beliefs regardless of the affiliation to any specific organization."

AL QAEDA: FROM TERRORIST ORGANIZATION TO GLOBAL JIHADIST MOVEMENT

Al Qaeda, from the time of its inception, has been almost entirely focused on a strategy of global jihad to establish a transnational Islamic caliphate.[36] They have also operated as facilitators and supporters of regional and global insurgency campaigns, providing training and logistical support to insurgents fighting in Chechnya, Kashmir, the Philippines, and serving as a propaganda tool to incite Muslims towards jihad.[37]

Based on active support for these various insurgent groups, Al Qaeda could more appropriately be defined as a hybrid organization, i.e., a state-based evolving global Islamist movement that not only inspires—but in some cases provides—funding, training, and logistical support. Additionally, Al Qaeda engages in terrorist tactics as well as guerrilla and subversive activity in an attempt to, "equal the playing field," to promote its violent agenda against far superior and technologically advanced Western military formations in places like Afghanistan and Iraq. Al Qaeda is state-based, in that since its formation, it has been supported in some respects by a state—first in Pakistan, then through six years in Sudan under Hassan al-Turabi, then back to Afghanistan in 1996 where the organization was provided "safe haven" by the Taliban until 2001, and presently in the heavily fortified Federally Administered Tribal Areas (FATA) region of Pakistan.[38] Al Qaeda, while indeed more fluid and decentralized, have stated that one of their parameters for success is the consolidation of territory (*Weekly Standard*, October 12, 2005).

This author maintains that a critical factor in the success of Al Qaeda, the Taliban, and affiliate groups lies in their ability to coerce, establish, and maintain an operational base sufficient for recruitment, training, and operational planning. This also requires a substantial amount of funding. This funding could come in the form of donations from wealthy individuals sympathetic to the insurgent's cause, commodity exchange—such as opium for arms, other forms of criminal activity, weapons and other war materiel confiscated from NATO/ISAF, or tax revenue and support received from segments of the Afghan population.[39] Evidence in the form of testimony suggests, and the 9/11 Commission report maintains, that Islamist groups e.g., Al Qaeda still receive assistance from charities and wealthy benefactors. Additionally, these groups, based primarily in Waziristan, continue to receive support from certain elements of the ISI and Pakistani army and to a lesser degree revenue from involvement in criminal activity, including the Afghan drug trade, primarily engaged in by rogue members of these organizations who derive revenue in the form of protection money from traffickers and conversion labs operating in areas controlled by these groups.

In a letter from Ayman al-Zawahari, Osama bin Laden's second in command, to Abu Musab al Zarqawi,[40] Al Qaeda's leader in Iraq, al Zawahari stresses several major points which provided an insight into the global objectives of Al Qaeda and affiliate groups. Al Zawahiri described a strategy for jihad in Iraq which involved more than driving foreign forces from the country. Indeed the ultimate goal of Al Qaeda, according to this piece of correspondence, is to establish an Islamic state in Iraq, conquering as much territory as possible thereby establishing a caliphate over a wide geographical area and, once this is accomplished, to extend the jihad to neighboring secular Muslim countries.[41]

Benjamin and Simon (2003, p.134) in *The Age of Sacred Terror: Radical Islam's War Against America*, wrote:

> A core tenet of al Qaeda's strategy is that radical Islamists must gain control of a nation from which they can then expand the area controlled by believers. Holding a state, in their view, is the prelude to knocking over the dominoes of the world's secular Muslim regimes . . . This craving for territory is one reason why al Qaeda carries out its own terrorist attacks and supports so many national insurgencies.

When one considers the political statements contained in the al Zawahiri letter (described below) and those made by Mansoor Dadullah, a clear picture develops of a potential emerging global threat with operational bases in the Pakistan tribal regions of North and South Waziristan and Iraq. These ongoing insurgencies serve as a training ground for present and future Islamic militants and provide fertile ground which conceivably could proliferate and expand beyond the borders of both countries. The objective of Al Qaeda, as expressed by Benjamin and Simon (2003), is stated by al Zawahiri (2005) and is perhaps the most significant revelation in his letter to Zarqawi, i.e., al Zawahiri envisions a global caliphate which initially focuses on Iraqi territory,[42] then the wider Middle East, including Israel. Citing Zawahiri's July 2005 letter to Zarqawi, John D. Negroponte, U.S. Director of National Intelligence, says Al Qaeda's vision:

> . . . portrays the jihad in Iraq as a stepping-stone in the march toward a global caliphate, with the focus on Egypt, Syria, Jordan, Lebanon, Saudi Arabia, the Gulf states, and Israel. Zawahiri stresses the importance of having a secure base in Iraq from which to launch attacks elsewhere, including in the US Homeland (Negroponte, 2006, p. 3).[43]

Negroponte suggests that with operating bases on the Pakistan-Afghan border and an alliance with al Zarqawi of Iraq this provides Al Qaeda with "added reach" to conduct operations and puts "new resources at its disposal" (Negroponte, 2006, p. 3). This notion of a merger is given additional credibility by the tactical shift in modus operandi relative to the types of attacks that are perpetrated in Afghanistan (Marzban, 2006c). For example, suicide bombings—which are now a regular occurrence in Afghanistan—were rarely heard of prior to the U.S.-led invasion of Iraq in 2003. This tactical shift suggests that the Taliban and others, including the HQN, have been subsumed under the Al Qaeda banner, possibly receiving training in the use of improvised explosive devices (IEDs) and suicide attacks from seasoned Al Qaeda operatives (Tran, 2006).[44]

The second point of interest relative to the al Zawahiri letter concerns finances. In his letter to al Zarqawi, Ayman al Zawahiri stressed that, "many of the lines have been cut off," and, "because of this, we need a payment while new lines are being opened"; al Zawahiri suggests a payment of "one hundred thousand" (*Weekly Standard*, October 12, 2005). This request for funds leads one to conclude that Al Qaeda may not be financially secure.[45] It may also indicate that, contrary to the views of those that advocate that the opium trade provides a substantial revenue source for the organization, this request may indicate that at the time the al Zawahiri letter was written Al Qaeda was not awash with revenue from criminal activity or any other source. However, the unknown here is contained in the word "lines" which could mean contributions from wealthy benefactors, opium profits, other criminally-derived revenue, or funds from allied groups, etc.

If indeed the Taliban–al Qaeda alliance is as Dadullah and international coalition officials have suggested, then by extension it can be assumed that members of this alliance are profiting to a greater or lesser degree from the opium trade. However, while providing some revenue in the areas controlled by insurgents, it does not yield the profits to these groups that many observers attribute to it. Moreover, as chapter 6 will show, while extremists may garner some revenue in the form of taxes, and possibly by providing protection services, indications are that the opium trade in Afghanistan is primarily controlled by warlords, national and internationally-based criminals, and corrupt local and provincial government officials including the Afghan National Police (ANP).[46]

AL QAEDA REDEFINED

In a treatise written over 2,000 years ago Sun Tzu, a Chinese philosopher and military strategist, said in effect, "Know Thine Enemy" (Carr, 2000, pp. 80–81). These words—although paraphrased from the original text—are particularly relevant today. It is important to consider the possibility that the Taliban and Al Qaeda, as defined prior to 9/11, may currently be a very narrow view of these two organizations as they have evolved since October 7, 2001, when their operational command infrastructure in Afghanistan was disseminated by U.S. and coalition forces.[47] For example, Bergen (2003, A29) argues that applying the pre-9/11 definition of Al Qaeda to the organization as it is presently constituted presents an inadequate depiction of the increased dangers it poses. Thus, he stresses the need to redefine post-9/11 Al Qaeda.

Peter Bergen, Cable News Network (CNN) terrorism analyst and author of *Holy War Inc.* was one of a handful of journalists who interviewed Osama bin Laden. He supports the view that Al Qaeda has undergone a major organizational transformation following the events of 9/11.

As stated above, defining Al Qaeda is significant because it impacts not only our military response but impacts international political and law enforcement responses as well. Bergen argues that defining present day Al Qaeda is critical to our understanding of the specific threat that we currently face. Bergen defines post-9/11 Al Qaeda by equating it to four concentric rings:

> First there is al Qaeda, the organization. Most non-specialists are surprised to learn that al Qaeda has only 200 to 300 members. These are the men who have sworn bayat, an oath of allegiance to serve their emir, or leader, bin Laden, even unto death. (It is al Qaeda, the organization that carried out the Sept. 11 attacks.) The second concentric ring spreading out beyond the inner core of al Qaeda consists of perhaps several thousand "holy warriors" trained in the group's Afghan camps in the terrorist black arts of bomb making and assassination. Beyond this circle are tens of thousands of militants who received some kind of basic military training in Afghanistan over the past decade. Many of these trainees went to Afghanistan for what amounted to little more than a jihad vacation. Most were to be cannon fodder in the Taliban's war against the Northern Alliance. Think John Walker Lindh. Finally, untold numbers of Muslims around the world subscribe to bin Laden's Manichean worldview that the West is the enemy of Islam. Some of these, too, may be prepared to do violence (Bergen 2003, p. A29).

Testimony by various experts and other knowledgeable government officials has revealed that there have been thousands of Islamic militants who have received training in camps supported and run by Osama bin Laden, thus supporting Bergen's assessment.[48]

In regard to Bergen's last point, Osama bin Laden's impact on disaffected Muslims, especially young men, and therefore his ability to influence and radicalize their thinking is perhaps best summed up by a Saudi official who was quoted in a report published by the *Wall Street Journal* (Europe). According to the authors' of this report, a local Saudi official made a significant statement that this author believes was both presented in very concise terms and presents a clear portrayal of some of the issues which spawn Islamist militancy, and hence the problems this type of extremist mindset causes. These points are certainly part of the ongoing propaganda campaign used by Osama bin Laden to engender alienated young Muslim men to rally to his cause. Moreover, this unique talent of Osama bin Laden was a major factor in revolutionizing the thinking of leading Taliban officials.[49] In addressing the state of affairs following the attacks on the United States, the aforementioned Saudi official was quoted as saying:

> . . . local Islamic preachers have been more strident than ever in mosques filled with fervent young people . . . "Osama bin Laden's a big hero, and

> if he gets killed, he'll be like a prophet," the official says. "The damage is already done. They are rebelling against the status quo, economic inequality, injustices, closed politics. They link themselves to God, and are so dogmatic they can't see anything else. They consider themselves occupied, that the Americans are in control of their daily lives. They want a Taliban regime" (Pope, Pearl, and Trofimov, 2001, p. A1).

In a report issued by RAND (Rabasa et al., 2006) titled, "Beyond Al Qaeda," the authors note:

> Indeed the term "terrorist" is inadequate to describe al-Qaeda which some analysts more correctly characterized as "global insurgency" that has successfully challenged the world's most powerful nations (Rabasa et al., 2006, p. 162 of Part 1).

Rabasa et al., argue that while U.S.-led attacks on Al Qaeda forces destroyed much of its leadership thus reducing its "functional ability," it did not destroy the core "ideology-based movement." From an organizational perspective, the authors point out that although the U.S. and coalition forces were successful in destroying Al Qaeda's operational base and a number of key members thereby reducing "the functional ability of al-Qaeda's leadership core" (Rabasa et al., 2006, pp. xx and 33 of Part 1),[50] this did not destroy what Bergen described as the outer rings of the base organization.

The point made by the authors of the RAND report cited above should not be construed to indicate that it is beyond the realm of possibilities that a scenario could develop which could raise the probability that a traditional group could converge with Al Qaeda if they deemed it strategically and/or operationally beneficial for them to do so.[51]

Due to the expanding and complex nature of the Afghan insurgency, the religious implications of the struggle, and the profound influence that the militant mindset of the actors involved has on certain segments of the world Muslim community, it appears that the ability of Al Qaeda and the Taliban to recruit more Sunni radicals and ordinary Afghans to their cause has been successful.[52]

Indeed, as Steven McGraw, assistant director, Office of Intelligence, Federal Bureau of Investigation (FBI), stated during a U.S. Senate hearing (cited above) on May 20, 2003, "The FBI, along with our state, local and federal partners, have identified hundreds of Islamic extremists and Sunni extremists tied to al-Qaeda, tied to terrorists" (McGraw, 2003, p. 11).

With respect to the above discussion it is clear that Al Qaeda has evolved into a movement which is capable of attracting like-minded Islamists, many of whom will operate individually or in small clandestine groups (Negroponte, 2006, p. 5). It is also important to note that based on Osama bin Laden's evolving relationship with the Taliban and that group's apparent shift in tactics, e.g., suicide bombings, and the employment of improvised explosive devices (IEDs), as well as a possible shift in objectives—from a national to more regional and perhaps global focus, the prospect of an expanding Islamist insurgency appears to this author to be gaining credibility. Kilcullen (2005, p. 597) notes:

> We must distinguish Al Qa'eda and the broader militant movements it symbolises—entities that use terrorism—from the tactic of terrorism itself. In practice, as will be demonstrated, the "War on Terrorism" is a defensive war against a world-wide Islamist jihad, a diverse confederation of movements that uses terrorism as its principal, but not its sole tactic.

Moreover, these local, regional, globally dispersed, and independently operating entities often seek funding through any available channels of opportunity, be they legal or illegal. This represents a different, elusive, and very dangerous threat. This point is based on the fact that Al Qaeda does not provide individual financial support to each entity operating under its banner. Al Qaeda is no longer a hierarchical organization but rather a movement, an ideology, a fluid entity, with cells evolving throughout the world taking up the Al Qaeda cause.[53]

The activities of these independent networks are not regulated from a central command-type structure. In the years following the initial invasion, the Al Qaeda network, which now includes former and newly recruited members of the Taliban as well as other foreign militants and a presence in the Pakistani tribal areas (North and South Waziristan),[54] has proven to be a highly adaptive and formidable foe for American and coalition forces. Moreover, the strength of Al Qaeda does not reside in the "core" organization but rather in its ideology, which has been adapted by numerous individuals and homegrown terror groups worldwide. Based on the information and data provided in this study, the threat posed by Al Qaeda can be equally applied to the transmuted Afghan Taliban and others who seek to align themselves with Al Qaeda and the insurgency presently underway in Afghanistan.

THE TALIBAN REDEFINED

Following the events of October 7, 2001, the Taliban became a Pakistani-Afghan-based insurgent group which has conducted terrorist attacks against Afghan civilians and foreign nationals. As illustrated above, many Taliban attacks are by definition acts of international terrorism; therefore, one would think that they should be included in the U.S. State Department's list of foreign terrorist organizations. RAND and U.S. State definitions of domestic and international terrorism have certainly been applied to other territorial-based groups (e.g., Irish Republican Army, Sri Lanka's

Tamil Tigers, Peru's Shining Path, and Colombia's FARC, ELN, and AUC,[55] etc.) which have perpetrated attacks within the confines of their national borders, and these incidents have been recorded as acts of terrorism. Furthermore, if a foreign entity was the recipient of such an attack, either by design or happenstance, then the group which perpetrated it is considered a foreign terrorist organization.

However, while evidence points to the fact that the Taliban have perpetrated attacks on foreign entities in Afghanistan there is a subtle difference between groups such as the Taliban—which attack foreign interests as part of their struggle to liberate their country from foreign occupation but do not threaten global security in the sense that the scope and focus of their attacks have thus far been confined to local objectives, and bin Laden's Al Qaeda—a terrorist group which has demonstrated its international reach and whose objectives have been and remain global in scope.

The Taliban have crossed an international border (from bases in Pakistan); they have also attacked foreign entities, but they have done so as part of the present insurgency and, for the moment, unlike Al Qaeda they have not attacked targets unrelated to their primary objective of regaining power in Afghanistan. Therefore, regardless of their national or global ambitions as expressed by Mansoor Dadullah, they have not at this writing demonstrated that they pose a level of international threat that Al Qaeda has and continues to demonstrate as evidenced prior to 9/11 and in the UK, Riyadh, Saudi Arabia, and Indonesia post-9/11. Among the Afghan-based groups which have committed terrorist attacks in Afghanistan Al Qaeda is the only group which has targeted, in addition to Afghanistan, several other countries, particularly Saudi Arabia.

Although the Taliban has focused most of their attacks within the borders of Afghanistan, evidence suggests that a number of Taliban attacks were perpetrated in Pakistan and no doubt had some relevance to the ongoing insurgency in Afghanistan. Based on the continued radicalization of the Taliban, tactical use of suicide bombers,[56] and their affiliation with foreign jihadists, the Taliban—along with their affiliates—do pose a grave danger to the region.[57]

Recognition of the subtle difference described above may raise some potentially significant policy implications regarding the nature of post-9/11 conflict, how we define terrorism, and specifically what constitutes acts of international terrorism. Certainly the wars in Iraq and Afghanistan have demonstrated that the line separating insurgent activity, criminality, and terrorism is becoming increasingly blurred. Moreover, how we *define* terrorism is intimately related to the *nexus* question, which is the primary focus of this study. The evolving nature of Islamist militancy no doubt has created new problems and requires new strategies from the intelligence community as well as academia.

EVOLVING SOUTHWEST ASIAN-BASED GLOBAL INSURGENCY

On September 24, 2001, shortly before the U.S. invasion, Osama bin Laden faxed a letter to Al Jazeera TV to be read on the air to the Pakistani people. In this communiqué Osama bin Laden called upon all Muslims to rise up for what he refers to as the "battle of Islam." He refers to Pakistan as: ". . . Islam's first line of defense in this region . . ." He further states:

> We hope those brothers are the first martyrs in the battle of Islam in this age. The new Jewish crusader campaign is led by the biggest crusader Bush under the banner of the cross. This battle is considered one of the battles of Islam . . . We incite our Muslim brothers in Pakistan to deter with all their capabilities the American crusaders from invading Pakistan and Afghanistan (Al Jazeera, September 24, 2001).

As discussed previously the Al Qaeda ideology has radicalized the ranks of the Taliban and expanded its revolutionary vision.[58] As an increasing number of Islamist militants take refuge in Pakistan's FATA[59] it appears that the insurgency in Afghanistan has all the hallmarks of an Al Qaeda-inspired movement.[60] As evidenced by the increasing lethality of Taliban attacks, i.e., suicide bombings[61] and the political declarations of Mullah Muhammad Omar and Mansoor Dadullah, it is becoming increasingly clear that the Al Qaeda banner is flying high over the Islamic Emirate of Waziristan. Statements by NATO/ISAF commanders, other coalition military officials, and Siraj Haqqani, leader of the Haqqani network, confirm the present Al Qaeda-Taliban alliance.[62]

On September 6, 2006, the Taliban signed a ceasefire agreement with the Pakistani government (Constable, 2006, p. A9). Since that time North and South Waziristan have become infiltrated with Al Qaeda sympathizers and future Islamists. This region has become an operational base from which Al Qaeda, the Taliban, and their affiliates launch cross-border attacks against international and Afghan forces in Afghanistan. North and South Waziristan also provide safe haven where Al Qaeda and affiliates can plan, coordinate, and perpetrate terror from Europe to the Middle East.[63]

According to Chaudhuri (2007) there are three factors which are fueling the growth of what he refers to as "al Qaedastan":

> First, a resurrected and more militant Taliban, which is supplanting traditional Pashtun chiefs in the border areas with its radical clerics. The second is the increasing number of global Islamic militant groups who are taking up residence there. The third is the inability of either Kabul or Islamabad to marshal a credible military response.

He further states that this phenomenon is self evident by the increased lethality of their tactics, i.e., "their use of suicide bombings, human shields and bloodier kidnappings, practices abhorrent in traditional Pashtun culture" (Chaudhuri, 2007). Said Tayeb Jawad, the Afghan ambassador to the United States, puts it more succinctly, "al Qaeda is the commander, the Taliban the foot soldier. Al Qaeda provides strategic guidance" (Chaudhuri, 2007).

Fueled in part by the lucrative trade in Afghan narcotics, the Taliban, according to several aforementioned reports, appears to have changed course on its drug prohibition policy declared by Mullah Muhammad Omar in 2000. Indeed, evidence suggests that the Taliban not only condone but may actively encourage the trade and to a certain degree profit by it, although the amount of revenue they are able to generate is at this writing unknown. The opium trade has no doubt furthered the insurgency as the Taliban have been able to coerce many rural farmers over to their cause.

This holds true particularly in the southern, and to some extent the eastern, provinces. Indeed the Taliban's transformed policies on opium cultivation have won the "hearts and minds," of rural inhabitants many of whom are angry at the Kabul government for not delivering on much needed aid and for efforts to eradicate their only viable means of livelihood, the opium poppy.

It appears that this new Islamist threat, partially based in Pakistan's FATA, has a regional as well as an international component. According to Rohan Gunaratna:

> The ground zero of terrorism has moved from Afghanistan to the tribal areas of Pakistan since 2001. . . . As long as al-Qaeda and the Taliban maintain a presence in the tribal areas there will be violence, not only in Afghanistan but also in Pakistan and beyond into Europe where there is a large Pakistani diaspora community . . . the terrorist group [al Qaeda] had replicated the operational, training and support structures it built in Afghanistan, where it had the protection of the Taliban regime, in Pakistan's tribal regions (Johnson 2007).[64]

Today's Taliban is tactically operating under an Osama bin Laden-inspired mindset which transcends Pashtun tribal traditions and by some accounts appears to be attracting local Afghans to their cause.[65]

The state of affairs in the FATA, the expanding opium trade in neighboring Afghanistan with its attendant criminal elements, and, as chapter 6 will detail, the corruption of public officials including the Ministry of Interior (MoI) and Afghan National Police (ANP), poses an extreme threat to the fragile government in Kabul and complicates efforts by international military and civilian authorities to establish security thereby impacting reconstruction efforts. In the words of Joanna Nathan of the International Crisis Group (ICG), "in places where they are strong the insurgents have been able to harass government operations and relief efforts—so much so that reconstruction has come to a virtual standstill in the south and east" (Wiseman, 2006). Current ISAF military and civilian operational policies are designed to counter Taliban military gains but more importantly win the support of the Afghan population. Time will tell.

The operational structure of Taliban and Al Qaeda forces enable them to operate as independent small guerrilla units employing terrorist tactics. They have been successful at exploiting weaknesses such as security gaps especially in the rural areas in the south (Gall, 2006, p. A1). As will be addressed further in chapter 6, the security situation throughout much of Afghanistan provides fertile ground for exploitation by corrupt government officials, provincial and district level commanders (warlords), criminals, drug traffickers, and terrorists.

CONCLUSION

The principal thrust of this work is to examine groups which commit acts of terrorism and most importantly are not only able, but indeed do, extend their destructive behavior across international borders, and to examine these type of groups (e.g., Al Qaeda) and determine if they are actively involved or being funded in part by the drug trade in Afghanistan.

The characterization of Al Qaeda and the Taliban is relevant to the central issue of this study: the nexus between international terrorism and drug trafficking. With regard to Al Qaeda, if this organization is defined as it was prior to September 11, 2001, as purely a terrorist group, then based on this author's research it appears that there is no documented empirical evidence available through open source channels directly tying the top-tier Al Qaeda leadership to the drug trade. However, if the definition is expanded to include individuals, groups of individuals, and splinter groups morphing into independent cells or affiliates operating under the post-9/11 Al Qaeda banner, then the evidence indicates that some of these Al Qaeda affiliates may indeed be deriving funding from the billions of dollars generated by Afghanistan's opium trade.[66] This view is supported in part by the activities of members of Jamiat ul-Ansar[67] in Afghanistan, and Taliban efforts at taxing opium poppy farmers and traffickers in the areas under their control.

Defining the global Islamist threat that Al Qaeda represents needs to take into account the global matrix of financial and logistical external support networks and state-supported sanctuaries (e.g., North and South Waziristan) and to address cooperation between Al Qaeda and like-minded non-state formations and individuals, i.e., with mutual interests no matter how narrowly defined, and others which may have different goals and objectives but are nonetheless staunch supporters of the Al Qaeda movement. These "outer rings," are important components of what appears to be a growing global movement. The key to thwart this modern day hydra is to understand its constituent parts. The words of Socrates and Sun Tzu are particularly relevant.

Defining Al Qaeda parallels the ambiguity surrounding the topic of terrorism. Many definitions of terrorism address specific actors and incidents in isolation of terrorist objectives. The focus is centered on "the act," apart from motivation since motivation is difficult to ascertain. Speaking specifically about Al Qaeda, it is obvious that Osama bin Laden's motivations, objectives, and intentions have been made clear through numerous venues over the past several years.

Finally, the attacks attributed to the Taliban[68] as illustrated above, the tactics employed by them in the present insurgency, the political pronouncements by Mansoor Dadullah, as well as the Al Zawahiri correspondence to the former Al Qaeda leader in Iraq as described above, may provide a window into the mentality of the post-9/11 Taliban. It is therefore wise to consider the Taliban as well as Al Qaeda and their allies to be very formidable and dangerous foes and mounting threats to global security. Furthermore, based on the nature of Al Qaeda's relationship with the Taliban, it is possible that the Taliban may eventually become a major player in global terrorism particularly in alliances with other militant groups based in Pakistan, China's Uighur province,[69] the Central Asian states[70] bordering Afghanistan, and Indian-controlled Jammu and Kashmir.

CHAPTER 6

Opium Industry in Afghanistan: Warlords, Criminals, and the Corruption of Public Officials

CRIMINAL SYNDICATES AND TERRORIST NETWORKS

The assessment by many that the end of the Cold War ushered in a new era where state sponsorship of terrorist proxies has ceased is not a completely valid argument. Indeed an argument can and has been made that Pakistan, Iran, Syria, as well as Saudi Arabia (knowingly or unknowingly) have and continue to sponsor various groups which advance their political and national objectives.[1] Be that as it may, there has been a decline in state sponsorship following the end of the Cold War. Subsequently, some insurgent and terrorist groups have been forced to seek alternative sources of operational revenue.[2] Therefore much recent political debate has focused on terrorist funding, as this topic has taken on a renewed urgency since September 2001.

Although criminal and terrorist groups both pose a danger to international security and are similar in many respects they are inherently different types of organizations.[3] A report prepared for the journal *Police Practice and Research* by American University's Louise Shelley and John Picarelli examined the often stated links between transnational organized crime[4] and international terrorism.

In part their findings suggest that both groups are capable of operating transnationally in a network type of organizational structure rather than a top-down hierarchical structure. This, the authors note, provides them more operational flexibility and greater efficiency while reducing the risk of penetration by law enforcement or other outside destabilizing influences.[5] With respect to the clandestine nature of both organizations, the authors state that both groups are very capable of employing and exploiting state-of-the-art information technology and are adept at conducting their operational and organizational activities in secret (Shelley and Picarelli, 2002, p. 307).

In a reference specifically addressing Al Qaeda the authors argue that criminal groups as well as terrorist organizations both use nation-states as "a means to an end" (Shelley and Picarelli, 2002, p. 307). This certainly was the case when Osama bin Laden and his associates took up residence first in Sudan (1991) and then Afghanistan (1996). This research will show that in both cases Osama bin Laden developed a symbiotic relationship with the existing governing establishment in order to advance his group's organizational and operational objectives. In both instances, Osama bin Laden provided financial assistance and undertook various projects designed to enhance the infrastructure of each country.[6]

Criminal activity is primarily motivated by profit. More specifically, the drug trade is driven by consumer demand; the product basically sells itself. It is profit-oriented and extremely competitive, whereas terrorist violence is driven by national, secular-based, or political concerns and objectives. Conversely, in the case of Al Qaeda and others whose ideology parallels that of Al Qaeda, religion is used as justification for their actions. Groups which fall into this category have apocalyptic[7] or revolutionary ambitions and may also harbor political aspirations as part of their overall objectives.

These groups, while not being motivated by profit, may be willing to pursue any financial avenue or area of opportunity regardless of whether it is legal or illegal in order to ensure enough revenue to support the particular needs (e.g., recruitment, training, logistical support) and further the objectives of their organization.[8] This is not meant to suggest that terrorist groups will arbitrarily align themselves with organized criminal elements in order to obtain operational revenue, although in some instances this has undoubtedly occurred.[9] As stated above, secrecy and trust are vital to the survival of criminal as well as terrorist groups.

When a relationship between criminal groups and specific terrorist organizations does exist it is usually born of necessity and a shared need that serves to further the objectives of both groups.[10] These arrangements can be short-term tactical alliances or longer-term based on the collective needs of each organization and the perceived and/or actual benefits of such cooperation. For example, in the case of a state with weak, corrupt, or non-existent internal security or law enforcement constraints—such as the situation which currently exists in Afghanistan—terrorists in control of certain territory may negotiate the movement of drugs by traffickers for arms, monetary imbursement, or other logistical consideration. Conversely, factors that may affect the decision by some terrorist groups to refrain from illegal activity (especially the drug trade) are increased susceptibility to law enforcement or military action,[11] and loss of public and benefactor support among those who view this activity as a violation of some religious or social tenet. Moreover, drugs have a corrupting effect on the individual. Not only are they physically addicting but the large sums of money that they command can pervert the groups raison d'être.

A 2005 study conducted by Mark Hamm, professor of criminology, Indiana State University, for the U.S. Department of Justice, examined the range of criminal activity engaged in by international jihad groups and right-wing domestic terrorist groups. Professor Hamm found that the types of crimes committed varied according to group type. Additionally, Professor Hamm (2005, p. 18) notes that, ". . . rarely are jihadists and domestic right-wingers the 'criminal masterminds' we have been led to believe they are."

In specific reference to South Asian criminal and terrorist networks, Rollie Lal of the RAND Corporation argues that some members belonging to South Asia criminal organizations have adopted the ideology of Islamist terrorist networks. He further notes that groups such as Dawood Ibrahim's D-Company,[12] "have adopted ethnic or ideological motives, especially in reaction to sharpening ethnic tensions or particular attacks on the Muslim community" (Lal, 2005, p. 302).

Finally, engaging in criminal activity to support operations and infrastructure, while organized in the sense that there is a consistent pattern and modus operandi at work, is not the same as establishing an ongoing operational alliance with groups such as the Albanian, Italian, or Russian mafias.

TERRORIST FINANCING: CHARITIES, DONORS, AND DRUGS

Since 9/11, the topic of terrorist financing has received international media attention and much public policy debate. A majority of these media reports have centered on Islamist extremist groups and their possible sources of funding.[13] Of these accounts a large percentage have focused on two sets of actors, the Taliban militia and Osama bin Laden's Al Qaeda network. This attention was primarily predicated on the fact that Al Qaeda, the principal suspect in the 9/11 attacks, had taken up residence in Afghanistan, a major source of the world's opium, following their ouster from Sudan in 1996. Following his arrival in May of that year, Osama bin Laden was eventually able to establish a symbiotic relationship with Taliban emir Mullah Muhammad Omar and other top Taliban officials. Additionally, the drug trade which had flourished in Afghanistan prior to and during the Taliban reign provided revenue in the form of tithes and agricultural taxes to that regime. While some argue that the Taliban's role in the opium trade was minor and the revenue garnished was not a major financial windfall, others maintain the position that opium was a major source of funding for this group and by extension served some of the financial needs of Al Qaeda.[14]

Prior to the events of 9/11, the purported linkage between Osama bin Laden and Afghanistan's opium trade had not received a lot of attention either in the halls of the U.S. Congress or in the international media, although evidence does indicate that Western intelligence agencies were alarmed following the Osama bin Laden-nuclear weapon-heroin debate in the latter 1990s and the possible role Afghan heroin may have played in this controversy.[15]

As previously discussed in chapter 3, much post-9/11 academic and political debate has focused on the mechanisms by which terrorists, specifically those with international reach, obtain funding to support the logistical and operational functions of their organizations. Investigations by various U.S. federal and international law enforcement agencies conducted post-9/11 have revealed that some of this funding comes from individual donors sympathetic to a particular cause or group. Terrorist organizations have also generated a considerable amount of revenue from both legitimate charities and those set up for the sole purpose of supporting a specific group or ideological agenda (Roth, Greenburg, and Wille, 2004). Expatriate communities also serve as a source of funding for groups espousing a nationalistic or ideological agenda (Levitt, 2005).

In addition to charitable contributions, and financing from wealthy patrons and sympathetic expatriates, funds are also generated through illegal activities.[16] This is especially true of independent cells, franchises, and individuals who form a bond based on shared beliefs relative to a particular group's ideology.

According to international crime expert Jeffrey Robinson, a terrorist operation engaging in criminal activity is not a recent phenomenon nor is this behavior restricted to Islamist or other religiously-motivated groups. For example, the Irish Republican Army (IRA) was engaged in crimes such as, "extortion, fraud, identity theft and cigarette smuggling" (Robinson, 2004)[17] and the Kosovo Liberation Army (KLA) and Turkey's Kurdistan Workers' Party (PKK) have both garnered revenue from the illicit drug trade (Cornell, 2005b, p. 23).

While numerous terrorist entities have sought funding through various channels be they legal or illegal, for the purposes of this study the focus on terrorist funding centers on the drug trade as a source of financing for terrorist groups operating or that have previously operated in Afghanistan.

NATIONAL, REGIONAL, AND INTERNATIONAL DRUG TRAFFICKING NETWORKS: AN OVERVIEW

As mentioned earlier, much of Afghanistan's opium output is converted into heroin either prior to leaving the country or in a processing facility during transit. Central Asia, the Russian Federation, and Europe are primary destination hubs for Afghan opiates.[18] Opiates originating in Afghanistan reach their destination points through a network of national, regional, and internationally-connected criminal groups which operate along main trafficking corridors.[19]

According to a U.S. government inter-agency report, *International Crime Threat Assessment*, issued in December 2000:

> Much of the Afghan opium industry and drug trafficking in Southwest Asia is controlled by a network of traffickers based in Pakistan and Afghanistan. Their ethnic, tribal, and political affiliations give them the connections and capability to negotiate drug transactions, assemble drug loads, and transport shipments to wholesale buyers in Turkey and other international markets. This network of loosely affiliated traffickers frequently cooperates with other traffickers based in Pakistan, Afghanistan, Iran, and the UAE.[20]

Additionally, the *Organized Crime Situation Report 2000* (OCSR 2000), prepared by the Council of Europe from input received by member states, cites some of the international criminal groups responsible for trafficking opiates throughout Europe. Chief among them are Turkish and Kurdish traffickers and most recently Albanian criminal groups have entered the fray, "especially in the central European and northern countries."[21] The report also states that trafficking groups emanating from the former Soviet Union are involved in the wholesale distribution of heroin (Council of Europe, 2001, pp. 45–46). These groups are usually collectively referred to as the Russian mafia.[22] In a June 2010 study issued by the United Nations Office on Drugs and Crime, the Russian Internal Affairs Ministry reported that there are approximately 450 such organizations comprising around 12,000 members (UNODC, 2010d, p. 116).

In June 2000, a conference was held in Bucharest, Romania. This forum was assembled to deal with the problem of organized crime and specifically, drug trafficking in the Balkans. Law enforcement representatives from Europol, Interpol, and the Council of Europe were in attendance. During the conference Uwe Kranz, an expert on East European criminal groups and head of Europol's organized crime projects in Eastern Europe, told the attendees that from his viewpoint, "Kosovar Albanians now dominate the heroin markets in Switzerland, Austria, Belgium, Germany, Hungary, Norway, and Sweden" (McMahon, 2000).

A similar albeit a more detailed perspective appeared in the *Boston Globe* in June 2001. In this article Whitmore, citing information generated by Interpol, reported that:

> Kosovo Albanians may control 40 percent of the European heroin trade. In Germany, Austria, Switzerland, and the Czech Republic, they may have as

> much as 70 percent of the market, according to the estimates. . . . In cities across Europe, smaller Kosovo Albanian gangs oversee storage, sale and distribution. To avoid risk, they hire local couriers, called donkeys or horses, to move the drugs across borders. (Whitmore, 2001, p. 14).[23]

The global drug trade is a complex and fluid enterprise which is subject to numerous external factors. Fluctuations in cultivation/production, demand, as well as the involvement, or degree of involvement, of various criminal organizations often occur over time and place.

Hence, since the end of the Macedonian uprising in 2001 and the signing of the Ohrid Agreement in August of that year Albanian criminal organizations, while still significantly involved in the trafficking of Afghan opiates, do not presently dominate the European heroin market (UNODC, 2010, p. 256).[24] Turkish groups, long involved in drug-related activity, appear to be the principal players in the trafficking of heroin throughout Europe (UNODC, 2010, pp. 123 and 252).[25]

It is also important to note that at the time the aforementioned *Boston Globe* article was written a considerable amount of Afghan opium was processed outside of the country. Today much of the raw opium is processed into heroin before it leaves the country, as labs have been set up inside Afghanistan especially along the border regions. Heroin is often paid for through the *hawala* system (money exchange) or used as barter exchange for licit as well as illicit commodities (e.g., arms for drugs).[26]

In 2002, Willy Deridder, executive director, Interpol General Secretariat, articulated Interpol's state of knowledge with respect to trafficking groups in Afghanistan and Central Asia. His comments were made while addressing the 17th Asian Regional Conference on the *Interpol Asian Threat Assessment*. He stated in effect that Interpol suspects that there are Afghan and Central Asian drug trafficking networks operating in the region because of the sheer volume of opiates transiting these countries with concomitant large amounts of money being exchanged; however, he acknowledged that Interpol has received relatively scant information on these groups (Deridder, 2002, p. 3).[27]

Indeed, information regarding specific drug actors remains fragmentary. Many globally inter-connected individuals and networks in Afghanistan and beyond its borders are involved in the distribution of Afghan opiates.[28] What is known is that heroin movement through Central Asia involves large as well as small ethnically-based groups. According to the aforementioned 2010 United Nations report, approximately 10 and 20 groups in Uzbekistan and Tajikistan, respectively, are responsible for the regional trafficking of Afghan opiates (UNODC, 2010d, p. 116).[29] U.S. congressional testimony in 2000 revealed that prior to 9/11 the Islamic Movement of Uzbekistan (IMU), which has been classified as a hybrid (criminal and terrorist in nature)[30] organization, was involved to a significant degree in the trafficking of opiates from Afghanistan into Central Asia.[31] IMU involvement in the trade post-9/11 cannot be confirmed.

The above cited United Nations report further notes that drug trafficking from Afghanistan to the borders of Central Asia is now dominated by "five major Afghan narcotics networks." These groups include Afghan public officials, Afghan-based criminals, warlords, and possibly Gulbuddin Hekmatyar's HIG. Additionally, the report states that most Afghan-based drug traffickers do not appear to move opiates beyond the border areas (UNODC, 2010d, p. 116). However, criminal networks based in, or operating out of neighboring border countries are well-connected to Afghan-based trafficking groups (UNODC, 2010d, p. 110). This undoubtedly creates security-related problems and perpetuates corruption among public safety and governing officials in Afghanistan as well as neighboring and destination countries.[32]

In the border areas of Afghanistan, Pakistan[33] and Iran, a region which provides sanctuary to extremists as well as drug traffickers, "Balochi and Pashtun networks"[34] smuggle heroin out of Afghanistan where it is handed off to organizations in Iran, "with greater regional and international ties such as Azeri, Arab, Persian and Kurdish groups" (UNODC, 2010d, p. 123).[35] Additionally, according to intelligence provided by NATO, the Kurdistan Workers' Party (PKK), a Kurdish militant group based in southeastern Turkey and northern Iraq, collects revenue by taxing drug shipments crossing Turkish areas under their control. Moreover, some reports suggest that they also receive donations from European-based Kurdish heroin traffickers. Total earnings are estimated at $50-$100 million per year (UNODC, 2010d). Of the approximately 140 tons of heroin trafficked through Iran each year an estimated 80–85 tons finds its way to various European countries (UNODC, 2010d, p. 125)[36]

UNODC estimates that the international heroin trade generates about $55 billion per year. A large percentage of this goes to criminal groups operating along the major smuggling corridors (i.e., Northern and Balkan routes). Furthermore, of the $55 billion generated annually, Afghan-based, "farmers and traders," earn approximately four percent or $2.3 billion (UNODC, 2010d, 111). Finally, very little heroin is seized within Afghanistan's borders. Of the 375 tons of heroin exported annually less than three tons were seized in 2008. This indicates a level of collusion between public officials, most notably the police, those responsible for border security, the cross-border transportation industry, and drug entrepreneurs (UNODC, 2010d, p. 249). This cooperation is essential in facilitating the movement of drugs to various global markets.[37] While the majority of heroin is exported to Europe and the Russian Federation, Afghan opiates are also exported to Africa, Australia, Canada, China, and the United States (UNODC, 2010d, p. 110; UNODC, 2009a, p. 125). This makes opium, primarily cultivated in seven Afghan provinces in 2009, an international concern (UNODC, 2010d, p. 248).

WARLORDS, CRIMINALS, AND INSURGENTS

In Afghanistan, there is a complex web of actors who dominate the expanding opium trade.[38] Barnett R. Rubin (2000, p. 1791) notes that, ". . . the Afghan war economy has generated a pattern of regional economic activity and associated social and political networks that compete with and undermine legal economies and states." This statement was relevant during the Soviet-Afghan war, the civil war years, the years of Taliban rule, and is still germane in the years following the October 2001 invasion by U.S. and coalition forces.

Opium production has risen steadily since the latter years of the Soviet-Afghan conflict and the civil war years.[39] During the Taliban ascendancy, beginning in November 1994, production peaked at over 3,400 metric tons (mt). In 1999 and 2000, the period prior to the Taliban enforced ban, production reached 4,565 mt[40] and 3,276 mt, respectively. In 2001, following the ban, production declined to 185 mt; a large percentage of this output being produced in Northern Alliance-held territory (UNODC, 2003a, p. 93).[41]

While the ban eliminated a large percentage of opium cultivation in Taliban-held territory, it did not impact the trafficking of opiates.[42] As Williams (2003, p. 84) notes, trafficking continued unabated, "partly because of extensive stockpiles and partly because the opposition Northern Alliance was heavily involved in the business." Additionally, it should be pointed out that with most of the country under Taliban control, security was enhanced which further facilitated the movement of drugs and other legal and illegal contraband (Williams, 2003, p. 127).

Following the U.S.-led invasion, production soared to over 3,200 mt. In the years 2002–2006 production reached 3,400, 3,600, 4,200, 4,100 and 6,100 mt, respectively(UNODC, 2007a, p. 12). The high yields of opium produced in 2007–2008,[43] existing stockpiles due to previous years of overproduction,[44] and market forces produced a decline in the amount of opium poppy cultivated in 2009. During 2009, opium was cultivated on 123,000 hectares (ha)[45] and production fell to 6,900 mt. This represents a 1,300-mt drop from the 8,200 mt high recorded in 2007.[46]

The United Nations Office on Drugs and Crime (UNODC) study, *The Opium Economy in Afghanistan: An International Problem*, states that one of the reasons traders enter the opium trade is "access to power, reputation and respect within the local community." According to the report these relatively young individuals "saw themselves as local heroes as they secured income for the local population, preventing them from starvation by smuggling locally produced opiates abroad and risking their lives for the community" (UNODC, 2003a, p.128).[47]

In Afghanistan's southern provinces where the insurgency and violence has not only maintained its presence but has increased in intensity the production of opium is most profound.[48] The *International Narcotics Control*

Strategy Report (INCSR) 2008, released by the U.S. Department of State in February 2009 reported that the southern provinces of Farah, Helmand, Kandahar, Nimruz, and Oruzgan were responsible for 95 percent of Afghanistan's opium poppy cultivation in 2008. The report also notes that 66 percent of this total was cultivated in Helmand province. Furthermore, the report adds, "nearly all significant cultivation now occurs in insecure areas with active insurgent elements."[49] The southern provinces are the nerve center of the drug trade and a region where security has been a major problem (Pajhwok News Agency, 2007). Moreover, due to the lax security, traffickers based in the southern provinces are purchasing and transporting opium from the northern province of Balkh to their operational bases in the south via unsecured drug corridors (Ibrahimi, 2005). As stated in Shaw (2006, p. 205):

> Significant changes have been occurring in the nature of drug trafficking and the criminal organisations that control it in the south. These changes also appear to have important implications for trafficking in other parts of the country and thus for Afghanistan as a whole.

In the eastern provinces, despite the ongoing insurgency, eradication efforts were successful in 2005.[50] General Daoud, Afghanistan's deputy interior minister, stated that, "efforts to wipe out crops in eastern provinces had been more successful because local officials acted earlier" (Ibrahimi, 2005). According to UNODC (2006, p. 211), "Afghanistan's first comprehensive eradication programme was initiated during the 2004–2005 growing season." Nevertheless, total production levels in 2005 dropped only 100 mt as production escalated in the northern and western provinces and favorable environmental factors allowed for a higher yield (UNODC, 2005b, p. 6).

As alluded to above, following the October 2001 invasion opium production increased over 1,700 percent from the previous year total of 185 mt. This rise can be attributed to the initial defeat of the Taliban regime, the "power vacuum" that ensued, and the decision on the part of the United States to align with former warlords in the war against the Taliban and Al Qaeda.[51] Rather than exposing a large number of U.S. government and Western allied forces to hostile action in Afghanistan, Washington sought cooperation with primarily Tajik and Uzbek warlords and their militias to engage the Taliban and Al Qaeda forces and drive them out of the major cities. This cooperation, usually sealed with a bag of U.S. currency, has come with a heavy price tag. Many of these "allies" are still in control of major portions of the country and are competing with each other for power and opium-generated wealth.[52] This threatens and undermines the central government in Kabul and presents a number of security-related issues for international forces.[53]

Political power in Afghanistan is concentrated in the hands of about a dozen regional warlords who command private armies and rule over opium-rich territory. This allows them to provide for their private militias and in turn increases their power base.[54] It is estimated that perhaps as many as 60 percent of these warlords are directly profiting from the opium trade (McGirk and Ware, 2004).[55] Although evidence does not indicate the existence of cartels[56] the trade is consolidated into a tight nucleus of people (Shaw, 2006, pp. 205–206).[57] While the fall of the Taliban created potential opportunities for development and reconstruction, much of this rebirth hinges on the ability of the Kabul government to curtail the increasing influence and power of local and regional warlords, their militias, and other armed factions.[58]

The rise of these regional commanders (warlords),[59] private militias, criminal groups, and other armed factions has created fertile ground for the uninhibited cultivation of opium poppy which in turn created an environment which spawned violence, corruption, and instability.[60] As noted above, a major causal factor for instability and lawlessness in Afghanistan was the decision by U.S. and allied forces to abdicate power to these former mujahideen commanders, essentially making them part of coalition war efforts. In the absence of a strong central government and in direct violation of the 2001 Bonn Agreement, which essentially called on all private militias and pro-coalition factions to unite under the central governing authority in Kabul, these regional and provincial commanders have basically turned territory under their control into their own "personal fiefdoms" (Dyer, 2003).

Khabir Ahmad, correspondent for *The Lancet*, notes that, "Warlords control much of the $2.3 billion dollar drug trade—more than 50% of the country's gross domestic product—are involved in systematic abuses of human rights, have private prisons, and still run private armies . . ."(Ahmad, 2004, p. 1304). With large portions of the country under their control and the income from poppy enhancing their stature and power, there is scant incentive for these individuals to cooperate with the unifying agenda of ISAF and President Hamid Karzai.

While provincial commanders (warlords) control much of Afghanistan and indeed play a dominant role in the opium trade, the above statement by Ahmad may be an oversimplification of the country's opium problem. According to a report issued by Barnett Rubin (2004a, p. 1) "there are disturbing signs that the opium industry is beginning to move toward greater vertical integration, with increased involvement by international organized crime . . . the opium economy is entrenched and pervasive in much of the country. . . ."[61] Indeed, opium cultivation has been escalating since the mid-1980s reaching a high of 4,565 metric tons in 1999.[62]

Over the past couple of years a major concern has been the increase in the amount of poppy being processed into heroin within Afghanistan.

According to counternarcotics officials and the UNODC this signals an expansion of organized criminal involvement which further aggravates ISAF counternarcotics efforts[63] and undermines state security as some public officials are actively involved in the trade or passively allow it to flourish. Shaw (2006, p. 206) notes that there are approximately 15 key trafficking groups based in the south of the country. According to Shaw these key individuals come from a "variety of backgrounds" and are united in their collective expertise in conducting this type of business and in their desire to generate vast wealth (Shaw, 2006, p. 206).[64] Shaw also adds that the security situation in the south has made media coverage difficult, therefore documentation relative to the opium trade in the southern provinces has been limited (Shaw, 2006, p. 206).

Interestingly the Shaw report, perhaps one of the most detailed exposés on the involvement of various state and non-state actors in the opium trade, was significant for what it did not say. This detailed report did not mention Al Qaeda or other extremist groups outside of the Taliban, which have been known to operate in the southern and eastern provinces. In this regard it is important to note that in the context of discussing the current strength of organized crime, the fluid political situation, and the overall security problems that continue to plague the southern provinces the only post-9/11 reference to the Taliban was the following statement: "The degree to which a resurgent Taliban seeks to provide protection for drug trafficking could be a key factor. . . . Thus it will be essential to continue to monitor developments" (Shaw, 2006, p. 211).

Reports by those who have investigated the opium phenomenon in Afghanistan reveal a complex and fractured enterprise which supplies opiates to global markets by employing the services of various internationally-connected criminal actors. It is also clear that in order to maintain its global reach, state, regional, and international actors are involved. Furthermore, due in part to our inability to fully understand the organizational complexity and the decision-making apparatus of Afghanistan's opium enterprise, disagreement exists relative to the specific role of various players.[65]

DISTRICT, PROVINCIAL, AND NATIONAL-LEVEL GOVERNMENT INVOLVEMENT IN THE DRUG TRADE

In April 2004, International Human Rights Law Institute (IHRLI) president and professor of law at DePaul University, Cherif M. Bassiouni was appointed by former UN Secretary General Kofi Annan to the position of "independent expert on human rights in Afghanistan." Among his responsibilities this position authorized him to obtain information with respect to human rights violations in Afghanistan and submit a report of his findings to the UN General Assembly and to the Commission on Human Rights. After spending a year in country Professor Bassiouni submitted his report to the Commission in April 2005.[66] A preliminary report was submitted to the UN in October 2004. Regarding the problem of government corruption and the drug trade, the report stated:

> The independent expert has received credible reports of corruption throughout the country and at various levels of Government. The problem appears particularly serious among the police and the judiciary, creating low levels of public confidence that negatively impact the operation and legitimacy of the State. Poorly coordinated justice institutions, low wages and related problems contribute to corruption, as does the financial and political power of factional commanders and those involved in the drug industry. If corruption continues to intensify, as is likely with the growing power of drug traffickers and organized crime, it will become virtually impossible to establish and sustain a meaningful commitment to rule of law in Afghanistan (Bassiouni, 2005, p. 8).[67]

According to the official views of the U.S. Department of State, Bureau for International Narcotics and Law Enforcement Affairs, as presented in their annual *International Narcotics Control Strategy Report* (INCSR) 2005 which covers all drug control, cultivation/production, and trafficking events for the year 2004:

> . . . most officials at the national level are believed to be free of direct criminal connection to the drug trade. At the provincial and district levels, however, drug-related corruption is pervasive. Involvement ranges from direct participation in the criminal enterprise, to benefiting financially from taxation or other revenue streams generated by the drug trade. The national government has officially condemned the illicit drug trade, but does not have sufficient power throughout the national territory to suppress it.[68]

Moreover, as evidenced by the 2010 U.S. Department of State INCSR, these views remain unchanged.[69] The statements contained in the INCSR and cited here may reflect a politically sensitive subject regarding the central government and the possible involvement of members of the Karzai administration.[70] Afghanistan's former interior minister, Ali Ahmad Jalali,[71] who resigned his post in 2005, also implicated "government officials" and pointed to the difficulty in combating corruption due to the "lack of investigative capacity"(Harnden, 2006, p. 25).[72] Moreover, comments made by Afghanistan's counternarcotics minister, Habibullah Qaderi, during an interview with *IRIN News Service*, part of the UN Office for the Coordination of Humanitarian Affairs, suggests government complicity in the drug trade. During that interview Qaderi conceded that government "channels and positions" were used to facilitate the trafficking of narcotics.[73] However, he was not specific in regards to the level of involvement i.e., district, provincial, or central government. Additionally, in an interview with *IRIN News Service* in October 2004, Mirwais Yasini, Counternarcotics Directorate (CND), claimed that the corruption of government officials is a major problem which impedes attempts at drug control.[74]

In the summer of 2005 the *Christian Science Monitor* (CSM) sent an investigative team into Takhar province in northeast Afghanistan.[75] The purpose of the investigation was to develop credible information on the extent of police corruption, i.e., participation and involvement in Afghanistan's opium trade.[76] The team questioned four high-ranking police officials during the course of their investigation and used a recording device which was unknown to the interviewees. Heroin is routinely smuggled into Tajikistan from Takhar province. According to the author of the June 2006 report:

> . . . the statements in these tapes—gathered by investigators who have excellent reputations collecting testimony for the Afghan Independent Human Rights Commission, among others—provide a rare inside view of how drug corruption has trickled down to the front lines in the country's faltering war on drugs (Baldauf, 2006, p. O1).

Through interviews the investigators learned that the drug trade in Takhar province is extremely competitive as various police commanders strive to control the lucrative trade. Moreover, the most powerful commanders often employ violence to minimize the competition. As one commander stated, "all the smuggling is now in the hands of these commanders, and no one can do anything without [their] permission" (Baldauf, 2006, p. O1). The offering and accepting of bribes are another corrupting component of the trade.[77] As revealed in the report, bribes are extorted on both sides of the Afghan-Tajik border, a major trafficking route.

The most powerful commanders move large shipments of heroin into Dushanbe, the capitol of Tajikistan, and are rewarded handsomely for their efforts. Another police official told the *CSM* that:

> . . . drug corruption has infiltrated deep within the Ministry of Interior, the chief law-enforcement organization, as top officials take bribes to appoint corrupt drug dealers into top police positions (Baldauf, 2006, p. O1).[78]

This same official further adds that in Takhar most police commanders have paid bribes to Ministry of Interior officials to initially secure their positions, and they continue to pay to retain their position (Baldauf, 2006, p. O1). Apparently they are more than willing to pay since the potential revenue generated from participating in the drug trade is far greater than the initial money they "invested" to secure the job.[79]

The author also reported that the Ministry of Interior, responsible for the nation's police and border guards, has done very little to end the corruption that exists within the security services (Baldauf, 2006, p. O1).[80] Paul Watson, a 1994 Pulitzer Prize winner and former South Asia bureau chief for the *Los Angeles Times*, reports that some former Northern Alliance members, territorial commanders (warlords), and former mujahideen are suspected of drug-related activity, including trafficking and "controlling networks that include producers, criminal gangs and even members of the counter-narcotics police force."[81]

Moreover, Watson notes that the present Afghan judicial system is unable to effectively prosecute drug offenders because of the practice of paying bribes to judicial officials who are poorly paid; judges receive approximately $100 US per month. He adds that individuals suspected of being involved in the opium business reach into the upper echelons of the national government (Baldauf, 2006, p. O1).[82]

The above accounts coincide with statements regarding the involvement of police officials, specifically in regard to the appointment of district and provincial level police officials, in the drug trade as cited in the aforementioned report by Shaw (2006, p. 199)[83] and provides support to allegations made by Afghanistan's former interior minister, Ali Ahmad Jalali, and counter narcotics directorate, Mirwais Yasini.

While much of the *CSM* report relied on hearsay evidence, and therefore is subject to scrutiny, it is nonetheless given additional weight by the strengths of the interviewers, other reporting agencies, independent analysts, and scholars whose similar views on this subject have been noted throughout this chapter.

Indeed, the views of government involvement in the narcotics business[84] as expressed above are not a new phenomenon. In a book titled *Deadly Transfers and the Global Playground: Transnational Security Threats in a Disorderly World*, author Robert Mandel (1999, p. 60) states that, ". . . the level of influence illicit drug sales provide for transnational criminal organizations over the governments of key source countries are a major source of instability . . ."[85]

While these words were written during the Taliban reign they certainly are germane to the current situation in Afghanistan.[86] Efforts at eliminating the opium trade by either eradication or alternative livelihood strategies have been circumvented by the ongoing insurgency and the political and socio-economic conditions in that country. The illicit narcotics industry provides much needed income for many rural Afghans, and is one source of funding available to insurgent forces and terrorists in Afghanistan.[87] Attempts at opium eradication would only serve to strengthen the insurgency. Ignoring the problem serves the same end.[88]

When addressing government-level complicity in the opium trade it is important to note that members of the Northern Alliance were known to engage in the drug trade prior to their involvement in the newly established government. Moreover, during the Taliban period, opium production hit its peak in 1999. Consequently, when we speak of government corruption we need to consider the following: Have drugs corrupted certain factions within the present government, or were some of the people appointed to powerful positions simply behaving as they always have? As noted previously, opium cultivation skyrocketed following the Taliban defeat.[89]

PAKISTAN GOVERNMENT SUPPORT FOR MILITANT GROUPS

Tensions and armed conflict between India and Pakistan have existed since Pakistan achieved statehood in 1947. The first Indo-Pakistani war in 1948, fought over the disputed region of Kashmir, ended the same year when the UN Security Council mediated an end to the conflict; a cease-fire taking effect on January 1, 1949 (Uppsala University, 2003). However, the Pakistani government continued to support insurgent forces in this contested region.[90]

An article written by Selig S. Harrison (1990),[91] of the Center for International Policy in Washington, D.C., stated that by 1988 Pakistan's ISI "had begun to set up training camps in Pakistan held Azad Kashmir[92] manned by retired Pakistan Army officers." Harrison also cited intelligence sources from India and the United States that claimed the existence of 63 training camps, "half located in Azad Kashmir and half in Pakistan" (Harrison, 1990, p. A11).[93] Stern (2000, pp. 117–118) notes that in 1992 following the end of the Soviet-Afghan war mujahideen, hardened from their 10-year struggle with Soviet forces, began infiltrating into Kashmir to assist insurgent forces there. She further states that, "What began as an indigenous, secular movement for independence has become an increasingly Islamist crusade to bring all of Kashmir under Pakistan control." Some of the groups comprising the Kashmir insurgency are Lashkar-i-Toiba, Jamiat ul-Ansar, Jaish-e-Mohammed, and Harkat-ul-Jihad Islami.[94] These groups are primarily Kashmiri-based, supported by Pakistan,[95] and have known ties to Al Qaeda (Ramachandran, 2006). Rashid (1999b) notes that:

> The Taliban, Deobandi groups in Pakistan, and bin Laden's terrorist network all give major support to Kashmir insurgents resisting New Delhi's control of Indian Kashmir. Islamabad therefore cannot drop its support for them without affecting the Kashmir cause it espouses.[96]

Additionally, it has been reported that foreign Islamists from various Middle Eastern countries have joined the fight for the liberation of Kashmir (Ehrlich, 1992, p. A10). In 1994, training camps in Khost province, Afghanistan, were run by Gulbuddin Hekmatyar with support from

Pakistan's Inter-Services Intelligence Directorate (ISI). In Amir Muawia, a camp located in Khost, Chechen militants among others received training in guerrilla tactics. These camps were established during the Soviet-Afghan war to train Afghan resistance fighters. Training facilities in Afghanistan also accommodated groups such as Harkat ul-Ansar,[97] a Kashmiri militant group (Sevunts, 1999, p. B1). Harkat ul-Ansar, a group purportedly tied to Osama bin Laden (Mir, 2005), conducts insurgent operations in Indian Jammu and Kashmir. Training camps (located in Khost and Jalalabad) utilized by this group were the target of U.S. retaliatory strikes following the simultaneous bombings of two American embassies in Africa in August 1998.[98]

Since Pakistan became a state it has often taken a defensive posture in international affairs. The catalyst for many of its policy decisions has been its own security concerns. This has been evidenced in its policies and actions in Afghanistan, Kashmir, and Punjab,[99] and its employment of Islamist militant groups to further its strategic interests.[100] On Pakistan's continued efforts in Kashmir, President Musharaaf issued the following statement in his Independence Day address on August 14, 2002:

> Pakistan supports the principled struggle of the people of occupied Kashmir for their right of self-determination, long promised to them by the international community. . . . The struggle for self-determination of our Kashmiri brothers is a sacred trust with us, which can never by [be] compromised (BBC News, August 14, 2002a).

The Kashmir issue is not likely to be resolved in the near future. Winchell (2003, p. 384) notes that Kashmir serves as an important information conduit for Pakistan's ISI to counter the regional activities of India's Research and Analysis Wing (RAW).[101]

Indeed, since the 1980s, Pakistan's Afghan policy has been motivated by its primary objective of providing "strategic depth" to counter any real or perceived Indian threat (Ahmad, 1998).[102] An additional effect of Pakistan's decision to utilize militant factions in pursuit of its national interests and to further its foreign policy agenda was succinctly articulated in a study conducted by author Rizwan Hussain.[103]

Documents acquired by the George Washington University, National Security Archive, through the Freedom of Information Act, cite several interesting facts concerning Pakistan's long-term relationship with the Taliban militia and militant groups operating in Kashmir, specifically Harakat-ul-Ansar (HUA), designated a foreign terrorist organization by the U.S. Department of State. These documents reveal that Pakistan's ISI provided this group with direct financial support of between $30,000 and $60,000 (US) per month. Additionally, the documents dated August 1996 stated that, "A senior HUA leader has publicly advocated an Afghan-style change of government in Pakistan that would remove the political, bureaucratic, and military hierarchies" (Elias, 2007, Doc. 10, p. 4).[104] The report notes that Pakistan, fearing inclusion in the U.S. Department of State's list of state sponsors of terrorism, may be drawing down on direct support to the group. This in effect could move HUA towards other channels of support including Osama bin Laden's Al Qaeda which shares HUA's "pan-Islamic" agenda (Elias, 2007, Doc. 10, p. 1).

These formerly classified documents also revealed that during the Taliban reign Islamabad provided direct financial and material support to the militia (Elias, 2007, Doc 8, p. 7) and specifically links HUA to Pakistan and terrorist training camps run by Osama bin Laden in Afghanistan.[105] Moreover, HUA is a signatory to Osama bin Laden's fatwa calling for attacks on U.S. facilities and citizens (Elias, 2007, Doc. 26, p. 3). Additionally noted is the assertion that the Taliban operated semi-independently of Islamabad. Although a tool of Pakistan's foreign policy, the Taliban was not subject to total control by the Pakistani government.[106] The Taliban for all intents and purposes operated under their own collective agenda (Elias, 2007, Doc. 7, p. 8).[107]

Pakistan support for the Taliban prior to 9/11[108] was also noted by the U.S. Department of State (2001, p. 19) in its annual report, *Patterns of Global Terrorism 2000*, released in April 2001. The report states that despite sanctions[109] imposed on the Taliban by the U.N. Security Council:

> . . . Pakistan is providing the Taliban with materiel, fuel, funding, technical assistance, and military advisers. Pakistan has not prevented large numbers of Pakistani nationals from moving into Afghanistan to fight for the Taliban. Islamabad also failed to take effective steps to curb the activities of certain madrassas, or religious schools, that serve as recruiting grounds for terrorism. Pakistan publicly and privately said it intends to comply fully with UNSCR 1333, which imposes an arms embargo on the Taliban (U.S. Department of State, 2001, p. 19).

Furthermore, support provided to the Taliban as noted in the above report of nine years ago appears to be ongoing. A recently released report by the London School of Economics claims that Pakistani support to the Afghan Taliban, including the provision of training and funding, is the "official policy" of Pakistan's ISI and "is approved at the highest levels of Pakistan's civilian government" (Burch, 2010).[110] According to the author of this report, the ISI provides various levels of support to the Afghan Taliban and the Haqqani network and may be instrumental in formulating policy and decisions regarding combat operations against NATO/ISAF (Waldman, 2010, p. 1).[111] Official Pakistani support to various militant groups presents a complex challenge to ISAF efforts in Afghanistan, further threatens regional stability, and complicates our present relationship with the Pakistani government. Recent U.S. efforts to convince Pakistan to do more to neutralize insurgent forces, e.g., the Afghan Taliban and Haqqani network based within their borders, has not brought much success.[112]

PAKISTAN INVOLVEMENT IN THE DRUG TRADE

As mentioned previously, it has been alleged that some members of both organizations (Pakistan's military and ISI), as well as former members who have retired, have been aligned to fundamentalist groups in Afghanistan. The ISI was created in 1948 and since its inception has become a powerful force in Pakistani governance. Its successful role as a conduit of men, arms, and materiel during the Soviet-Afghan war was a major factor in its rise to prominence.

According to Yousaf and Adkin (2001, p. 96), "The entire planning of the [Afghan] war, all types of training of the Mujahideen and the allocation and distribution of arms and supplies were the sole responsibility of the ISI . . ."[113]

Towards the end of the Soviet-Afghan war and continuing through the present there have been allegations that members of the Pakistani military and ISI have been involved in the drug trade[114] as a funding mechanism for various insurgent movements. An article, which appeared in the *Washington Post* on September 12, 1994, stirred a lot of controversy in the U.S. Congress when it reported that Prime Minister Nawaz Sharif (1990–1993; 1997–1999), stated in an interview that he had been approached by Pakistan's army chief of staff and the head of its military intelligence service (the ISI), both of whom "proposed a detailed 'blueprint' for selling heroin to pay for the country's covert military operations in 1991 . . ." (Anderson and Khan, 1994, p. A13).

Additionally, a report prepared by a consultant for the CIA in 1992, "warned that drug corruption had permeated virtually all segments of Pakistani society and that drug kingpins were closely connected to the country's key institutions of power, including the president and military intelligence agencies."[115] Moreover, it has been alleged that members of the government under former President Zia (1977–1988) and senior Army officials were involved in the transportation of drugs from Afghanistan during the Soviet occupation of that country.[116] Allegations of official Pakistani involvement in the drug trade emerged during the 1980s when Pakistan's ISI was serving as a conduit for delivery of U.S. covert arms and material to Afghan insurgents (Lifschultz, 1988, pp. 477–496).

Furthermore, reports from the international media suggest that Afghan heroin has been making its way into the Kashmir valley. According to Deputy Inspector General (DIG) Dilbag Singh, "a number of foreign mercenaries and Pakistan-trained militants have been caught in Kupwara and Baramulla areas carrying heroin." Singh also stated that heroin had been recovered from the bodies of militants killed in the conflict. According to this report the recovered heroin had "the stamp of Afghanistan on it." It was also reported that "ISI guided militants" are enlisting young boys and local residents into the insurgency, and these newly recruited militants, addicted to heroin, are being used in smuggling operations (Mishra, 2000).

Moreover, the director-general of the Jammu and Kashmir police, Gurbachan Jagat, accused Pakistan of narcotics trafficking. Speaking about the ISI Jagat said, "The ISI has increasingly been using the Line of Control in Kupwara and [an] International Border in Jammu for this narcotic trade, which to some extent is funding the military also" (Suri, 2000).[117]

Allegations of official Pakistani government involvement in the drug trade also appeared in the June 2002 issue of *Defence Journal*, a Karachi monthly publication, which examines Pakistani national security and defense-related issues. In an article examining the drug trade and the impact of narcotics on the Pakistani economy, author Hassan Bashir (2002) notes that the narcotics trade has permeated all levels of society and has had a detrimental impact on not only the political process but has infiltrated state institutions responsible for public safety and order.[118] Bashir alleges that, "drug lords, with the help of narco-money have developed strong connections in the administration, law enforcing agencies, military and the political elite of the country." He further states that Pakistani "airlines and sea vessels" have been used to transport this illegal contraband. Moreover, he reports that the majority of poppy grown in Pakistan occurs in the "tribal belt" where the government has very little influence.[119]

The U.S. Department of State (2004b) reported that in Pakistan, "Cultivation took place both in the traditional growing area, the Bara River Valley of Khyber Agency, and in new areas where it had not been seen before—Orakzai, Kurram, and North and South Waziristan in the FATA and Gulistan and Qila Abdullah in Baluchistan."[120] Additionally, groups based primarily in the Federally Administered Tribal Areas (FATA) continue to receive support from certain elements of the ISI and Pakistani army and to a lesser degree revenue from involvement in criminal activity, including the Afghan drug trade (Norell, 2007, pp. 78–81). This is disturbing considering the influx of foreign militants following the October 2001 invasion and the current Talibanization of this strategic area. The following statement by Bashir presents an equally disturbing assessment:

> . . . even if the anti-narcotics strategies become effective and poppy cultivation in Pakistan controlled, the trafficking and production of narcotics will not be hampered. Because the supply line for the narcotics industry will shift across the border in Afghanistan . . . the political instability in Afghanistan makes it impossible for Washington to pressurize Kabul on the issue and local and international drug enforcing agencies to gain any positive results regarding the control of poppy cultivation. In fact, instead of having any

> success in controlling the drug menace, it has been reported that most of the international aid to Afghanistan for developing the agricultural infrastructure for the purpose of providing substitute crops for poppy, had been used to improve the yield of the latter! (Bashir, 2002).

U.S. government information also ties these rogue actors to the Afghan drug trade and the insurgency in Kashmir. In a hearing before the U.S. House of Representatives on March 20, 2003, Wendy Chamberlain, assistant administrator, Bureau for Asia and the Near East, Agency for International Development, stated that the ISI involvement in the drug trade over the past six years had been "substantial" (Chamberlain, 2003, p. 52).[121]

Finally, according to the U.S. Department of State (2005b), Pakistan's cultivation of opium poppy has increased since 2001, when the UN declared Pakistan, "poppy free," and the U.S. Drug Enforcement Administration (DEA) suspects that heroin processing labs have been established in the Federally Administered Tribal areas (FATA). Moreover, according to the U.S. Department of State 2009 *INCSR* opium poppy in Pakistan is primarily cultivated in the FATA.[122]

CONCLUSION

The meteoric rise in opium poppy cultivation in Afghanistan since the ouster of the Taliban is not an isolated event nor can it be solely attributed to their demise. When the Soviet-Afghan war ended and foreign assistance began to diminish, the major mujahideen factions—the recipients of much of this aid—needed a ready source of cash to continue the internecine fighting amongst themselves and the Soviet-sponsored government in Kabul, which did not fall until 1992. As the civil war continued, these warring factions vied for power and territory and further damaged an already devastated country.

With the ascendancy of the Taliban in November 1996 many of the obstacles that existed in the transiting of commodities both licit and illicit were removed. As the trade became more entrenched, criminal groups expanded their operations gaining influence in the major poppy producing provinces. Indeed, as noted above, some of these groups—such as the Quetta-Chaman transport mafia—played a significant role in the Taliban's overall success. As more territory came under their direct control, the Taliban were able to derive a significant amount of revenue by taxing all aspects of the trade (farmers, producers, and traffickers).

With the October 2001 invasion, U.S. and allied forces elicited many former Soviet-era commanders (warlords) to assist in the war effort against the Taliban and Al Qaeda. Many of these former warlords and mujahideen used this alliance to rebuild their private militias, essentially carving out their own fiefdoms. With the persistent decades-long abject poverty of the Afghan people, a lack of alternative livelihoods, and the availability of a cash crop that offers them both an income and a system whereby they are able to secure credit (salaam), i.e., an advance on their harvest, which could not be generated in other economic endeavors given the infrastructure devastation wrought by 25 years of continuous war, many rural Afghans opted to cultivate opium poppy. Opium poppy cultivation not only generated income for the poor farmer and his family but allowed provincial and regional strongmen (warlords) to personally enrich themselves and provided sufficient revenue to arm and pay those that served in their private militias. This has presented additional problems for the central government as well as NATO/ISAF forces.

Additionally, and perhaps equally if not more important, the drug trade provides these power holders a measure of political leverage and independence from the central government in Kabul, which many Afghans view as ineffective and limited. As fighting continued, opium cultivation expanded to areas that had not previously grown the crop and large quantities of raw opium were being processed in-country. Eradication efforts, which primarily impact the poorest farmers and those who are not connected or otherwise unable to influence the eradication process by the paying of bribes, began in the southern provinces and were often met with armed resistance. Moreover, measures taken to eradicate opium have a "boomerang effect." As the population becomes more closely allied with the Taliban, due in part to the protection they provide for their opium harvests, cooperation and actionable intelligence to ISAF and Afghan government forces is less forthcoming.

Given the insecurity in the region and the animosity of the farmers towards the Karzai administration and foreign forces, the Taliban—particularly in Helmand and Nangarhar, two major poppy growing provinces—began a concerted campaign to use the trade as a source of revenue by earning protection money from traffickers and conversion labs in areas that they controlled and in some cases physically threatening those who did not harvest the crop.

Perhaps the most significant contribution the opium poppy has made to Taliban war efforts in the south is the support they have been able to achieve through a concerted propaganda campaign.[123] Cornell (2005c, p. 757) argues that in areas of narcotics cultivation where there is an ongoing insurgency, narcotics production is likely to change the "dynamics" of that conflict and concomitantly be changed by it. Cornell concludes that most insurgent groups fighting a protracted battle in narcotics-producing areas will seek to reinforce and strengthen their "capabilities" by becoming involved in some aspect of the narcotics production process (Cornell 2005c, p. 757).[124]

Moreover, it has been alleged that current members of the government are involved in the trade. Many senior government officials who rose to positions of power in the new government were members of the previous anti-Taliban Northern Alliance. As presented in this study, the Northern Alliance had not only allowed and encouraged the opium trade during the 2000 ban instituted by the Taliban but in some instances various members of the Alliance were actively involved in it. This chapter has shown that national and international criminal gangs, warlords, corrupt government officials, and public service personnel are all part of the multifaceted opium problem in Afghanistan.[125]

CHAPTER 7

Terrorism and the Opium Trade in Afghanistan

TALIBAN INVOLVEMENT IN THE DRUG TRADE: PRE-9/11

As illustrated throughout this study, prior to the U.S.-led invasion in October 2001 numerous media accounts and official reports cited both Taliban and Northern Alliance involvement in the drug trade to fund their ongoing war effort; the Taliban also received financial support from Osama bin Laden.[1] In addressing Taliban and Northern Alliance involvement in the drug trade prior to 9/11 Makarenko (2002d, p. 9) claimed that while both groups collected funds from the drug trade the Taliban's revenue emanated from collecting taxes from farmers and a prearranged agreement established with the opium traders. These traders or "drug mafias" paid a percentage of their profits to the Taliban in return for the right to move their commodity across Taliban-controlled areas.[2]

By 1998, the Taliban were effectively in control of much of the country. The United Nations Office on Drugs and Crime notes that between 1996 and 1999, a period when the Taliban were the major political and military force in Afghanistan, production of opium doubled and in 1999, a record year, production reached 4,600 mt (2003, p. 5)[3]. This may have been due in part to the Taliban's policy of encouraging cultivation and to their success at providing security along major trafficking routes where prior to their arrival transporters often found themselves at the mercy of warlords, their armed militias, and opportunity-seeking criminal elements. The increased security and reduced delays in the transportation process may have spawned an increase in the amount of opium cultivated (Stepanova, 2002, p. 38; UNODC, 2003a, p. 128; Rubin, 2000).

The United Nations Report of the International Narcotics Control Board for 2001 released in 2002 cites an interesting point:

> In Afghanistan, the harvest in the crop year 2000/2001 is estimated to be less than one tenth of the harvest in the previous crop year. As a result of the implementation of the ban, opium and morphine had become much less available on illicit markets in West Asia; however, in response to the military events after September 2001, large quantities of opiates were made available from illicit stocks. The availability of heroin originating in Afghanistan remained high in the region, even following the ban . . . Seizure statistics for countries throughout West Asia show that opium had been increasingly processed into other opiates in Afghanistan (UN, 2002, p. 67).

This statement suggests three things. First, an established infrastructure was converting opium into heroin prior to leaving the country. Secondly, the fact that heroin was still available in large quantities suggests that even with the apparent success of the ban there were stockpiles of opium available for conversion. This is indicated by the seizure data alluded to above. Finally, the fact that the Taliban were engaged in an ongoing struggle with the Northern Alliance suggests that other forces were at work ensuring that this demand-driven trade would continue.

Additionally, it may also be suggested that prior to 9/11 neither Al Qaeda nor the Taliban appear to have been in direct control of the opium industry in Afghanistan.[4] Taliban involvement, which was a direct result of territorial control, was limited primarily to taxing various aspects of the trade and possibly encouraging cultivation (UNODC 2003a, p. 10) with both the Taliban and possibly members of Al Qaeda drawing revenue by providing security for shipments along the main transporting routes. Additionally, the U.S. Department of State, Bureau of International Narcotics and Law Enforcement Affairs, reported in its 2001 issue of the *International Narcotics Control Strategy Report 2000* that the Taliban continued to encourage poppy cultivation despite proclamations to the contrary (U.S. Department of State, 2001a).[5]

According to the U.S. Department of State, revenue generated from the trade helped to support the Taliban war effort against Northern Alliance forces (U.S. Department of State, 2001a). This opinion was also reached in May 2001 by a UN panel of experts who concluded that the Taliban, despite their July 2000 ban, were stockpiling opium and using proceeds from the sale of opiates to fund their war effort against the Northern Alliance. Furthermore, the five-member panel concluded that opium sales were providing revenue to "buy weapons" and "finance the training of terrorists and support the operations of extremists in neighboring countries and beyond" (Lederer, 2001).[6]

In reference to the Taliban encouraging the cultivation of opium poppy Maley (2000, p. 11) reports that, "eyewitness testimony pointed to

Taliban involvement not only in compelling farmers to grow opium, but in distributing fertilizer for the crops."[7] The Northern Alliance, according to Makarenko (2002d, p. 9), was involved in the production as well as the trafficking phase of the trade. Regarding the Taliban she adds that the major portion of their revenue was derived, "from the cross-border smuggling of licit commodities" (Makarenko, 2002d, p. 9).

Makarenko (2002d, p. 9) goes on to state that, although several former high-ranking members of the Taliban may have personally profited due to their strong ties with various traders and warlords,[8] there is no evidence which supports the assertion that the Taliban controlled the trade.[9]

ISLAMIC MOVEMENT OF UZBEKISTAN INVOLVEMENT IN THE DRUG TRADE: PRE-9/11

In addressing terrorist group involvement in the drug trade prior to 9/11, Makarenko (2002d, p. 9) finds that the only terrorist group which had direct involvement in the trade prior to 9/11 was the Islamic Movement of Uzbekistan (IMU).[10] Moreover, she argues that prior to 9/11 IMU incursions into Kyrgyzstan and Uzbekistan in 1999 and 2000 were designed to divert government forces away from key drug trafficking routes. According to Makarenko these incursions occurred at a time of the year when Afghanistan's opium had been harvested.[11]

Information on IMU involvement in the drug trade also came from the testimony of Ralf Mutschke, assistant director of Interpol's Criminal Intelligence Directorate before the U.S. House of Representatives Committee on the Judiciary, Subcommittee on Crime, in December 2000.[12]

Mutschke's assessment closely parallels that of Makarenko (2002b; 2002d).[13] Thus, according to Mutschke (2000) and Makarenko (2002) the IMU prior to 9/11 was a hybrid organization.[14] They were a terrorist organization as evidenced by their cross-border attacks (e.g., kidnapping incidents involving Japanese and American citizens) and criminal in that they had been involved in the cross-border trafficking of narcotics. This view is held by Rashid (2003, p. 154) who asserts that, while based in Afghanistan, the Islamic Movement of Uzbekistan was deeply involved in the opium trade and controlled trafficking routes "from Afghanistan through Central Asia to Europe using its network of militants across the region as couriers."

Based on the IMU's involvement in the trafficking of Afghan opiates (Mutcshke, 2000; Makarenko, 2002d; Stepanova, 2005; Baran, Starr, and Cornell, 2006; Curtis, 2002; Rashid, 2003) and their campaign of terror prior to 9/11, they could be considered a group "where a single entity simultaneously exhibits criminal and terrorist characteristics" (Makarenko, 2005, p. 173).

TALIBAN AND ISLAMIC MOVEMENT OF UZBEKISTAN INVOLVEMENT IN THE DRUG TRADE: POST-9/11

Since the initial defeat of Taliban and Al Qaeda forces, the drug trade has not only been revived but has increased dramatically. Makarenko (2002a, p. 28) notes:

> . . . it is unsurprising to find that the displacement of Taliban and Al Qaeda forces did not significantly alter the organization or operations of the vast narco-networks responsible for the cultivation, processing and trafficking of Afghan opiates to the international market.

Additionally, it appears that in the period of the Taliban's reconstitution (2002–2004) large drug profits do not appear to have had a major impact on Taliban expansion or operations.[15]

This suggests that forces—other than Al Qaeda and the Taliban—at work prior to 9/11, remained operational following the U.S.-led invasion.[16] The resilience of the trade, as evidenced by pre- and post-2001 UNODC and U.S. Department of State production data,[17] indicates that any possible role that the Taliban and/or Al Qaeda played in the opium trade was not a necessary or sufficient factor in its sustainability or continued success.

For example, as the international coalition's attention focused on the Taliban and Al Qaeda, the Afghan opium trade began to flourish as farmers began harvesting the only crop they knew would yield immediate and financially lucrative returns, the opium poppy. Indeed, the first post-invasion crop (2002)—which yielded 3,400 mt—surpassed the 2000 production total of 3,300 mt, and the area devoted to opium poppy cultivation in 2002 surged to 74,000 ha.[18] Helmand province in the south and Nangarhar province in the east are traditional Taliban strongholds and account for a large percentage of Afghanistan's opium output.[19]

As the insurgency continued and fighting intensified, specifically in the southern and eastern provinces where Taliban forces were entrenched and beginning to garner a certain amount of local support, reports began to circulate that the strength of the insurgency was directly related to the region's opium output (Bergen, 2007, pp. 22–29). Press reports indicated that the Taliban and other allied factions were not only encouraging residents to plant poppy but in some instances threatening farmers who chose not to cultivate the crop.[20]

Moreover, in Baramchah, a drug bazaar and Taliban stronghold located near the Pakistan border in Helmand province, insurgents collected substantial revenue from criminal groups seeking safe passage. According to Helmand Governor Mohammad Daud, the Taliban and drug traffickers support each other and have a very close relationship in the province (Galeotti, 2006).[21]

An article advocating similar views appeared in the *Christian Science Monitor*. That report alleges that the Taliban, and those associated with them in the areas that they control, are not only involved in the taxation of the trade but are controlling and organizing farm poppy output,[22] protection of shipments, and also operating labs[23] that convert raw opium into heroin.[24]

The article further claims that the drug trade, particularly in the south, has breathed new life into the ongoing Taliban insurgency.[25] In addressing possible involvement of other extremist groups in the drug trade the reporting correspondent wrote:

> Hezb-Islami Gulbuddin, run by the fundamentalist Gulbuddin Hikmatyar, is now "a full-fledged smuggling organization," moving everything from heroin to people, says a US official. There's fragmentary evidence that Osama bin Laden has instructed his people not to get wrapped up in narcotics, apparently fearing it would harm his movement. "Some say that Osama and his people have specifically stayed away from it," says the Western official (Peters, 2006b, p. O4).[26]

Inspector Paul Richards of the Royal Canadian Mounted Police (RCMP) spent a year in Afghanistan as a counter-narcotics adviser for Canadian forces. In this role Inspector Richards investigated the potential ties between Islamist insurgents and drug traffickers. In an interview with CanWest News Service Inspector Richards refers to the profit-driven "symbiotic" relationship between these two factions:

> The Taliban is not, as some western officials maintain, a narco-terrorist group directly involved in producing heroin itself, Richards said. It does, however, receive an estimated $10 million a year for guarding drug labs and smugglers and for generally creating an atmosphere of permissiveness around the business, he told CanWest News Service. "They work very, very closely together and that's how the Taliban funds what they're doing . . . whether it's paying a suicide bomber's family, whether it's buying bullets, whether it's buying food," said the officer. "The Taliban have become very reliant on the narco-economy. They are completely dependent on it." In turn, the instability sown by the insurgent attacks—many of which have killed Canadian troops—aids the drug lords by making it easier for them to carry out their illicit activities, he noted (Blackwell 2007a, p. A3).[27]

Elizabeth Rubin, an investigative journalist for the *New York Times*, was in Afghanistan in December 2001 and returned in the summer of 2006 to investigate the drug trade. In an article titled, "'In the Land of the Taliban," Rubin (2006, pp. 86–97 and 172–174) reports:

> When I asked Manan Farahi, the director of counterterrorism efforts for Karzai's government, why the Taliban were so strong in Helmand, he said

> that Helmandis had, in fact, hated the Taliban because of Mullah Muhammad Omar's ban on poppy cultivation. "The elders were happy this government was coming and they could plant again," Farahi told me. "But then the warlords came back and let their militias roam freely. They were settling old scores—killing people, stealing their opium. And because they belonged to the government, the people couldn't look to the government for protection. And because they had the ear of the Americans, the people couldn't look to the Americans. Into this need stepped the Taliban." And this time the Taliban, far from suppressing the drug trade, agreed to protect it.

The view that the Taliban has reversed its position regarding opium cultivation is shared by Dr. David Kilcullen,[28] former lieutenant colonel in the Australian army currently serving as chief strategist for the U.S. Department of State, Office of the Coordinator for Counterterrorism. According to Dr. Kilcullen, "the Taliban has a political strategy of defending the poppy fields, in order to detach the people from the government . . ." (Reynolds, 2007). In essence, the Taliban strategy of thwarting government attempts at eradication is designed to gain public support by protecting the livelihoods of rural Afghans.[29]

Furthermore, opium eradication successfully implemented on a wide enough scale could spawn an increase in violence against international forces by initiating a widespread propaganda campaign by the Taliban and other factions linked to the insurgency, and others who derive substantial revenue from the trade. Additionally, the drug trade is demand-driven and the drug industry in Afghanistan is the mainstay of various powerful national, regional, and international interests, therefore eradication would only initiate cultivation in other areas.

Eradication without alternative livelihood strategies would further alienate a large percentage of the rural population from the central government in Kabul. Hence, the Karzai regime would find itself hard-pressed to maintain national legitimacy and avoid further erosion of public support. Anecdotal evidence suggest that the Taliban is recruiting fighters among Afghans[30] who feel betrayed by the Karzai government and what they believe to be an insincere commitment by the international community and occupation forces charged with providing security.

In comparison, the poppy farmer is a small cog in a big wheel. There are other much more powerful players who reap huge financial and political benefits from Afghanistan's opium. It is these actors, e.g., anti-coalition factions, regional warlords, sub-commanders, criminal elements such as the Afghan drug mafias, former members of the Northern Alliance who now hold government positions, and international criminal networks[31] who would present an equal if not greater challenge to the central government and NATO/ISAF. Disrupting the cash flow to these people would be a good thing provided Afghanistan was sufficiently stabilized with non-corrupt security forces in place to counter the violence that would no doubt ensue.

On the issue of IMU post-9/11 militant and drug activity[32] recent reports note that while the group is not considered to be a major threat to Afghan and international forces, the current expansion of the drug trade in Afghanistan could serve as a catalyst and provide IMU remnants with a means to acquire sufficient funds to rebuild their military capabilities and recruit new followers. Moreover, in the absence of alternative sources of financing (Makarenko, 2002d, p. 12) and IMU remnants occupying drug-producing provinces, this is a real possibility. As noted by Cornell (2005a, pp. 637–638) many IMU fighters were eliminated in the battle for Kunduz in November 2001.[33] However, IMU detachments remain in Afghanistan's Paktia and Kunar provinces, and are reportedly mobilized in Pakistan's tribal areas thereby posing a potential threat to the Pakistani government.[34]

AL QAEDA, THE DRUG TRADE, AND SOURCES OF FINANCING: EVOLVING LINKAGE

Allegations regarding Osama bin Laden's affiliation with the narcotics trade began to surface around 1998. In the aftermath of 9/11 these allegations became a media target and a national and international concern. However, prior to 9/11, while the Taliban was mentioned as profiting from opium, Osama bin Laden for the most part was not.

An interview given by Ahmed Rashid to CNN International prior to the 9/11 events was one of the few media events which did address the possible involvement of Osama bin Laden in the Afghan opium trade. During this short exchange Mr. Rashid discussed Osama bin Laden's sources of finance, his relationship with the Taliban, and claimed a bin Laden-opium trade connection but provided no details as to how he arrived at this conclusion.[35] Other prominent individuals shared this same concern while others refuted the allegation based on a lack of corroborating evidence.

Since 1998, the intelligence community was at least open to the possibility that Al Qaeda may be implicated in the drug trade.[36] This concern was voiced by former CIA Director George Tenet in February 2000. In a prepared statement before the Senate Select Committee on Intelligence then CIA Director George Tenet (2000) made the following comment relative to Afghanistan's opium trade:

> Explosive growth in Afghan opium production is being driven by the shared interests of traditional traffickers and the Taliban. And as with so many of these cross-national issues, Mr. Chairman, what concerns me most is the way the threats become intertwined. In this case, there is ample evidence that Islamic extremists such as Usama Bin Ladin use profits from the drug trade to support their terror campaign.[37]

In terms of "ample" evidence linking Al Qaeda to unmentioned aspects of the Afghan drug trade, CIA Director Tenet did not specify what the nature of that evidence was, however, since the events of September 11, 2001, anecdotal evidence connecting the two has been promulgated extensively in the international media.[38]

PLAUSIBLE CONNECTIONS

Another view of Osama bin Laden's possible connection to the drug trade is provided by Michael Scheuer, a 22-year veteran of the CIA and the head of the agency's Osama bin Laden unit from 1996–1999. Basing his assessment on several media accounts, Scheuer states in effect that Osama bin Laden's purported involvement may have entailed providing technical assistance to the Taliban. Scheuer cites this explanation as a more "plausible link," of Osama bin Laden's possible involvement in the Afghan drug trade. In his book, *Through Our Enemies Eyes: Osama bin Laden, Radical Islam, and the Future of America,* Scheuer acknowledges that the available information regarding Osama bin Laden's ties to the opium trade are "of varying quality, some obviously true, some analysis by assertion, and some propaganda meant to defame bin Laden" (Scheuer, 2006b, p. 42). A close examination of some of the reports referenced by Scheuer provides some interesting insights. For example, an article which appeared in the January 31, 2000, issue of the *Financial Times* discusses the rapid expansion of the opium trade during the Taliban's ascendancy. It was also during this period (1996) that Osama bin Laden sought and was given refuge by that militant group:

> Over the last five years Afghanistan has been converted from a normal agricultural economy into a poppy-based economy and the proceeds from opium production are seen as financing an "explosion" of Islamic radicalism in several neighbouring Central Asian states. Osama bin Laden, the international terrorist linked to several US embassy bombings, is the best known Afghan immigrant, but the number of other militant movements seeking sanctuary in Afghanistan has increased rapidly. None of these organisations could survive without the income from the drug trade, says Mr. Rashid . . . (Hall, 2000, p. 2).[39]

This study shows that the increase in poppy cultivation, spawned by the Soviet-Afghan war, became an intrinsic part of Afghanistan's social and economic fabric prior to 1995. Indeed, data provided by UNODC indicates that production has been rising steadily since 1987 and increased to over 3,400 mt in 1994, the year the Taliban began their ascendancy. However, the 1994 increase over the previous year could not have been attributed to the Taliban as they did not emerge as a military and political force until October of that year in Kandahar; at the start of the 1995 planting season. Nevertheless, the drug trade has been expanding steadily since the latter years of the Soviet-Afghan war. Opium cultivation increased by almost 60 percent and production more than doubled between 1996 and 1999, a period when the Taliban were gaining substantial control over the country (UNODC, 2007c, pp. 196–197).

Additionally, in May 1996, Osama bin Laden returned to Afghanistan. In September 1996, the Taliban took power by capturing Kabul. Whether Osama bin Laden had an impact on increasing opium production remains an open question. Robert Fisk, a journalist for the *Independent*, interviewed Osama bin Laden in 1993 in Sudan. During that interview bin Laden told Fisk, "I am a construction engineer and an agriculturalist" (Fisk, 1993, p. 10).[40] With a background in economics and management,[41] and experience in business and agriculture, it would be reasonable to assume that Osama bin Laden had the capabilities and could have provided the technical expertise to increase opium production in Afghanistan as a service to the Taliban who provided him safe haven since May 1996. It should be noted that Osama bin Laden undertook and was successful at several agricultural projects during his stay in Sudan (Scheuer, 2006b, p. 43). In an interview with Osama bin Laden conducted in December 1998, and aired on al Jazeera television on June 10, 1999, author Jamal Isma'il provides the following insight into Osama bin Laden's agricultural expertise:

> He [bin Laden] told me about his days in Sudan and the challenge he faced when Arab aid to Sudan stopped and how he was able to survive with limited local resources. He told me about the agricultural projects he carried out in the al-Jazirah area in Sudan. He told me that this country can feed the whole world if it were allowed to be properly invested. He told me about how he was able to produce a record number of sunflowers. His agricultural projects were many and included cotton farms (Najm, 1999).

Applying these same agricultural skills in Afghanistan would have had the effect of further reinforcing Osama bin Laden's relationship with the Taliban[42] by providing them with the technical expertise to increase the amount of opium cultivation, thereby creating an additional revenue stream in the form of collectable taxes on the production and trade of opium and its derivatives. Additionally, it is noted that the Taliban set up experimental opium farms with the intent of perfecting techniques which would maximize opium yield (Rashid, 1999b, p.29). If true, what if any impact Osama bin Laden had in this process remains a mystery. The premise whereby bin Laden provided support without actually engaging in the trafficking of the product was emphasized in an investigative report published by a U.S weekly news magazine.

In a report published in the weekly *U.S. News & World Report* the authors support the view that Osama bin Laden's involvement in the drug trade was more of a supportive role in that he provided protection services for drug shipments leaving the country.[43] This "good will gesture" could be viewed as similar to providing fighters to the Taliban in their struggle with the Northern Alliance. It has been previously established that Osama bin Laden provided fighters from his elite 055 Brigade to the Taliban in their ongoing conflict with the Northern Alliance. This force fought with the Taliban from 1997 to 2001 (Gunaratna, 2002, p. 58).[44] An excerpt of this report states:

> His [bin Laden's] ties to the illicit drug trade have been difficult to pin down. But American authorities are now convinced of the accuracy of foreign intelligence reports detailing his involvement. "He sees it as a way to poison the West," says one U.S. official. Experts say bin Laden has profited from the drug trade by taking payment for providing armed fighters to protect opium and heroin shipments moving from Afghanistan to the West, primarily Europe. They also say that the intelligence reports link bin Laden's people to the labs in Afghanistan where heroin is produced.
>
> Officials maintain that bin Laden does not need the drug trade to finance his terrorism, but instead became involved as a good will gesture designed to cement his relationship with the militant Islamic Taliban government. The Taliban—which controls most of the impoverished nation—has provided bin Laden with a safe haven for more than five years (Pound, Ragavan, and Robinson, 2001).

This is a plausible scenario given bin Laden's prior negative experience in Sudan. It is also important to note that the Taliban also provided protection services to convoys carrying commodities other than opium or its derivatives, therefore it is equally plausible that Osama bin Laden could have aided in this endeavor as well.[45] Notwithstanding the veracity of this report it is important to note that it was published prior to the U.S.-led invasion when such reporting, i.e., Osama bin Laden's purported ties to the drug trade, especially in Britain, was at its peak and Western public sentiment along with the international media was immersed in the "demonization"' of Osama bin Laden.

Interestingly, a more recent article in *U.S. News & World Report* titled, "Paying for Terror," adopts an entirely different viewpoint. In this updated report, investigative journalists David Kaplan, Bay Fang, and Soni Sangwan echo the sentiments of Blanchard (2006, p. 15). According to the authors, counterterrorism officials reported that interrogations with captured Al Qaeda militants revealed that the organization decided not to become involved in the lucrative opium trade for fear of drawing the attention of law enforcement. Moreover, the authors note that Al Qaeda top leadership does not trust the individuals at the high end of the business (Kaplan, Fang, and Sangwan, 2005, p. 47). However, the report also points out that while Al Qaeda may be averse to participating in the drug business, "nearly everyone else in the region—from warlords to provincial governors to the Taliban—is not" (Kaplan, Fang, and Sangwan, 2005, p. 48).[46]

An article in the *New York Times* shortly after the October 2001 invasion addressed Osama bin Laden's fundraising and financial efforts in southern Europe following the 1995 Balkan peace accord in Dayton, Ohio. The author points out that since the inception of Al Qaeda Osama bin Laden has been able to successfully exploit political unrest and garner the funds necessary to expand his network.[47] Moreover, the author notes that a linkage exists between Bosnian organized crime and various militants tied to the Al Qaeda organization. He further stated that unnamed "officials" assert that through these linkages Al Qaeda and the Taliban were able to locate "a route for the trafficking of heroin from Afghanistan into Europe through the Balkans." Furthermore, these purported linkages with criminal groups have provided extremists with weapons and other related hardware (Eichenwald, 2001, p. A1). This would have been a plausible scenario prior to 9/11 since most of the country was controlled by the Taliban, and by extension Al Qaeda, both of whom were actively engaged in armed action against the Northern Alliance. This control of territory would certainly include key trade routes.

OPEN SOURCE REPORTS AND OFFICIAL INVESTIGATIONS

A previously classified U.S. Defense Intelligence Agency (DIA) intelligence information report (IIR) apparently written in October 1998 was obtained through the Freedom of Information Act and acquired by Judicial Watch, an organization located in Washington, D.C., and devoted to checking government related corruption. In addressing Osama bin Laden's potential links to individuals and groups in the former Soviet states this report, while by no means a "smoking gun" or a product of final "evaluated intelligence," does provide valuable information regarding Al Qaeda's activities and objectives and Osama bin Laden's relationship with the Chechen insurgency.[48] According to the report, bin Laden allegedly met several times with representatives of the "Islamic Way" specifically Movladi Udugov, former Chechen foreign minister. The meetings were held in Afghanistan in 1997. The report notes that during these meetings an agreement was formed that involved the exchange of "financial supplies" to Chechen militants. Furthermore, these meetings also stressed the need to train "terrorists drawn from among 'converted' Europeans, Russians, Ukranians, Cossacks and Ossetians in Khattab's[49] training camps to conduct kidnappings and terrorist acts against French, Israeli, U.S., and English citizens" (DIA, 1998, p. 5, item 8).

This report goes on to state that the purpose of the Khattab camps was to train terrorists for jihad and that the objective of these militants was to generate panic and disorder with the intent of "creating an uprising against Russia" for the ultimate purpose of establishing an "Islamic state of Northern Caucasus."[50] The following section of this document is particularly enlightening. It states that:

> A direct route has been established to Chechnya from Pakistan and Afghanistan through Turkey and Azerbaijan. Abu Sayaf . . . coordinates this traffic of "volunteers" as well as drug trafficking, working as a representative of Ben

> [Bin] Laden in the Chechen foreign ministry under the protection of Movladi Udugov . . . After an adaptation period they (Afghan Arabs) would go to the Central Asian Republics [] "for diversion" and to create Wakhabites and Taliban cells, spreading terror against U.S., Russian, and other Western officials and businessmen (DIA, 1998, p. 5, items 9–10).[51]

On November 20, 2004, following the release of the Judicial Watch report, Movladi Udugov, chief of External Subcommittee of Informational Council (Command Council) of the Chechen Republic of Ichkeria (CRI), issued a denial of its contents in an article published by the Kavkaz Center News Agency.[52]

As stated previously, the National Commission on Terrorist Attacks upon the United States (2004, p. 171) concluded that although the Taliban received revenue from the drug trade there was no convincing evidence linking Al Qaeda to the drug trade. The report further states:

> Although some reporting alleges that bin Laden may have been an investor, or even had an operational role, in drug trafficking before 9/11, this intelligence cannot be substantiated . . . No evidence indicates any such involvement in drug trafficking, and none of the detained Al Qaeda operatives has indicated that this was a method of fund-raising (9/11 Commission, 2004, p. 499, footnote 128).

The Commission's final report was released on July 22, 2004. However, the Council on Foreign Relations (CFR), a non-partisan think-tank which informs members of Congress, the executive branch, government officials, and others on matters of foreign policy, released its report titled, *Update on the Global Campaign Against Terrorist Financing*, second report of an Independent Task Force on Terrorist Financing, on June 15, 2004, five weeks prior to the final 9/11 Commission report. This report states:

> The United Nations Monitoring Group, in its second required report to the UN's al-Qaeda and Taliban Sanctions Committee, also found that "al-Qaeda continues to receive funds it needs from charities, deep-pocket donors, and business and criminal activities, including the drug trade" (Roth, Greenburg, and Wille, 2004, p. 7).[53]

Additionally, in its first report, *Terrorist Financing*, report of an Independent Task Force, Greenberg, Wechsler, and Wolosky (2002, p. 7) note that, "Al-Qaeda also earns money from a wide range of criminal enterprises. Some of these have been grand, such as its symbiotic relationship with the heroin trade in Afghanistan."

Two highly regarded and competent investigative bodies charged with conducting a senior-level inquiry into these important matters appear to have reached different conclusions relative to Al Qaeda's role in the Afghan opium trade. Moreover, both reports addressed the issue of Al Qaeda financing. This should cause some concern given the probability that the investigative components which input to each of these reports were more than likely being carried out simultaneously given the date each report was released. If this was not the case then those preparing the reports were relying on different intelligence or disagreed on the information that was presented for input into these reports. Finally, the information cited by the Independent Task Force contradicts what an official of the United Nations told this author in an e-mail communication in October 2006.[54]

OBSERVATIONS AND OPINIONS OF INVESTIGATORS, VARIOUS EXPERTS AND OTHER KNOWLEDGEABLE SOURCES

Perhaps the best source of information pertaining to a possible Al Qaeda-drug nexus came from news and wire service reports. However, given their subjective nature and in the spirit of critical intersubjectivity[55] these reports were examined multi-dimensionally, i.e., in relation to other reported accounts of the same event.[56] In this context they do serve as a good "event data" source and provide useful incident-specific detail for further follow-up and analysis. In an effort to establish the credibility and accuracy of reports, which were particularly germane to this study, discussions were held with some of the leading authorities on this particular issue and in some cases interviews and follow-up interviews were conducted with the authors of specific articles. Additionally, this section contains information obtained from interviews and correspondence with individuals who had previously written and commented on the subject and those with onsite experience in Afghanistan investigating this problem.[57]

Perhaps the most incriminating article alleging a connection between Al Qaeda and the drug trade was written by Tim McGirk, investigative journalist for *TIME* magazine. In this article McGirk reports that U.S. forces had arrested and subsequently released Juma Khan,[58] a top-level drug trafficker who investigators later learned "is employing a fleet of cargo ships to move Afghan heroin out of the Pakistani port of Karachi." The report further states that at least three of these ships returned from the Middle East with armaments including "plastic explosives and anti-tank mines which were secretly unloaded in Karachi and sent overland to Al Qaeda and Taliban fighters" (McGirk, 2004, p. 41).[59] McGirk also cites a statement by Mirwais Yasini,[60] head of Afghanistan's Counternarcotics Directorate (CND), who claims that terrorists "provide gunmen" to protect traffickers and heroin processing labs in exchange for a cut of the profits. The article cites additional incidents which may link terrorists in Afghanistan to the growing opium trade. McGirk reports:

> Recent busts have revealed evidence of al-Qaeda's ties to the trade. On New Year's Eve, a U.S. Navy vessel stopped a small fishing boat in the Arabian

> Sea. After a search, says a Western antinarcotics official, "they found several al-Qaeda guys sitting on a bale of drugs." In January U.S. and Afghan agents raided a drug runner's house in Kabul and found a dozen or so satellite phones. The phones were passed on to the CIA station in Kabul, which found that they had been used to call numbers linked to suspected terrorists in Turkey, the Balkans and Western Europe. And in March U.S. troops searching a suspected terrorist hideout in Oruzgan province found opium with an estimated street value of $15 million (McGirk, 2004, p. 41).[61]

In a question from this author regarding a direct link between Al Qaeda and drug traffickers McGirk provided the following response:

> I think it's an informal fluid link. In Afghanistan it exists more between Taliban and the drug industry but, indirectly with Al Qaeda too. Al Qaeda may not necessarily get direct financing from drugs, but al Qaeda and drug traffickers almost certainly share the same channels for moving money and guns. AQ also relies on drug smugglers, particularly along the Iranian-Baluch border, to move from one country to another. (McGirk, 2004, p.41 and e-mail communication, September 15, 2006).

McGirk further added that within the al Qaeda organization they view the trafficking of drugs to the West as a, "legitimate weapon of jihad" (McGirk, 2004, p. 41 and e-mail communication, September 15, 2006). The point here is that both groups may share common smuggling networks to move not only drugs but fighters, weapons, and other war materiel as well.[62]

As noted in chapter 3, the ship seizure incidents in the Persian Gulf were also reported by Barbara Starr, CNN Pentagon correspondent on the news show *Anderson Cooper 360°*, on January 5, 2004.[63] A follow-up e-mail reply from Ms. Starr indicated that she did not know of any additional information regarding these seizures nor was she aware of any subsequent incidents (e-mail communication, January 22, 2007). If indeed there had been subsequent seizures they did not receive the press coverage that the December 15, 2003, incident received.[64] Peter Bergen, CNN terrorism analyst, who provided commentary during the broadcast of the aforementioned CNN report, could not provide additional detail on the allegations other than there was a "very complex interplay of various actors" involved in the drug business in Afghanistan (interview with author, November 28, 2006). Subsequent attempts by this author did not uncover updated information on this story.

This apparent lack of follow-up coverage in the open-source literature where these revelations initially surfaced is disturbing and raises several questions, which to date appear to have gone unanswered. For example, the CNN report stated that an initial investigation showed "clear links" between the drugs seized and Al Qaeda members, while the February 2004 article by Crawley stated essentially the same thing, i.e., the Pentagon cites clear links to Al Qaeda; the 9/11 Commission report disregarded at least one of these seizures as irrelevant on the issue of Al Qaeda and drugs. The three seizures resulted in the capture of 33 crew members, 10 of whom were held and questioned at Bahram Air Base in Afghanistan.

The article did not provide the name of the Navy spokesperson who made the comments, nor did it provide information relative to what evidence the Navy had to back up the claim that some of those detained had ties to Al Qaeda. What, if any, additional information was gathered as a result of the interrogation of these 10 men? Why did this story not receive adequate follow-up? Was Juma Khan, purported drug trafficker cited in the McGirk *Terrorism's Harvest* article and in Blanchard (2004, 2005, 2006, and 2007), affiliated with any of the seized dhows? These questions have gone unanswered.

While this story did not receive a significant amount of media follow-up, these incidents in the Persian Gulf did become an issue at a U.S. congressional hearing and have been cited a number of times by proponents of the nexus. Regarding the December 15, 2003, seizure the 9/11 Commission concluded in their final report that the resulting investigation (DEA, CIA) did not shed evidence of a direct tie-in to the Al Qaeda organization.[65]

Although the 9/11 Commission report mentions the December 15, 2003, seizure by U.S. Navy personnel there was no mention of three subsequent seizures by the U.S. Navy.[66] Two of these seizures were made with the assistance of Australian and New Zealand air support. On two separate occasions on December 20, 2003, U.S. Naval forces seized two dhows, confiscating 95 pounds of heroin, 50 pounds of methamphetamines, and took 21 crewmen into custody. On December 31, 2003, a fourth ship was seized carrying more than 2.5 tons of hashish. Fifteen crewmen were apprehended during this seizure. These seizures were reported in the international media by various news organizations. The media reported that a total of 48 men were initially detained and 10, allegedly tied to Al Qaeda, were taken to Bagram Air Base in Afghanistan.

If indeed Al Qaeda members were passengers on these vessels it is uncertain if the "clear ties" cited in the report link Al Qaeda personnel to the transport or the drugs or both. In other words, these seizure incidents may not link Al Qaeda directly to the trafficking chain of the drug trade but they do suggest an opportunistic symbiotic relationship between narcotics traffickers and Al Qaeda i.e., that the same routes used by drug traffickers are being accessed by Al Qaeda to transport men and materiel including arms. Though each group is motivated by different factors, they both share the same environment and have similar operational and logistical needs. Al Qaeda fighters, while in transit, may be available to provide protection services to drug couriers. Conversely, drug traffickers, who know the geographical landscape, could provide valuable assistance in the way of safe passage and intelligence for Al Qaeda members and their affiliates.

Moreover, as stated in chapter 3, David Osler of *Lloyd's List*, an international maritime publication, stated that he had "not previously heard claims of AQ [al Qaeda] being deeply involved in narcotics trade" (e-mail communication, January 30, 2007). However, he did acknowledge in an article titled, "Investigators closing in on bin Laden vessels" that, "Associates of Osama bin Laden have built up a fleet of around two dozen ships in recent years, primarily to facilitate the smuggling of high quality heroin and hashish from Afghanistan to the West" (Osler, 2001, p. 1). This may provide substance to McGirk's statement regarding Juma Khan's smuggling operations. Attempts at determining whether any of the seized vessels were registered to Juma Khan, cited in the McGirk article above, were unsuccessful.

Concerning the issue of U.S. forces seizing large quantities of stockpiled opium, Mazzetti and Smucker (2002, pp. 14–15) reported that during a raid on Al Qaeda and Taliban hideouts in Paktika province in February 2002 U.S. Special Forces uncovered a large cache of weapons, satellite phones, computers containing Al Qaeda operational information, and two pounds of opium.[67] Also, an article published in the *Washington Times* on September 13, 2004, cites several incidents where U.S. troops seized large quantities of opium gum while conducting raids in what was reported as Al Qaeda and Taliban hideouts. The article states that the *Washington Times* received photographs and an e-mail from a U.S. Army Special Operations soldier stating: "Attached are photographs summarizing the linkage between [anti-coalition militants] and the drug trade, . . . The soldier described the militants as renegade warlords and members of Taliban and Al Qaeda." The article claimed that the photographs were taken in Helmand and Uruzgan provinces following three separate raids conducted by U.S. forces against anti-coalition factions.[68] According to the report opium stockpiles, purportedly belonging to Gulbuddin Hekmatyar,[69] were also confiscated in Zabul province (Scarborough, 2004c, p. A11).[70]

During a discussion with this author, Rafael Perl—at the time of the interview a drug policy expert at the Congressional Research Service—stated that claims of Al Qaeda direct involvement with drugs are mostly speculative. He further added that, "There is no concrete evidence directly linking them with the drug trade" (interview with author, January 10, 2007).[71] This view parallels that of Blanchard, an analyst specializing in Middle Eastern Affairs with the Congressional Research Service. In an e-mail communication received on March 8, 2005, Blanchard emphasized discussions he had with senior government officials in Kabul in January 2005. In his correspondence he presented the following argument against an Al Qaeda-drug nexus:

> As far as al Qaeda's connection to the drug trade go[es] my sources in Kabul indicated to me that the central leadership of al Qaeda considered

> becoming directly involved in the trade but ultimately decided against it based on ideological and practical reasons. Involvement would have left them vulnerable to critique by traditional Islamists opposed to drug use on religious grounds and involvement would have created new temptations/priorities for operatives as well as leaving more footprints and antagonizing new authorities in the West.

The above views were presented in Blanchard's updated report, "Afghanistan: Narcotics and U.S. Policy," released on May 26, 2005. In a follow-up phone discussion Blanchard stated that, "there is no concrete evidence directly linking Al Qaeda to the drug trade"; however, he cautioned that Al Qaeda may benefit tangentially from the trade, "because groups in the tribal areas control the smuggling routes, i.e., drugs, weapons, etc."[72] He further added that, "this is where some experts believe bin Laden is provided safe haven" (interview with author, January 10, 2007).

SYMBIOTIC RELATIONSHIPS AND THE OPIUM TRADE

In a questionnaire submitted by Dr. Svante Cornell, research director for the Central Asia-Caucasus Institute, the issue of Taliban and Al Qaeda's possible control of the drug trade was addressed. Cornell stated that prior to 9/11, "al Qaeda was not strongly involved in the drug trade in the sense of controlling it or deriving its main sources of funding from it." However, he further adds that, "it [al Qaeda] probably benefited from it tactically." An interesting point brought out by Cornell has to do with the issue of territorial control and parallels a prior statement made by Felbab-Brown (2005, p. 59). Cornell stated that since Al Qaeda is, "transnational in nature they cannot control producers to the same extent [as the Taliban] and do not want to be dependent on them" (e-mail communication, December 7, 2006). This point was also addressed by Roth, Greenburg, and Wille (2004 pp. 22–23).

As stated earlier in this chapter Mark Corcoran, ABC News foreign correspondent, has produced several documentaries inside Afghanistan. Additionally, Mr. Corcoran has extensive experience reporting from Southwest Asia. During an interview with this author on November 11, 2006, Corcoran stated that there exists a symbiotic relationship between the Taliban and drug traffickers. He asserted that the opium trade was probably the Taliban's only source of income. He also stated that Haji Bashir Noorzai, indicted and subsequently convicted in New York for importing $50 million (US) worth of heroin into the United States, was closely aligned to the Taliban both prior to and following the 9/11 attacks.[73] He explained that relationship by stating that prior to 9/11 both Haji Bashir Noorzai and the Taliban moved drugs into Iran; post-9/11 the Taliban provided protection services for Noorzai.[74] Addressing "terrorists" (al Qaeda et al.) and possible connections to drug traffickers, Concoran stated that he was told by the police chief in Kandahar that based on his [police chief] investigations there was a linkage between the two groups.

This statement took on additional significance when Concoran told the author that by 2000–2001 Al Qaeda was providing combat troops to the Taliban in the south, i.e., Kandahar.[75] Kandahar, according to Concoran, was a key operating base for Noorzai. Moreover, between 2001–2002 heroin was being smuggled in convoys with the support of Noorzai. The Taliban was passing it off to Iranian Kurds for further transport to Turkey where, according to Corcoran, the drugs were delivered to Albanian gangs. During his investigation Corcoran also learned that heroin was processed inside Afghanistan. Corcoran advised this author that this information was obtained from the Iranian revolutionary guard and the Iranian police.

Based on the statements made by Corcoran, an interesting point emerged from this interview: in Kandahar province in 2001 Al Qaeda provided troops to the Taliban, who were moving drugs for Noorzai, who was based in Kandahar. This could possibly indicate indirect Al Qaeda involvement in the drug trade, i.e., members of Al Qaeda aiding Taliban efforts to protect in-transit drug shipments.[76]

On the issue of territorial control, as discussed by Cornell (2006b) and Felbab-Brown (2005), and Al Qaeda providing troops to the Taliban (as cited by Concoran above) Galeotti (2006) in an article written for *Jane's Intelligence* Review[77] states:

> The connection between Al-Qaeda and the drug trade, while real, is much more indirect, anti-drug officials say. Al-Qaeda has neither the capacity nor, it appears, the desire to attempt to control territory in Helmand. Whereas in neighbouring Kandahar province it has established its own opium collection and smuggling operation, in Helmand it largely relies on "taxing" autonomous or associated criminal groups, according to anti-drug officials. This has been strengthened by its growing presence in the Pakistani border region of Baluchistan, where it has training and logistical centres as well as a constituency of allies and supporters. By building bridges with nationalist and criminal groups in Baluchistan, who also operate in Helmand, Al-Qaeda is able to make inroads into the province's opium trade without extensive local structures or areas under its control.[78]

Mark McDonald, former bureau chief for Knight Ridder newspapers and current professor of journalism at the University of Michigan, spent time on the Afghan-Tajik border investigating the trafficking of opiates from Afghanistan. His article, "Tajikistan at the Crossroads of the Drug Trade," was based on statements made by Major Aviz Yuldashov, head of the border guard contingent on the Afghan-Tajik border, and other security officials manning the Afghan-Tajik border whom McDonald had interviewed. Yuldashov's position is similar to the claims made by the Kandahar police chief as expressed by Corcoran above. Aviz Yuldashov sees a clear link between international terrorism and the drug trade, describing the relationship as the primary financial support mechanism for international terrorism (McDonald, 2004c).[79] According to McDonald, this claim is based on informant information received by Yuldashov and other agents working the Afghan-Tajik border.[80]

Another potential insight provided by Yuldashov was in reference to Al Qaeda. Yuldashov stated that he believes that Al Qaeda was receiving funds from various warlords. When McDonald asked him why Afghan warlords would want to help finance Al Qaeda, Yuldashov cited two reasons: Islamic solidarity and, by giving Al Qaeda and other extremist groups a tithe of the drug proceeds, these groups would stop seeking sanctuary in the regions that they (the warlords) controlled. In turn, this would reduce coalition presence and thus attacks by coalition forces.

The problem with McDonald's account from the standpoint of this research is that, according to McDonald, he had not seen any seizure or arrest data and was not certain if it indeed existed given the very low-tech, low budget operating conditions of the Tajik border guard. McDonald used the term, "very rudimentary police work" (interview with author, February 3, 2005, and November 16, 2005).

Finally, after nearly three decades of reporting and writing about events in Afghanistan and Central Asia, Ahmed Rashid takes the position that both Al Qaeda and Hezb-i-Islami (HIG) are involved in the drug business. This study has shown that this is a position he held prior to the events of 9/11. However, he informed this author during an interview that it is "very hard to prove." He claimed that there were "a number of ongoing investigations but obtaining access to this information is next to impossible." Therefore, he stated that to his knowledge "there is no empirical documentation that can be accessed which directly ties Al Qaeda to the drug trade." He notes that the drug trade involves many individuals comprising a very complex network. He further states that "these people are performing a function for the coalition and they are too influential to be arrested." Furthermore, "if some of these people were apprehended," and thereby put out of business, "it could destabilize certain provinces or districts (interview with author, May 18, 2005).

ISLAMIST GROUPS, HOLY WAR, AND THE DRUG TRADE

Some researchers who have investigated possible links between Al Qaeda and the Afghan drug trade take the position that Al Qaeda's involvement prior to 9/11 was minimal[81] in that some of its members exploited an existing criminal opportunity and used their affiliation with Al Qaeda to personally enrich themselves through a limited involvement in the trade. While not specifically addressing Al Qaeda, Stepanova (2005, p. 166) argues that Islamist groups are not naturally drawn to the drug trade or any other criminal activity for operational revenue. All terrorist organizations need money to operate. Non-Islamist or secular groups are just as likely to engage in some aspect of the illegal narcotics business as Islamist or other religious-based groups.

With respect to specific sources of financing, what separates Islamist groups from the more traditional secular organizations is the method by which the former are funded. Stepanova (2005, pp. 166,167) notes that the primary source of finance for traditional Islamist groups [82] remains charitable or religious donations (*zakat*).[83] She also notes that groups located in narcotics-producing areas or along main supply channels are more prone to engage in some aspect of the trade to finance their cause.[84] She states that Islamist groups which do participate at some level in the drug trade generally view their involvement as part of the overall struggle (jihad) and as a tool to weaken Western societies. More specifically, Stepanova asserts that there are Islamist organizations which have "degraded to semi-criminal status. . . ." She cites the Abu Sayyaf Group [85] in the Philippines and the previously mentioned Islamic Movement of Uzbekistan which she classifies as a group which combines, "criminal activities and Islamist ideology" (Stepanova, 2005, p. 168).[86]

While the Koran specifically disavows intoxicants in any form, including their production and use,[87] Osama bin Laden has been able to justify many of his actions through his interpretation of Islam. On this point Stepanova notes that, "There is no known fatwa specifically sanctioning the use of funds generated from drug smuggling and other shadow activities in a jihad against infidels" (Stepanova, 2005, p. 167).[88] Professor James Pavlin, a specialist in Islamic Studies at Rutgers University, stated, ". . . the production, sale, transportation and use of intoxicants is forbidden in Islam, there is no justification for their activities according to the Shariah" (e-mail communication, December 9, 2004).

However, the argument that Osama bin Laden would refrain from engaging in the narcotics trade or other illegal activity which had the potential to further his cause, based on religious grounds, does not hold much credibility. Osama bin Laden has often spoken of the need to use all available resources in an effort to achieve the objectives established by Al Qaeda in Sudan. Again, if we want to know what his future plans are we need to listen or read what he has said. Osama bin Laden has stated many times in various venues that his "clear strategic goal" is defeating the United States by whatever means possible. "While bin Laden may not exactly be a proponent of an 'ends justify the means' policy, he is within arm's length of it" (Scheuer, 2006b, p. 57).[89]

OTHER AVENUES OF POSSIBLE FINANCE

As stated in the previously cited reports and also in the aforementioned Rashid interview, it has been alleged that numerous charities have served to channel funds to terrorist organizations including Al Qaeda.[90] In October 2003, one of several hearings were held by the U.S. Senate Committee on Banking, Housing and Urban Affairs. These hearings addressed the subject of terrorist financing. In a statement before the committee, Jean-Charles Brisard, an investigator and an international expert on terrorist financing, cited evidence compiled by several countries on behalf of the 9/11 victims' families. The hearing transcript reveals that—according to Brisard—the evidence gathered during the aforementioned investigation implies that Al Qaeda is heavily financed by wealthy Saudi businessmen and bankers. He also claimed that various Saudi charities served as fronts for terrorist organizations.[91] Brisard further stated that during the course of their investigation:

> We recovered thousands of documents from Saudi charities which are archives of Al Qaeda, showing their involvement in every stage of terrorism, acting as an umbrella, safe houses, and even military bases for Al Qaeda operatives, to the point of creating a symbolic relationship with the terrorist organization through its resources, management, members or facilities. Charities have, for example, provided military training for Al Qaeda terrorists. From intelligence sources, the investigation of the September 11 families established that 10 terrorist training camps in Afghanistan have been funded by Saudi charities. The International Islamic Relief Organization funded at least six terrorist training camps, including the Darunta camp, a facility used for chemical and biological weapons testing. Others, such as the Muslim World League and the Saudi Red Crescent, were part of an Al Qaeda financial committee (Brisard, 2003, p. 71).[92]

In addition to charities and wealthy financiers there is some evidence which indicates that Al Qaeda "sleeper cells" located in many countries throughout the world operate legitimate businesses to support themselves and help finance operations (Levitt, 2002, p. 43). Indeed, Osama bin Laden and his Al Qaeda organization have been able to build a sophisticated and resilient financial and support network which has been extremely difficult to penetrate (Gunaratna, 2002, p. 61).[93] Since the events of 9/11 many Saudi-based charities have been and are currently being investigated by numerous international agencies relative to allegations that a portion of their donated revenue was supporting various terrorist organizations either overtly or covertly (GAO, 2003, p. 15).[94]

AL QAEDA-DRUG TRAFFICKERS NEXUS: NARCOTICS REVENUE OR SMUGGLING ROUTES

It may be true that in the period following 9/11 members of Al Qaeda provided protection to drug traffickers for personal enrichment or to gain access to various smuggling corridors for moving money, men, and arms.

It has been previously established that during the period 1997–2001 Al Qaeda provided the Taliban with fighters (al Qaeda's 055 Brigade) during their battle with Northern Alliance forces. It has also been established that Mullah Muhammad Omar ordered Osama bin Laden to relocate from Jalalabad to Kandahar in 1997.[95] Therefore, it is not inconceivable that the Taliban opium security/protection detail could have included Al Qaeda fighters.[96] In September 2001, an article in the *New York Times* citing information received from "two senior Congressional aides with access to intelligence reports" stated that Osama bin Laden supplied men to provide security for heroin processing labs and protect, "drug convoys" (Gordon and Schmitt, 2001, p. B4).[97]

The Haji Bashir Noorzai investigation and subsequent indictment, trial, and conviction revealed that the Taliban were providing protection to Noorzai's drug convoys and labs in exchange for manpower, weapons, and other war materiel in Kandahar, Noorzai's base of operations. Additionally, Haji Baz Mohammad—who was allied to the Taliban and controlled opium production in Afghanistan's Nangarhar province—and Haji Juma Khan, both major drug traffickers, were arrested and subsequently indicted in the United States for providing material support to the Taliban in exchange for protection of opium, conversion labs, and smuggling routes; this provides further evidence of Taliban complicity in the drug trade.[98] These smuggling channels may indeed have been used by Al Qaeda forces to transfer men and equipment.

As far as senior level Al Qaeda direct involvement in the drug trade there are several possibilities. First, just because the intelligence community does not have evidence linking certain actors to a given series of events does not mean that the actors in question are not involved. It only means that it is not possible to confirm or negate the alleged involvement of certain individuals or groups. Second, it could also be true that the intelligence community may indeed have specific knowledge which links certain actors to these events but for a reason or reasons unknown it is not being shared with the general public.

Interestingly, the international media cite various incidents where U.S. forces seized drugs during combat operations with Al Qaeda and/or Taliban forces. These articles were published by separate news agencies over a two-year period. Moreover, the author of one of these reports confirmed its accuracy during an interview with this author.[99]

If an Al Qaeda-drug nexus were empirically established this would in effect alter the measures that have been recently implemented as part of the revised ISAF Afghanistan strategy since this involvement would more than likely be in the Pakistani tribal areas. To date such involvement has not been empirically established in the open sources.

However, if it can be established that Afghan drug profits are supporting Al Qaeda in the tribal areas, then engaging the drug situation would present ISAF with an additional front that would most likely entail a military component. Given the complexities of the opium trade in Afghanistan, such an eventuality would more than likely expand the present insurgency to include various factions of the rural population that depend upon opium for their livelihood.[100]

Former director of the Office of National Drug Control Policy in the Clinton administration and current professor at West Point, General Barry McCaffrey (U.S Army, retired), upon his return from the region, stated, "Is there a relationship between $2 billion in this impoverished 14th-century desperate land, and the appearance of brand-new guns and shiny camping gear? Of course there is . . . "The article goes on to state:

> The larger problem, emphasized the general, are the unmistakable signs that opium and heroin money is energizing both Al Qaeda and the Taliban in Afghanistan, and widening the drug trade into the Persian Gulf and Iraq (Behn, 2005, p. A07).[101]

Based on this author's research in the open sources, evidence linking the Al Qaeda leadership directly to the Afghan drug trade is anecdotal and speculative. However, the Taliban and others allied with them are indeed profiting financially from the drug trade.

CONCLUSION

While questions of direct senior-level Al Qaeda involvement in the opium trade cannot be substantiated with any degree of certainty it is clear by the testimony and statements of key individuals with on-site experience and events, which have occurred on the ground in Afghanistan, that the Taliban are indeed deriving financial benefit from the trade, particularly in the southern provinces where poppy cultivation has expanded in direct proportion to an upsurge in anti-coalition activity.[102]

How much revenue finds its way into the Taliban "war chest" is open to speculation and debate. However, based on current available data such as the aforementioned Shaw (2006) report, it appears that the considerable revenue the Taliban received from the opium trade prior to October 2001 has shifted from the Taliban to regional and provincial commanders (warlords), drug traders (mafias), organized crime, and criminal groups which include local, provincial, and national government officials. Indeed the evidence suggests[103] that an unholy alliance between drugs, criminals, insurgents/terrorists, and various political institutions and actors currently exists in Afghanistan. Moreover, opium provides political currency to warlords, corrupt government officials, and Taliban-led insurgents.

CHAPTER 8

The Drug Trade in Afghanistan: A Complex System

THE AFGHAN OPIUM TRADE: A COMPLEX SYSTEM

Very little is known regarding the internal dynamics of terrorist and drug trafficking groups. Accessible (open-source) information often focuses on the external activity of these groups and this is often subject to speculation and misleading information.

In the current effort it would appear that, due in part to its clandestine nature, the "complexity" of the Afghan opium trade makes it very difficult to draw specific and precise propositions regarding the involvement of certain non-state and state actors. In a broader sense, this may apply to the operational characteristics of many complex organizational networks such as Al Qaeda in that the more decentralized and amorphous it becomes, its "complexity" increases, thereby making it very difficult to predict its behavior and future actions. Fay (1996, pp. 214–215) notes that judgments, which examine all of the available evidence including rival explanations, can be objective[1] in the sense that they were reached utilizing "available and relevant procedures for obtaining and weighing evidence" yet not garner universal acceptance or for that matter guarantee that judgments reached through this process are true.[2] However, this is not a basis for concluding that previous and present assumptions and propositions put forth to describe the purported nexus carry equal weight or are based on an in-depth examination of the issue.

NETWORK OF NETWORKS

The drug trade—whether in Afghanistan, Myanmar, Colombia or the Tri-border region of South America—is made up of a complex network of national and international actors. The role of terrorists/insurgents in the drug trade cannot be isolated from other drivers. The picture is large and very complex.[3] The forces that are shaping and benefiting from the drug trade in Afghanistan comprise many different groups and individuals with similar and also diverse motivations. This study has also shown that since the early 1980s the drug trade in Afghanistan has played a dominant role in that country's social and economic fabric, has been nurtured by ongoing conflict, and—concomitantly—has provided the economic resources to perpetuate and sustain it. The available evidence indicates that the primary agricultural commodity in that country, the opium poppy, has also undergone a not so gradual and indeed profound rebirth which was initiated by the U.S.-led invasion and the near simultaneous decision to utilize former commanders, mujahideen, and other assets from the 1980s Soviet-Afghan war in U.S. and coalition initial efforts to expel Taliban and Al Qaeda forces from Afghanistan.[4]

As recent Afghan history has shown, the common variable between pre- and post-9/11 is the continuation and expansion of the opium trade—notwithstanding the July 2000 ban. This lucrative commodity has spearheaded a criminal economy which has attracted both domestic and international criminals; corrupted public officials, local commanders, and warlords; supported terrorists and the facilities which trained them; and provided revenue for arms and other weaponry for terrorists, insurgents, criminal factions, and others intent on maintaining an environment of chaos. Indeed, the drug trade continues to promote an atmosphere of violence and lawlessness and thus is conducive to the often narrow self-serving interest of those cited above.[5]

Opium production prior to the Taliban ban, and immediately following the invasion and initial defeat of Taliban and Al Qaeda forces, indicates that other factions were not only operational but served as the catalyst for the revival and subsequent expansion of opium cultivation and processing. Indeed, opium production surged to record levels in the years following the invasion.[6]

This study was undertaken to examine various non-state actors in Afghanistan and their possible relationship with the opium trade.[7] This was done in order to achieve a broader understanding of the dynamics of this enterprise.[8] Conversely, understanding the intricacies inherent in clandestine associations is at best a difficult endeavor. The drug industry in Afghanistan is supported by a complex network comprising adaptable and unpredictable links between constituent groups with divergent long-term objectives but short-term reciprocal interests. The drug trade by design breeds symbiotic and often strange alliances among disparate factions including state political actors.

Concerning possible Pakistani involvement in the trade, during the Soviet-Afghan war heroin became an economic mainstay of the Pakistani government and a major revenue producer which helped finance the war effort. Narcotics production and heroin conversion labs in Baluchistan and the North-West Frontier Province have a long history, dating back to the early 1980s when the area was flooded with Afghan refugees (Harshe, 2003, p. 3622).

This region is known for weapons, drugs, and licit commodity smuggling.[9] The literature shows that there is a clear nexus between arms purchases and drug profits.[10]

Pakistan, opium, and Afghanistan have been enmeshed since the early 1980s. According to Goodson (2000, p. 121), during that decade local drug merchants with links to international criminal networks fostered and encouraged the production of poppy in the border region.[11] Regarding the Pakistani-supported Taliban movement and its impact on the state, Goodson (2000, p. 123) notes:

> Talibanized Islamism is a virulent social movement in Pakistan. It espouses an ideology of intolerance and hatred, is enforced by the weapons of Kalashnikovization, and is funded by foreign interests and narcotics traffic. The rise of the militant religious right has combined the worst legacies of Pakistan's adventurist Afghan policy of the 1990s to create severe disorder in Pakistani politics and civil society.

Pakistan has had and continues to maintain a relationship with various Islamist factions through the intelligence and military services. Elements within the ISI and the Pakistani military have provided logistical and military support to various extremist factions, and since the 1980s have used the drug trade to finance insurgent efforts against the Indian government.[12] Moreover, if recent reports of Al Qaeda and Taliban forces taking up sanctuary in Karachi are true, this could have only been possible with the full knowledge of the ISI and possibly hands-on assistance from organized criminals—specifically Dawood Ibrahim who has purportedly been based there since 1994 and whose illegal activities include drugs and the trafficking of persons.[13]

This symbiotic relationship between the ISI and Islamist militants became a tool of Pakistani policy in Kashmir and Punjab throughout the 1990s. During the present conflict in Afghanistan and the turmoil in Pakistan, these organizations have attracted other would-be jihadists into a movement whose tentacles span the globe. Pakistan, the epicenter of this movement, is becoming increasingly vulnerable to Islamist indoctrination especially in the border regions, areas occupied by Afghan and Pakistani Taliban[14], Al Qaeda, and other foreign Islamists. These areas are also home to numerous madrassas where radical indoctrination of new recruits occurs and support for existing groups of extremists exists.

During the course of this research, information was uncovered which pointed to alleged corruption of public officials and agencies within the Afghan government.[15] This could have a direct impact on the terror-drug nexus question. For example, if officials within the present government are indeed involved in the drug trade, a number of interesting questions arise, e.g., what specific individuals and/or agencies are involved, what is the extent of involvement, and who are they involved with? Moreover, are bribes being paid to elicit silence or to circumvent legal channels or sanctions, or does this involvement include "hands-on" participation? Does involvement reach the provincial or national level, or is it confined to specific districts and low-level officials? Furthermore, does this relationship with criminal elements tangentially involve an indirect alliance with terrorists/insurgents, specifically in reference to the southern provinces—a Taliban stronghold and nerve center of the Afghan drug trade?

Thus, an expansion of the original theoretical framework was necessary to inform discussion of the corruption factor as it relates to the possible role of public officials in Afghanistan's opium trade. Most importantly, an examination of other relevant actors may shed additional insights into the opium trade and offer additional and/or alternative interpretations on possible insurgent/terrorist involvement which is the primary focus of this study.

In reference to official Afghanistan government involvement in the opium trade, the evidence seems to indicate that some high-level Afghan public officials, local commanders, and police are working in concert with various drug criminals who themselves may be linked to various insurgent factions.[16] Government and public safety workers profit by taking an active role in the trade (e.g., protection of labs and transport) or are compensated by turning a blind eye to the activity. This activity is most evident in the Ministry of Interior (MoI), responsible for counter-narcotics operations, and the Afghan National Police (ANP).[17] Often these criminal-political alliances are formed out of opportunity, convenience, or coercion.

Indeed, endemic corruption and crime is deeply embedded in the Afghan drug economy. Afghanistan's criminal groups, having international contacts and alliances with other powerful criminal organizations and distribution networks, are often supported and protected by politicians, regional warlords, and members of law enforcement.[18] Additionally, turf battles over opium and the land used to grow it create a dangerous and oftentimes distracting and destabilizing element which provides insurgents and terrorist factions with large ungoverned areas from which they can plan, stage, and conduct offensive action against Afghan and coalition forces and terrorize domestic as well as Afghan-based international entities.

Other players are local, regional, and international criminal groups within Afghanistan and other states that serve as transit corridors. Although criminals and insurgents/terrorists have different strategic objectives, ad hoc alliances between the two undermines the present government and hence promotes the long-term goals of each. For example, violent acts by criminal groups against government eradication teams and coalition forces are designed to insure that the illegal enterprise they are engaged in continues. Criminals also gain by the instability caused by insurgents' and terrorists' control over opium-rich territory, which allows them safe passage to move their contraband.

Terrorists, such as Al Qaeda, the Haqqani network,[19] and the Taliban benefit from the resulting chaos by the further destabilization of the region which forces coalition troops to expend time and resources against drug criminals and others who are attempting to further limit the authority and legitimacy of the central government. Insurgent forces and terrorists, specifically the Taliban and their allies, gain revenue by controlling territory where opium is produced, encouraging cultivation—albeit by threats and intimidation, and providing protection to drug entrepreneurs and traffickers.

More than 90 percent of the world's opium is cultivated in Afghanistan (BBC News, November 28, 2006b). The drug trade in Afghanistan operates on the basic principle of supply and demand. The demand for opium and its derivatives, primarily heroin, is global. An enterprise of this magnitude is not unlike other major global conglomerates. Multinational corporations require the expertise and participation of many diverse actors engaged in various roles—a network of networks drawn together for a common purpose: the generation of profit and the expansion of corporate power.[20]

UNODC seizure data for opiates[21] indicates involvement of international criminal networks, since it would take a transnational network to move the product from Afghanistan into Russia, Europe, Africa, the Middle East, Oceania, and to a lesser degree North America. This amalgamation of global actors may be ideologically diverse. Some of these groups are pure criminals, others terrorists, and some as embodied by the IMU prior to 9/11, an amalgamation of the two. The global trade in narcotics could not function or proliferate without the cooperation, albeit short-term mutually beneficial alliances, of many actors, some with ancillary motives in addition to profit. For the criminal and corrupt politician—money and power; for terrorists' ideological convictions drive behavior, although individual members may seek to exploit various opportunities for self-enrichment. For armed groups engaged in an insurgency or other forms of armed conflict, drugs provide a revenue source for weapons purchases, recruitment of fighters, the expansion of territorial control, and political capital with the rural population.

Hence, the violent and destabilizing activities of both groups merge into a mutually beneficial alliance which seeks to further destabilize the government and thwart attempts to create a democratic society based on the rule of law. In an environment which lacks security and has been rife with lawlessness for three decades, cooperation between political, criminal, and ideologically-motivated groups is in many respects the natural order of things.[22]

Armed groups in Afghanistan operate in an environment conducive to mutual cooperation. *Jane's Intelligence Review* reports that drug barons have established a complex system of protection which includes police and government officials mostly at the provincial level (Wright, 2006, pp. 6–7). The direct involvement of government officials—including members of the ANP—in drug trafficking, and others who are paid bribes to turn a blind eye to the activity, has undermined government and NATO/ISAF efforts at establishing security, has strengthened the insurgency, and has provided the Taliban and its allies a certain degree of legitimacy. According to *Jane's*, the Taliban are provided shelter, food, revenue, transportation, and satellite phones, and in a quid pro quo type of arrangement protect drug convoys and farmers from eradication teams (Wright, 2006, p. 10).

The inability of the central government to exert control over large swathes of Afghan territory provides a favorable environment which contributes to and furthers a symbiotic relationship between terrorist/insurgent factions and drug criminals. This creates a more lethal insurgency as both groups with often diverse ambitions and objectives fight against a common enemy. Therefore, from an operational standpoint, both groups out of tactical necessity further the objectives of the other in a mutually beneficial alliance. The various organizations and actors comprising the opium trade in Afghanistan are an integral part of the global jihadist movement either by design or happenstance. Terrorist organizations operating in Afghanistan and Pakistan can be viewed as a consortium of like-minded militants, ideologically inseparable and part of the same global movement. In addition to sharing a similar ideological mindset, these groups often share men, materiel, training regimens, logistical and financial resources, and key transportation routes, thus maintaining an active support and supply infrastructure which benefits all factions.

Additionally, evidence indicates that funding for terrorist infrastructure comes from numerous sources and is not solely dependent upon the drug trade or other criminal activity.[23] For example, Al Qaeda and the Taliban were able to reestablish themselves in Pakistan's tribal belt following their initial defeat with no evidence that the drug trade in Afghanistan played a significant role in their ability to reconstitute. Moreover, the drug trade skyrocketed in the period following the October 2001 invasion (UNODC 2003a). This indicates that the above cited organizations were not necessary players in the overall success of Afghanistan's opium industry; therefore, one could conclude that they did not control the trade prior to or following the events of 9/11.[24] Furthermore, if they did not control the trade, then other entities were operating to insure the continuation and expansion of this illicit enterprise.

The opium trade in Afghanistan had been in place since the Soviet-Afghan war and has expanded and become more entrenched in the economic fabric of the country since that time. The Taliban inherited the trade and opened up supply routes which had been previously controlled by warlords and criminals trying to exploit cross-border trade.[25] However, the Taliban did play a supporting role in the ongoing process as opium cultivation increased significantly under their rule.[26]

Evidence also suggests that in the post-9/11 period the Taliban reversed their stand (2000 ban) on poppy cultivation and are now encouraging farmers to grow the crop.[27] This is often accomplished through threats, intimidation, and violence. Moreover, investigative reports and statements by senior NATO/ISAF military officials have illustrated that there is a strong link between the Taliban insurgency, members of terrorist groups, and the opium trade in the southern and southeastern provinces where poppy is most abundant.[28] The insurgency comprises a number of different groups both terrorist and criminal.[29] As stated previously, drug smuggling corridors have no doubt been used by Al Qaeda and the Taliban to transport fighters and weapons to Afghan and Pakistani-based Islamist groups.[30] Furthermore, foreign Islamists based in Pakistan constitute an important component in Taliban efforts throughout Afghanistan's southern provinces and portions of the east.

AL QAEDA-DRUG NEXUS: OVERVIEW OF FINDINGS

After conducting an evaluation and analysis of the documentary and interview data compiled in this study, including the statements and arguments of U.S. congressional witnesses, trial testimony, government and non-government officials, investigative reports, and those with on-site knowledge regarding the situation in Afghanistan, it appears that much of the basis for believing that a direct linkage between Al Qaeda and drugs in Afghanistan exists is based upon the following facts.

First, Afghanistan began its dominance as a major global supplier of opium and its derivatives during the Soviet-Afghan war. Secondly, opium poppy cultivation continued its expansion through the civil war period up to and including the Taliban ascendancy period; in fact cultivation doubled during their reign. Moreover, the Taliban have been drawing revenue from, and involved in some aspect of the opium trade since 1996. Third, the Al Qaeda organization has been in Afghanistan since May 1996 and began developing a symbiotic relationship with the Taliban, specifically Mullah Muhammad Omar, in September of that year. Fourth, due to the Taliban's support of terrorist groups and training facilities operating in territory under their control, ideological similarities with Al Qaeda, the close relationship between the Taliban and Osama bin Laden during the years 1996–2001, and their similar modus operandi Al Qaeda has at least benefitted indirectly from the opium trade through Taliban involvement in the major poppy producing southern and southeastern provinces.

Finally, in or around 1998, the intelligence community was open to the possibility that Osama bin Laden was actively pursuing a nuclear component, and therefore the assumption was that heroin may have been part of the negotiating equation. For many public officials and media outlets the events of 9/11 followed by the continued refusal on the part of Taliban officials to turn Osama bin Laden over to the United States for prosecution further tied Al Qaeda to the Taliban militia. Moreover, the fact that opium cultivation doubled during the Taliban years with a record crop in 1999 followed by a ban that many regarded as an attempt to drive up the price of opium, fueled speculation regarding the nature of their relationship. Hence, many international journalists and public officials increased their focus and concomitant reporting on these two groups, ultimately concluding that Al Qaeda and the Taliban were essentially a single entity; therefore, both were benefiting substantially from the lucrative narcotics trade in Afghanistan.

Direct evidence in the form of testimony by expert witnesses was evaluated and determined to be informative in regard to the general issue of drugs and terrorism but lacked supporting evidence relative to Osama bin Laden or Al Qaeda involvement in Afghanistan's drug trade. Furthermore, some of these statements regarding a direct link between terrorists—specifically Al Qaeda—and the opium trade, may have been made to serve a politically-motivated agenda spawned by the events of 9/11. This study finds that there is no documented evidence in the open-source literature which directly ties Osama bin Laden or the top-tier leadership of Al Qaeda to the drug trade before or after 9/11.[31] Some media reports and government officials have alleged that Osama bin Laden is the world's principal supplier of heroin.[32] This would indicate that Osama bin Laden and his Taliban hosts had controlling interests in the trade, which is an oversimplification of the drug problem in that country. Based on available evidence, or lack thereof, in the open-source literature these claims are simply untrue. It is unlikely that Al Qaeda would be inclined to participate directly in an activity inside Afghanistan which had the potential to draw the attention of NATO/ ISAF and Afghan government forces thus jeopardizing their long-term objectives.

It is also unlikely that Osama bin Laden and his deputy, Ayman al Zawahiri, would form financial alliances with groups which did not share their radical views. This is not to imply that individual members of the group or individuals who share similar goals would not seize an opportunity for personal enrichment. However, as a matter of policy, it is highly unlikely that Osama bin Laden and/or his immediate associates would become directly involved in a high-profile illegal activity. Additionally, available open-source information indicates the contrary, or at the very least judgment on this issue needs to be suspended until further information becomes available.[33] Direct involvement could certainly have a negative impact on Al Qaeda's long-range regional and global ambitions cited below:

- The creation and deployment of an international jihadist force
- Remove U.S. forces and allies from the Middle East
- Replace existing regimes considered "apostate"
- Establish a caliphate throughout the Middle East, North Africa, and Asia
- Spread their ideology throughout the world

Evidence suggests that following the U.S.-led invasion certain groups and individuals allied to Al Qaeda became involved in the expanding drug trade.[34] While empirical evidence directly tying Osama bin Laden to the drug trade is lacking, what is apparent and indeed has been espoused by him on numerous occasions in various venues is his hatred of the West, particularly the United States, and his desire and indeed his obsession to engage in global jihad to right the centuries-long wrongs (whether real or perceived) that have been perpetrated by Western powers against Muslims. He has stated that he would strive to attain this goal by all available means. His 1998 fatwa calling for the establishment of the International Islamic Front for Jihad Against the Jews and Crusaders effectively was a declaration of war.[35]

What he does seek and considers to be an important goal of his long-term ambition of defeating the West and establishing an Islamic caliphate throughout the greater Middle East and beyond has been previously noted in this study and stated by al Zawahiri[36] on a number of occasions: a pure Islamic state, a country governed and based on a strict interpretation of the Koran. This reality was almost achieved in Afghanistan prior to October 2001.

Many open-source reports, which cite a direct Osama bin Laden link to the Afghan drugs trade, have originated in the international media or from an unconfirmed "security source."[37] These claims have often served as a source of many allegations and statements made by senior-level government and non-government officials. However, these reports often lack corroborating information and therefore their credibility becomes questionable. Nevertheless, indirect links tying Osama bin Laden to the drug trade vis-à-vis the Taliban though fragmented are compelling reasons to conclude that either he or members of his organization as it existed prior to 9/11 were involved at some level in the narcotics trade in Afghanistan.

If Osama bin Laden is personally involved in the drug trade he has probably coordinated this activity through various operatives and intermediaries.

This would not be beyond the realm of possibilities. Historically, his modus operandi has been that of a facilitator or catalyst rather than a direct hands-on conspirator. For example, anecdotal information exists that Osama bin Laden encouraged the Taliban to export heroin to the West. This information was apparently picked up by the U.S. National Security Agency (NSA) in an intercepted message that Osama bin Laden placed from his satellite phone (Campbell, 2001, p. 1).

Notwithstanding the lack of corroboratory information, the account provided above is very important given the response of former senator, Joseph Biden (D-Delaware). As cited in chapter 3, then Senator Biden—during a U.S. Senate hearing conducted on May 20, 2003, which focused on the global terror-drug nexus—made the following statement:

> What bothers me about your collective testimony, not any of you individually, is everybody knows that is for sure one of the revenue streams for the Taliban, particularly in the Pashtun area, and in turn Al–Qaeda, although we don't know for certain. None of you know enough to tell me. The intelligence community doesn't know enough to tell me. We don't know even what we don't know . . . (Biden, 2003, p. 24)

This is a powerful statement. Certainly if the aforementioned report citing an NSA intercept of Osama bin Laden encouraging the Taliban to export more heroin to the West had any basis in fact it most surely should have been made part of the hearing record or at the very least one would think that Senator Biden would have had access to this information which was reported in the media 20 months prior to this hearing.

Even more powerful is the statement, "there is ample evidence that Islamic extremists such as Usama Bin Ladin use profits from the drug trade to support their terror campaign," made by former CIA director George Tenet (Senate Select Committee on Intelligence, February 2, 2000) three years prior to the above cited U.S. Senate Judiciary hearing and 17 months prior to 9/11. Since the Tenet statement was made in an open hearing, it should have been made part of the official record in the May 2003 U.S. Senate hearing or at the very least the statement should have been cited by those conducting the hearing.[38]

Concerning the NSA intercept mentioned above, there are two possibilities: the report is true or it is not true. Moreover, if this piece of reporting is true then it could possibly suggest that the Taliban were involved in aspects of the trade which exceeded taxation. The statement suggests that they were possibly involved in trafficking as well or at the very least exercised control over quantities produced, smuggling corridors, and possibly destination points. Furthermore, if this intercept did occur it could possibly imply a nexus, albeit one of convenience between the Taliban and international criminal elements.

Secondly, if this intercept occurred then it also speaks to the nature of the Al Qaeda-Taliban relationship, i.e., it further corroborates information that Osama bin Laden had some input into Taliban policies and activities. While this communication does not directly implicate Osama bin Laden in the drug trade, it does reveal what others have pointed out—that he views Western consumption of narcotics as a way of weakening and destroying infidels and therefore justifiable and part of the overall jihad.

The argument by some that in the process of harming Westerners Afghan opium is destroying the lives of countless numbers of Muslims would not be a valid argument against Osama bin Laden's alleged support for this action. This view is based on some of his statements regarding secular Arab states[39] and the fact that in many attacks in which Al Qaeda was involved the collateral damage included Muslims and other non-Westerners. Finally, if the information regarding the intercept is valid, then it also supports the argument that Osama bin Laden had an indirect rather than a "hands on" role in the opium trade. Nevertheless, without having more specific source information it is impossible to conclude that the above anecdotal information is nothing more than uncertain and unverifiable speculation. Another piece of evidence which provides additional insight into Al Qaeda operations prior to 9/11 is the report released by Judicial Watch in October 2004.[40]

Furthermore, it is conceivable that information linking Osama bin Laden directly to the drug trade is available in the classified information even though the 9/11 Commission stated that at present no such evidence exists (Roth, Greenburg and Wille, 2004, p. 19).[41] Post-9/11investigations, including the aforementioned, have revealed that there is much we do not know about the organizational and operational structure and sources of finance of various terrorist groups.[42]

This point was made during a July 31, 2003 U.S. Senate hearing which discussed the Saudi role in financing various extremist factions. During this hearing Jonathan Winer of Alston and Bird, a U.S. law firm serving national as well as international clientele, made the following statement: "Saudi Arabia has been the most significant source of terrorist funds for Al-Qaeda."[43] In his opening remarks Senator Norm Coleman (R-Minnesota) asked John Pistole, acting assistant director for counterterrorism, Federal Bureau of Investigation, if he agreed with Mr. Winer's assessment regarding Saudi Arabia's possible role as a leading financier of Al Qaeda. Mr. Pistole's response was:

> . . . the FBI does not have enough intelligence or law enforcement information to agree or disagree with that. There is obviously a tremendous amount of money that has flown through NGOs and charitable organizations. As

> Mr. Newcomb mentioned, the question is how much of that has gone specifically for terrorist activity. And in limited situations, we can document that, and I can tell you affirmatively, yes, that this money has gone for this act. But to trace it from the government to a particular terrorist, I can not sit here and tell you that has been done (Pistole 2003, p. 17).[44]

Post-9/11 reports which merge Al Qaeda, the Taliban, and drugs do little to determine the extent or degree of possible Al Qaeda involvement. Moreover, the argument which directly links Osama bin Laden to the drug trade by virtue of his association with the Taliban lacks credibility.[45]

Certainly if the claim made by some that Al Qaeda is deriving substantial funding from heroin trafficking were true, then it would seem that this activity was taking place across the border in Pakistan's tribal areas where Al Qaeda is based thereby minimizing risks of detection and possible capture of Al Qaeda operatives. This study concludes that allegations of Al Qaeda drawing revenue from traffickers as they transit Pakistani territory in the Khyber PakhtunKhwa cannot be substantiated.

However, a case can be made through compelling circumstantial evidence that Al Qaeda was from 1997–2001, involved in an indirect capacity.[46] The circumstantial evidence consists of opportunity, motive, ability, and documented patterns of conduct prior to 1996.[47] Evidence also indicates that Al Qaeda has and continues to utilize other non-state factions, both criminal and terrorist, to further its objectives.

Finally, the testimony and statements of various government officials, members of academia, and other private sector "experts" who have studied and researched Osama bin Laden's possible revenue sources reveal a financially amorphous and savvy organization. Based on formal investigative efforts such as the 9/11 Commission and statements by knowledgeable individuals who have dedicated much time and effort investigating the financial network of Al Qaeda, two points stand out. First, much remains to be known relative to terrorist financing and Al Qaeda in particular.[48] However, based on what is known, it is apparent that neither Osama bin Laden nor his organization required active participation in the Afghan drug trade to generate operational revenue. Second, Osama bin Laden had and continues to have wide support throughout the Muslim world[49] and among global Muslim diaspora. Much of this support was generated in the 1980s during the Soviet-Afghan war. That said, there has been some post-9/11 evidence which suggest that rogue elements either within his organization or operating under the Al Qaeda banner have seized the opportunity provided by the lucrative opium trade to enrich themselves by participating at the protection and/or transport stages of the process.

EVIDENCE-BASED LINKAGES

Furthermore, this study finds that there is a direct link between the opium trade and terrorist groups such as the Taliban, the Islamic Movement of Uzbekistan, and rogue members of Osama bin Laden's International Islamic Front. Drug involvement has included activity in the cultivation process through refinery and transportation protection services. This study has shown that prior to 9/11 the Taliban collected revenue by taxing the trade and providing protection services to Haji Bashir Noorzai, Haji Juma Khan, and Baz Mohammad, all of whom were Afghanistan-based drug traffickers. All three individuals have been arrested and indicted in U.S. federal court in New York.[50] According to U.S. Attorney Michael Garcia the evidence which led to the indictment of Baz Mohammad shows a direct link between him and the Taliban but does not directly implicate Al Qaeda. Furthermore, the Taliban continue to reap financial benefits by imposing taxes on the trade and in some instances controlling production in the areas that they control or maintain a substantial presence.[51] Documentary evidence indicates that Taliban involvement has taken many forms e.g., coercion, night letters, offers of protection from crop elimination, and quid pro quo security arrangements with farmers and local commanders, especially in the southern and southeastern provinces.[52]

The opium trade provides terrorist and insurgent factions more than operational revenue. It gives them power and influence over the population that they have been able to infiltrate and coerce. Since opium is the agricultural crop, which provides a ready cash income and access to much needed credit, the Taliban, in the areas that they control, are able to draw significant political capital and legitimacy from all aspects of the process: cultivation, refinement, and transportation. Additionally, drug money has allowed the Taliban to recruit new fighters and afford to compensate them at a higher rate than the average member of the Afghan National Army.[53]

This study also finds that there is a geographic linkage based on territorial control as both groups often share the same well-established logistical (smuggling) routes to transport not only drugs but fighters, arms, and other war materiel.[54] As McGirk (2004, p. 41) notes, "AQ [al Qaeda] also relies on drug smugglers, particularly along the Iranian-Baluch border, to move from one country to another." In addition to providing safe passage to Afghan- and Pakistan-based insurgents, this interaction with criminal elements may also serve to provide insurgent and terrorist forces valuable intelligence regarding troop movements and coalition counterinsurgency activity in specific areas. Additionally, traffickers often create instability and turmoil in an attempt to further weaken the ability of state law enforcement agencies to hinder or obstruct their illegal operations (Kleiman, 2004, p. 5).[55] Moreover, the areas where the

Taliban insurgency is most entrenched are the principal poppy producing areas, namely Helmand and Kandahar provinces.[56] Prior to 9/11 the Taliban, supported by members of Al Qaeda, provided protection services to drug convoys and processing labs.

In regard to the Taliban and other Pakistani-based extremist groups rogue elements within the ISI and Pakistan's military establishment have been and continue to support various militant groups including the Taliban[57] Moreover, according to U.S. Congressional testimony, the ISI has had an ongoing relationship with drug lords.[58] This relationship had its genesis in the Soviet-Afghan war and has been reported in various publications such as the *Washington Post* (1994) and *The Nation* as early as 1988. The Pakistani government is unable or unwilling to exert control over these groups. While Pakistani efforts against Al Qaeda have yielded some success, the group is still able to direct and provide guidance to various affiliates throughout the world.[59]

Finally, the nature of Islamist terrorism has changed. This evolutionary process began in the 1980s at the end of the Soviet-Afghan war and has morphed into a global movement whose ideology rather than its leadership serves as a catalyst for "'global jihad." Likewise, the Taliban has become more radicalized since their ascendancy in the late 1990s and today both groups and the ideology they espouse pose not only a direct threat to Afghanistan and Pakistan but have the potential to further destabilize Central and Southwest Asia.[60]

Additionally, credible reports show that the Taliban are deriving funds from the cultivation of opium, particularly in the southern and southeastern provinces, areas that are currently under their direct or partial control. It has also been shown that the opium trade has provided them with a tremendous amount of political capital and legitimacy.[61] This study has shown that the insurgency comprises many factions, which have been lumped under the rubric Taliban.[62] To the extent that some Al Qaeda operatives are part of the insurgency, and evidence from onsite military officials indicates that they are, they too are deriving indirect benefits from this source of funding.

This is not a new phenomenon; insurgency and drugs have a long history.[63] According to Cornell (2007, p. 208), "the bulk of the global cultivation of opium and coca is taking place in conflict zones, while the trafficking of their derivatives has come to heavily involve insurgent and terrorist groups operating between the source and destination areas of illicit drugs." Indeed, the evidence suggests that the Northern Alliance profited from opium during their struggle with the Taliban. Evidence also indicates that when the Taliban instituted their ban in July 2000 this ban did not extend to northeast Afghanistan—specifically Badakhshan province, an area controlled by Northern Alliance forces—nor did the ban affect existing stockpiles and the transporting and sale of the drug.[64]

Evidence linking the Taliban to the Afghan drug trade was presented in part by the former head of the U.S. DEA, Asa Hutchinson (2001, p. 13) and the U. S. State Department's William Bach[65] and Michael Sheehan[66] among others during U.S. Congressional venues. This study also provided corroborating information relative to Taliban involvement in the opium trade by Rohan Gunaratna[67] and Ahmed Rashid,[68] two leading authorities on the Taliban. While their views on the extent of involvement differed, both ascertained that indeed the Taliban derived funding from the cultivation, production, and transport of opium and its derivatives. It is also questionable that this was their primary source of funding. Evidence indicates that they received income by imposing taxes on other commodities as well. A study conducted by the World Bank (1999) concluded that the Taliban derived significant income from "large scale regional contraband of regular goods" (Transnational Institute, 2001, p. 8).[69] Additionally, according to World Bank calculations for the year 1997, this enterprise was estimated to generate revenue of $2.5 (US) billion from which it is estimated that the Taliban received approximately $75 million (US) from cross-border smuggling operation (UNODCCP, 2001, p. 41). Additionally, this study has shown that prior to 9/11 Al Qaeda was providing revenue and other services to the Taliban. Furthermore, Osama bin Laden, through his long-established contacts, was able to generate revenue from a wide range of sources.[70]

In order to address the principal question presented in this research it was important to address the nature and definition of terrorism and examine various Afghan-based groups to determine if they indeed fit the definition as stated in chapter 1. In this regard chapter 5 illustrated, examined, and concluded that the Taliban,[71] Al Qaeda, the Islamic Movement of Uzbekistan, Hezb-i-Islami (HIG), and the Haqqani network are, by the definition used in this study, foreign terrorist organizations which have perpetrated acts of international terrorism. Hezb-i-Islami (HIG) headed by Gulbuddin Hekmatyar, is a terrorist group which has perpetrated attacks against domestic targets inside Afghanistan and, as noted in chapter 4, the organization has conducted attacks against UN "personnel and facilities" and NGOs.[72]

The opium trade in Afghanistan has indeed been a funding source for the Taliban, certain Al Qaeda operatives, the Islamic Movement of Uzbekistan, Hezb-i-Islami (HIG), as well as rogue members of other foreign jihadist's organizations with ideological ties to Al Qaeda. Opium cultivation, especially in Helmand province, has served as a "force multiplier" for Taliban and allied forces.[73] The Taliban benefited financially by taxing all facets of the opium trade,[74] forming symbiotic relationships with traffickers and other opium trade actors (e.g., Quetta-Chaman transport mafia).[75] This study supports the fact that during the years 1996–2001 Al Qaeda was providing support to the Taliban, not vice versa. It has also been noted that Osama bin Laden provided various services to the regime including the provision of some of his most experienced and highly trained cadre, the 055 Brigade, to assist Taliban combat efforts against the Northern Alliance.[76] Moreover, it has been established that Osama bin Laden provided training and various labor-intensive services to the regime.[77] Hence, there is sufficient compelling circumstantial information which indicates that prior to 9/11 Osama bin Laden played an indirect role in the opium trade, e.g., providing Al Qaeda fighters to the Taliban, who were providing protection to Haji Bashir Noorzai's controlled shipments of opiates,[78] in exchange for arms, demolitions, and men and may have assisted in efforts to increase the amount of cultivated poppy in the latter 1990s.[79]

In the period immediately following the October 7, 2001, invasion Al Qaeda's relationship with the Taliban becomes less clear. Additionally, almost immediately after the invasion Al Qaeda held no territory within Afghanistan. It has been established that Osama bin Laden and many of his followers were able to escape the onslaught by crossing into Pakistani territory.

Concerning other terrorist entities which have operated from Afghan soil, evidence presented in the form of testimony by Interpol's Ralf Mutschke and supported by various experts such as Cornell (2005a), Makarenko (2002d), Rashid (2003), and Stepanova (2004) clearly indicates that the IMU, basically a hybrid organization, was deriving income from the drug trade and was directly involved in transport operations prior to 9/11. According to Mutschke (2000) the IMU may have been responsible for up to 70 percent of the heroin transiting from Afghanistan through Central Asia. Information in the form of documentation and interview data also confirms that Gulbuddin Hekmatyar, leader of Hezb-i-Islami (HIG), has been involved in the drug trade since the 1980s and continued this activity following the U.S.-led invasion.[80]

Moreover, it has been established that Taliban tactics of suicide bombings,[81] kidnappings, and the use of improvised explosive devices (IEDs) against NATO/ISAF forces and foreign and domestic non-combatant targets, are new modes of attack recently added to their modus operandi.[82] Evidence shows that these tactics have been taken directly from the playbook of an Osama bin Laden affiliate, "al Qaeda in Iraq."[83] This provides additional support for the argument that Al Qaeda and the Taliban have merged ideologically and tactically. Thus, Osama bin Laden, Al Qaeda, and the ideology which drives this movement has commanded mass appeal to the point that its influence has indeed controlled the actions and lives of those who have perished in martyrdom-type operations. This is the greatest asset that charismatic and revolutionary-driven leaders such as Osama bin Laden and others like him possess.

Additionally, this study finds that acts of violence, specifically in the main poppy producing regions of the south and southeast, are in many cases spawned by criminal entities, often in concert with territorial warlords,[84] the Taliban, and affiliated factions in order to further weaken the government and thwart international efforts to suppress the opium trade, thus ensuring that the cultivation, production, and transportation of illegal narcotics continues unabated. Corrupt officials, individual power-holders, local criminal groups, and associated national and international-based criminal networks are motivated by profit rather than ideological considerations.

CONCLUSION

While terrorist organizations in general need money to purchase weaponry and pay for logistical and operational support, terrorism by its very nature is not an expensive endeavor. Although it is uncertain how many individuals and organizations throughout the Middle East and the world are supportive of the Al Qaeda, the Taliban, and like-minded ideologies to the point that they are willing to invest large sums of money to insure that the movement and others like it are able to continue operating, it does appear that with or without the lucrative Afghan drug trade there is enough support within the larger Muslim community to sustain continued militant efforts by these groups. Testimony and statements made by various national and international investigative agencies have confirmed this fact.

Statements have also been made that tie the nexus to a curtailment of cash flow brought about by the reduction of state-sponsored terrorism at the end of the Cold War and the freezing of various militant assets following the 1998 African embassy attacks and the events of September 2001. There are several reasons why this argument does not in my opinion carry much credibility with regard to hard-core religiously-motivated extremists. Islamic fundamentalism is not driven nor is it dependant on money to the extent that it serves as a deterrent or catalyst for what happened on 9/11. Extremists of this persuasion are driven more by ideology and religion. The Taliban, Al Qaeda, Pakistani-based Islamists, and other Osama bin Laden and Taliban affiliates are fomenting violence in various parts of the world through a complex financial network that includes rich patrons, front companies, charities, and legal and illegal enterprises. In fact, some of these Afghan-Pakistan-based groups/individual members could be considered criminals with a political agenda.

In Afghanistan a number of threats converge and when viewed holistically, provide a formidable menace to NATO/ISAF, the democratic process, the rule of law, and negatively impacts reconstruction efforts. These threats, no doubt spawned by different motivations among various state and non-state actors (criminals, corrupt public officials, insurgents/ terrorists, and angry unemployed and often displaced Afghans), coalesce in an often unplanned alliance of convenience and opportunity; each player or group is individually or collectively motivated by money, power, territory, ideology, or a combination of several if not all of these dynamics.[85]

This study finds that much of what has been written relative to the drug-terror nexus in Afghanistan rarely goes beyond reports published in the international media and uncorroborated and questionable statements of various law enforcement and government officials. Many of these reports have lacked specific detail and credible corroborating information. Furthermore, there are no data in the open-source literature which suggests that a direct operational alliance exists between internationally-based criminal groups engaged in drug trafficking and international terrorists in Afghanistan either prior to or following the events of 9/11.[86] Additionally, on the specific issue of Al Qaeda or Taliban involvement in the international trafficking of opiates from Afghanistan, there is no empirically-based evidence which directly links either group to this activity.[87]

The drug trade and the terrorist threat are extremely diffuse and constitute separate but intertwined multidimensional problems. Criminals, drug traffickers, terrorists, and insurgent factions exploit territorial and regional security vacuums, creating violence and instability which further influences and encourages the opium process at the cultivation level as well as processing and transport operations.[88] Moreover, opium revenue exacerbates and strengthens the insurgency by providing these actors with a degree of political leverage and legitimacy.[89] Furthermore, destabilization and the lack of security prevent NATO/ISAF and Afghan forces from exerting control over insurgent-infested areas, thereby challenging government reconstruction efforts and keeping the population in these areas dependent upon the Taliban.

The opium trade in Afghanistan is a more critical and complicated issue than what appears in daily press reports. Providing a funding source for enemy combatants is only the tip of the proverbial iceberg. Indeed, the burgeoning trade in opium has international ramifications as globally-based and violent non-state groups are empowered and use drug revenue to purchase weapons and armament through the global black market thereby arming some of the world's most dangerous groups. Additionally, these armed elements are often supported by individuals holding powerful government positions in Central and Southwest Asia and beyond.

The fact that drugs and conflict feed off of each other has been well documented.[90] However, in the case of Afghanistan, a country with very few income-producing resources available to the principally agrarian population, the opium trade has taken on profound importance in income-generation for the poor; plays a major role in provincial and local governance; serves as a propaganda tool and revenue-producing source for the Taliban and its allies, national and internationally-based criminals, and some district, provincial, and national-level government officials.[91] Furthermore this complex and expanding enterprise which has fueled and intensified insurgent and terrorist violence in Afghanistan, Pakistan, Central Asia, and possibly Iraq[92] is an immediate threat to regional and global security.

A number of challenges exist in Afghanistan and Pakistan in the near term which will impact the stability of the entire region well into the future. The current U.S. strategy to turn back and reverse Taliban momentum by introducing more troops into theater will take a considerable amount of time, money, and unfortunately lives. Moreover, it will not address the larger context in which the Afghan Taliban, Tehrik-i-Taliban (Pakistani Taliban), and other violent factions thrive. Problems such as FATA, outside support for militant groups, corruption within the Afghan government, and Pakistan's unwillingness to confront the Quetta Shura Taliban and Haqqani network will require more than a strictly military effort. U.S. ground action within Pakistan's borders does not appear to be an option which would garner much support in the United States, Pakistan, or other allied countries.

Pakistan, a nuclear-armed country and hotbed of terrorism, presents a very serious threat to U.S. and global security. We need to get smarter on how to manage this growing problem, its often volatile relationship with India, and the massive financial assistance we are pouring into this country. These are tough issues. There are no quick fixes or easy answers. One thing is clear; success in Afghanistan is contingent on Pakistan's policies and actions regarding its support of militant factions and the safe haven they enjoy in FATA and Baluchistan province. This will require a reversal of a 60-year-old mindset which entails among other things a negotiated settlement to the Kashmir problem. Pakistan is a reluctant ally in the "war on terror" and as time passes they view cooperation with the United States and its NATO allies to be detrimental to their national interests. Furthermore, the Pakistan government and a majority of its population do not trust the United States regardless of the amount of aid flowing into their coffers.

Finally, insurgent forces in Afghanistan are receiving support from a number of sources, one of which is the opium trade and other criminal activity. Additionally, in Pakistan elements of the ISI and possibly senior civilian officials are providing various levels of support to groups they view as critical components in their policy towards India and Afghanistan.

Hard choices need to be made in Southwest Asia because how the Afghanistan-Pakistan problem is ultimately decided will, in part, determine how the global community will live in the 21st century. This war could conceivably go on for years, if not decades. First, there needs to be a clear vision of what needs to be achieved in Afghanistan in order to consider this monumental national effort a "success." Second, a realistic and objective assessment needs to be made of the likelihood that these targets can be realized and, finally, a determination needs to be made regarding how much of our national resources—both blood and treasure—will be required to realize this intended outcome. The situation in Afghanistan will require a tremendous effort by NATO, the Afghan and Pakistan governments, and neighboring countries just to bring some measure of security and stability to a country that has known only war for three decades. Without confronting some of the issues enumerated above, the outlook for a successful outcome in Afghanistan appears bleak as the possibility of a wider conflict including deadly attacks upon our homeland and other Western nations seems possible.

Appendix: Maps

Map No. 3958 Rev. 6 UNITED NATIONS
July 2009

Department of Field Support
Cartographic Section

Afghanistan, No. 3958 Rev. 6 United Nations July 2009

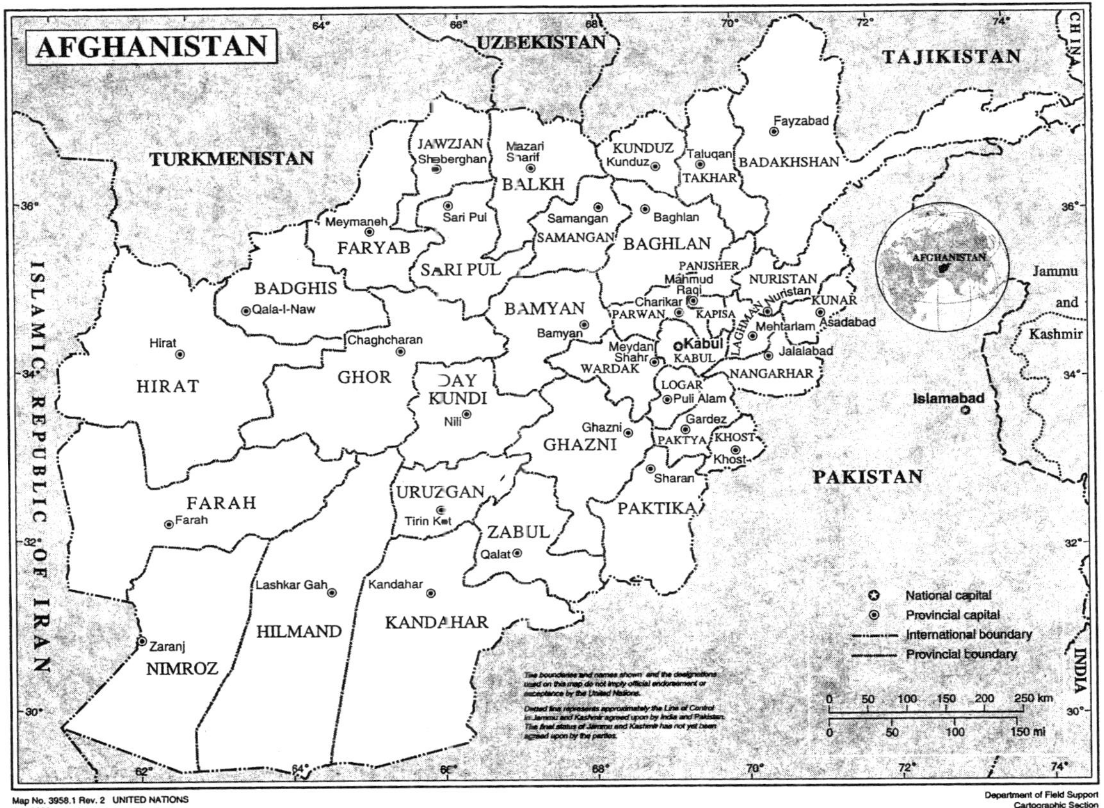

Afghanistan, No. 3958.1 Rev. 2 United Nations July 2009

Notes

PREFACE

1. Sections of this study have been updated to reflect events from 2006 to August 2010.

2. See Fay, 1996, pp. 212–214.

3. See Yin, 2003; and Yin, 1998, pp. 229–259.

4. See Fay, 1996, p. 213; see also Haskell, 1998, pp. 145–173; and Bevir, 1994, pp. 332–337.

5. Fay (1996, p. 213) defines "critical intersubjectivity" as an "ongoing dialogue among rival inquirers" which "involves the systematic examination of rival accounts and methods in a careful, probing, and open-minded way." Fay further notes that "Objectivity is thus a feature of co-operative conversations bent on collectively exploring the worth of various theories and modes of inquiry from a detached (but not necessarily disinterested) perspective"; see also Goldman, 1994, p. 30.

6. Each examined account or theory represents the subjective views of the author, journalist, area/subject expert, and others whose words, written or verbal, have been used in this study: an attempt to comprehensively explain the drug-terror phenomena through an exchange of ideas between and among a variety of individuals thereby enhancing knowledge regarding the purported nexus between drug criminals and international terrorists in Afghanistan; for a discussion on critical subjectivity and four ways of knowing see Heron, J. and Reason, 1997a, pp. 274–294, and Kratochwil, 2007, p. 50; concerning objectivity Little (1995) states that, "Objectivity invokes an assertion of rational credibility for the theories advanced within the social sciences . . . however, that objectivity is not the same as certainty."

7. See Schmid, 2004, pp. 43–44, and 56; for a general discussion on terrorism and criminal activity see Dishman, 2003, pp. 59–72, and Makarenko, 2004, pp. 129–145.

8. The news media is a competitive profit-oriented business. Each media outlet seeks to present the news based on the particular biases and preconceptions of the readership. Furthermore, media reports present the specific authors' interpretation of events; therefore it becomes critical that alternative sources of information regarding the same events are used to evaluate conflicting information and viewpoints. Since all authors have biases and may slant the story to reflect a particular view or position, the process of triangulation can somewhat ameliorate this problem by comparing other perspectives on the same issue or event.

9. Media reports do provide a wealth of anecdotal evidence. While some of this information is misleading, the fact that the information has not been subjected to rigorous examination does not make it totally extraneous. Information must be relevant and reliable. The credibility of a particular source may be established by the use and reference to that source in other scholarly works. An article which appeared in the *Oregon Law Review* addressed the issue of evaluating anecdotal evidence. Lisa S. Roy, Assistant Professor of Law at the University of Mississippi, School of Law states: "I have no problem evaluating anecdotal evidence. Most of us draw conclusions about the world around us based on our own personal experiences, so it seems to make perfect sense to listen to the stories of others, particularly when the stories are different than our own. Some of the most compelling stories have moved the Court's jurisprudence in groundbreaking directions that now seem correct as a matter of social policy" (Roy, 2004, p.31).

10. Lichbach (2007, p. 268) notes: "This then is the fundamental indeterminacy of empirical work: important questions cannot be entirely arbitrated by the sciences of deductive and inductive logic. . . . As best as they can scientists rely on judgment to establish that a model of a theory is consistent with a model of the data"; see also p. 277 footnote 4; Kratochwil (2007, p. 50) argues that, "Aside from the issue of interpretation that precedes those of inference and proofs, the social element plays a significant part in the communication among practitioners, particularly when the criteria of logic are not helpful in solving the puzzles that scientists address."

11. See Fay, 1996, p. 208.

CHAPTER 1

1. For detailed information on "networks" and "netwar" see, Arquilla and Ronfeldt, 1996; and Arquilla and Ronfeldt, 2001.

2. See United Nations Office on Drugs and Crime, 2007a, p. 12; see also Jelsma and Kramer, 2009, p. 2; and Blanchard, 2009, p. 14.

3. See also Rubin, B. R., 2002, pp. 179–195; and Rashid, 2003, pp. 137–155.

4. For a concise historical description of the opium factor in Afghanistan during the Soviet-Afghan War period through the U. S.-led invasion in October 2001 see McCoy, 2003, pp. 461–531; Rashid, 2001f, pp. 117–127; and Cooley, 2002, pp. 105–134.

5. For a holistic and comprehensive discussion of Afghanistan's economy see Nyrop and Seekins, 1986, eds., pp. 141–207.

6. See also Rubin, 1995, pp. 117–119.

7. The Taliban (religious students) emerged in Afghanistan in November 1994 as a result of internecine fighting between various mujahideen factions

and pervasive criminal activity and lawlessness that was engulfing the country. From their base in Kandahar the Taliban rapidly gained public support; for a report on the origins of the Taliban as a political force see Magnus and Naby, 2002, pp. 179–211; Rashid, 2001f, pp. 17–30; and Tanner, 2002, pp. 271–287.

8. See Rashid, 2001f, pp. 17–80, 139–140; Tanner, 2002, pp. 271–288; Magnus and Naby, 2002, pp. 181–188; and Gunaratna, 2002, pp. 39–53.

9. The International Security Assistance Force (ISAF) is under the direct command of the North Atlantic Treaty Organization (NATO), is mandated by the United Nations (UN), and was established to provide security to the elected government of Afghanistan; see http://www.jfcbs.nato.int/htm/operations/isaf.htm.

10. See also McCoy, 2003, pp. 461–487, 500–531.

11. See Lichbach, M. I., 2007, pp. 261–284, at p. 267 for two interrelated difficulties inherent in empirical inquiry.

12. Epistemological issues related to testimony are discussed in chapter 4 of Goldman, A. I., 1999, pp. 103–130; see also Audi, R., 2003, pp. 132–152. The term testimony in the context of this study means, "the transmission of observed information from one person to others" (Goldman, 1999, p. 103).

13. Audi (2003, p. 260) argues that, ". . . scientific knowledge does not automatically arise as we observe our surroundings. Normally, we must first raise questions about the world; they direct our inquiry."

14. Yin (2004, p. 21) states that, "The more that your questions are descriptive ("what has been happening?") or explanatory ("how or why has it been happening?"), the more that the case study method will be relevant."

15. The term "non-state actors" refers to groups or organizations which operate "beyond state control". These actors are transnational in scope and have the ability to "affect political outcomes either purposefully or semi-purposefully, either as their primary objective or as one aspect of their activities" (Josselin and Wallace, 2001, pp. 3–4).

16. Yin (2003, pp. 111–112) regards the use of theoretical propositions as the most preferred analytical strategy. He states that, "The original objectives and design of the case study presumably were based on such propositions, which in turn reflected a set of research questions, reviews of the literature, and new hypotheses and propositions."

17. Sarantakos (1993, p. 309) notes that, "Establishing valid relationships between variables provides a sound basis for drawing conclusions about the research findings."

18. Yin (2004, p. 9) notes that, "In collecting case study data, the main idea is to 'triangulate' or establish converging lines of evidence to make your findings as robust as possible . . . The most desired convergence occurs when two or more independent sources all point to the same set of events or 'facts.'" See Yin, R. K., 2004, "Case Study Methods", COSMOS Corporation, revised draft, October 1; King, Keohane and Verba (1995, pp. 479–480) note that, "Triangulation involves data collected at different places, sources, times, levels of analysis, or perspectives, data that might be quantitative, or might involve intensive interviews or thick historical description . . . Triangulation, then, is another word for referring to the practice of increasing the amount of information to bear on a theory or hypothesis."

19. See Fay, 1996, pp. 212–214; and Hopf, 2007, p. 68.

20. See Yin (2003, pp. 33, 37, and 38).

21. For a definition of the case study and its application see Yin (2003, pp. 13–14); in discussing the value of case study research in the learning process Flyvbjerg (2006, p. 223) argues that ". . . there does not and probably cannot exist predictive theory in social science. Social science has not succeeded in producing general, context-independent theory and, thus, has in the final instance nothing else to offer than concrete, context-dependent knowledge. And the case study is especially well suited to produce this knowledge."

22. Bernstein et al., 2007, pp. 230–236.

23. This term taken from Raab and Milward, 2003.

24. See Goodhand, n.d; see also Dupree, 1980, p. 43.

25. See Yin (2003, p. 15); see also Eisenhardt, 1989, p. 538.

26. The definition further adds that "all types of evidence are dependent on circumstances for its credibility". See U.S. Legal, n.d., "Definitions and Legal Terms Defined", viewed September 9, 2006, and May 10, 2008, http://definitions.uslegal.com/.

27. See Aristotle, 350 BCE, *Metaphysics*, Book 4, Part 6, trans. W. D. Ross, viewed May 15, 2008, http://classics.mit.edu/Aristotle/metaphysics.4.iv.html; and Goldman, 2007.

28. Courts are frequently mentioned as an analogy for epistemology in the social sciences. For instance, see Kratochwil, 2007, p. 51.

29. Bevir (1994, p. 333) asserts that "a fact is a piece of evidence which nearly everyone in a given community would accept as true. . . . Facts typically are observations embodying categories based on the recognition of similarities and differences between particular cases."

30. See Scarborough, 2004c, p. A11.

31. See MSN Encarta World English Dictionary [North American Edition] 2007, viewed April 20, 2008, http://encarta.msn.com/dictionary_/anecdote.html.

32. See also Goldman, 1999, p. 124, footnote 17.

33. Both documentation and interview data were triangulated to insure that the findings were corroborated by different individuals across various data sources and times.

34. See Yin (2003, pp. 112–113); see also the discussion on "Objectivity Through Comparison," in Bevir, 1994, pp. 332–337; Haskell, 1998, pp. 149–152, 384, footnote 4; and 385, footnote 12.

35. For a discussion of the triangulation process in mixed-methods research see Jick, 1979, pp. 602–611.

36. See Little, 1995; see also Fay (1996, pp. 212–214) for a detailed discussion on objectivity as "critical intersubjectivity."

37. Fay (1996, p. 214) further states that . . . "at any one time the evidence may be interpreted in many objectively acceptable ways, may support even quite antagonistic theories. No method, no matter how cogent and responsive to evidence and criticism, can insure answers which any rational knower must accept"; Bevir (1994, p. 336) notes that, "Our standards of evidence require us to try to support our interpretations by reference to as many clearly identified facts as we can. An accurate web of interpretations is one with a close fit to the facts supporting it." He further states that, "A comprehensive web

of interpretations is one that fits a wide range of facts with few outstanding exceptions, and especially one that fits facts from different areas, or from areas that previously seemed unrelated."; Goldman (1999, p. 117) states that, "There is little agreement among philosophers about when, or under what precise conditions, statements have determinate objective probabilities."

38. As national defense priorities shifted from a post-Cold War mentality to an anti- and counterterrorism focus, the label terrorism has become rhetorical in efforts to sustain and increase funding for various government agencies. See Council on Hemispheric Affairs, 2004.

39. The UN draft resolution as cited above is a long overdue but positive step because it specifically includes in its proposed wording what constitutes a terrorist act.

40. This information can now be accessed at the U.S. Department of Homeland Security, National Consortium for the Study of Terrorism and Responses to Terrorism, University of Maryland, College Park, MD, available online at http://www.start.umd.edu/gtd/.

41. RAND adds that "all terrorist acts are crimes. Many would also be violation of the rules of war if a state of war existed. This violence or threat of violence is generally directed against civilian targets. The motives of all terrorists are political, and terrorist actions are generally carried out in a way that will achieve maximum publicity. Unlike other criminal acts, terrorists often claim credit for their acts. Finally, terrorist acts are intended to produce effects beyond the immediate physical damage of the cause, having long-term psychological repercussions on a particular target audience. The fear created by terrorists may be intended to cause people to exaggerate the strengths of the terrorist and the importance of the cause, to provoke governmental overreaction, to discourage dissent, or simply to intimidate and thereby enforce compliance with their demands." See Memorial Institute for the Prevention of Terrorism, 2005d.

42. "The US Government has employed these definitions of terrorism for statistical and analytical purposes since 1983" (U.S. Department of State, 1999, p. 7); see also Kalic, 2005, p. 2.

43. The term "noncombatant," which is referred to but not defined in Title 22 USC 2656f (d) (2), is interpreted to mean, in addition to civilians, military personnel (whether or not armed or on duty) who are not deployed in a war zone or a war-like setting; see United States Department of State, 2005a, *Country Reports on Terrorism 2004*, p. 1; State further defines "terrorist group" to mean "any group practicing, or which has significant subgroups which practice, international terrorism. The term 'international terrorism' means terrorism involving citizens or the territory of more than one country."

44. Baltic Defense Review, 2002, p. 42; and Schmid and Jongman, 1988, p. 5.

45. This quote has been attributed to British author Gerald Seymour, former US President Ronald Reagan, and former US Attorney General Ramsey Clark among others.

46. Ibid

47. This follows the RAND definition of terrorism in its emphasis on the "nature of the act." See the discussion in Hoffman and Claridge, 1998, p. 139.

48. This study notes that some of these acts may be perpetrated by drug criminals in concert with insurgents/terrorists in order to spawn or maintain an

atmosphere of intimidation and lawlessness. It is also noted that a by-product of this mutual alliance is the advancement of their criminal objectives and concomitantly the provision of a potential funding source for Taliban and affiliates.

49. See Shanty and Picquet, 2000, p. 6; Shanty and Picquet, 2004, pp. 7–8; and United States Department of State, 1999, p. 18.

50. See U.S. Department of State (2005a, p.1); RAND defines a "terrorist group" as "a collection of individuals belonging to an autonomous non-state or subnational revolutionary or anti-governmental movement who are dedicated to the use of violence to achieve their objectives." RAND further states that: "Such an entity is seen as having at least some structural and command and control apparatus that, no matter how loose or flexible, nonetheless provides an overall organizational framework and general strategic direction. This definition is meant to include contemporary religion-motivated and apocalyptic groups and other movements that seek theological justification or divine sanction for their acts of violence"; see Memorial Institute for the Prevention of Terrorism, 2005d.

51. International terrorism is defined by RAND as "incidents in which terrorists go abroad to strike their targets, select domestic targets associated with a foreign state, or create an international incident by attacking airline passengers, personnel or equipment"; see Memorial Institute for the Prevention of Terrorism, 2005d.

52. RAND defines domestic terrorism as, "incidents perpetrated by local nationals against a purely domestic target" (RAND/MIPT); see Memorial Institute for the Prevention of Terrorism, 2005d.

53. To view the full report see United States House of Representatives, 2006, *Al-Qaeda: The Many Faces of an Islamist Extremist Threat*, report of the U.S. House Permanent Select Committee on Intelligence, viewed April 5, 2008, http://www.fas.org/irp/congress/2006_rpt/hrpt109-615.pdf; see also GlobalSecurity.org, viewed April 5, 2008, http://www.globalsecurity.org/intell/library/congress/2006_rpt/al-qaeda_hpsci109-615-02.htm.

54. For other definitions of organized crime see Von Lampe, K., n.d., "Definitions of Organized Crime," viewed January 12, 2006, http://www.organized-crime.de/OCDEF1.htm.

55. Williams, 2002, p. 195.

56. See United Nations Convention Against Transnational Organized Crime, 2000, United Nations, New York, NY, viewed June 20, 2006, http://www.uncjin.org/Documents/Conventions/dcatoc/final_documents_2/convention_eng.pdf.

57. "Although use of the term 'narco-terrorism' has only recently been advanced to describe what is alleged to be an emerging Afghan scenario, it seems that the term itself was first used by former Peruvian President Belaunde Terry in 1983 to describe terrorist-type attacks against his own nation's anti-narcotics police by the Shining Path Marxist rebels. Later, in 1986, then U.S. President Ronald Reagan also spoke of narco-terrorism when referring to purported links between international drug trafficking and terrorism among allies of the Soviet Union (Cuba, Nicaragua);" see Chouvy, 2004, p. 7.

58. See Ehrenfeld, 1990; Ehrenfeld, 2003; and Napoleoni, 2003.

59. See Rabasa and Chalk, 2001, p. 16; United States Department of Justice, 2008; Krauss, 1992, p. 4; Trujillo, 1992, p. A25; and Brodzinsky, 2005, p. 13.

60. See Rashid (2001f, pp. 118–124).

61. See United States Senate, Committee on Foreign Relations, 2009, *Afghanistan's Narco War: Breaking the Link Between Drug Traffickers and Insurgents*, A Report to the Committee on Foreign Relations, One Hundred Eleventh Congress, First Session, U.S. Government Printing Office, Washington, D.C., August s0, p. 9, viewed December 15, 2009, http://www.newsweek.com/media/5/Afghan-Narco-War.pdf.

62. See United States Department of Defense, 2001, *Department of Defense Dictionary of Military and Associated Terms*, Joint Publication 1–02 amended through June 9, 2004, p. 355.

63. See Hutchinson, 2002a; and Hutchinson, 2002b, pp. 9–15.

64. See also Shanty, 2009b, p. 188.

65. The International Narcotics Control Board (INCB) is the "independent and quasi-judicial control organ established by treaty, for monitoring the implementation of the international drug control treaties." INCB works to insure that, "adequate supplies of drugs are available for medical and scientific uses and that the diversion of drugs from licit sources to illicit channels does not occur" (INCB, 2005, p. 113); see also Shanty. 2009c, p. 92.

66. The principal international instruments that address the issues surrounding the distribution of illicit narcotics are the 1961 Single Convention on Narcotic Drugs and the 1988 United Nations Convention against the Illicit Traffic in Narcotic Drugs and Psychotropic Substances. The Single Convention assigned drugs into four Schedules depending upon their addictive properties and potential for abuse. The Schedule 1 drugs are the most dangerous in terms of their ability to cause addiction and their likelihood of abuse is high. Raw opium and heroin are listed in Schedule 1 of the Convention. Schedule II drugs are addictive and subject to abuse but do not rise to the level of substances listed in Schedule I. Narcotic drugs are those substances listed in Schedules I and II of the 1961 Convention on Narcotic Drugs (INCB, 2005, p. 37); the 1988 Convention against Illicit Traffic in Narcotic Drugs and Psychotropic Substances provides a list of chemical and other precursor agents which may be utilized in the manufacture and production of narcotic and psychotropic drugs. These substances are under international control and regulation. This list is prepared and updated periodically by the International Narcotics Control Board; see United Nations Convention Against Illicit Traffic in Narcotic Drugs and Psychotropic Substances, 1988, United Nations, New York, NY, p. 22, viewed February 2, 2007, http://www.unodc.org/pdf/convention_1988_en.pdf; and United Nations, 2007.

CHAPTER 2

1. Border areas of Afghanistan, Iran, and Pakistan.

2. See also Chouvy, 2002; McCoy, 2003, p. 4; and Shanty, 2007b, p. 84.

3. Johnson and Leslie (2004, p. 112) note: "In the 1930s only three provinces grew poppy (even in 1994 it was grown in only eight), but by 2003 it had become an integral part of the rural economy, with twenty-eight of the country's thirty-two provinces growing it. All ethnic groups were by now involved, and the exponential rate of expansion was reflected in the fact that thirty-one districts cultivated it for the first time in that year."

4. Haq (1996, p. 948) further notes that, "Afghanistan's experience with the modern international drug trade commenced in the 1970s when large numbers of Westerners descended on the Asian country to 'drop out and turn on' inexpensively. . . . The growth of the hashish trade at local levels became a major source for international drug links, particularly to Europe, as foreign visitors paved a way for close connections with Afghan opium producers. Later on, this proved to be a major source of opium and heroin smuggling from this part of the world."

5. Ahmed Rashid has been an investigative journalist covering Afghanistan since the Soviet invasion in December 1979.

6. See also Reuters News Agency, 1985; Yates, 1987, p. 32; Associated Press, 1987; Ispahani, 1987, p. A1; Kamm, 1988, p. A16; and Atlas, 1988, p. 4.

7. The United Nations Office for Drug Control and Crime Prevention (UNODCCP) became the United Nations Office on Drugs and Crime (UNODC).

8. See Lamour and Lamberti, 1974, pp. 177–200.

9. Prior to this time opium in the Crescent was produced primarily for domestic use and to supply the increasing demands of Iran's addict population. See McCoy (2003, p. 428).

10. See Kerry, J. F., et al., 2009, *Afghanistan's Narco War: Breaking the Link Between Drug Traffickers and Insurgents*: a report to the Committee on Foreign Relations, United States Senate, One Hundred Eleventh Congress, first session, August 10, U.S. Government Printing Office, Washington, D.C., pp. 3–4, viewed November 15, 2009, http://www.newsweek.com/media/5/Afghan-Narco-War.pdf.

11. By the late 1970s Afghanistan was producing a significant amount of opium and was a major global supplier of heroin. The author of an article, which appeared in the *Washington Post* thirteen months prior to the December 1979 Soviet invasion, notes that Afghanistan was producing an estimated 300 tons of opium annually while Pakistan's estimated annual production was 400–600 tons. While a large portion of this crop supplied local addict populations in Afghanistan, Pakistan, and Iran, "experts estimate that . . . more and more opium is being refined into heroin for the European trade in laboratories in western Iran, southern and eastern Turkey and possibly western Afghanistan" (Randal, 1978, p. A30). While the Soviet invasion and occupation of Afghanistan in December 1979 was indeed a key event which initiated a surge in opium cultivation a close examination reveals that opium's importance to the Afghan people predates the events which occurred in the latter part of 1979; see Auerbach, 1979, p. A1; Chouvy, 2002; and Shanty, 2007b, p. 88.

12. See McCoy, 2003, pp. 464–466; Roy, 1995, p.107-110; and Beaty and Gwynne, 1993, p. 295.

13. See Booth, 1996, p. 312; this action by the Iranian government, coupled with increased opium cultivation in Pakistan and Afghanistan during the Soviet occupation, triggered a market for Afghan-produced opium to feed the growing addict population in that country. See UNODCCP, 2002a, p. 4; and Shanty, 2007b, p. 84.

14. McCoy (2003, p. 471) notes that, the new Islamic regime, "reflecting Iran's traditional tolerance for the drug, did not place opium in the same forbidden category as alcohol, creating an ambiguity that allowed the traffic to flourish."

15. The Hadd Ordinance was introduced by Pakistani President, General Zia ul-Haq in 1979 in an attempt to address the country's growing opium problem.

It prohibited the cultivation, production, and consumption of illicit drugs. At the time of its enactment cultivation along the border regions was considerable. It was during this period that the expansion of opium cultivation in Afghanistan began; see Armenta, et al., 2001, pp. 8 and 19.

16. See Armenta, et al., 2001, p. 474; and Kaplan, 2000, p. 72.

17. In this context and speaking specifically about Afghanistan, McCoy (2003, 465–466) further states, ". . . that the rising opium harvests in Afghanistan and Pakistan, America's major suppliers, were unintended 'fallout' from the CIA covert Afghan war. . . . The agency's aid to mujaheddin guerrillas now expanded opium production in Afghanistan and linked Pakistan's nearby heroin laboratories to the world market."

18. See Ahmed Rashid, 2001f, p. 20; regarding Soviet impact on Afghanistan's agrarian economy see Keegan, 1985, pp. 94–105; and Urban, 1990, p. 110.

19. Pakistan's NWFP is presently referred to as Khyber PakhtunKhwa. This updated information was provided by Dr. Rohan Gunaratna and Halimullah Kousary in an e-mail communication dated September 20, 2010.

20. See Dietz, 1980; Thornton, 1982, p. A3; and Arnett, 1980.

21. See Bearden, 2001, pp. 17–30; see also Rubin, M., 2002a; and Rubin, M., 2002b, pp. 1–16.

22. See Gunaratna (2002, pp. 3–6); Muhlberger (1999) notes that, "In the context of the growth of political Islam, the [Soviet] invasion had a special significance. In Iran, Islamic forces had just begun a showdown with one of the superpowers, when, suddenly, right next door, the other superpower intervened to crush the Islamic movement. [This] heightened the sense of crisis. In the wider Islamic world, these crises gave special prestige to Iran's religious movement and others who had a similar orientation. It was Islamic revolution rather than national revolution."

23. According to Ahmed Rashid (1999b, p. 28) "With the active encouragement of the CIA and Pakistan's ISI, who wanted to turn the Afghan jihad into a global war waged by all Muslim states against the Soviet Union, some 35,000 Muslim radicals from 40 Islamic countries joined Afghanistan's fight between 1982 and 1992. Tens of thousands more came to study in Pakistani *madrasahs*. Eventually more than 100,000 foreign Muslim radicals were directly influenced by the Afghan jihad"; see also Gunaratna, 2002, pp. 3–6.

24. The author emphasizes the extent of the problem when he states, "it is not uncommon for Russian soldiers or airmen to negotiate the exchange of ammunition for drugs with the very people they are supposed to be fighting" (Freemantle, 1986, p. 180); see also Grau and Gress, 2002, p. 292.

25. See Shanty, 2007, p. 81.

26. This view is also supported by Rashid (2001f, p. 121).

27. See also UNODC, 2004a, p. 4.

28. See Shanty, 2007b, pp. 81 and 88.

29. This hostile environment has made serious research of the country very difficult. Dupree (1980, p. 43) has noted that, "statistics on Afghanistan abound, but most consist of 'intelligent estimates,' i.e., wild guesses based on inadequate data."

30. See Gunaratna and Kousary, 2010.

31. According to Rashid (1999b, p. 10) the United States basically abandoned Afghanistan following the Soviet defeat. With American involvement for the most

part absent, Saudi Arabia and Pakistan would continue to exert their influence based on their own domestic agenda.

32. As Goodson (2001, p. 97) so aptly noted, "The long Afghan War profoundly altered and in some cases even obliterated important components of Afghanistan's economic and political framework . . . much of the economic infrastructure has been destroyed by war, including urban factories, power supply and transportation links, and important agricultural areas . . . the war so shattered the traditional Afghan economy that an opium-heroin economic sector based on drug trafficking emerged to replace it."

33. See UNODC, 2005a, p. 23.

34. In fact, according to Booth (1996, p. 291), global heroin production tripled between 1982 and 1990; regarding the Russian Mafia's possible involvement in Afghanistan see Risen, 1998, p. A1; Cornell (2006, p. 43) notes that during the turbulent period 1994–1998, "most Afghan factions were implicated in the drug trade in one or another way."

35. See UNODC, 2005c, p. 184, for a map depicting Afghanistan opium poppy cultivation in 2001.

36. The International Crisis Group recounts that there have been no reports concerning initiatives taken by the Northern Alliance to curtail or eliminate opium production in territory they controlled. A considerable amount of speculation exists as to the reasons the Taliban instituted the ban. Some analysts believe that it was implemented to raise prices while others saw it as an attempt at acquiring legitimacy and international recognition. ICG reports that by the time the ban went into effect the Taliban was estimated to have stockpiled over 220 tons of heroin, "the equivalent of a nearly two-year supply for the needs of the Western Europe market." See International Crisis Group, 2001, pp. 3–4 and footnote 20.

37. See Ehrenfeld, 2003, p. 52; Rashid, 2001f, p. 124; and Gunaratna, 2002, p. 61.

38. See Hutchinson, 2001, p. 18.

39. Following the U.S.-led invasion opium poppy cultivation returned to pre-2001 levels and had spread throughout the country. See Curtis, 2005; and Kerry, et al., 2009, pp. 4–5.

40. See Felbab-Brown, 2005, pp. 58–62; and McGirk and Ware, 2004.

41. He further notes that, "the intervention by U.S. and Coalition forces strengthened the position of many regional warlords and 'Afghan commanders' by attempting to obtain their loyalty and support through financial means. To that end: thirty-five warlords were said to have received a total of $7 million in an effort to buy their loyalty in the 'fight against terrorism.' Whilst warlords control the illicit smuggling and drug trades, which in turn fund their own private militias, there are few incentives for engaging with the embryonic central state" (Goodhand, 2003, p. 8).

42. According to Townsend (2005, p. 18) in 2000 approximately 82,000 hectares were allocated to poppy cultivation. In 2004 this number rose to almost 126,000 hectares.

43. The provinces of Daikondi and Panjshir were officially added as administrative entities by President Hamid Karzai in June 2004.

44. See Ward and Byrd, 2004, p. 20.

45. See Kerry, J. F., et al., 2009, p. 26.

46. According to the Afghanistan National Development Strategy, "Opium remains a significant proportion of the national economy. UNODC estimated that in 1383 (2004/5), Afghanistan's opium economy earned US$ 2.8 billion, 79% of which went to traffickers, not local Afghan farmers. This is a fraction of the value of Afghanistan's opium sold on the international market, estimated to be worth around US$ 30–50 billion" (ANDS, 2006, p. 43).

47. A U.S. Department of State report released in 2002 notes that, "Traders offer growers advances to finance inputs and to tide growers over while the crop is in the ground. They visit households to buy opium. This credit, or advance payment on future opium production, is an integral part of livelihood strategies in poppy-producing areas of Afghanistan" (U.S. Department of State, 2002b).

48. According to Rubin (2004, p. 4): "a farmer who had been advanced $300 in the fall of 2000 to deliver 10 kilograms of opium in the spring of 2001 at the prevailing average price of $60/kg before the ban, owed his creditor as much as $6,750 at the peak average price of $675/kg that prevailed after the ban; see also MacDonald, 2005, p. 96.

49. The Afghanistan Relief Organization, an organization which provides food, clothing, and other basic humanitarian services, reported that despite the fact that, "Wheat production was an estimated 58% higher than in 2002. . . . The country still needed to import an estimated one million tons of wheat to meet its requirements for the 2003 year. Millions of Afghans, particularly in rural areas, remained dependent on food aid" (ARO, 2006).

50. During the Taliban period (1994–2000) the average number of hectares producing poppy was approximately 68,000. In 2001, following the Taliban imposed ban in July 2000, the number of hectares cultivating poppy was approximately 7,600. See United Nations Drug Control Program, 2001; the opium trade contributed to the Taliban's success against the Northern Alliance in the mid-late 1990s. According to the UN Committee of Experts on Resolution 1333, "funds raised from the production and trade of opium and heroin are used by the Taliban to buy arms and war materials and to finance the training of terrorists and support the operation of extremists in neighboring countries and beyond." See Mack, 2001, p. 35; and Farah and Constable, 1998, p. A15.

51. See UNODC, 2004a, p. 23.

52. See Felbab-Brown, 2010, pp. 92–93.

53. Ward and Byrd (2004, p. 3) report that, "Based on the changing pattern of seizures of opiates in neighboring countries, it appears that much more opium is now processed into morphine and heroin within Afghanistan"; an updated report by the United Nations Office on Drugs and Crime indicates that there are, "at least," 90 processing labs operating inside Afghanistan. See United Nations Office on Drugs and Crime, 2007b, p. 3; see also Felbab-Brown, 2010, p. 99; anecdotal reports indicate that the processing of opium into heroin may involve input from "chemists" based outside of Afghanistan (Toosi, 2008); see also Johnson, 2008.

54. See Rubin, B. R., 2004, p. 5.

55. The United Nations Office on Drugs and Crime was formerly the United Nations Office for Drug Control and Crime Prevention.

56. Small mobile labs consist of a few barrels and basins, a press, water, opium, and a precursor agent (Ibrahimi, 2008).

57. See also Gunaratna and Kousary, 2010.

58. See Neighbour, 2010, p. 013.

59. It is noteworthy to point out that demand along with addiction rates is high along the main smuggling routes as is the incidence of HIV infection.

60. See Center for Geopolitical Drug Studies, 2001, 2002a, and 2002b; see also Chouvy, 2003.

61. See Haq, 2005; Radhakrishnan, 2003; and Abbosov, 2002.

62. See Gunaratna and Kousary, 2010.

63. See Gunaratna and Kousary, 2010.

64. UNODC (2010d, p. 249) estimated that $1 billion per year is trafficked in Pakistan. Drugs traversing the NWFP are under the control and indeed are taxed by Tehrik-e-Taliban (Pakistani Taliban) and other extremist groups, some linked to Al Qaeda; see also Gunaratna and Kousary, 2010.

65. See Integrated Regional Information Networks, 2004, p. 47, for a map outlining major drug trafficking routes out of Afghanistan.

66. See also Townsend, 2006, pp. 69–91.

67. According to UNODC (2010d, p. 114) of the estimated 95 tons of opiates that are trafficked annually through the Central Asian states approximately 11 tons are consumed by regional users especially along key trafficking routes.

68. See Swanstrom, 2003.

69. In March 2005, the annual International Narcotics Control Strategy Report was renamed. Starting with the March 2005 issue the annual report's title reflects the release date. Therefore, no 2004 report was issued. The 2005 report covers events which occurred in 2004. Subsequent annual report titles cover events which occurred in the previous year; see http://www.state.gov/p/inl/rls/nrcrpt/.

70. See Makarenko (2002d, p. 7, footnote 21).

71. According to Haq (1996, p. 950): "In the late 1980s, there were reports of a drug-trade route through Azad Kashmir from the adjacent NWFP that went up the Karakoram Pass into China's Xinjiang Province and Tibet, then down into Nepal. Nepal sources confirmed the existence of this route . . ." see also Gunaratna and Kousary, 2010.

72. With respect to the ease with which drugs are smuggled out of Afghanistan, much of the problem is a direct consequence of the lack of reach of the government in Kabul and the immutable fact that smuggling has been a part of the Afghan culture for centuries. See Walsh, 2005, p. A42; see also Gunaratna and Kousary, 2010.

73. This diversion is accomplished in a number of ways: "ranging from front companies to purchase the chemicals, pressuring legal manufacturers, and outright theft of the chemical. . . . New routes from Central Asia seem to be indicated by the increasing captures of acetic anhydride in Central Asian nations like Turkmenistan and Uzbekistan." See Raghavan, 2005; Redo (2004, p. 102) concludes that, "there is no doubt that Central Asia has become a major trafficking route for drugs as well as precursors"; Neighbour (2010, p. 013) reported that in 2008 approximately, "14,000 litres," of acetic anhydride was confiscated in Afghanistan.

74. See United Nations Office on Drugs and Crime, 2010c, p. 33.

75. See Cornell, 2006b, pp. 38–39; and Cornell and Swanstrom, 2006, p. 10.

76. For a similar view, see Makarenko (2002d, p. 4).

77. See also Rashid, 2000.

78. For an early report which addressed Afghanistan's growing opium problem and its negative repercussions for the Central Asian states, see chapter 3 of the United States Government Interagency Working Group, 2000.

79. For example, Rashid (1999b, pp. 22–35) argues that, "China, too, has been affected by the ascendance of the Taliban. Beijing shunned the civil war in Afghanistan until February 1999, when it first made overtures to the Taliban in an attempt to stem the tide of Afghan heroin flooding Xinjiang. The heroin was helping fund Islamist and nationalist opposition to Beijing among the Uighurs and other Muslim ethnic groups. Uighur militants have trained and fought with the Afghan mujahideen since 1986 and Chinese officials say the arms and explosives the rebels have used against Chinese security forces come from Afghanistan"; See *China Daily*, 2010, for additional information on heroin smuggling through China's Xinjiang province.

80. See Shanty, 2009c, p. 92.

81. See Cornell and Swanstrom, 2006, pp. 10–28.

82. See also Central Asia-Caucasus Institute Analyst, 2005, Herman, 2004; and Dikaev, 2007.

83. Additionally, the International Crisis Group (2001, p. 15) reported that the, "Tajik ambassador to Kazakhstan . . . was caught twice transporting drugs, the second time in Kazakhstan with 62 kilograms of heroin and U.S. $1 million in cash. Just after the ambassador was expelled, Tajikistan's trade representative was caught with 24 kilograms of heroin."

84. See Peuch, 2001.

85. See also Makarenko, 2002d, p. 7, footnote 20.

86. Based on a July 2001, interview with Sergiy Ratushnyy, the United Nation's Chief Technical Advisor in Tajikistan, Russian involvement in the Afghan drug trade has declined since the end of the Tajik civil war (ICG, 2001, p. 6 and footnote 39).

87. The FATA is a semi-autonomous region located on the Pakistan-Afghanistan border where the Pakistani government exerts little if any authority.

88. On Afghanistan's rise to global opium dominance, see Booth, 1996; Coll, 2004; McCoy, 2003; and Schetter, 2004; see also UNODC, 2003a; and Ward and Byrd, 2004.

CHAPTER 3

1. On May 11, 1997, the *Washington Post* reported that, "More than 90% of Afghanistan's poppy-growing areas are under Taliban control. The country's biggest poppy-producing province, Helmand, borders Kandahar province to the east. Yet despite the Taliban's professed religious convictions, it has not acted with customary zeal to stop poppy cultivation. Its reluctance stems from the damage Afghanistan's economy has suffered during nearly two decades of war, the revenue derived from a 10 percent tax collected on opium and a fear of losing popular support from hundreds of thousands of small growers of poppies" (Cooper, 1997, p. A22).

2. See Cilluffo, 2000, pp. 60–77.

3. Yin (2003, p. 87) notes "that even the 'verbatim' transcripts of official U.S. Congress hearings have been deliberately edited—by the congressional staff and others who may have testified—before being printed in final form."

4. In testimony before the United States Senate, Committee on Foreign Relations, Rubin (1998) noted that, "The Taliban also receive support from traders based in Quetta, Peshawar, and Karachi who are engaged in the transit and drug trade. These traders include both Afghan and Pakistani Pashtuns. The removal of checkpoints and the establishment of public order in southern and western Afghanistan was of great benefit to them, and they have contributed to the Taliban's treasury and are also regularly assessed as needs arise. Afghan, Pakistani, and Arab traders based in the United Arab Emirates have contributed to the Taliban as well. These traders also affirm their new-found social status through contributions to the *madrasas* where Taliban are trained. They are linked to the local administrations of Northwest Frontier Province and Baluchistan, who are remunerated for permitting smugglers' markets to continue. Officials of these provinces also benefit from the system of permits in force for the export of food and fuel to the Taliban-controlled areas of Afghanistan. The Taliban thus have a broad set of links to Pakistan's society and polity"; see also Labrousse, 1999.

5. It should be noted that the United States Department of State had previously acknowledged that the Taliban had ordered bans (1997 and 2000) on poppy cultivation, though the State Department's message also indicated a skeptical outlook on the sincerity of the heroin ban.

6. Perl (2001, p. 2) argues that, "Some members of the U.S. drug enforcement community suggest that a new strategy may have been adopted by the Taliban in the wake of their July 27, 2000 announced ban on cultivation. This strategy would reflect a desire by the Taliban to use their 'monopoly' position to maximize profits, i.e., restrict supply by restricting cultivation; drive prices up dramatically; and sell from an extensive supply of stockpiled opium. According to the United Nations Drug Control Program (UNDCP) personnel, in the past, up to 60% of opium stock has been stored for sale in future years"; see also Shanty, 2007b, p. 86.

7. On Al Qaeda's efforts at raising and moving money see Roth, Greenburg, and Wille, 2004, pp. 17–29, [an addendum to the 9/11 Commission's final report]; see also Comras, 2005, pp. 1–16; Greenberg, Wechsler, and Wolosky, 2002; Greenberg et al., 2004; and Hamilton, 2004, pp. 5–10.

8. On August 23, 2004, the *Wall Street Journal* reported that, "... efforts within the financial industry to create financial profiles of terrorist cells and terrorist fundraisers have proved unsuccessful, and the ability of financial institutions to detect terrorist financing remains limited.... As of spring 2004, the FBI has generated very little quality finished intelligence in the area of al Qaeda financing" (Simpson, 2004, p. B2); see also Roth, Greenburg, and Wille, 2004, p. 42; U.S. House of Representatives, 2004; and Reuter and Truman, 2005, p. 36.

9. With respect to the dossier and the conventional view of intelligence Burke (2003, p. 20) provides the following underlying rationale, "Oddly, a convention seems to have developed whereby something from a 'security source' acquires a degree of veracity. Such material thus appears to be exempted from normal journalistic practices. The fact that it cannot be confirmed independently is seen as a confirmation of the utility of the information rather than the opposite ... I know from experience that selling a story to a news editor is a lot easier if you can involve bin Laden."

10. Due to the explanatory nature of this research and the numerous statements made confirming or denying the existence of a drug-terror nexus in Afghanistan,

this chapter cites "direct quotes" taken from official transcripts made by public officials and others with firsthand knowledge of the events covered in this study. A principal reason for examining these statements and transcripts is to determine how some of the leading thinkers in the field view the nexus issue, thereby spawning additional discerning questions for inquiry.

11. It is important to note that the statements and testimony presented below are taken from open source hearing transcripts and press reports.

12. See McCarthy, 2003, p. 13; and Taylor, 2002, pp. 23 and 25.

13. See Souder, 2001, pp. 3–5; to view later statements by Representative Souder on this topic see, Souder, 2004, pp. H729–H730; and Souder, 2006, pp. H6511–H6513.

14. Hutchinson (2002b, p.13) provided the committee with a copy of a Taliban receipt. He noted that while the tax for cultivated opium was 10 percent the rate for transporting and processing varies.

15. See also MacDonald, 2005, p. 95.

16. See MacDonald, 2005, p. 95; and Souder, 2006, pp. H6511–H6513.

17. This hearing focused on the global problem of drug trafficking and terrorism and while addressing Afghanistan and neighboring countries it was not specific to Central and Southwest Asia.

18. These two cases, along with several others, will be examined in more detail later in this chapter.

19. Rensselaer W. Lee is a world renowned expert on the narcotics trade and drug trafficking, and has co-authored *The Andean Cocaine Industry*, an in-depth analysis of the cocaine industry in Latin America.

20. Larry Johnson is also a former CIA employee and has worked for the U.S. State Department Office of Counterterrorism.

21. Raphael Perl is a specialist in foreign policy and international affairs.

22. See also Ehrenfeld, 2003, pp. 35–38.

23. See Lee, 2003, p. 43.

24. Senator Biden added, "I think we need some harder data in order to make priority judgments about the extent to which there is a fundamentalist Islamic/terrorist nexus with drug trafficking. That is the key because if that is to be established and if we are unwilling in this or future administrations to spend the resources necessary to cover all the bases, then guys like me are left in a position of deciding how to best spend the limited resources" (Biden, 2003, p. 42).

25. See McCraw, 2003, pp. 103–106.

26. See also Kerry, et al., 2009, p. 10.

27. Regarding Taliban involvement in Afghanistan's opium trade, recent testimony by a former senior official with the U.S. DEA confirmed direct Taliban involvement. In a prepared statement delivered to the U.S. Senate Caucus on International Narcotics Control on October 21, 2009, Michael Braun, former chief of operations for the U.S. DEA, stated that as early as 2005 the DEA had, "clearly identified the Taliban's involvement in protecting," heroin processing labs and drug caches. He also claimed that in 2009 the Taliban had expanded their drug involvement to manufacturing and trafficking. To support the allegation of Taliban involvement in heroin manufacturing, Braun cited a joint U.S. military/DEA raid on an opium conversion lab in southern Afghanistan which uncovered, "approximately 1.8 metric tons," of opiates (opium and heroin). Furthermore, he noted that during the attack on this site, which was conducted two weeks prior

to this statement, 16 Taliban were killed. See Braun, 2009, p. 3; Weinberger, 2009; and Erwin, 2009, p. 6.

28. The information cited in this chart was presented to members of Congress by officials from the U.S. Department of State in April 2004 and February 2005. See Blanchard, 2004, p. 16; 2005, p. 19; 2006, p. 16; 2007a, p. 16.

29. Ms. Tandy's statement and testimony before the U.S. House of Representatives was criticized by some Central Asian drug agents. An article which appeared in *Asia Times Online* cites reaction by some members of Tajikistan's Drug Control Agency (DCA) to Ms. Tandy's remarks. They were perplexed by some of her "on the record" statements. More specifically these agents refer to Tandy's references to "potential links" as absurd. Colonel Alexander Kondratiyev, who spent nearly ten years on the Afghan-Tajik border monitoring and interdicting drug traffic, countered that the link between narcotics and terrorism "is absolutely obvious to us . . . Drugs, weapons, ammunition, terrorism, more drugs, more terrorism—it's a closed circle";. in 2003, prior to Ms. Tandy's statement, Major Avaz Yuldashov of DCA expressed similar views and in fact was even more specific in his appraisal of the drug-terror nexus. He stated in part that "drug trafficking from Afghanistan is the main source of support for international terrorism now." See Maitra, 2005.

30. See also Charles, 2004, pp. 26–27.

31. Secretary O'Connell further stated that, "Poppy cultivation and the revenues generated from the different aspects of the narcotics trade provide fresh resources for extremists and terrorists. The infrastructure of smuggling that supports narcotics trafficking, which can expand and become more capable as the trade increases, also services terrorist transportation and logistics needs. Local leaders and commanders can use profits from narcotics to oppose coalition efforts to establish a unified Afghan government that provides full security to its citizens" (O'Connell, 2004, p. 22); see also Shanty, 2007b, p. 83.

32. At this hearing Tandy stated that, "the Afghan drug trade has the capability of financing terrorists and those who support them," noting that the, Taliban's association with the opium-and heroin-smuggling trade continues today. She said the Taliban continues to use the proceeds from the sale of drugs, which it taxes and protects, as a source of revenue for the anti-coalition activities" (Seper, 2006, p. A03).

33. Representative Mark Kirk is presently Senator-elect after having won the November 2, 2010 election.

34. The primary purpose of this trip was to review the U. S. Department of State's "Rewards Program" implemented to assist in the apprehension of wanted terrorist suspects and identify areas for improvement.

35. At a press conference in Manhattan, N.Y., on April 25, 2005, U.S. Attorney David Kelley announced the indictment of Haji Bashar Noorzai, charging him with "conspiring to import $50 million worth of heroin from Afghanistan and Pakistan into the U.S. and other countries . . . Kelly further said that, "Noorzai had an 'unholy alliance' with deposed Taliban leader Mullah Mohammad Omar, trading drugs and weapons for protection of his operation . . . The indictment further said that 'Noorzai and the Taliban had a symbiotic relationship,' The Taliban 'protected his drug operations in return for demolitions, weaponry and manpower.' Kelly went on to say that, 'In 1997, Taliban officials seized a truckload of morphine base owned by Noorzai, according to the indictment. Upon learning

it was his, they returned it to Noorzai with personal apologies from Mullah Mohammad Omar,' the indictment said. As far as a link to bin Laden or Al Qaeda 'Kelley would not confirm a link to bin Laden, and no mention is made of it in the indictment'" (Rovella and Weidlich, 2005); see also United States District Court, Southern District of New York, 2005a.

36. See Kirk 2004a, pp. 9–12; see also Scarborough 2004a, p. A01; it should be mentioned that this article also stated that a Pentagon drug policy official backed up the findings expressed by Rep. Kirk by stating that, "Mr. Kirk is 'on target' . . . We know of individuals in Afghanistan who continue to fund Al Qaeda with drug proceeds." The article did not cite the official's name; see also Scarborough 2004b, p. A07.

37. This figure has been cited elsewhere as $24 million (US) and is based on statements made by U.S. Congressman Kirk.

38. See Bevir 1994, pp. 328–344.

39. This conclusion is based on the 2004 and 2006 congressional statements of U.S. Drug Enforcement Agency (DEA) Administrator Karen Tandy as cited above.

40. See Weiser, 2008, p. B4 and Weiser, 2009, p. 10.

41. The views expressed by Blanchard in the May 2005, January 2006, and December 2007, updates were based on interview data with U.S. officials in Kabul in January 2005; in the summary section of Blanchard's 2009 report released on August 12 he states, "The trafficking of Afghan drugs also appears to provide financial and logistical support to a range of extremist groups that continue to operate in and around Afghanistan, including resurgent Taliban fighters and some Al Qaeda operatives."

42. This view has been shared by others. See Olcott, 2002, p. 51.

43. Goldman (1994, p. 36) states that, "It is widely recognized that the vast majority of arguments presented in genuine discourse are enthymemes. Many premises are commonly left tacit or unexpressed. A speaker's strength of support for a conclusion may not be captured, therefore, in the support conferred by the stated premises. Notice that a stronger rule, namely, that speakers should state all premises on which they base a given conclusion, would be unfeasible. Inductive inferences normally involve too many background premises to state fully, in any reasonable length of time, and it is probably impossible to retrieve from memory all assumptions on which one's conclusion belief is based."

44. See Souder, 2006, p. H6513.

45. See Kirk, 2004, pp. 8–11 at p. 9.

46. To view full text of statement, see Souder, 2004, pp. H729–H730.

47. See Susnjara, 2005, p. 4; and Grusich, 2002, p. 4.

48. Gunaratna (2002, p. 40) further notes that, "Al Qaeda's guerilla component of 1,500–2,000 Arabs was integrated into the Taliban fighting forces, with the result that al Qaeda and Taliban fighters camped, trained and operated together. Although they functioned strictly as two separate organizations, the structures were integrated for the purpose of fighting the Northern Alliance."

49. In this respect it was noted in the 911 Commission Report [cited above] released on August 21, 2004, nearly three years after the terrorist attacks upon the U.S. that, "after careful review of all of the evidence available to us, including some of the most sensitive information held by the U.S. government, we have

judged that such theories cannot be substantiated (Roth, Greenburg, and Wille, 2004, p. 19); see also Kerry, et al., 2009, p. 10.

50. See Tandy, 2004a, pp. 17–21 at p. 20.

51. This point will be addressed in more detail in chapters 7 and 8.

52. See also Makarenko, 2002d; and Rashid, 2001f.

53. See also Shanty, 2007b, p. 82.

54. See Scarborough, 2004b, p. A07.

55. For example, Congressman Kirk's statement before the U.S. House of Representatives Committee on International Relations on February 12, 2004, that: "These ships carried probable al-Qaeda agents and $10 million worth of methamphetamine, hashish and heroin. If this cargo had made it to Turkey, Al-Qaeda would have been able to sell its heroin for five times the price it receives in Pakistan. If the network was able to reach New York, the profit would be multiplied by 40 times," has not been confirmed by either the U.S. DEA or the CIA. As a matter of fact, according to the 9/11 Commission Report released on July 22, 2004, the DEA and CIA both discounted this as evidence linking the two. According to the report: "We are aware of the December 2003 seizure of two tons of hashish from a ship in the Persian Gulf, and of the initial press reports that three individuals on board had purported al Qaeda links. Both the CIA and the DEA discount the significance of those links, and neither agency believes that this seizure is evidence that al Qaeda is financing itself through narcotics trafficking. We have seen no evidence to the contrary" (Roth, Greenburg, & Wille, 2004, p. 23, footnote 13). It is interesting to note that the above statement by Rep. Kirk was made in February 2004, five months prior to the release of the 9/11 Commission Report.

56. It is possible that members of Al Qaeda and drug traffickers are using the same smuggling channels. This point will be discussed in chapter 7.

57. Interestingly, while some media outlets reported the Persian Gulf incidents as late as the end of 2005 these later reports cited previously disseminated information but failed to break new ground relative to the initial report findings. Most media coverage of drugs/possible Al Qaeda members seized in the Persian Gulf occurred in the December 2003 to February 2004 time frame.

58. See also McGirk, 2004, p. 41.

59. The actual indictment confirms this account: "During the course of the conspiracy, the Noorzai Organization provided demolitions, weaponry, and manpower to the Taliban in Afghanistan. In exchange for its support, the Taliban provided the Noorzai Organization with protection for its opium crops, heroin laboratories, drug-transportation routes, and members and associates." See United States District Court, Southern District of New York, 2005a, p. 3; Ehrenfeld (2003, p. 52, footnote 94, and p. 218) claims that Al Qaeda provided protection to opium poppy growers; this issue will be addressed in chapters 7 and 8.

60. According to U.S. attorney Michael Skerlos, "Both defendants who pleaded guilty Wednesday knew that the Taliban and al-Qaida, Osama bin Laden's terrorist network, were 'virtually synonymous'" (Hettena 2004, pp. 53–54).

61. The suspects in this case may have been motivated by money rather than ideology and may have sold the weaponry to the highest bidder regardless of where it would ultimately be used.

62. See Shanty, 2007, p. 89.

63. The term "non-state actors" refers to groups or organizations which operate "beyond state control," and are transnational in scope with the ability to "affect political outcomes either purposefully or semi-purposefully, either as their primary objective or as one aspect of their activities" (Josselin and Wallace, 2001, pp. 3–4).

CHAPTER 4

1. Mujahideen are holy warriors; Tanner (2002, p. 273) states that, "the mujahideen were predominantly Muslim fundamentalist, part of a loose movement that had become increasingly dangerous since the fall of the Shah of Iran. . . . Most Islamic terrorists were from the Mideast, where the Israeli-Palestinian conflict fueled the fire, but the CIA was aware that many of the most vicious terrorists had acquired the nickname 'Afghans.' These were Arabs who had joined the jihad in Afghanistan, emerging afterwards with training, weapons, and combat experience. Most Arab volunteers had been affiliated with the parties of Sayaf and Hekmatyar, though one Saudi aristocrat, Osama bin Laden, had set up his own organization"; some scholars such as Marsden (1998, pp. 27–28) note that the mujahideen can include all Afghans who took up the struggle against the Soviet-backed People's Democratic Party of Afghanistan (PDPA) and Soviet occupation forces; while this definition can be viewed as a more comprehensive and concise description of the anti-Soviet formations for the purposes of this study Tanner's (2002, p. 273) definition will be used.

2. See Gunaratna and Kousary, 2010.

3. According to Wilke (2004, p. 10) Pakistan's government and military intelligence agency (ISI) "hoped that the Taliban would give them more political and military influence, while trucking companies and traders hoped for a revival of economic relations that had been paralyzed by the war."

4. Stern (2000, p. 119) states that many of these religious schools ignored basic educational instruction in math and the sciences. Their primary focus was on religious indoctrination. She further notes that some of these madrassas taught jihad which was equated "with guerrilla warfare."

5. Saudi Arabia's funding of these religious schools ensured that the curriculum was Wahhabist. Wahhabism is a fundamentalist Saudi sect which, "fiercely opposed anything they viewed as bida, an Arabic word, usually muttered as a curse, for any change or modernization that deviates from the fundamental teachings of the Koran." See MacFarquhar, 2001, p. 1B.7; and Stern, 2000, p. 119.

6. Pakistan supported the Taliban movement since its inception in 1994. The Pakistani government, particularly the ISI, provided the Taliban with arms, training, and weapons. In addition to providing "strategic depth" they [ISI] viewed the Taliban as a strategic asset in their ongoing struggle with India over Kashmir. Militants recruited to fight in the insurgency in Kashmir underwent training in camps in Afghanistan run by Al Qaeda. See Benjamin and Simon, 2003, p. 275.

7. According to Norell (2007, p. 80) "The mullahs of the Jamiat Ulema-e-Islam-Fazlur Rehman (JUI-F) are known to be aiding the Taliban by offering logistical support for the drugs industry. Afghan President Hamid Karzai has attempted to negotiate with the JUI-F in order to stop support for the drug trade and especially

the regrouping of the Taliban in Quetta (also one of the major bases for the drug trade), but without avail"; see also Raman, 2003.

8. The Deobandi movement was named after an Indian town, Deoband. Deobandism began in British India as a reform movement which still exists today. The Deobandi tradition is a branch of Sunni Islam which rejects secular society and believes in following the dictates of traditional Islam. See Schwartz, 2006.

9. In October 2001, shortly before the U.S. and coalition offensive in Afghanistan began, Rashid (2001e) provided some insight into the Taliban's emergence, their reclusive leader Mullah Muhammad Omar, and his relationship with Osama bin Laden: "Omar fought with the mujahideen guerrillas against Soviet occupying forces in the late 1980s. He and other former mujahideen soon became disillusioned with the rampant warlordism, crime and mayhem that followed the departure of the Soviet troops in 1989, and in 1994 helped form the Taliban, literally Islamic students, who pledged to impose law and order and create a pure Islamic society. . . . Osama bin Laden introduced Omar to the wider world of Islamic radicalism, global jihad and hatred of the non-Muslim world. Bin Laden also provided funds and recruited thousands of Arabs to fight in the Taliban army."

10. A burka is a total body garment with a screen mesh that enables women to see. The Taliban's gender policies aroused international concern and were a contributing factor in their failed attempts to gain international recognition (Rubin, 1998).

11. "Afghan Arabs" was a term given to foreign Islamists who volunteered to fight in the Soviet-Afghan war; see Ghazi, 2002.

12. Many of the Arab volunteers who descended upon Afghanistan and Pakistan during the 1980s were recruited through the Maktab al-Khalimat (Afghan Service Bureau), an organization set up by Osama bin Laden and Abdullah Azzam, a former activist in the Palestinian struggle with Israel, to recruit, train, direct, and otherwise support mujahideen efforts to combat the invading Soviet forces.

13. Among them the 1993 murder in Somalia of 18 U.S. Army Rangers, the 1998 bombing of two U.S. embassies in East Africa, the October 2000 attack on the Navy destroyer USS *Cole* in Aden, Yemen—which left 17 American sailors dead and 39 others injured, and the September 11, 2001, attacks on the World Trade Center and the Pentagon, and the crash of a fourth commercial airliner in Pennsylvania. These four events claimed the lives of over 3,000 people (Shanty, 2003, pp. 605–606).

14. For a description of Al Qaeda's ties to other like-minded jihadist groups see Caruso, 2001.

15. Hezb-i-Islami (HIG) was formed by Gulbuddin Hekmatyar, a former engineering student at Kabul University in the 1970s. HIG was one of seven factions that were financed by the U.S. and Saudi Arabia to counter Soviet military operations in Afghanistan. Considered to be the most radical of the anti-Soviet Afghan groups, HIG received a large percentage of U.S. and Saudi funding channeled through Pakistan's Inter-Services Intelligence Agency (ISI). During the present campaign Hekmatyar, staunchly anti-American, has aligned himself with the Taliban, a former opponent, and Al Qaeda against U.S. and coalition forces. See, GlobalSecurity.org, http://www.globalsecurity.org/military/world/para/hizbi-islami.htm; for more information on HIG and other Afghan Islamist movements formed in the 1970s see Roy, 1990, pp. 69–83.

16. As noted in chapter 1, for the purposes of this study the terms "Islamist militant groups" and "Islamist extremists" are interchangeable.

17. See Rubin, M., 2002b, pp. 1–16.

18. Concerning direct CIA support for the "Afghan Arabs," see Rubin, M., 2002b, pp. 1–16; see also Rubin, M., 2002a; and National Commission on Terrorist Attacks upon the United State, 2004 p. 467, Note 23.

19. Roth, Greenburg, and Wille (2004, p. 20) report that: "From about 1970 until 1993 or 1994, Usama Bin Ladin received about a million dollars per year—adding up to a significant sum, to be sure, but not a $300 million fortune. In 1994 the Saudi government forced the Bin Ladin family to find a buyer for Usama's share of the family company and to place the proceeds into a frozen account. The Saudi freeze had the effect of divesting Bin Ladin of what would otherwise have been a $300 million fortune. Notwithstanding this information, some within the government continued to cite the $300 million figure well after 9/11, and the general public still gives credence to the notion of a 'multimillionaire Bin Ladin.'"

20. Caruso (2001) states: "From its inception until approximately 1991, the group was headquartered in Afghanistan and Peshawar, Pakistan. Then in 1991, the group relocated to the Sudan where it was headquartered until approximately 1996, when Bin Laden, Mohammed Atef and other members of Al-Qaeda returned to Afghanistan. During the years Al-Qaeda was headquartered in Sudan the network continued to maintain offices in various parts of the world and established businesses which were operated to provide income and cover to Al-Qaeda operatives."

21. See McGeary, 2001; and Weiser, 2001, p. A1.

22. See also United States District Court, Southern District of New York, 2001b, pp. 1041, 357, and 528.

23. Gunaratna (2002, p. 31) notes that, "While in Sudan, Osama played a dual role, both as terrorist and businessman. In keeping with Sudan's clandestine support for Islamist movements around the world, he [bin Laden] built a powerful organization to augment Khartoum's efforts. After establishing links with about twenty Islamist groups engaged in guerrilla warfare and terrorism, he supported them with funds, training and weapons."

24. See the National Commission on Terrorist Attacks Upon the United States, 2004, p. 67.

25. See also Rashid, 2001b, Rashid, 2001c; Gunaratna, 2002, p. 40; and O'Harrow, Hilzenrath, and DeYoung, 2001, p. A13.

26. See United Nations Security Council Resolution 1267, dated October 15, 1999; and UN Security Council Resolution 1333, dated December 18, 2000.

27. A bi-monthly report issued by the Jamestown Foundation, an independent research institute.

28. Peter Bergen is the author of *Holy War, Inc.* and a recently published book, *The Osama bin Laden I Know: An Oral History of al Qaeda's Leader*; to view this interview in its entirety see CNN, 2006.

29. See Gunaratna and Kousary, 2010; Mansoor Dadullah replaced his brother, Mullah Dadullah, when the latter was killed in Helmand province in May 2007. See *Daily Times*, 2007; for information on Mullah Dadullah, see Marzban, 2006b, pp. 3–4; and BBC News 2007a; Mansoor Dadullah was reportedly relieved of his command by Mullah Muhammad Omar in December 2007. See Roggio, 2007;

Dadullah was subsequently wounded and captured by the Pakistani military in February 2008. See Roggio, 2008a.

30. See Gehriger and Yousafzai, 2007; Associated Press, September 20, 2007b; and *USA Today*, September 20, 2007.

31. See also Kohlmann, 2007.

32. See also http://www.msnbc.msn.com/id/20880736/; and *USA Today*, September 20, 2007.

33. See *Daily Times* (Pakistan), 2007; Marzban, 2006b, pp. 3–4; and BBC News, 2007a.

34. See U.S. Department of State, 2000, pp. 7–8.

35. Bruce Riedel, a senior fellow of the Brookings Institution notes, "The ideology of global jihad has been bought into by more and more militants, even guys who never thought much about the broader world. And this is disturbing, because it is a force multiplier for Al Qaeda" (Sanger 2010, p. WK1).

36. For more on this topic see Rosenau 2007; and O'Neill 2005.

37. See also Byman et al., 2001.

38. Rohan Gunaratna argues that in many respects the Taliban is still providing safe haven to Al Qaeda. See Zabriskie, 2003.

39. Although responsible for attacks on United Nations (UN) "personnel and facilities" and non-governmental organizations (NGOs) Hezb-i-Islami has not been designated a foreign terrorist organization by the U.S. Department of State; Gulbuddin Hekmatyar, founder of Hezb-i-Islami, has also trained terrorists in Afghan-based camps for service in various "Islamic conflicts." See United States Department of State, 2003d; on February 19, 2003, the U.S. Department of State issued a press release designating Gulbuddin Hekmatyar as a "specially designated global terrorist under authority of Executive Order 13224." The statement released by Richard Boucher, U.S Department of State spokesman, further adds that, "Gulbuddin Hekmatyar has participated in and supported terrorist acts committed by al-Qaida and the Taliban." See United States Department of State, 2003b; see also Poole, 2005, p. 98; and Burns, 2005b.

40. See Brewster, 2009; and Gopal, 2009.

41. See Escobar, 2004.

42. Gunaratna and Kousary, 2010 note that Hezb-i-Islami (HIG), "was the largest Afghan Mujahideen faction fighting against the Soviet forces and it had the largest representation of the Pashtun ethnic group in Afghanistan. Pashtun ethnic group in Afghanistan is the majority and Pakistan is believed to be seeing its strategic interests vis-à-vis Afghanistan in the Afghan Pashtun groups. Pakistan itself has Pashtuns as its largest minority, which could also be a reason for Pakistan's support for the Afghan Pashtun groups. Also, Hezb-i-Islami leadership had close ties with the Pakistani religious groups like Jamiat-i-Islami (Islamic party of Pakistan) in 1980s and these religious groups had been considerably influential in Pakistani establishment during General Zia's regime."

43. See also Booth, 1996, p. 289; and UNODC, 2009a, p. 103.

44. According to a report which appeared in the *Terrorism Monitor*, an unnamed senior official in the Parwan province told the Jamestown Foundation that, "the most recent government investigation shows that Hekmatyar is leading the insurgency in the northern and eastern parts of Afghanistan, while Mullah Omar and his al-Qaeda ally, Osama bin Laden, operate in the south

and the west. It is believed that these three leaders form a group that has been labeled the 'Triangle of Terror'" (Marzban, 2006a, p. 7); according to a previously cited report issued by the Jamestown Foundation: "There are indications that both the remnants of the Taliban and al-Qaeda militants have combined forces with Gulbuddin Hekmatyar's Islamic Party and have been rapidly building up their military capabilities. Hekmatyar and the Talibs have joined forces . . . some reports suggest that previously isolated and scattered Taliban armed groups have accepted Hekmatyar as their commander, and the number of such units is growing" (Korgun, 2003, p. 5); see also Brewster, 2009 and Gopal, 2009; additionally, a report by National Public Radio cites a "deeper and more collaborative relationship" between the Al Qaeda and the Haqqani Network. See National Public Radio, 2009; and UNODC, 2009a, p. 103.

45. Jones further elaborates on the organizational composition of the Afghan insurgency. See Jones, 2008, pp. 37–66; and DuPee and Azizpour, 2006.

46. The UN Secretary General provides additional detail regarding these five, "command and control," centers. See United Nations General Assembly Report, 2006, p. 2.

47. For information regarding the strength of the insurgent forces see Pant, 2006.

48. On August 4, 2006, the Magazine Publishers of Australia honored *TIME* magazine's Rory Callinan with the Story of the Year award for an article he wrote on the war in Afghanistan; see http://www.magazines.org.au/default.asp?page=/news/latest+news/nw+judged+magazine+of+the+year; Callinan was also a finalist in the 2004 Walkley awards (Australia) feature writing category; see http://www.time.com/time/magazine/article/0,9171,1138022,00.html?iid=chix-sphere; and http://www20.sbs.com.au/walkleys/assets/2004%20Walkley%20Awards%20Finalists.pdf.

49. According to information provided by the Memorial Institute for the Prevention of Terrorism Knowledge Base (MIPT) the group's current main objective is "to continue the armed struggle against non-believers and 'anti-Islamic forces.'" Their sources of financing consist of "donations from Pakistanis and Kashmiris. Inter-Services Intelligence (ISI), Pakistan's external intelligence agency, also contributes to the organization's funding." Additionally, they are involved in a number of legal businesses; see Memorial Institute for the Prevention of Terrorism, 2005b.

50. See McChrystal, S., 2009, "Commander's Initial Assessment," (Unclassified) NATO International Security Assistance Force, Kabul, Afghanistan, August 30, viewed October 10, 2009, http://media.washingtonpost.com/wp-srv/politics/documents/Assessment_Redacted_092109.pdf

51. See Walsh, 2010; and Schmitt and Mazzetti, 2009; for a detailed perspective on the Quetta Shura Taliban in Afghanistan, see Dressler and Forsberg, 2009.

52. See Gopal, 2009.

53. Although the top leadership of the QST is based in Quetta, Pakistan, they have a "governing structure in Afghanistan" and "appoint shadow governors for most provinces." In areas under their control they administer justice, levy taxes, and recruit fighters. According to the assessment, HQN and HIG share a similar objective with the QST (driving foreign forces from Afghanistan), however, they do not arbitrarily accept the "QST governing framework and have yet to develop competing governing structures" McChrystal (2009, p. 2–7).

54. See Sciutto and Perez, 2010; regarding new measures to control/eliminate corruption see Shanker and Schmitt, 2010, p. A1.

55. A travel alert issued by the U.S. embassy in Kabul on 9 January 2006 describes very concisely the security situation wrought by non-state actors in Afghanistan. See United States Department of State 2006c.

56. For information regarding civil wars and warlords, see Makarenko, 2002, p. 8, footnote 24.

57. A report issued by the U.S. Congressional Research Service in May 2010 notes that of these 1,800 IAGs "several hundred" are considered "significant." Additionally, U.S. military and Afghan officials estimate that there are approximately 20,000 Taliban fighters, 1,000 HQN fighters, and 1,000 fighters belonging to Gulbuddin Hekmatyar's HIG operating against coalition forces in Afghanistan (Katzman, 2010, p. 51).

58. See also Government of Afghanistan, 2006, pp. 56 and 114.

59. See UNODC, 2009b, p. 10.

60. See Eikenberry, 2006; and White, 2006, p. A14; the views of Lt. Gen. Eikenberry are shared by ICG's Joanna Nathan who argues: "What is often labeled as Taliban violence is not . . . It's a whole set of fluid alliances, cross-border attacks from Pakistan, drugs, tribal feuds, and of course the Taliban . . . The state we're in now is because of the policy decision to co-opt those people who in the past committed human rights abuses. There's a culture of impunity" (Montero, 2006, p. 7). Ms. Nathan further adds that these problems are not isolated in the southern provinces but are widespread throughout the country.

61. See Government of Afghanistan, 2006, p. 44.

62. A fatwa is a legal opinion or statement usually rendered on a point in Islamic law. To view Osama bin Laden's 1996 fatwa titled, "Declaration of War against the Americans Occupying the Land of the Two Holy Places" see Bin Laden, O., 1996, from the Arabic-language daily *Al-Quds al-Arabi* (London), August 1996, reproduced in "Bin Laden's Fatwa," *Online News Hour with Jim Lehrer,* Public Broadcasting Service (PBS), viewed transcript July 5, 2007, http://www.pbs.org/newshour/terrorism/international/fatwa_1996.html.

CHAPTER 5

1. This information was retrieved, in part, from the Memorial Institute for the Prevention of Terrorism (MIPT) Terrorism Knowledge Base, MIPT/RAND terrorist incident reports (incidents by groups), viewed May 30–June 5, 2007, http//www.tkb.org/incidentgroupmodule.jsp; see Memorial Institute for the Prevention of Terrorism, 2005e.

2. Al Qaeda in this context is defined as the "core" organization, responsible for 23 of the above cited 46 attacks.

3. See United States Department of State, 2003c; the term "Terrorist Exclusion List" is derived from the "USA PATRIOT ACT of 2001, Section 411 (8 U.S.C. § 1182); see United States Department of State, 2004d; the term Other Terrorist Organizations, "includes other selected terrorist groups also deemed of relevance in the global war on terrorism"; see Memorial Institute for the Prevention of Terrorism, 2005b; to view the U.S. Department of State's list of "Other Selected Terrorist Organizations" see United States Department of State, 2005a, pp. 113–129.

4. This action, pursuant under Executive Order 13224, blocks assets and provides an instrument which is designed to restrict support to terrorist groups; according to Guitta (2006) a specially designated global terrorist is, "Anyone determined to 'act for or on behalf' of a listed entity or to 'provide financial . . . support for, or financial services to or in support of . . . entities designated in or under the Order' or '[t]o be otherwise associated with certain individuals or entities designated in or under the Order' may be designated a SDGT. In other words, soliciting funds or even being associated with an SDGT is enough to get someone designated an SDGT"; see also Kellerhals, 2004.

5. According to the U.S. Department of State's report, *Patterns of Global Terrorism 1999*, this incident was perpetrated by Kashmiri militants. This author's research indicates that members of Jamiat ul-Ansar, a militant group which operates primarily in Kashmir, were responsible for the hijacking of the Indian airliner. The Taliban were instrumental in the final stages of the hijacking and it is highly possible, given the ties the Taliban had with other militant factions, that collusion between these two groups existed, as the perpetrators were allowed to go free after the aircraft landed in Kandahar (U.S. Department of State, 2000).

6. The Fergana Valley is a mountainous region which spans three Central Asian states: Kyrgyzstan, Tajikistan, and Uzbekistan.

7. See Rashid, 2001a.

8. See Mutschke, 2000, pp. 85–120; Makarenko, 2002d; and Napoleoni, 2003, pp. 88–91.

9. According to the U.S. Department of State (2004c, p. 122): "the IMU is closely affiliated with al-Qaida and, under the leadership of Tohir Yoldashev, has embraced Usama Bin Ladin's anti-US, anti-Western agenda"; see also prepared statement of Olcott (2003, p.56) delivered before the U.S. House of Representatives.

10. See U.S. Department of State, 2001b, p. 68.

11. See also Mutschke, 2000; Napoleoni, 2003, p. 89; and Ehrenfeld, 2003, pp. 54 and 219, footnote 111.

12. In October 2003, Dr. Victor Korgun, a terrorism analyst for the Jamestown Foundation, reported that, "Afghan Taliban and their foreign allies—mainly Arabs and Pakistanis—are developing a cohesive command structure in an effort to control the militia's armed units and coordinate its operations. For example, remnants of Uzbek and Tajik militants have reportedly been brought under the command of Tahir Yuldash, a former deputy of Juma Namangani, the leader of the Islamic Movement of Uzbekistan who was killed in October 2001 in the course of the US bombing campaign. Shortly before the American attack, Mullah Omar had appointed Namangani commander-in-chief of Taliban forces in Afghanistan's northern provinces" (Korgun, 2003); see also Rashid, 2002, pp. 34–42.

13. See Raman, 2004.

14. According to the U.S. Department of State, *Country Reports on Terrorism 2005*, issued in April 2006, the IMU was implicated in three attacks in Kyrgyzstan since 9/11. These attacks occurred in 2002, 2003, and 2004. According to the U.S. Department of State (2006a, p. 200) ". . . it is difficult to differentiate between IMU and Islamic Jihad Group members . . ." This may be the basis for the discrepancy between MIPT/RAND and U.S. State Department accounts; the discrepancy may also be due to source information. It is noteworthy to point out that according to this report [U.S. State Dept] "Since Operation Enduring Freedom, the IMU has been

predominantly occupied with attacks on U.S. and Coalition soldiers in Afghanistan and Pakistan.... Pakistani security forces continue to arrest probable IMU operatives in the Federally Administered Tribal Areas (FATA). Suspected IMU members have also attacked Pakistani Government forces in the FATA and been discovered fighting Coalition forces in Afghanistan"; according to Makarenko (2002d, p. 12, footnote 41) "Prior to the events of September 11th there were indications the IMU was splitting between the criminal and ideological—between Namanganiy and Yuldashev. Reports that the IMU had changed its name to the Islamic Party of Turkestan was evidence of the shifting internal dynamics of the IMU"; the U.S. Department of State designated the Islamic Movement of Uzbekistan (IMU) a foreign terrorist organization (FTO) in 2000; see also U.S. Department of State, 2004c, p. 122.

15. See also Gall, 2004, p. 13; and Campbell, 2004, p. 17.

16. At the time this data was compiled, May 1, 2007, was the last date that terrorist incident data was entered into the MIPT/RAND database Web site.

17. See Gall, 2008b, p. 1.

18. See Dupee, 2008.

19. The Serena hotel in Kabul is frequented by international visitors such as foreign journalists, aid workers, etc. See Baker, 2008; see also Rogio, 2008b.

20. See Gall, 2008b; and UNODC, 2009a, p. 103.

21. These provinces were primary poppy-producing areas prior to the Taliban 2000 ban.

22. See Robichaud, 2006; Carl Robichaud of the Century Foundation used the RAND definition of terrorism, cited in chapter 1 of this study, to compile this data; on January 15, 2006, a Canadian diplomat was killed and three soldiers were wounded in Kandahar when a Canadian Provincial Reconstruction Team came under attack; Ghafour (2006) notes that the Canadian team, "is operating in a region where a combination of Islamist terrorists, organized criminals and drug traffickers have created an environment which makes it increasingly difficult to carry out combat operations or humanitarian work. The extent to which these groups work together is not clear, but it is in their collective interest to keep Kandahar, and the entire southern Pashtun belt, unstable."

23. Since these numbers are subject to change as more information became available, the data presented here was collected on August 31, 2007. The date of February 2, 2007, is an arbitrary date which was selected to allow for at least a 6–7 month period to provide those maintaining the database sufficient time to incorporate any additions, deletions, and/or modifications. The date of October 7, 2001, was chosen as that date represents the beginning of the U.S.-led attack on Afghanistan.

24. That is, "incidents in which terrorists go abroad to strike their targets, select domestic targets associated with a foreign state, or create an international incident by attacking airline passengers, personnel or equipment" (MIPT, 2005); terrorist incidents information was provided by the RAND Corporation through MIPT.

25. See Eikenberry, 2006.

26. See Government of Afghanistan, 2006, p.114 of Vol. 1.

27. See Memorial Institute for the Prevention of Terrorism, 2005a.

28. According to the CIA (2007) Web site, accessed on October 1, 2007: "The Intelligence Community is guided by the definition of terrorism contained in

Title 22 of the US Code, Section 2656f(d): 'The term "terrorism" means premeditated, politically motivated violence perpetrated against noncombatant targets by subnational groups or clandestine agents, usually intended to influence an audience.' The term 'international terrorism' means terrorism involving the territory or the citizens of more than one country. The term 'terrorist group' means any group that practices, or has significant subgroups that practice, international terrorism"; see https://www.cia.gov/news-information/cia-the-war-on-terrorism/terrorism-faqs.html.

29. The definition further states that, "The common denominator of most insurgent groups is their desire to control a particular area. This objective differentiates insurgent groups from purely terrorist organizations, whose objectives do not include the creation of an alternative government capable of controlling a given area or country" (https://www.cia.gov/news-information/cia-the-war-on-terrorism/terrorism-faqs.html).

30. This point was well noted by McChrystal, 2009.

31. Attacks by criminals against Afghan and NATO/ISAF forces could also be designed to create an environment conducive to the trafficking of narcotics.

32. This assessment has been confirmed by McChrystal, 2009, and the Pakistani government. See *Press TV*, 2009.

33. See Escobar, 2004.

34. See Memorial Institute for the Prevention of Terrorism, 2005a.

35. "The Government of Pakistan accused AQ, along with the Taliban, of being responsible for the October 2007 suicide bombing attempt against former Pakistani Prime Minister Benazir Bhutto that killed at least 144 people in Karachi, Pakistan. On December 27, 2007, the Government of Pakistan stated that Baitullah Mahsud, a leading Pakistani Taliban commander with close ties to AQ, was responsible for the assassination of Benazir Bhutto." See United States Department of State, 2009a, p. 318.

36. See United States Department of State, 2005a, p. 7 of chapter 3.

37. Prior to the death of its co-founder, Abdullah Azzam, Al Qaeda had been interested in training foreign fighters for global jihad—particularly against the United States and Israel. Moreover, the Egyptian members of MAK, Afghan Service Bureau, and forerunner to Al Qaeda, wanted to train Islamists to launch a terrorist campaign in Egypt; Azzam disagreed; he wanted their available funds to be used in Afghanistan. This struggle over the future operational direction that Al Qaeda would take ended with the untimely death of Azzam in November 1989 (Gunaratna, 2002, pp. 22–23); this dispute over operational tactics and organizational objectives was to surface again in Sudan. See al Fadl testimony in United States District Court, Southern District of New York, 2001a; and United States District Court, Southern District of New York, 2001b.

38. During an interview conducted by Afgha.com, Dr. Seth Jones (RAND) who has made numerous trips to Afghanistan stated that, "all major insurgent groups enjoy a strong base of support in Pakistan" (DuPee and Azizpour, 2006).

39. See UNODC, 2009a, p. 106; and Bakier, 2010, p. 5.

40. Abu Musab Zarqawi was killed in an air strike launched by U.S. forces on June 7, 2006, in Iraq. See Knickmeyer and Finer, 2006.

41. To view the entire text of this correspondence see *Weekly Standard*, 2005, "Ayman al-Zawahiri's letter to Abu Musab al-Zarqawi" (English translation), October 12, viewed June 12, 2007, http://www.weeklystandard.com/Content/

Public/Articles/000/000/006/203gpuul.asp; during an interview with Robert Fisk (1996) of *The Independent*, a British daily newspaper, conducted shortly after his return to Afghanistan from Sudan Osama bin Laden "declared that killing the Americans [in Khobar (Dhahran), Saudi Arabia in May 1996] marked 'the beginning of war between Muslims and the United States.' He also stated during that interview that 'he would carry on a campaign from Afghanistan to set up a 'true' Islamic state under sharia law in Saudi Arabia which, he said, had been turned into 'an American colony.'"

42. At this writing it appears that Al Qaeda's organization in Iraq has been disabled, if not defeated, through joint American-Iraqi (Sunni) combat operations in 2006–2007.

43. For a discussion of Al Qaeda's modus operandi see Negroponte, 2006, p. 5.

44. Pape (2003, p. 14) notes that, "Although the United States successfully toppled the Taliban in Afghanistan in December 2001, Al Qaeda launched seven successful suicide terrorist attacks from April to December 2002, killing some 250 Western civilians, more than in the three years before September 11, 2001, combined."

45. Although not supported by empirically-based data, the United States Department of the Treasury and some media reports suggest that Al Qaeda is struggling financially. See Bartolf and Finel (2009, p. 13); in June 2009, Al Qaeda appealed to supporters for assistance noting a shortage of food, equipment, and ancillary supplies. See Maclean 2009; see also Bruno, 2010; and Bliss and Capaccio, 2010.

46. Incidents of widespread corruption and drug abuse have been reported among members of the ANP. See Oppel, 2009, p. 1; and Brady, 2010.

47. Prior to the US-led invasion, the Taliban was a territorial-based militia which controlled approximately 90 percent of the country. Al Qaeda was a terrorist group with global ambitions implicated in many attacks on foreign, mostly Western, targets. They were based in Afghanistan and were operating training facilities (camps) for future Islamists. The Taliban provided "safe haven" for this group as well as some others (e.g., Islamic Movement of Uzbekistan).

48. Regarding testimony, see Audi, 2003, p. 148; extremists from Chechnya, the Balkans, the Middle East, Europe, North Africa, and North America have received training in these camps. Osama bin Laden has ties to various other extremist groups such as the Egyptian Islamic Jihad, the Islamic Group of Algeria, the Abu Sayyaf group based in the Philippines, the Chechen resistance, the previously mentioned IMU, groups operating in Kashmir, and others. Many of these groups are ideologically tied to bin Laden in that they share his global vision. Moreover, there are shifting alliances among many of these radical groups. It is not known how much control bin Laden and the Al Qaeda leadership have over the myriad of people that presently identify with them ideologically, nor how much influence Al Qaeda actually has over the collective or individual actions of other ideologically-minded organizations or individuals.

49. This issue was addressed in chapter 4.

50. See Rabasa et al., 2006, pp. xx–xxi, and 73 of Part 1.

51. See Rabasa et al., 2006, pp. xxiv–xxv of Part 2.

52. Al Qaeda's ability to reconstitute itself following the October 2001 invasion points to the sustained appeal the organization continues to have throughout the world. See Brimley, 2006, p. 35.

53. For example, Shelley and Picarelli, et al., (2005, p. 112, endnote 85) note: "The members of the March 11th 2004 Madrid bombing group are an exemplar of the evolving nature of terrorism. While they held a strong affinity for the goals of Al Qaeda and were influenced early on by a member of the September 11th conspiracy, but there is no evidence that they ever obtained direct assistance from Al Qaeda."

54. A U.S. intelligence report issued in July 2007 confirmed what military commanders on the ground in Afghanistan have been saying regarding the various extremist components infiltrating into Afghanistan from Pakistan's North West Frontier Province (NWFP). See Whitlock, 2007, p. A1; and Nasir, 2006, pp. 5–7; see also Gunaratna and Kousary, 2010.

55. These are the Spanish acronyms for the Revolutionary Armed Forces of Colombia (FARC), the National Liberation Army (ELN), and the United Self-Defense Forces of Colombia (AUC).

56. On September 29, 2007, the Associated Press reported that Taliban spokesman, Zabiullah Mujahid, claimed responsibility on behalf of the Taliban for the September 29, 2007, suicide bombing aboard a bus carrying members of the Afghan military. The Associated Press (2007a) also reported that: "Taliban attacks typically target international and Afghan military and police, though civilians are often killed or wounded as well. The Taliban have launched more than 100 suicide attacks this year, a record pace."

57. See National Public Radio, 2009.

58. An Afghan official recently noted that, "Today's Taliban are fighting for an extremist ideology" (Chaudhuri, 2007).

59. See Fair, Malhotra, and Shapiro, 2009, p. 39; and Blair, 2010, pp. 18–20.

60. According to Rashid (2009, pp. 278–279) most, "latter-day Al Qaeda terrorist plots," are linked in some way to Pakistan's tribal areas.

61. According to a UN report, suicide attacks have become a common tactic in the Taliban arsenal: "The tribal areas of Pakistan remain an important source of human and material assistance for suicide attacks in Afghanistan" (Fair, 2007, pp.10 and 89). The report also highlights the fact that the Taliban often recruit children for suicide attacks and Mullah Dadullah Mansour, a Taliban commander runs one such school; see also Williams, 2007, pp. 1–4; and Pape, 2003, pp. 1–19.

62. See Roggio, 2010; and UNODC, 2009a, p. 103.

63. See Maples, 2007a, p. 5; and Maples, 2007b, p. 8.

64. See also Gunaratna, 2002, p. 11; and Dollard, 2007.

65. See Fair (2007, pp. 68 and 86) for a discussion of suicide attacks by Afghan civilians and the use of Pakistan as a recruitment base for suicide bombers.

66. Anecdotal reports indicate that Al Qaeda in the Islamic Maghreb (AQIM), an Algerian group active in North Africa, is involved in protecting drug convoys and other illegal activity to generate funds. See Chikhi, 2010; and Neighbour, 2010, p. 013.

67. See chapter 4.

68. For example see Harden, 2007, p, A 17.

69. Chinese militants from the Xinjiang region in northwestern China seek to establish an autonomous state in China's Uighur province. A report published by *Newsline* suggests that Uighur militants are closely aligned with bin Laden and were part of the anti-Coalition force in 2001. Additionally the report states that

some Pakistani officials believe that "nearly 1,000 Uighur militants from China's Xinjiang region have made their way to South and North Waziristan" and have been responsible for attacks targeting Chinese nationals in Pakistan. The article further notes that according to Pakistani officials "militants have sought shelter in the lawless tribal zones for decades, never before had they used Pakistani soil to fight their 'ideological' battles" (Ansari 2007); see also Wolfe, 2004.

70. See Levy, C. J., 2009, p. A4.

CHAPTER 6

1. This chapter, while not addressing all instances whereby states may be supporting various terrorist factions, will address Pakistan's purported support of militants in Kashmir and Punjab and support provided by various individual actors and charities in Saudi Arabia.

2. See Shanty, 2007b, pp. 81–82.

3. See Schmid, 1996, pp. 40–82; for a discussion on the links between drug criminals and terrorists including some of the Middle Eastern groups see, Lee, 2003, pp. 30–32.

4. For definition used in this study see chapter 1.

5. See Shanty, 2007b, p. 83.

6. See Rashid, 2001c and 2001f, p. 139 and Gunaratna, 2002, pp. 58–62.

7. The Japanese religious sect Aum Shinrikyo, responsible for the 1995 Sarin nerve agent attack inside the Tokyo subway system, is an example of such a group.

8. See Iselin, 2004.

9. See Makarenko, 2002, endnote 51.

10. See O'Malley and Hutchinson, 2006, pp. 2 and 13; and Shanty, 2007b, p. 82.

11. Terrorists are much more likely to encounter military reprisals than are criminal organizations. This is another factor that makes long-term alliances between these two groups unlikely.

12. See *U.S. News & World Report*, 2005; BBC News, 2006a: United States Department of the Treasury, 2003; on possible links between Dawood Ibrahim and Osama bin Laden see Scheuer, 2006b, pp. 43–44.

13. See for example, Sumii et al., 2005.

14. See Gardner, 2001, p. C3; Kaplan, Fang, and Sangwan, 2005, p. 44; and United States Defense Intelligence Agency, 1998.

15. See Shanty, 2007, pp. 350–357; concerning bin Laden's possible involvement in the Afghan drug trade the *Drug War Chronicle* (2001) stated that, "According to various sources, Osama bin Laden and Al-Qaeda have pocketed some of the proceeds. 'There are increasing reports out of the region that, indeed, he is replenishing his coffers with drug money and helping move drugs across Afghanistan,' Congressional terrorism researcher Kenneth Katzman told *CBS News* back in May."

16. See Baldor, 2010b; Lormel, 2001, p. 2; Schmid, 2001, p. 126; and Gunaratna, 2001, pp. 182–185.

17. According to Robinson (2004) the World Trade Center attack in 1993 cost about $25,000 and, "the money, which funded the planning of the attack, was stolen through credit card and other types of low-level fraud. It was much the same with

the 'Millennium Plot' to blow up Los Angeles International Airport in December 1999. The conspirators lived off check fraud, credit card fraud and identity theft."

18. The main source of imported opiates for many European countries is Afghanistan. In a 2001 report, the U.S. Drug Enforcement Administration (2001a) estimated this number to be 80 percent.

19. See UNODC, 2009a, p. 114.

20. Europol (2009, p. 19) states that various groups' involvement in the heroin trade is primarily due to, "geographical and historical proximity to the main source country"; regarding Afghan trafficking networks Shaw (2006, p. 208) notes: "There is general agreement among those interviewed that Afghan trafficking groups control the drug trade up to the borders of Afghanistan, from where consignments are sold to trafficking networks in the surrounding countries. There is, however, substantial evidence that the networks and contacts of Afghan traffickers, particularly those based in the south, extend well beyond the borders of the country, with Dubai serving as a key financial hub for transactions conducted outside of Afghanistan. There is limited evidence that some Afghan trafficking groups have sought to transport drugs to their end destinations in Europe (where some arrests have been made), but this is not yet a widespread phenomenon"; see also, Makarenko, 2002d, p. 7, footnote 18.

21. See, Council of Europe (2001, pp. 45–46) on the extent of involvement of Albanian trafficking groups in the early part of the decade.

22. While not directly addressing the drug trade Ahmad Shah Massoud, former commander of Northern Alliance forces, in interviews conducted prior to his death in September 2001 had said that, "he receives much of his equipment from the Russian mafia, not the Russian government" (Risen, 1998, p. A1).

23. Whitmore further states that, "Kosovars became Europe's heroin kingpins by dominating the 'Balkan route,' a series of roundabout highways that run from Turkey through Bulgaria, the former Yugoslavia, Hungary, Slovakia, the Czech Republic, Germany, and then, it is said, into Austria. . . . At the top of the drug-smuggling hierarchy, according to Interpol, is a group of gangsters known as 'The Fifteen Families,' who are based in northern Albania, near the Yugoslav border" (Whitmore, 2001, p. 14); during his testimony before the U.S. House of Representatives in December 2000 Mr. Ralf Mutschke expanded on the role that Albanian criminal groups play in the trafficking of Afghan opiates throughout Europe. See Mutschke, 2000, p. 96.

24. See also Europol, 2005, p. 11.

25. See Europol, 2009, pp. 28, 31 and 35; UNODC, (2010d, p. 124) reports that after the drugs reach specific destination countries in Europe national criminal groups control the local drug markets.

26. For additional insight into the movement of heroin and other commodities through Afghanistan's borders see U.S. Department of State, 2005, p.65 (Vol. 2); see also UNODC, 2010d, p. 117; and UNODC, 2009a, p. 112.

27. In a questionnaire submitted to this author Mitch Prothero, investigative reporter for United Press International, stated that although the drug trade in Afghanistan consisted of, "very organized groups of people with international connections,", criminal gangs operating inside Afghanistan tend to be nationally and regionally based, i.e., Afghanistan, Iran, Pakistan, and Tajikistan (e-mail communication, October 2, 2006); see also UNODC, 2009a, p. 104; due to the competitive

nature of the drug trade Swanstrom (2007, p. 3, footnote 10) argues that since the 2001 invasion there has been an increase in the number of internationally-based criminal groups (Albanian, European, Turkish) in Afghanistan.

28. See Felbab-Brown, 2009, p.12.

29. Since 2008 trafficking organizations moving drugs through Central Asia have become more operationally sophisticated. Seizure data indicates that much larger quantities have been confiscated than in preceding years. See UNODC, 2010d, p. 115.

30. Jacobson and Levitt (2010, p. 119–120) note that senior officials with the U.S. Drug Enforcement Agency state that "hybrid" organizations may provide opportunities for law enforcement as cooperation between international law enforcement agencies is more forthcoming in criminal matters than purely terrorist activities.

31. See Mutschke, 2000, pp. 85–120.

32. See UNODC, 2010d, p. 245.

33. Europol (2009, pp. 13 and 29) notes that Pakistan is playing an increasingly important dominant role in the international heroin trade.

34. These disparate ethnic groups cooperate with each other to generate drug revenue. See UNODC, 2009a, pp. 133 and 136.

35. UNODC (2010d, p. 123) reported that 10–12 Afghan trafficking networks, with links to trafficking groups inside Iran, are based in the border regions. UNODC (2010d, p. 121) estimates that approximately 140 tons of heroin are trafficked through Iranian territory each year.

36. UNODC (2010d, p. 125) estimates that Europe consumes approximately "87 tons of heroin" per year. Furthermore, 60 percent of this total is consumed in France, Germany, Italy, and the United Kingdom.

37. See UNODC, 2009a, pp. 140–141.

38. See Shanty, 2009a, p. 256.

39. See Shanty 2009a, p. 256; and UNODC, 2003a, p. 6; Chandra (2006, p. 78) states that during the civil war years ". . . a well-knit network evolved between poppy cultivators, local commanders, warlords, government officials, heroin processors, smugglers, drug dealers and traders."

40. The Associated Press reported that a five-member UN panel concluded that, "Afghanistan supplied as much as 79 percent of the world's opium in 1999. Between October 2000 and March 2001, the panel said 12,980 pounds of heroin were seized in Europe, the majority from Afghanistan. It said that indicates the Taliban still has large quantities of the drugs in stock" (Lederer, 2001).

41. See also Shanty, 2009a, p. 256.

42. Shanty, 2009a, p. 256.

43. The UNODC (2008, p. 3) reported that in 2008, 157,000 hectares were cultivating opium poppy. This represents a 19 percent decrease from the 193,000 hectares which cultivated poppy in 2007.

44. See Felbab-Brown, 2010, p. 110, footnote 5.

45. See Ahrari, et al., 2009, p. 4; and United Nations Office on Drugs and Crime, 2010a, pp. 1–2.

46. See UNODC, 2009, p. 78.

47. The report goes on to state: "Some research undertaken in northern Afghanistan (which would be probably true for other parts of the country as well) also indicated that there was a link between local commanders and opium traders.

While the position as a local commander was often acquired through prowess in battle and entailed status and respect, the opium trader secured respect by making economic contributions to the locality" (UNODC 2003a, pp. 128–129).

48. Prior to the Taliban opium ban in 2000, the southern and eastern provinces of Helmand and Nangarhar respectively accounted for over 75 percent of Afghanistan cultivated opium (UNODC, 2003a, p. 38).

49. See United States Department of State, 2009b: (Afghanistan).

50. See Shaw, 2006, p. 207.

51. See Shanty, 2009a, p. 257; and Kerry, et al., 2009, p. 4.

52. See Lee (2003, p. 31) for a discussion of the alliances which have contributed to the opium problem in Afghanistan; see also Chouvy, 2002; and Favre, 2005.

53. See Shanty, 2009a, p. 257.

54. See Shanty, 2009a, p. 257; and Chandra, 2006, p. 78.

55. Mark Galeotti, Director, Organized Russian & European Crime Research Unit, Keele University, UK, indicates that the opium trade is controlled by "warlords, local criminal entrepreneurs, tribalized criminal structures . . . often paying tribute to political groups for the use of routes and areas . . ." He further notes that the relationship between traffickers and terrorists is more "alliances of convenience" (e-mail communication, February 9, 2007).

56. See Ward and Byrd, 2004, p. 3.

57. See Buddenberg and Byrd, 2006, pp. 189–214; see also World Bank, 2004, p. 84.

58. See Shanty, 2009a, p. 257; and Suyono and Zuhaid, 2001.

59. See Rubin, B. R., (2004b) interview given to Bernard Gwertzman (Council on Foreign Relations) in July 2004.

60. See Shanty, 2009a, p. 257; following the fall of the Taliban various factions competed for power and influence. The fallout from these events was an increase in the level of instability throughout the country. See Johnson and Leslie (2006, p. 15).

61. See also Shaw, 2006, pp. 206–208.

62. See UNODC, 2003a, p. 6; and Blanchard, 2009, p. 5.

63. See Burnett, 2004, p. A10; for information on criminal groups involved in the cross-border smuggling of Afghan opiates see, Makarenko, 2002a, pp. 28–31.

64. As alluded to by Shaw (2006, p. 201), in most parts of Afghanistan local commanders (warlords) do not directly participate in the trafficking of opium/heroin. Their role is usually limited to providing protection; see also, United States Department of State, 2005c; UNODC (2004a, p. 66) reports that local commanders receive a variable percentage of the farmer's income; according to Robert Templer, Director of the Asia Program, International Crisis Group, "Warlords keep the farmer in a cycle of debt and poverty, while doing everything possible to keep the farm-gate prices down; same as any other exploitive agricultural system" (e-mail communication with author, February 7, 2007); Michel Chossudovsky (2006) professor of economics at the University of Ottawa argues that an enterprise (opium trade) of this magnitude could not function as efficiently without the help of public officials.

65. See Afghanistan Justice Project, 2005, p. 8.

66. See Bassiouni, 2005.

67. See Bassiouni, 2005, pp. 7 and 10; see also discussion on corruption in Asia Foundation, 2006, pp. 14–16; Watson, 2005a, p. A3; Coghlan, 2005, p. O17; Glantz, Rohde, and Gall, 2006, p. 1; Ghafour, H., 2006, p. A1; Afghan.com, 2007;

and Burch, 2009; accusations of drug involvement have also been made against the aforementioned brother of Afghan President Hamid Karzai. See Kerry et al., 2009, pp. 11–12.

68. The United States Department of State, 2009b (Afghanistan) vol. 1, reported that in 2008, "nine public officials," including senior officials of the Afghanistan National Police (ANP), were convicted of drug related and corruption charges; also reported in Blanchard, 2009, p. 27; see also, U.S. Department of State, 2005c, p. 267; Blackwell, 2007a, p. A3; Blackwell, 2007b, p. A16; Blackwell, 2007c, p. A9; Grimes, 2007, p. E9; Holloway, 2006, p. 27; and Otis, 2004, p. 1.

69. The U.S. Department of State (2010, p.98, Vol. 1) notes that, ". . . many Afghan government officials are believed to profit from the drug trade, particularly at the provincial and district levels of government. Corrupt practices range from facilitating drug activities to benefiting from revenue streams that the drug trade produces."

70. Cornell (2006b, p. 60) states: "Clearly, the drug trade influences the decisions taken by numerous individuals in high positions involved directly or indirectly in the trade, involving most obviously Afghan warlords whose private militias are undoubtedly costly to maintain. In February 2006, Afghanistan's counternarcotics minister Habibullah Qaderi stated that several members of President Hamid Karzai's cabinet are deeply implicated in the drug trade"; see also, Harnden, 2006, p. 25; De Borchgrave, 2005, p. A19; Taylor, 2006, p. 8; Gall, 2008a, p. 12; Risen, 2008, p. A1; Smith, 2008, p. A11; *Australian*, 2008, p. 11.

71. Minister Jalali, upon leaving his post as Afghanistan's interior minister in September 2005, accepted a position at the National Defense University Institute for National Strategic Studies in Washington, D.C. and is a member of the faculty; see Afgha.com (2007) for interview given by Jalali on August 12, 2007.

72. Afgha.com (2007); see also, Gutterman, 2005; and Pennington, 2005.

73. See IRIN News Service, 2005; and Baldauf and Bowers, 2005, p. O1.

74. See also Schweich, 2008, p. MM45.

75. To view how the information for this story was compiled see: "A note on how we reported this story," (Baldauf, 2006, p. O1).

76. See also Coghlan, 2005, p. O17; Gutterman, 2005; and Holloway, 2006, p. 27.

77. See Kerry, et al., 2009, pp. 11–12.

78. According to the United Nations Office on Drugs and Crime (UNODC), two activities which generate the most income in Afghanistan are drugs and the taking of bribes. UNODC reports that, "together they amount to about half the country's (licit) GDP." See United Nations Office on Drugs and Crime, 2010b, pp. 4 and 31.

79. Some positions require payments of several hundred thousand dollars. See, Loyd, 2007; Sommerville, 2010; and BBC News, 2010.

80. The article further states: "At a press conference announcing his resignation last fall, Interior Minister Ali Jalali said that the ministry had a list of 100 top officials who were being watched for evidence of drug trafficking. The result is a government that is either incapable or unwilling to prevent a trade that is rapidly undermining the country's rule of law and the Afghan people's faith in their leadership." The report concludes that while it may be difficult to prove a particular individual's involvement in the drug trade, "Top Afghan officials privately admit that perhaps 80 percent of the personnel at the Ministry of Interior,

Afghanistan's chief law-enforcement agency—from local police chiefs up to the top bureaucrats—may be benefiting from the drug trade" (Baldauf, 2006, p.O1); see also, Wilder, 2007, specifically section 5.3: Reforming the Ministry of Interior, pp. 52–53; Baldauf and Bowers, 2005, p. O1; Morarjee, 2006; Smith, 2009; and Erwin, 2009, p. 7 and footnote 23.

81. See Watson, 2005b, p. A1.

82. A human rights official working in eastern Afghanistan reported that, "drug traffickers and other well-connected criminals are often ignored by Nangarhar police." Moreover, the warlord who commands the provincial police "provided the bulk of the Afghan ground force that aided U.S. soldiers in the attempt to capture Osama bin Laden at Tora Bora in late 2001" (Watson, 2005a, p. A3).

83. Additionally, the report noted that based on interview data a majority of police chiefs, often through intimidation and death threats, are involved in the opium trade (Shaw, 2006, p. 199).

84. Cornell notes that among the states where drugs are produced evidence suggests that there is some level of "corruption or collusion" of public officials in the narcotics trade, often at the highest levels of government. See Cornell, 2006b, p. 42; see also, Mandel, 1999, pp. 55–62; and Land, 1996, pp. 20–22.

85. Makarenko (2002c) notes that, "Transnational criminal groups have gained control over most trafficking routes bringing Afghan opiates to world markets. These groups have ties throughout Central Asia, including relations with high-level government and law enforcement officers."

86. See Cornell, 2006b, p. 39.

87. See Shanty, 2009a, p. 257; and Senlis Council, 2006b.

88. Mandel (1999, p. 59) argues that, "Without popular support and understanding of these anti-drug initiatives, the result can easily turn into political and social turmoil."

89. Prior to the October 2001 invasion, the U.S. and coalition forces made a decision to incorporate these people (warlords and former mujahideen), already angry at the Taliban because of the ban, into the alliance to help defeat Al Qaeda and Taliban forces. This decision, perhaps a good idea at the time, has contributed to the current security problems—most notably in the southern and eastern provinces, and has thwarted the governing capacity and authority of the Karzai administration. No doubt former Northern Alliance members, pre-Taliban era commanders (warlords), and former mujahideen, who were involved in the trade prior to the 2000 ban, seized the opportunity provided to them when the Taliban were removed and subsequently many rural Afghans began cultivating opium poppy.

90. See Stern, 2000; and U.S. Department of State, 1994, p. 5.

91. Harrison was the South Asian correspondent (1951–1954) for the Associated Press and served as South Asia bureau chief (1962–1965) for the *Washington Post*. He has over 50 years experience in East and South Asian affairs.

92. Azad Kashmir is the Pakistani-controlled portion of the disputed territory of Jammu-Kashmir.

93. Harrison (1990, p. A11) further notes that interrogations of captured fighters revealed a direct Pakistan-militant link and the diversion of weaponry, originally designated for the Afghan conflict, and subsequently stockpiled, to Kashmiri insurgents. Additionally, Harrison reports that some of the captured insurgents

were members of the Pakistani-supported Hezb-i-Islami, a radical Islamist faction run by Gulbuddin Hekmatyar, beneficiary of a large portion of U.S. and Saudi Afghan war funds; the Conflict Database, an ongoing project of the Department of Peace and Conflict Research, Uppsala University, maintains that: "In 1989, the first year of recorded conflict, the Jammu and Kashmir Liberation Front (JKLF), was the single dominant rebel group. By January 1990, the rapidly escalating circle of violence was said to include as many as 40 different militant outfits . . . many of those crossing the Line of Control have been Arab veterans of the Afghan war wanting to join Kashmir insurgents in their 'jihad' (holy war) against the Indian government. It should be noted that the foreign-based groups have been among the most reluctant to embrace any initiative to find a political solution to the problem."

94. For additional information about terrorist groups operating in Kashmir see South Asia Terrorism Portal (SATP); and Fair, Malhotra, and Shapiro, 2009, pp. 1–36.

95. See Stern, 2000; see also, United States Department of State, 2000, pp. 102 and 113; United States Department of State, 2003d, pp. 126 and 132; and Fair, Malhotra, and Shapiro, 2009, pp. 1–36.

96. For a discussion on Pakistan and radical Islam see, Weaver, 2002; and Abbas, 2005; for a discussion on Pakistan and Kashmir, see Rashid, 1999, pp. 22–35.

97. Harkat ul-Ansar changed its name to Harakat ul-Mujahideen (HUM); see United States District Court for the Eastern District of Virginia (Alexandria Division), 2002, Item 2, p. 3.

98. See Embassy of India, n.d., *Global Terrorism: Attack on Democratic Societies*, A Note on Global Terrorism, viewed December 18, 2007, http://www.indianembassy.org/policy/Terorism/pak_terrorism.htm.

99. See *Bangalore Deccan Herald*, 1999.

100. See Winchell, 2003, pp. 379–380; and Fair, Malhotra, and Shapiro, 2009, pp. 1–36.

101. The Research and Analysis Wing (RAW) is India's intelligence agency. Like Pakistan's Inter-Services Intelligence Directorate (ISI) it serves India's domestic as well as international interests.

102. In a study conducted by the Pakistan Institute of Legislative Development and Transparency, author Tahir Amin (2001, p. 10) contradicts the widely held belief that Pakistan's Inter-Services Intelligence Agency (ISI) played a dominant role in Afghan policy. He asserts that, ". . . the policy of support of the Taliban was in fact conceived by (retd.) Naseerullah Babar, the Interior Minister during the PPP regime (1993–1996)"; The Pakistan People's Party (PPP) is a secular socialist party created by Pakistani Prime Minister Zulfikar Ali Bhutto (1928–1979) in 1967. See Husain, 2001, p. 14.

103. In this study, Hussain (2005, pp. 123–124) concludes that, "A significant outcome of Pakistan's role in the Afghan conflict was to further legitimise the use of irregular warfare and terrorism by states in the pursuit of ideological and strategic goals. The utilization of religious groups as instruments to achieve strategic objectives at the tail end of the twentieth century was to ensure that Afghanistan would remain one of the foremost epicentres of religiously inspired militant groups in the post-Cold War era"; see also Risen and Miller, 2001, p. 1; see also Fair, Malhotra, and Shapiro, 2009, p. 39.

104. See Elias, 2007, Documents 1–35.

105. See also Rashid, 2001f, p. 186; and BBC News, 2002c.

106. See also Cornell, 2006a, p. 269.

107. In further reference to the information provided in these documents relative to the Taliban and Kashmiri militants, see Elias, 2007; for additional information on these documents and Pakistan's relationship with the Taliban, see Afghanistan Conflict Monitor, 2007.

108. Mark Corcoran, ABC News foreign correspondent and producer of documentaries inside Afghanistan, stated that the, "Taliban is still supported by the ISI" (interview with author, November 11, 2006).

109. Sanctions on the Taliban were imposed in January 2001 for harboring terrorist fugitive Osama bin Laden and for allowing Afghanistan to become a haven and training infrastructure for international terrorists. An additional resolution (1363) was passed in July 2001. This resolution sought to put teeth into the original resolution (1333) by posting UN monitors on Afghanistan's borders to insure arms embargo compliance (Rashid, 2001f, p. ix).

110. See Mazzetti and Schmitt, 2008, p. 1; Woodward, 2009, p. A1; BBC News, 2010; *The Australian*, 2010, p. 10; and Lamb, 2008b, p. 4.

111. For complete report see Waldman, 2010; see also Mazzetti et al., 2010, p. A1.

112. See Perlez, 2009, p. A1.

113. According to the authors the ISI was responsible for all intelligence involving Pakistan's national interests. This included matters involving the military as well as internal politics. The authors further state that, "The ISI was considered all powerful, and the Director General second only in authority to President Zia . . ." (Yousaf and Adkin, 2001, p. 22).

114. See Parthasarathy, 2003; for information on the National Logistic Cell see, Pakistan Planning and Development Ministry; according to Robert Templer, "most Afghan drugs go through Pakistan, Iran and Central Asia . . . members of the ISI and the Pakistani army control drug trafficking through Iran and Turkey" (interview with author, January 19, 2007); see also Napoleoni, 2003, pp. 91–92; and Booth, 1996, p. 289.

115. The report titled, "Heroin in Pakistan: Sowing the Wind," also alleges ISI use of drug money to fund insurgencies in Punjab and Kashmir; see Vora,1994, p. 48; see also Federation of American Scientists Web site, "Terrorism in India: extracts from independent reports from the Western, Pakistani, and Indian Press'; Kranti, 1997 and Prabha, 2001.

116. See Lifschultz, 1988, pp. 477–496; see also Burger, 1999; McCoy, 2003; and Rupert and Coll, 1990, p. A01.

117. Approximately one year later another report appeared in the *Nezavisimaya Gazeta*, a Russian daily newspaper. This report, published by the *Press Trust of India*, cites ISI involvement in the drug trade to help finance the insurgency in Kashmir. The report also accused the Pakistani military of playing a direct and significant role in Taliban efforts against Northern Alliance forces. Additionally, it was reported that senior Pakistani officials received kickbacks from the drug trade during the Afghan-Soviet conflict (*Press Trust of India*, May 14, 2001). This report supports the views of the 1988 article published in *The Nation* and reported by Lifschultz (1988, pp. 477–496).

118. See also Balfour, 2001.

119. See also United States Department of State, 2004a.

120. See United States Department of State, 2004a; United States Department of State, 2009b; and Norell, 2007, p. 80; see Felbab-Brown, 2010, pp. 101–106 for a discussion of the ramifications of large-scale opium cultivation in FATA, NWFP, and Punjab province; as noted elsewhere in this study, the NWFP is presently referred to as Khyber PakhtunKhwa. See Gunaratna and Kousary, 2010.

121. This statement was made in response to a question by Congressman Rohrabacher (R-CA). The testimony by Ms. Chamberlain confirms what many believed was the case for some time, despite denials from the Pakistani government.

122. See United States Department of State, 2009b, p. 265, Vol. 1.

123. In addition to increasing their war chest, the Taliban have been able to exploit the government and coalition forces eradication campaign by promising the farmer that they (Taliban) would resist attempts at eradication thereby assuring them an uninterrupted source of income from the crop. In many respects the opium poppy virtually guaranteed the return of the Taliban especially in the southern province of Helmand, as local Afghans, becoming more critical of the central government, began to join their ranks by providing material support or taking up arms thereby strengthening the insurgency. See Erwin, 2009, p. 6.

124. See also, Stepanova, 2005, p. 167.

125. See United States Government Accountability Office, 2006, p. 8.

CHAPTER 7

1. See McCaffrey, 1999, p. 17.

2. When the Taliban began their ascendancy in October 1994 they were immediately supported by, "Pakistan's trucking cartels," which were previously subjected to the influence and greed of territorial warlords who controlled access to various, "trade routes" (HRW, 2001, p. 25).

3. UNODC (2003a, p. 89) also reported that "opium production in Afghanistan grew at an average rate of 15% per annum over the 1980–2000 period, almost twice as fast as the global opium production growth rate of 8%. While Afghanistan produced about 19% of world opium in 1980, this proportion grew to 52% by 1995, the year prior to the Taliban takeover, and rose to 79% by 1999."

4. Opium production in Afghanistan has been increasing steadily since the mid-1980s, a decade before the Taliban and Al Qaeda were a force in Afghanistan. See also Taylor, 2004, p. A03.

5. In March 2000, the UN Office for Drug Control and Crime Prevention (UNODCCP)—now the UN Office on Drugs and Crime (UNODC)—released a report prepared by the executive director, Pino Arlacchi. The report stated that although the Taliban impose taxes on the trade, earning between $10 and $30 million per year, no evidence exists that the Taliban leadership is receiving drug profit revenues (Crossette, 2000, p. A6); Frank Cilluffo, senior policy analyst and deputy director for the Center for Strategic and International Studies, offers a contradictory view. According to Cillufo, Taliban earnings from the drug trade went beyond imposing, "taxes on traders." He noted that the opium harvests are taxed at the rate of approximately 12 percent by the Taliban. Additionally, according to Cilluffo the Taliban earn about $70 per kilogram from the labs that process the raw opium into heroin and earn an additional $250 per kilogram by charging transporters for a permit which needs to be presented at all Taliban checkpoints

(Cilluffo, 2000, p. 73); Favre (2005, p. 21, footnote 38) states: "The transport smuggling mafia based in Quetta/Pakistan which is made up largely of Pakistani but some Afghan Pashtuns drawn from the same tribes as the Taliban leadership had become increasingly frustrated by the warring warlords around Kandahar; these warlords prevented the expansion of their smuggling between Pakistan and Afghanistan further afield into Iran and Central Asia. The Quetta-Chaman mafia funded the Taliban handsomely and significantly contributed in their initial success in controlling southern Afghanistan and opening the smuggling roads. 'The one-time all inclusive customs duty the Taliban charged trucks crossing Afghanistan from Pakistan became the Taliban's major source of official income'"; see also UNODC, 2003a, p. 91; and Hasnain, 2000.

6. See also Hussain, 1999, p. 7; and Makarenko, 2002d, p.1, footnote 3.

7. See also Meier, 1997, p. 4.

8. See also UNODC, 2003a, p. 92.

9. In reference to the Northern Alliance (NA) and purported links to the opium trade, Makarenko (2002d, p. 10) notes that many former NA commanders, who occupy various positions in the present government, increased the amount of opium cultivation in the areas of the north under their control (Badakhshan province) following the Taliban enforced ban. She states that opium cultivation increased, "by over 200 percent on their [Northern Alliance] territories in 2001."

10. Makarenko, 2002d, p.11; Makarenko, 2002b; see also Rashid, 2003, pp. 154–155; and Felbab-Brown, 2010, p. 100.

11. See Makarenko, 2002d, p. 11.

12. A statement by Mutschke (2000, p. 100) reflects the hybrid nature of the IMU: ". . . according to some estimations IMU may be responsible for 70 % of the total amount of heroin and opium transiting through the area"; a similar claim was made by Bolot Januzakov, Chairman of Kyrgyzstan's Security Council; see Manayev, 2000; Miller, 2003; and Kaplan, Fang, and Sangwan, 2005, p. 50.

13. See also Curtis, 2002; and Inciyan, 2001; Dr. Felbab-Brown stated in an interview with the author that up until 2001 the IMU probably transported drugs from Northern Afghanistan and provided protection for traffickers. She also stated that the operation was broken up in 2002 (Interview with author, December 7, 2006).

14. See Gold, 2005, pp. 11 and 21, footnote 29; and Ballentine and Sherman, 2003.

15. See Felbab-Brown, 2009, p. 3.

16. Makarenko, 2002c, p. 14 notes that, ". . . few groups realistically control the trade from field to international market, but are forced—at one point or another—to interact with other actors. As a result of this understanding, the common myth (increasingly spread post 9/11) that the Taliban and al-Qaeda single-handedly controlled the Afghan drug trade is dispelled."

17. See United States Department of State, 2001a; United States Department of State, 2005c; United Nations Office on Drugs and Crime, 2003c; United Nations Office on Drugs and Crime, 2005b; United Nations Office on Drugs and Crime, 2003a; and United Nations Office on Drugs and Crime, 2006.

18. See United Nations Office on Drugs and Crime, 2003c, pp. 167 and 172.

19. As noted in the U.S. Department of State's *International Narcotics Control Strategy Report 1994*, Helmand and Nangarhar provinces have traditionally been major opium-producers. The report states that in some years these two provinces

collectively combine to produce "as much as 88 percent—of Afghan poppy and opium production"; data for 2005 taken from the UNODC World Drug Report (2006, p. 55) indicates that ". . . five provinces (in order of magnitude: Helmand, Kandahar, Balkh, Farah and Badakshan) accounted for 65 per cent of the total area under opium poppy cultivation in 2005."

20. See Tohid, 2003, p. O6; and Rohani, 2005.

21. See also Lamb, 2006, p. 13; and Holloway, 2006, p. 27.

22. Mitch Prothero (UPI) stated that in areas that the Taliban had a controlling presence local growers were provided protection by them [Taliban] and in return received a tithe for providing a "supportive atmosphere" (interview with author, September 18, 2006); in a subsequent e-mail communication with the author, Prothero expanded on his original comment by pointing out that the Taliban encourage farmers to plant poppy in order to collect revenue from the trade and to further weaken the central government (e-mail communication, October 2, 2006); this view is also held by *TIME* magazine's Tim McGirk who told this author in an e-mail correspondence that "over the past year the Talibs have come out publicly and threatened farmers who've stopped growing poppy." McGirk also confirmed Prothero's comment (above) that the Taliban provided protection for drug traffickers when they moved their product (e-mail communication, September 15, 2006); see also UNODC, 2009a, p. 107, footnote 53.

23. Johnson and Leslie (2005, p. 116) claim that some of these conversion labs are directly tied to "foreign heroin markets" which increases the profit margin. The authors further state that these laboratories are frequently operated by "warlords and local commanders although there are also rumours of Russian Mafia connections."

24. The article quotes General Ali Shah Paktiawal, director of criminal investigations for the Kabul police: "It's reached the point where about half of the opium we seize in the provinces has some link to the Taliban." The article goes on to state that, this assessment is based in part on Taliban confessions upon capture. The report also notes that opium production in the Taliban stronghold of Helmand province increased dramatically in 2006 (Peters, 2006b, p. O4); see also UNODC, 2007c, p. 196; Franco, 2007, p. 14, footnote 21; Franco, 2008, p. 1.

25. See Senlis Council, 2006a, p. 7; Kerry et al., (2009, p. 9) reports that, "the biggest source of drug money for the Taliban is the regular payments made by large drug trafficking organizations to the Quetta shura, the governing body of the Taliban whose leaders live in Quetta, the Pakistani border city"; see also UNODC, 2009a, p. 104.

26. Gulbuddin Hekmatyar had been implicated in the drug trade during and immediately following the Soviet-Afghan war. See Rupert and Coll, 1990, p. A01; during an interview with the author, drug policy expert Rafael Perl added that the group run by Gulbuddin Hekmatyar, Hezb-i- Islami, is heavily involved in the trade, drawing between 60–70 percent of their revenue from this source (interview with author, January 10, 2007). This appraisal coincides with statements made by Dr. Svante Cornell, who maintains that the group has been heavily involved in the trade since the 1980s (e-mail communication, December 7, 2006); see also McCoy, 2003, pp. 478–487; and Griffin, 2003, p. 111.

27. See also Blackwell, 2007b, p. A16; Blackwell, 2007c, p. A9; and Peters, 2006b, p. O4.

28. See Packer, 2006, pp. 60–69.

29. See Holloway, 2006, p. 27; Jun, 2006; and *Boston Globe*, 2006.

30. See Senlis Council, 2006c; and Associated Press, October 8, 2006.

31. For information regarding criminal networks in Afghanistan see Swanstrom, 2007, pp. 1–25.

32. During an interview with the author (January 10, 2007) Rafael Perl stated that he was uncertain if the Islamic Movement of Uzbekistan were currently involved in the drug trade as they had been prior to 9/11.

33. According to Robert Templer, "The IMU appears to have disintegrated as a formal, coherent group but it is believed by police in Tajikistan and elsewhere that some of their members may be using their knowledge of infiltration routes to smuggle drugs" (interview with author, January10, 2007).

34. Mark McDonald addressed the IMU during an interview with this author. During this exchange McDonald spoke about a discussion he had with an IMU member, the former driver for Juma Namangani, leader of the group until his purported death in late 2001. During a conversation with McDonald he [driver] stated that the group was presently reconstituting itself in the Ferghana Valley and would ultimately join forces with Hizb ut-Tahrir. This statement may be relevant and possibly provide insight into the Islamic Movement of Uzbekistan's future plans. McDonald was told by Major Yuldashov of the Tajikistan Drug Control Agency that many radicals who had formerly taken up residence in Afghanistan were now in Uzbekistan setting up training camps (interviews with author, February 3, 2005, and November 16, 2005); regarding Hizb ut-Tahrir see International Crisis Group, 2002; for additional information on the IMU see Baker, 2003, p. A19; Yegorov, 2004; Kimmage, 2004; Sidikov, 2008; Tynan, 2009; and Felbab-Brown, 2010, p. 100.

35. See Makgabo and Feyerick, 2001; regarding Osama bin Laden's business interests in Sudan a counterclaim was provided in a report published in Australia's *Gold Coast Bulletin* (2001, p. 58); see also Rashid (2001g) for additional detail regarding bin Laden's finances.

36. See Shanty, 2007a, pp. 350–357.

37. For an alternative view see Tandy, 2004a, p. 20; and Lee, 2002b.

38. See Al-Oraifij, 2010.

39. For a detailed account of Osama bin Laden and Al Qaeda see Scheuer, 2006b; and Gunaratna, 2002.

40. See Fisk, 1993, p. 10.

41. Some media accounts state that Osama bin Laden graduated in 1979 with a degree in economics and management from King Abdul Aziz University in Jedda, Saudi Arabia. According to Gunaratna (2002, p. 17) bin Laden left school in his 3rd year and therefore did not receive a degree. However, Gunaratna further states that prior to leaving the university he did study economics and management and had planned to enter the family construction business; see also, Forbes.com, 2001.

42. Other direct beneficiaries of this effort would be those engaged in the trafficking and distribution of the commodity, i.e., drug criminals.

43. See Ehrenfeld, 2003, p. 52 and footnote 94, p. 218.

44. See also Rashid, 2001f, p. 139.

45. *Houston Chronicle* journalist Michael Hedges (2001, p. 1) reported that the CIA's former chief of counterterrorism, Vince Cannistraro, stated, "'Opium has been

a way for the Taliban to finance its operations since the mid-1990s . . . It appears that bin Laden's organization has provided security for the shipments and has collected a tax from the sales.' The Taliban, backed by bin Laden's organization, reaped a substantial cut of the profits from an opium crop with an annual wholesale value of more than $90 million, according to U.S. and U.N. officials."

46. It is important to note that this report was published five years after the U.S.-led invasion when many Al Qaeda members were in the "tribal areas" of Pakistan.

47. Eichenwald (2001, p. A1) also reported that, "Charities around the Arab world proclaimed that they were raising money for humanitarian purposes in Bosnia, but in fact portions benefited Islamic extremist groups in the area, including Al Qaeda."

48. This previously classified Defense Intelligence Agency (DIA) intelligence information report (IIR) report, obtained by Judicial Watch in October 2004, is a transcript "verbatim" of handwritten documents from October 1998. This document follows the establishment of the "International Islamic Front" (an alliance of terrorist organizations) and the bin Laden issued fatwa in February 1998 urging armed action against the U.S. and its allies. It also follows, by two months, the attacks on U.S. embassies in Africa. Most notably in October 1998 it was planting season in Afghanistan for the 1999 opium crop, which was harvested in the spring of 1999. This harvest yielded a record opium crop. These documents shed light on the activities and objectives of the Al Qaeda organization and their purported ties to Chechen militants. They also confirm reports of Al Qaeda's desire to acquire weapons of mass destruction (WMD) and the desire to create a global Islamic caliphate. The reference to a global caliphate provided in this report closely parallels more recent statements by Al Qaeda's al Zawahiri and the Taliban's Mansoor Dadullah (now deceased) and Mullah Muhammad Omar. Providing financial support to various Islamist networks including the Taliban movement in Afghanistan is also addressed. See United States Defense Intelligence Agency, 1998, p. 4, items 5 and 6, p. 5, item 6.

49. Amir al-Khattab, now deceased, was an Islamist militant leader in Chechnya who participated in the Soviet-Afghan war and has been reported to have ties to Al Qaeda. See Erikson, 2002; for an opposing view see McGregor, 2005.

50. In February 2003, the U.S. Department of State issued a statement on Chechen terrorist groups and their possible ties to Al Qaeda and the Taliban. See United States Department of State, 2003a; for additional information on Khattab's purported ties to Al Qaeda see Council on Foreign Relations, 2006; Khalilova, 2002; BBC News, 2002b; for another perspective on Khattab's ties to Al Qaeda and a discussion on the purported ideological rift (near and far enemy) on the advancement of "jihad" see Tumelty, 2006, pp. 8–10.

51. Abu Sayaf [also spelled Sayyaf] was a mujahideen fighter during the Soviet-Afghan war. The Abu Sayyaf Group (ASG) is an Islamist terrorist organization based in the Philippines; see BBC News, 2000.

52. See Kavkaz-Center News Agency, 2004; according to the U.S. Department of State, the Kavkaz-Center News Agency Web site is affiliated with Chechen militants. See U.S. Department of State, 2003a.

53. See also Roth, Greenburg, and Wille, 2004, p. 18; Simpson, 2004, p. B2; and United Nations Security Council; Second Report of the Monitoring Group

established pursuant to resolution 1363 (2001) and extended by resolutions 1390 (2002) and 1455 (2003), on sanctions against Al-Qaida, the Taliban, and individuals and entities associated with them.

54. Perhaps the present state of knowledge relative to the drugs/terror nexus in Afghanistan is best summed up in an e-mail communication with Doris Buddenberg, Afghanistan's representative for the United Nations Office on Drugs and Crime (UNODC). In a response to this author's statement: *I have read or scanned numerous open source publications (i.e., government reports, past and current U.N. reports, U.S. Congressional testimony, conference papers, research reports, scholarly articles, books, news accounts, etc.). Many of these reports make claims of a nexus between groups and drug trafficking networks. Problem: there seems to be very little empirical data (outside of a few newswire reports) linking the two* [emphasis added]. Ms. Buddenberg replied, "you placed your finger on exactly the right spot: There is no empirical data to support the link. That is the reason why everybody and each and every agency can use 'data', myths and legends for or against its preferred thesis/objective. No empirical research has taken place, neither at a local/provincial level, nor at national level." This communication ended with her assurance that she would ask her colleagues "regarding a very few, very specific cases of either involvement/link or none" (e-mail communication, October 28, 2006). On November 26, 2006, the following reply was received: "even my colleagues' information is anecdotal. The situation remains amazing" (e-mail communication, November 26, 2006).

55. Fay (1996, p. 221) notes that, Critical intersubjectivity ". . . demands that cognizers be open to others, engage them, seek out and hearken to their observations, discoveries, and criticisms."

56. As noted in chapter 1, a sound epistemology requires a "triangulation" approach to assessing corroboration that embodies the principles of "critical intersubjectivity," that are analogous with determination of contested issues based on evidence by a court; courts are frequently mentioned as an analogy for epistemology in the social sciences; see for instance, Kratochwil, 2007, p. 51.

57. Fay (1996, p. 208) notes that, "Any theory we believe, even ones for which we have excellent reasons to believe, may be false. This conclusion is at the heart of the philosophical thesis called fallibilism. According to fallibilism nothing about the world can be known for certain; certainty is not something which science can provide us. This is not because science is currently flawed . . . it is an inherent feature of the epistemology of science and scientific reasoning itself: no amount or quality of empirical confirmation or disconfirmation is sufficient to guarantee ascertainable truth or falsity."

58. See Walsh (2008) for a more detailed profile of Haji Juma Khan; Khan was arrested on October 23, 2008, by Indonesian authorities who turned him over to U.S. federal agents. He was transported to New York City where he was charged with "conspiracy to distribute narcotics with intent to support a terrorist organization." See press release issued by United States Drug Enforcement Administration, 2008; and United States District Court, Southern District of New York, 2008; Kearney, Nichols, and Eastham, 2009; see also Peters, 2009, p. 162; and the indictment and superseding indictment at *The Investigative Project on Terrorism* (court cases); and Kerry, et al., 2009, p. 16.

59. To view article see McGirk, 2004, p. 41; the U.S. Department of State's International Narcotics Control Strategy Report (2005b) indicates that according

to Pakistan's Anti-Narcotics Force (ANF), "drugs are being smuggled in the cargo holds of dhows to Yemen, Oman and United Arab Emirates via the Arabian Sea."

60. In October 2003, Carl Robichaud, program officer for The Century Foundation, spoke with Mirwais Yasini. During the interview Yasini told Robichaud that we "proved AQ and the Taliban are funded by drug traffickers." Yasini cited upper Helmand and southern Jalalabad and mentioned heroin labs, protecting delivery routes, and Al Qaeda. According to notes taken by Robichaud during the interview Yasini stated, "We know individuals who are financiers . . . we cannot disclose names." Yasini further stated that these comments were, "positive, definitive—I would say before Congress." Robichaud informed this author that when he questioned Yasini regarding supporting evidence to back up his allegations the most he [Yasini] would offer is, "drug trafficking requires instability, terrorism creates instability, terrorism needs money" (interview with author, October 25, 2006; e-mail communication, November 9, 2006).

61. See Starr and Courson, 2003; Cable News Network (CNN), 2004; *Washington Post*, 2003, p. A04; Osler, 2001, p. 1; and Meo and Crichton, 2004, p. 18.

62. See Farah, 2008, p. 97.

63. As previously discussed, the U.S. Navy intercepted three ships in the Persian Gulf. When Navy personnel boarded the vessels they found heroin, hashish, and other illegal substances that when combined were estimated to be valued at more than U.S. $20 million. Furthermore, CNN reported that, "After the first seizure on December 15, [2003] the U.S. Navy said an initial investigation uncovered clear ties between the smuggling operation and Al Qaeda" (CNN, 2004); a report of the seizures published on December 19, 2003, included a statement by Dr. Bruce Hoffman, former corporate chair in counterterrorism and counterinsurgency at the RAND Corporation and current professor at Georgetown University's Edmund A. Walsh School of Foreign Service: "This is the first empirical evidence I've seen that conclusively links Al Qaeda with the drug trade . . . Monday's seizure was the first indication that Al Qaeda was smuggling hashish, a drug made from the resin of marijuana plants that has a long history in the Middle East" (Associated Press/CBS News, December 19, 2003a); see also Oziewicz, 2003; and Starr, 2004.

64. Cable News Network (CNN), January 5, 2004.

65. See Roth, Greenburg, and Wille, 2004, p. 23, footnote 13.

66. Starr and Courson, (2003) reported that 12 individuals were taken into custody in the December 15, 2003 seizure.

67. See Mazzetti and Smucker, 2002, pp. 12–17; see also McGirk, 2003, p. 18.

68. See also Kabul Afghan Radio Kelid, 2004; Peters, 2006, p. 4; Gall, 2006b, p. 1; and Gall, 2006a, p. 4.

69. For additional information on Hekmatyar's pre-9/11 involvement in the drug trade, see Booth, 1996, p. 289; Chouvy, 2004, p. 8; and McCoy, 2003, pp. 478–487.

70. See Scarborough, 2004c, p. A11. Rowan Scarborough confirmed the accuracy of his report in an interview conducted on October 27, 2006. This author was not able to obtain a copy of the photographs cited in the article (interview with author, October 27, 2006).

71. This view was expressed by Dr. Felbab-Brown of the Brookings Institution, who stated in an interview with this author, "There is no concrete evidence linking Al Qaeda to the drug trade" (December 7, 2006); Dr. Pierre-Arnaud Chouvy,

international drug expert who has been to Afghanistan, echoed similar sentiments and further added that attempts to link drugs and terrorism in Afghanistan are a "political use of non-existent links of intelligence data by political leaders in an effort to drive the military deeper into Afghanistan" (interview with author, October 8, 2004); Tom Gouttierre, director of the Center for Afghanistan Studies at the University of Nebraska-Omaha, told the author that he has not seen "credible research linking drugs to terror in Afghanistan" (interview with author, March 9, 2005, and July 12, 2005).

72. The U.S. Department of State, *International Narcotics Control Strategy Report 2005b*, reported that, "Pakistan remains a substantial trafficking country for heroin, morphine, and hashish from Afghanistan, and according to DEA, Pakistani financiers/traffickers may also play an important role in financing and organizing opium production in Afghanistan. . . . Cultivation was almost completely contained in 2004 in the 'nontraditional' areas in which significant cultivation occurred in 2003 (Orakzai, Kurram, and North Waziristan—no estimates for South Waziristan are available due to ongoing counterterrorism operations)."

73. See United States District Court, Southern District of New York, 2005a, pp. 2–3; Risen, 2007, p. A1; see also Weiser, 2008, p. B4; and Weiser, 2009, p. A10.

74. As previously noted in chapter 6, UNODC (2009a, p. 111) reported that, "after 2005," some Taliban groups earned revenue by trafficking drugs to the Afghanistan-Pakistan border; see also UNODC, 2010d, p. 248.

75. See also Rashid, 2001f, p. 139 and Gunaratna, 2002, p. 58.

76. See Gunaratna, 2002, p. 58.

77. See Galeotti, 2006; in an e-mail follow-up to this article, Galeotti states: "anti-drug officials is a euphemism for intel officers I spoke to. That said, they have been working on the ground, and not only has this been the experience on [of] UK forces in Helmand, but this is also what the Afghan government is reporting to the UNODC" (e-mail communication, February11, 2007).

78. This information could not be verified as it was provided by an unnamed intelligence official (Galeotti e-mail communication with author, February11, 2007).

79. See also McDonald, 2004a, p. A01; and McDonald, 2004b.

80. McDonald told this author that, "based on what he has learned Major Aviz Yuldashov is probably one of the best sources of information relative to terrorist's involvement in the drug trade" (interview with author, February 3, 2005, and November 16, 2005).

81. See Makarenko, 2002d, p. 10; this view is also held by Robert Templer, who believes that Al Qaeda is a very minor player in the drug trade and not a controlling force. This view is based on the assumption that involvement in the drug trade would necessitate interaction with a wide range of actors, thereby leaving them very exposed and vulnerable to law enforcement penetration (interview with author, January 10, 2007); and Mitch Prothero, United Press International investigative journalist, who argues that Al Qaeda involvement is "low-level retail and wholesale stuff to raise money for specific attacks . . . Madrid bombing for example" (e-mail communication, September 18, 2006); see also Kaplan, Fang and Sangwan, 2005, p. 47; and Blanchard, 2006, p. 15. In the above reference to the Madrid bombing, Spanish investigators have established that those responsible for this attack "were part of a local Islamist militant group inspired by

al-Qaeda, but had no direct links to the terror organization" (BBC News, October 31, 2007b).

82. Stepanova (2005, p. 166) defines traditional Islamist groups as those "formed on the basis of radical Islamist theology."

83. The CIA estimates that in 2009, "Taliban leaders and their allies," received $106 million from foreign donations. See Whitlock, 2009, p. A1; and Schmitt, 2009, p. A1.

84. See also Cornell, 2005c, p. 757.

85. The Abu Sayyaf Group (ASG), an Islamist group which operates primarily in the southern Philippines and Malaysia, provides an example of an Islamist organization which for years has engaged in kidnapping for ransom and extortion, similar to the criminal activities perpetrated by Colombia's Fuerzas Armadas Revolucionarias de Colombia (FARC).

86. See Mutschke, 2000, pp. 85–120; Makarenko, 2002d; Napoleoni, 2003, pp. 88–91; Jacobson and Levitt, 2010, p. 117; and Baran, Starr, and Cornell, 2006, p. 49.

87. See Bagader, et al., 2006 (part 7 of 7); and Chaudhry, 1999 (chapter 3).

88. Stepanova (2005, p. 167) further notes that among Islamist militant leaders the mere nature of "global jihad" circumvents the generally accepted Muslim view that drugs and other intoxicants are banned. Moreover she states that fatwas relative to jihad are "interpreted as sufficient justification," for utilizing revenue generated by illegal activity.

89. See Scheuer, 2006b, pp. 57–58, for additional detail regarding bin Laden's view on this issue.

90. Hirschkorn et al., 2001 notes that, "Al Qaeda physically and/or ideologically penetrates international and domestic Islamic NGOs throughout the world. Thus the Al Qaeda infrastructure is inseparably enmeshed with the religious, social and economic fabric of Muslim communities worldwide."

91. Brisard (2003, p. 70) notes that, "Al Qaeda receives as its foundation massive financial support of about $500 million from businesses, banks, charities, or wealthy sponsors. This money primarily originates from donors in the Middle East. One single example can demonstrate the reach of this support. In the course of our investigation, and as part of a judicial cooperation process with Bosnia-Herzegovina, we uncovered an internal document, known as the Golden Chain, that lists the top 20 Saudi financial sponsors of the group, including 6 bankers, 12 businessmen, and 2 former ministers, whose assets were valued at $85 billion. They include leading Saudi bankers and businessmen who represent the backbone of the Saudi economy"; see also Kohlmann, 2004, pp. 35–52; Comras, 2005; Ehrenfeld, 2003, pp. 35–38; and Gunaratna, 2002, pp. 60–69; on the general issue of terrorist funding see Carisch and Napoleoni (2005, p. 28).

92. In further reference to Saudi support for Islamist militant groups see Greenburg, Wechsler, and Wolosky, 2002, p. 8; Dick Gannon, former deputy director for operations for the U.S. Department of State Office of Counterterrorism, claimed that bin Laden was funded in part by the Saudi royal family which numbers in the thousands. Gannon stated that "There are certain factions of the Saudi royal family who just don't like us . . . They may have the same father or grandfather, but they can have very different agendas" (Auster and Kaplan, 1998); see also United States Government Accountability Office, 2009, pp. 33 and 40; *World Tribune*, 2009; and Savage, 2009.

93. Al Qaeda's support network enhances its operational capabilities and makes it a more fluid and flexible organization; see Brimley, 2006, pp. 34–36; on the difficulties of penetrating terrorists financial networks see Raphaeli, 2003, pp. 77–78.

94. Concerning Saudi Arabia's prosecutorial efforts to curtail terrorist fundraising see Roth, Greenburg, and Wille, 2004, p. 113; see also United States Government Accountability Office, 2003.

95. See Brown, 2007; and Gunaratna, 2002, p. 42.

96. See Ehrenfeld, 2003, p. 52, p. 218, footnote 94.

97. See also Hedges, 2001, p. 1.

98. See United States District Court, Southern District of New York, 2005d; United States District Court, Southern District of New York, 2008; and Kerry, et al., 2009, p. 9.

99. See Scarborough, 2004c, p. A11; Kabul Afghan Radio Kelid, 2004; McGirk, 2003, p. 18; as previously noted, this author was not able to obtain a copy of the photographs cited in the article (Rowan Scarborough interview with author, October 27, 2006).

100. Moreover, it could impact our relationship with Pakistan and our overall objectives in the region. This factor along with President Karzai's attempts at national reconciliation and the potential political ramifications of adopting such a policy may be a factor in the U.S. Department of State's apparent decision not to designate the Taliban as a foreign terrorist organization. For discussions of Karzai's attempts at national reconciliation see Tarzi, 2005a and Tarzi, 2005b.

101. This same article brings out a very interesting point which has been discussed above: "The intelligence community was reluctant to link increased drug production money in Afghanistan to either the terrorist organization or the militant fundamental Muslim organization that supports it . . . the *Washington Times* reported last month that defence officials were reluctant to make the link for fear of being forced to take a direct, but unwanted, role in interdiction." See Behn, 2005, p. A07.

102. See Peters, 2006a.

103. Fay (1996, p. 220) notes that, ". . . even though we cannot achieve 'objective truth' as objectivism conceives it, we needn't conclude that all attempts at knowledge are biased or the mere expression of interest or power . . . objectivity understood as critical intersubjectivity—harmonizes with a theme of multicultural philosophy of social science: the theme of interaction and appropriation."

CHAPTER 8

1. See Fay, 1996, p. 200.

2. Napoli (1992) argues that, "Empirical science is a *hermeneutic* enterprise in all its aspects. There are objective standards, but they are never free of interpretation. It is always possible to reinterpret them."

3. In an effort to obtain a more comprehensive understanding of Afghan opium trade dynamics it was often necessary to corroborate information in an effort to gain additional insight on statements cited in certain published reports. Therefore, it was often necessary to speak with the authors who generated the reports. These exchanges often provided additional detail regarding a specific interview, statements made in articles they wrote, events that they covered, or

scholarly work that referenced a specific group's involvement in the drug trade. This was a necessary step in the process of establishing the accuracy of certain media accounts since many news reports often originate from the same source, e.g. Reuters, Associated Press, United Press International. Upon questioning the author of a specific article concerning a statement or claim it was sometimes determined that the statement in question was based on uncorroborated sources such as informant information relayed to the journalist during the course of an interview. Additionally, a direct exchange between this author and the person who wrote the report often revealed additional facts not addressed in the article. Some of this information was valuable and provided a venue for additional inquiry. In a few instances it was necessary to conduct follow-up interviews in order to obtain clarification on points addressed in earlier discussions. Some of the initial discussions focused on a specific statement or a particular incident cited in the article or report. The objective of these discussions was to determine the reasoning which spawned the statement and ascertain if the statement in question could be supported by corroborating evidence.

4. See International Monetary Fund, 2003, pp. 43–44; see comment by Joanna Nathan of the International Crisis Group (Kabul) in Montero, 2006, p. 7.

5. See Felbab-Brown (2010, pp. 96–97) discussion of illicit economies.

6. According to the 2010 World Drug Report, production totals for 2009 indicate that, "Afghanistan remained by far the largest opium producing country, representing 89% of the global illicit opium production" (UNODC, 2010e, p. 140).

7. This study addressed the terrorism and drug problems employing a multi-dimensional data and interview triangulation data collection strategy and alternative explanations as outlined in chapter 1. Much of this information was derived from individuals with relevant direct experience in Afghanistan.

8. The opium trade is providing a catalyst for a terror-crime-political nexus which could become powerful enough to completely destabilize and undermine the fragile Pakistani government and prevent Afghanistan from achieving political unity and nationwide security.

9. See Lee, 2004, p. 14.

10. See Curtis and Karacan, 2002, p. 6; Honwana and Lamb, 1998; and Makarenko, 2004, p. 132.

11. According to the U.S. Department of State (2004a, p. 258), "After being declared a 'poppy-free nation' by the United Nations in 2001, opium poppy cultivation in Pakistan increased in 2003. Ground and aerial surveys conducted by NAS (U.S. Embassy Narcotics Affairs Section), the NWFP Home Department, and the ANF indicated that the opium poppy crop remaining in NWFP was in the range of 2,000–2,600 hectares after eradication of some 1893 hectares . . . While insignificant compared to neighboring Afghanistan (and to the many thousands of hectares under cultivation in Pakistan in the 1990s), the increase is troubling, not only because cultivation increased overall (from 622 hectares in 2002), but also because it expanded into new areas in Orakzai, Kurram, and North and South Waziristan in NWFP and Gulistan and Qila Abdullah in Baluchistan"; see also Gunaratna and Kousary, 2010.

12. Pakistan continues to be a major transportation hub for Afghan processed opiates with some reports indicating that drug money is financing militant activities in Afghanistan, Pakistan, and Kashmir (Kronstadt, 2006, p. 12).

13. B. Raman, counterterrorism chief in India's Research and Analysis Wing (RAW), points out that Ibrahim's relationship with the ISI goes back to the early 1990s. See Raman, 2002; *Press Trust of India*, 2003; Indo-Asian News Service, 2005; and Moreau and Yousafzai, 2006, pp. 32–35.

14. The Pakistani Taliban, collectively referred to as Tehrik-i-Taliban, was formed in 2007. The organization is based in FATA, has close ties to Al Qaeda, and poses a direct threat to the Pakistani government. See Abbas, 2008a, pp. 1–4; and Abbas, 2008b, pp. 3–5; on September 1, 2010, Tehrik-i-Taliban was designated a foreign terrorist organization (FTO) and a specially designated global terrorist (SDGT) by the U.S. Department of State. See United States Department of State, 2010b; see also Peters, 2010.

15. See Farmer, 2010; Harnden, 2006; Baldauf and Bowers, 2005, p. O1; and Center for the Study of the Presidency, 2008, p. 33.

16. Regarding a criminal-political linkage see Shaw, 2006, p. 210.

17. See chapter 6 for detailed information relative to this point.

18. See Zakaria, 2004, p. 39; Rubin, 2004b; Buddenberg and Byrd, 2006; and McGirk and Ware, 2004, pp. 46–61; concomitantly, some public officials draw drug revenue through malfeasance and in some instances alliances with anti-government factions. See Waldman, 2004, p. A1; United States Department of State, 2005c, pp. 267–268; Bassiouni, 2005; Harnden, 2006, p. 25; Gutterman, 2005; De Borchgrave, 2005, p. A19; Asia Foundation, 2006, pp. 14–16; Baldauf and Bowers, 2005, p. O1; Baldauf, 2006, p. O1; Taylor, 2006, p. 8; Gall, 2008a, p.12; Risen, 2008, p. 1; Smith, 2008, p.A11; and *Australian*, 2008, p. 11.

19. UNODC, 2009a, pp. 103–104 reports that in addition to funding from Al Qaeda and Gulf state contributors, the Haqqani network receives revenue from drug couriers for providing protection services.

20. See UNODC, 2010, p. 247.

21. See United Nations Office on Drugs and Crime, 2009c (Seizures).

22. See Shanty, 2007b, p. 88.

23. See, Caulkins, Kleiman, and Kulick, 2010, p. 8.

24. The expansion of the drug trade since the mid- to late 1980s, and the escalation of production following the removal of the Taliban in October 2001, provides circumstantial evidence against the Taliban and/or Al Qaeda controlling the trade; according to Shaw (2006, p. 205) trafficking is controlled by a handful of individuals who are tied to powerful political actors; as noted by Makarenko (2002a, p. 28) "it is unsurprising to find that the displacement of Taliban and Al Qaeda forces did not significantly alter the organization or operations of the vast narco-networks responsible for the cultivation, processing and trafficking of Afghan opiates to the international market"; see also Makarenko, 2002b; Makarenko, 2002d; and Shanty, 2007b, p. 88.

25. See Olcott, 2002; Hutchinson, 2001, pp. 16–24; and Cilluffo, 2000, pp. 60–77.

26. See Tandy, 2006; UNODC, 2003a; and Rashid, 1999b, pp. 22–35.

27. See Packer, 2006, pp. 60–69; and Rubin, 2006, pp. 86–97 and 172–174.

28. The subsequent expansion of opium poppy particularly in the south has coincided with the expansion and spread of the Taliban-led insurgency. This has been substantiated by various NATO/ISAF force commanders and also evidenced by the number of attacks perpetrated in the south and attributed to the Taliban since 2003. Although testimony presented in chapter 3 established that extremist

elements do not control Afghanistan's drug trade, they do control territory within the country which undoubtedly includes smuggling corridors; see Kaplan, Fang, and Sangwan, 2005, p. 48; correlations between patterns of increasing opium/heroin production and increasing insurgent/terrorist activity in a region provides circumstantial evidence of the possibility of a nexus; see chapter 1; see also Rubin and Sherman, 2008, p. 54.

29. The Afghan drug trade involves many actors, state as well as non-state, and has a profound impact on the present insurgency and government and coalition efforts to undermine and defeat it. Due to shifting alliances, organizational secrecy, and the complexities inherent in obtaining a comprehensive understanding of the opium problem, it is difficult to determine precise linkages between various actors in any specific place and time; see Chouvy, 2004, p. 8; Blanchard, 2006, p. 15; and Shanty, 2007b, p. 83; regarding the issue of government corruption see Harnden, 2006, p. 25; Baldauf and Bowers, 2005, p. O1; De Borchgrave, 2005, p. A19; Taylor, 2006, p. 8; Gall, 2008a, p. 12; Risen, 2008, p. 1; Smith, 2008, p. A11; and *Australian*, 2008, p. 11.

30. See statement of Rear Admiral Bruce Clingan, Deputy Director, Naval Air Warfare Division in *Channel News Asia*, 2004; and McGirk, 2004, p. 41.

31. This is not to say that bin Laden or other senior Al Qaeda officials do not have ties or are not affiliated with other Islamic groups or individuals that are involved in the drug trade.

32. See also Scarborough, 2004b, p. A07.

33. See Burke, 2003, pp. 19, 20, and 252; Simpson, 2004, p. B2; and Roth, Greenburg and Wille, 2004, p. 18.

34. As noted in chapter 4, members of Jamiat ul-Ansar, a foreign terrorist group known to have strong ties to Al Qaeda, have generated revenue from the lucrative opium trade.

35. See Lewis, 1998, pp. 14–19; Kilcullen (2004, p. 7) notes that, "The Declaration of War of 23 February 1998 was co-signed by leaders from Afghanistan, Pakistan and Bangladesh, and South Asia has long been a key jihad theatre. Afghanistan was the principal Al Qa'eda sanctuary until October 2001. A symbiosis developed between the Taliban government and numerous Islamist groups which shared facilities, and allied themselves, with Al Qa'eda. Prominent among these was Lashkar e Toiba, which since the fall of the Taliban has become Al Qa'eda's principal South Asian ally. The Provincially Administered Tribal Areas (PATA) and Federally Administered Tribal Areas (FATA) on the Afghan-Pakistan border have become a haven for Al Qa'eda, who are cooperating with Taliban remnants fighting as guerrillas in the area"; see also Kilcullen, 2005, pp. 597–617.

36. *Weekly Standard*, 2005, "Ayman al-Zawahiri's letter to Abu Musab al-Zarqawi" (English translation), October 12.

37. Burke (2003, p. 20) notes, "Oddly, a convention seems to have developed whereby something from a 'security source' acquires a degree of veracity. Such material thus appears to be exempted from normal journalistic practices. The fact that it cannot be confirmed independently is seen as a confirmation of the utility of the information rather than the opposite . . . I know from experience that selling a story to a news editor is a lot easier if you can involve bin Laden."

38. This hearing focused on the global problem of drug trafficking and terrorism and, while addressing Afghanistan and neighboring countries, it was not specific to Central and Southwest Asia.

39. See for example De Young, 2006, p. A23; Bin Laden, 1996; Associated Press, 2007b; and *USA Today*, 2007.

40. See United States Defense Intelligence Agency, 1998.

41. See also Roth, Greenburg, and Wille, 2004, p. 19 and pp. 5–6.

42. See also Greenberg, Wechsler, and Wolosky, 2002; and Greenberg, Factor, Wechsler, and Wolosky, 2004.

43. See also Ehrenfeld, 2003, pp. 35–38; and Loyd (2010) for information regarding Saudi support for the Taliban.

44. See Pistole, 2003, pp. 4–7 and 13–33; see also Brisard, 2003, p. 70; Kohlmann, 2004, pp. 35–52; Comras, 2005; Greenberg, Wechsler, and L. S. Wolosky, 2002; Greenberg, Factor, Wechsler, and Wolosky, 2004; Hamilton, 2004, pp. 5–10; and Gunaratna, 2002, pp. 60–69.

45. See Hutchinson, 2001, pp. 16–24; and Transnational Institute, 2001, p. 8.

46. Compelling is defined as "demanding attention, convincing." (*Merriam-Webster's Collegiate Dictionary*, 10th ed. 2001); as noted in chapter 1, circumstantial evidence is defined as "indirect evidence which creates an inference from which a main fact may be inferred. . . . When circumstantial evidence is cumulative, the weakness [weight] of such circumstantial evidence is strengthened" (U.S. Legal).

47. Documentary evidence such as the *Judicial Watch* Defense Intelligence Agency (DIA) papers, firsthand in-country accounts provided by investigative journalists, and statements made by various experts during the interview process have provided a compelling case for an indirect relationship between Al Qaeda and the drug trade.

48. See Roth, Greenburg, and Wille, 2004, p. 18; Simpson, 2004, p. B2.

49. See Reeves, 1999, p. 203; and Pope, Pearl, and Trofimov, 2001, p. A1.

50. Three major Afghan "drug kingpins" were extradited to the United States and faced indictments for drug trafficking and related offenses: Haji Bashar Noorzai, April 25, 2005; Baz Mohammad, October 24, 2005; and Haji Juma Khan, October 24, 2008. All three individuals have been tied to the Taliban regime in a symbiotic relationship which furthered the Taliban's political and military ambitions vis-à-vis the opium trade. See *United States of America v. Noorzai*, 05-CR-19, pp. 2–3, April 25, viewed April 15, 2007, http://www.house.gov/kirk/pdf/NorzaiIndictment.pdf; United States District Court, Southern District of New York, 2005d; TEXT: US GRAND JURY INDICTMENT AGAINST Baz Mohammad, a/k/a "Haji Baz Mohammad," and Bashir Ahmad Rahmany, October 24, S14 03 Cr. 486 (DC), viewed March 17, 2008, http://www.investigativeproject.org/documents/case_docs/101.pdf; in this indictment Baz Mohammad equated the selling of heroin to a jihad. See United States District Court, Southern District of New York 2005a; United States District Court, Southern District of New York, 2005d; and Synovitz, 2005; see also United States District Court, Southern District of New York, 2008, *United States of America v. Haji Juma Khan*, S1 08 Cr. 621, October 24, viewed April 15, 2010, http://www.justice.gov/usao/nys/pressreleases/October08/usvkhansignedindictment.pdf; superseding indictment at: *The Investigative Project on Terrorism* (court cases), viewed April 22, 2010,

http://www.investigativeproject.org/cases.php#281; Peters, 2009, p. 162; and Kerry, et al., 2009, p. 16.

51. Estimates of Taliban revenue from the drug trade run from $70 million on the low end to $500 million per year. See Kerry, et al., 2009, p. 10; according to UNODC (2009a, p. 113) "the Taliban must find at least 85 per cent of its funding from non-opium sources"; Caulkins, Kleiman, and Kulick (2010, p. 5) note that a relatively small percentage of total drug revenue finds its way into Taliban coffers.

52. See United States Government Accountability Office, 2006, p. 8; and Packer, 2006, pp. 60–69.

53. See Senlis Council, 2006c, p. 18; and Associated Press, 2006.

54. See statement of Rear Admiral Bruce Clingan; and UNODC, 2009a, p. 105.

55. Many of the "perpetrator unknown" terrorist attacks cited in chapter 5 could very well have been conducted by criminal entities to hinder and/or obstruct counternarcotics efforts or create an environment conducive to the movement of drugs.

56. However, these provinces have been traditional Taliban strongholds and major poppy producers prior to the Taliban ban (2000) and subsequent to their ascendancy; see U.S. Department of State, 1995.

57. In September 2000, Operation Medusa, a NATO operation targeting Taliban forces in Panjwai district, uncovered an extensive ISI operated "Taliban support structure," run out of Quetta in Balochistan province, Pakistan. Additionally, captured Taliban fighters interviewed by NATO claimed direct ISI support to the Taliban (Rashid, 2006c, p. 16); Jones, 2007, pp. 15–22.

58. See Chamberlain, 2003, p. 52; and Napoleoni, 2003, pp. 91–92.

59. See Borum and Gelles, 2005, p. 474.

60. See Baldor, 2010a.

61. See author interview with UPI investigative reporter Mitch Prothero, September 18, 2006, and author e-mail communication on October 2, 2006; see also e-mail communication with *TIME* magazine investigative reporter Tim McGirk on September 15, 2006; Tohid, 2003, p. O6; and Shaw, 2006, p. 211.

62. See O'Connell, 2004, pp. 22–25; Hsu and Cole, 2006; Jones, 2008, pp. 37–66; McChrystal, 2009; and Kerry, et al., 2009.

63. See Rabasa and Chalk, 2001, pp. 751–760.

64. See UNODC, 2003a, p. 93; Williams, 2003, p. 84; Cornell, 2006b, pp. 43–44; and International Crisis Group, 2001, p. 3.

65. See *Pakistan Newswire*, 2001; and Global Security.org, 2001.

66. See Sheehan, 2000, pp. 33–45 and 45–58; see also Olcott, 2002.

67. See Gunaratna, 2002, p. 61; and Chouvy, 2004, pp. 7–9.

68. See Ahmed Rashid interview with author, May 18, 2005, in chapter 7.

69. See also UNODCCP, 2001, p. 41; Zaqvi, 1999, p. 1802; also cited in Rubin, 2000, p. 1802.

70. See Brisard, 2003, p. 70; Kohlmann, 2004, pp. 35–52; Comras, 2005; Greenberg, Wechsler and L. S. Wolosky, 2002; Greenberg, Factor, Wechsler, and Wolosky, 2004; Hamilton, 2004, pp. 5–10; and Gunaratna, 2002, pp. 60–69.

71. Regarding the proposition established in chapter 1, that the Taliban is by definition a terrorist group, it has been established in chapter 5 of this study that their modus operandi has involved attacks on Afghan civilian targets as well as suicide attacks against NATO/ISAF forces, international aid agencies, the UN, and

other non-combatants, as well as the kidnapping and killing of foreign nationals. These attacks against civilian and international targets are by design perpetrated with the intent of promulgating fear in the affected population and the wider international community, particularly the citizenry of countries allied with U.S. and NATO-led expansion ISAF forces. Taliban use of suicide bombings draws wide media coverage thus insuring the broadest possible international exposure. Furthermore, it should be clear that when the "nature of the act" involves suicide bombing attacks on civilian or non-combatant domestic and international targets, these attacks should be classified as "terrorism" and therefore the group perpetrating these actions should be designated a "terrorist group" by the international community. The United Nations Assistance Mission in Afghanistan (UNAMA) reported that suicide attacks in Afghanistan are being perpetrated by Al Qaeda, Hizb-i-Islami, and the Taliban (Fair et al., 2007, p. 16; and p.120, footnote 5).

72. Fair et al., 2007, p. 16; and p.120, footnote 5; see also United States Department of State, 2003b; Poole, 2005, p. 98; and Burns, 2005b.

73. The Taliban insurgency is primarily being fought from the opium-producing southern provinces and from territory in northwest Pakistan and supported by foreign militants, including Al Qaeda and disaffected Afghan peasants; see Korgun, 2003; Marzban, 2006b; Hsu and Cole, 2006; Schneider, 2004; United Nations General Assembly Report, 2006; O'Toole, 2006; and Jones, 2008, pp. 37–66.

74. See, for example, Porter, 2001; UNODC, 2003a, p. 10; and Cilluffo, 2000, pp. 60–77.

75. See Rashid, 2001f, p. 191; and Rubin, 1998.

76. See Gunaratna, 2002, pp. 58–59.

77. According to Rashid (2001c) "Bin Laden quickly ingratiated himself with Omar, building a new bomb-proof house and mosque for Omar in Kandahar and training his bodyguards. He then began to fund Taliban military campaigns and the building of roads and wireless facilities, and recruited some 3,000 Arabs who now fight for the Taliban."

78. See U.S. District Court, Southern District of New York, 2005a, pp. 2–3; Risen 2007, p. A1; and Farah and Constable, 1998, p. A15.

79. See Fisk, 1993, p. 10; Najm, 1999; and Rashid, 1999, pp. 22–35.

80. Gulbuddin Hekmatyar, leader of Hezb-i-Islami, had been implicated in the drug trade during and immediately following the Afghan-Soviet war; see Rupert and Coll, 1990, p. A01; during an interview with this author, drug policy expert Rafael Perl added that the group run by Gulbuddin Hekmatyar, Hezb-i- Islami, is heavily involved in the trade, drawing between 60–70 percent of their revenue from this source (interview with author January 10, 2007). This appraisal coincides with statements made by Dr. Svante Cornell, who maintains that the group has been heavily involved in the trade since the 1980s (e-mail communication, December 7, 2006); see also McCoy, 2003, pp. 478–487; Griffin, 2003, p. 111; Waldman, 2004, p. A1; and UNODC, 2010d, p. 116.

81. Suicide terrorism is not restricted to Islamists groups. It has been used by secular groups as well. For example, Sri Lanka's Tamil Tigers have been employing this tactic in mass killing operations and targeted assassinations since the 1980s.

82. Fair et al. (2007, p.38) reports that, "Despite the fact that Afghanistan has been in a state of conflict for over 30 years, suicide attacks came to prominence

only in mid-2005. The Afghan mujahadeen commanders never used suicide attacks against the Russians, nor did the Taliban and the Northern Alliance use it against each other. In fact, the first suicide attack occurred on September 9, 2001, when Al Qaeda suicide operatives, posing as journalists, assassinated Ahmad Shah Massoud"; a study released by the Center for the Study of the Presidency (2008) notes that in 2007 the Taliban launched more than 140 suicide attacks. Many of these attacks were perpetrated in Kabul; see also Williams, 2007, pp. 1–4; and Harden, 2007, p. A17.

83. Suicide bombings have been a highly effective insurgent tactic on the battlefield and have also drawn international attention. See Rahmani, 2006a, pp. 7–9.

84. See UNODC, 2009a, p. 106.

85. See Shanty, 2009b, p. 188.

86. The opium trade and its ability to provide financial and political support to various insurgent forces and terrorist factions is a small part of a much larger and far more serious international problem. In addition to opium, militants operating in Afghanistan and the border regions of Pakistan receive support from wealthy Arab benefactors, religious contributions (zakat), the global jihadist movement, and a host of other illegal activities such as credit card fraud, extortion (protection money from government contractors and local businesses), and kidnapping. See Baker, 2009; Lamb, 2008, p.1; and Roston, 2009, pp. 12–16; moreover, many of the logistical and support structures prevalent prior to 9/11 are still active.

87. See Ahrari, et al. (2009, p. 12); the Transnational Institute (2001, p. 8), an international global policy research forum, reported that allegations of international drug trafficking have been made against the IMU's Juma Namangani, Afghan drug lord Haji Bashar, and former Northern Alliance warlord Abdul Rashid Dostum; UNODC (2009a, p. 111) notes that, "After 2005," some Taliban groups earned revenue by trafficking drugs to the Afghanistan-Pakistan border; see also UNODC, 2009a, p. 108.

88. The 2000 edition of the UN *World Drug Report* expresses quite succinctly the impact that conflict may have on drug cultivation and production: "The cases of Afghanistan and Myanmar, in particular, demonstrate with unusual clarity that wartime may under certain conditions minimize the costs while raising the benefits of illicit drug production into a large-scale, income-generating enterprise" (UNODCCP, 2000, p. 156).

89. See Felbab-Brown, 2006a.

90. See Chouvy, 2004, pp. 7–9; Favre, 2005; Armenta et al., 2001; Cornell, 2005a, pp. 619–639; Cornell, 2005c, pp. 751–760; and Cornell, 2006b, p. 37–67.

91. See Grono and Nathan, 2007, p. 9; and Center for the Study of the Presidency, 2008, p. 31.

92. See *CBS News*, May 12, 2005; and Hussein, 2005.

Bibliography

Abbas, H., 2005, *Pakistan's Drift into Extremism: Allah, the Army and America's War on Terror*, M.E. Sharpe, Armonk, New York.

Abbas, H., 2008a, "A Profile of Tehrik-i-Taliban." *CTC Sentinel*, Volume 1, Issue 2, pp. 1–4.

Abbas, H., 2008b, "From FATA to the NWFP: The Taliban Spread their Grip in Pakistan." *CTC Sentinel*, Volume 1, Issue 10, pp. 3–5.

Abbosov, F., 2002, "Drug Problems in Central Asia." Papeles del Este, Number 4, Universidad Complutense, Madrid, viewed November 11, 2006, http://www.ucm.es/BUCM/cee/papeles/04/33.doc.

Afgha.com, 2007, "Exclusive Interview: Former Interior Minister Ali A. Jalali on Afghanistan's Security." August 12, viewed January 4, 2008, http://www.afgha.com/?q=node/3891.

Afghanistan Conflict Monitor, 2007, "Declassified documents detail Pakistan-Taliban ties." Human Security Research Project, viewed January 7, 2008, http://www.afghanconflictmonitor.org/2007/08/declassified-do.html.

Afghanistan Justice Project, 2005, *Casting Shadows: War Crimes and Crimes against Humanity: 1978–2001*, p. 8, viewed October 13, 2007, http://afghanistanjusticeproject.org/warcrimesandcrimesagainsthumanity19782001.pdf.

Afghanistan National Development Strategy, 2006, *Macroeconomic and Poverty Diagnostic*, Volume I, Part 2, Ch. 3, pp. 43–44, viewed February 5, 2007, http://www.nps.edu/programs/ccs/Docs/Pubs/unands_Jan.pdf.

Afghanistan Relief Organization, 2006, *Afghanistan facts, Culture and History*, ARO, Cypress, CA, viewed February 2, 2007, www.afghanrelief.org/about-afghanistan/afghanistan-facts.

Ahmad, E., 1998, "What after 'strategic depth?'" August 23, viewed July 6, 2007, http://www.geocities.com/CollegePark/Library/9803/eqbal_ahmad/eqbal_strategic_depth.html.

Ahmad, K., 2004, "'Aiding the aiders." *The Lancet*, Volume 364, Issue 9442, October 9–15, pp. 1303–1304.

Ahrari, E., V. Felbab-Brown, L. I. Shelley and N. Hussain, 2009, *Narco-Jihad: Drug Trafficking and Security in Afghanistan and Pakistan*, National Bureau of Asian Research, Seattle, Washington.

Alexiev, A 1988, *Inside the Soviet Army in Afghanistan*, RAND Corporation, Santa Monica, CA.

Al Jazeera TV, 2001, "Letter by Usama Bin Laden to the Pakistani People." September 24, viewed September 23, 2006, http://www.pbs.org/newshour/bb/military/terroristattack/binladenletter_9-24.html.

Al-Oraifij, A., 2010, "Drugs cache linked to Al-Qaeda network." *Saudi Gazette* [Internet Edition], April 22, viewed April, http://www.saudigazette.com.sa/index.cfm?method=home.regcon&contentID=2010042270128.

Al-Zawahiri, A., 2001, *Knights Under the Prophet's Banner: Meditations on the Jihadist Movement*, London, UK; excerpts available through the Foreign Broadcast Information Service (FBIS) as "Al-Sharq Al-Awsat Publishes Extracts from Al-Jihad Leader Al-Zawahiri's New Book." December 2; see also: Federation of American Scientists Web site http://fas.org/irp/world/para/aymanh_bk.html.

Amin, T., 2004, *Development of Pakistan's Foreign Policy: Study on Recognition of Taliban*, Pakistan Institute of Legislative Development and Transparency, Foreign Policy Case Study, Number 3, p.10.

Amnesty International, 2007, *Afghanistan: All Who Are Not Friends, Are Enemies: Taleban Abuses Against Civilians*, April 19, viewed October 15, 2008, http://www.amnesty.org/en/library/info/ASA11/001/2007.

Anderson, J. W., and K. Khan, 1994, "Heroin Plan by Top Pakistanis Alleged; Former Prime Minister Says Drug Deals Were to Pay for Covert Military Operations." *Washington Post*, September 12, p. A13.

Anderson, T. S., 2004, "Transnational Terror and Organized Crime: Blurring the Lines." *SAIS Review*, Volume 24, Issue 1, pp. 50–52.

Ansari, M., 2007, "The New Face of Jihad." *Newsline*, August 3, (Special Report), viewed June 12, 2007, http://www.newsline.com.pk/NewsAug2007/specrep3aug2007.htm.

Aristotle, 350 B.C.E., *Metaphysics*, Book 4, Part 6, trans. W. D. Ross, viewed May 15, 2008, http://classics.mit.edu/Aristotle/metaphysics.4.iv.html.

Armenta, A., M. Jelsma, T. Blickman, and V. Montanes, eds., 2001, *Merging Wars: Afghanistan, Drugs and Terrorism*, Transnational Institute, Drugs & Conflict Debate Paper 3, TNI Briefing Series, pp. 8 and 19, viewed August 20, 2005, http://www.tni.org/reports/drugs/debate3.pdf.

Arnett, P., 1980, "Heroin: U.S. is Battling 3rd Heroin War.", *Boston Globe*, November 18.

Arquilla, J., and D. F. Ronfeldt, 1996, *The Advent of Netwar*, RAND Corporation, Santa Monica, CA, p. 43, viewed March 15, 2005, http://www.rand.org/pubs/monograph_reports/MR789/MR789.ch3.pdf.

Arquilla, J., and D. F. Ronfeldt, eds., 2001, *Networks and Netwars: The Future of Terror, Crime, and Militancy*, RAND Corporation, Santa Monica, CA.

Asad, A. Z., and R. Harris, 2003, *The Politics and Economics of Drug Production on the Pakistan-Afghanistan Border*, Ashgate Publishing Co, Burlington, VT.

Asia Foundation, 2006, *Afghanistan in 2006: A Survey of the Afghan People*, Kabul, Afghanistan, pp. 14–16, viewed December 12, 2007, http://www.asiafoundation.org/pdf/AG-survey06.pdf.

Asia Today, 2002, "The Drug Trade in Central Asia." April 26, viewed June 15, 2006, http://www.asiasource.org/news/at_mp_02.cfm?newsid=72136.

Associated Press, 1987, "Drug Production Rose Worldwide in '86, Report Says." published in the *Dallas Morning News*, March 3, p. 6A.

Associated Press, 2003a, "Navy Makes Persian Gulf Drug Bust." as reported on *CBS News*, December 19, viewed February 2, 2006, http://www.cbsnews.com/stories/2003/12/19/terror/main589500.shtml.

Associated Press, 2003b, "Taliban Teaming With Al-Qaida Again." September 3.

Associated Press, 2004, "Madrid Bombers Financed Operation With Drug Sales, Spain Says." published in *USA Today*, April 14.

Associated Press, 2005, "U.N. seeks first political definition of terrorism." as reported on *MSNBC*, July 23, viewed October 26, 2006, http://www.msnbc.msn.com/id/8676132/.

Associated Press, 2006, "NATO: Afghanistan at a Tipping Point." as reported on *CBS News*, October 8, viewed December 27, 2007, http://www.cbsnews.com/stories/2006/10/08/terror/main2072505.shtml?source=RSSattr=World_2072505.

Associated Press, 2007a, "27 killed in suicide blast on Afghan bus." September 29.

Associated Press, 2007b, "'Bin Laden urges war on Pakistani president." September 20, viewed November 17, 2007, http://www.msnbc.msn.com/id/20880736/.

Associated Press, 2007c, "Suitcase Nukes? Probably a Myth." November 10.

Atlas, T., 1988, "Pakistan Poppy Crop Signals New Heroin Harvest." *Chicago Tribune*, May 9, p. 4.

Audi, R., 2003, *Epistemology: a contemporary introduction to the theory of knowledge*, Routledge, New York, NY and London, UK.

Auerbach, S., 1979, "'New Heroin Connection." *Washington Post*, October 11, p. A1.

Auster B. B., and D. Kaplan, 1998, "'Saudi royalty gives money to bin Laden." *U.S. News & World Report*, October 19, viewed July 8, 2007, http://www.usnews.com/usnews/news/articles/981019/archive_004977.htm.

Australian, 2008, "Drug claim on Karzai brother." October 6, p. 11.

Australian, 2010, "Pakistan Intelligence 'funds the Taliban.'" June 14, p. 10.

Babcock, C. R., and J. Kotkin, 1980, "Opium: Troubling Export From Troubled Golden Crescent." *Washington Post*, January 31, p. A8.

Bagader, A., A. El-Sabbagh, M. Al-Glayand, and M. Samarrai, 2006, "Environmental Protection in Islam: Protection of Man and Environment from Harm" (part 7 of 7). *The Religion of Islam*, April 17, viewed October 26, 2006, http://www.islamreligion.com/articles/312/.

Baker, A., 2008, "Losing Kabul: A Bombing's Legacy." *Time*, January 16, viewed March 15, 2010, http://www.time.com/time/world/article/0,8599,1703984,00.html.

Baker, A., 2009, "How Crime Pays for the Taliban." *Time*, September 7, viewed April4,2010,http://www.time.com/time/magazine/article/0,9171,1919154-3,00.html.

Baker, P., 2003, "Renewed Militancy Seen in Uzbekistan, Government Crackdown Threatens to Radicalize Previously Non-Violent Groups." *Washington Post*, September 27, p. A19.

Bakier, A. H., 2010, "Taliban Spokesman Discusses Relations with al-Qaeda and Opium Production in Afghanistan." *Terrorism Monitor*, Volume 8, Issue 25, June 24, pp. 4–6, viewed June 25, 2010, http://www.jamestown.org/uploads/media/TM_008_49.pdf.

Baldauf, S., 2003, "Afghans yet to lay down arms; A deadly skirmish between warlords last week points to the perils of slow disarmament." *Christian Science Monitor*, October 14, p. O7.

Baldauf, S., 2006, "Inside the Afghan drug trade; In a northern province, four law-enforcement officials describe life built around trafficking." *Christian Science Monitor*, June 13, p. O1.

Baldauf, S., and F. Bowers, 2005, "Afghanistan riddled with drug ties; The involvement of local as well as high level government officials in the opium trade is frustrating efforts to eradicate poppy fields." *Christian Science Monitor*, May 13, p. O1.

Baldor, L. C., 2010a, "Terrorist attacks spike in Pakistan, Afghanistan." Associated Press, as reported on *MSNBC*, April 28, viewed May 23, 2010, http://www.msnbc.msn.com/id/36820196/.

Baldor, L. C., 2010b, "US Treasury beefing up staff in Afghanistan." Associated Press, April 7, viewed April 7, 2010, http://www.google.com/hostednews/ap/article/ALeqM5gjnDGpz2XrTOD_dlzX4oOaUWvp0gD9EUFBP80.

Balfour, F., 2001, "Dark Days for a Black Market." *Business Week*, October 15, viewed May 10, 2010, http://www.businessweek.com/magazine/content/01_42/b3753016.htm.

Ballentine, K., and J. Sherman, eds., 2003, *Political Economy of Armed Conflict: Beyond Greed and Grievance*, Lynne Rienner Publishers, Boulder, CO.

Bangalore Deccan Herald, 1999, "'Pakistan's ISI Trying to Revive Militancy in Punjab." Internet version, FBIS-NES-1999-0728, July 28, viewed July 2, 2007, http://www.fas.org/irp/world/pakistan/isi/punjab.html.

Baran, Z., F. S. Starr, and S. Cornell, 2006, "Islamic Radicalism in Central Asia and the Caucasus: Implications for the EU." *Central Asia-Caucasus Institute & Silk Road Studies Program*, Silk Road Paper; Occasional Papers Series, July 2006, viewed June 30, 2007, http://www.silkroadstudies.org/new/docs/Silkroadpapers/0607Islam.pdf.

Barrett, R. 2008, "Seven Years After 9/11: Al Qaida's Strengths and Vulnerabilities." *The International Centre for the Study of Radicalisation and Political Violence/Eden Intelligence*, Future Actions Series, September 2008.

Bartolf, C., and B. I. Finel, 2009, *Are We Winning? Measuring Progress in the Struggle against al Qaeda and Associated Movements*, American Security Project, December 15, Washington, DC, viewed April 12, 2010, http://www.americansecurity project.org/content/publications/2009/are-we-winning-measuring-progress-in-the-struggle-against-al-qaeda-and-associate-movements/.

Barwich, N., M. Bauer, S. Hummel, G. Lakus, and D. Nytra, 2004, *Voices of Muslim Scholars against Terrorism* in "Ethics, 9/11 and History of American Nation." viewed September 2, 2008, http://www.acsonweb.de/hd/content/pres_c5/section2/Ethics_and_911BarwichBauerHummelLakusNytraDFH.html.

Bashir, H., 2002, "Political Economy of Narcotics—An Overview." *Defence Journal*, viewed January 18, 2008, http://www.defencejournal.com/2002/june/narcotics.htm.

Bassiouni, C. M., 2005, *Report of the independent expert on the situation of human rights in Afghanistan*, United Nations Commission on Human Rights (UNCHR), viewed December 16, 2007, http://www.law.depaul.edu/institutes_centers/ihrli/pdf/Bassiouni_Afghanistan_Final_05.pdf.

Bazzi, M., 2001, "'A Network of Networks' of Terror."', *Newsday*, September 16, p. W.05.

BBC News, 2000, "'Who are the Abu Sayyaf?" December 30, viewed October 20, 2007, http://news.bbc.co.uk/2/hi/asia-pacific/719623.stm.

BBC News, 2002a, "Excerpts from Pakistan President Pervez Musharraf's independence day speech on 14 Aug 2002." August 14, viewed January 15, 2008, http://news.bbc.co.uk/1/low/world/south_asia/2192902.stm.

BBC News, 2002b, "Obituary: Chechen Rebel Khattab." April 26, viewed January 15, 2008, http://news.bbc.com.uk/2/hi/europe/1952053.stm.

BBC News, 2002c, "Profile: Pakistan's military intelligence agency." January 9, viewed http://news.bbc.co.uk/1/hi/world/south_asia/1750265.stm.

BBC News, 2006a, "Profile: India's fugitive gangster." September 12, viewed January 2, 2008, http://news.bbc.co.uk/2/hi/south_asia/4775531.stm.

BBC News, 2006b, "Warning over Afghan Drug Economy." November 28, viewed February 13, 2008, http://news.bbc.co.uk/2/hi/south_asia/6190922.stm.

BBC News, 2007a, "Afghan Taliban commander killed." May 13, viewed May 19, 2007, http://news.bbc.co.uk/2/hi/south_asia/6650755.stm.

BBC News, 2007b, "Madrid bombers get long sentences." October 31, viewed August 1, 2007, http://news.bbc.co.uk/2/hi/europe/7070827.stm.

BBC News, 2007c, "Pakistan Taleban vow more violence." January 29, viewed January 22, 2008, http://news.bbc.co.uk/2/hi/south_asia/6292061.stm.

BBC News, 2010, "Afghans 'paid $2.5bn in bribes'." January 19, viewed January 30, 2010, http://news.bbc.co.uk/2/hi/south_asia/8466915.stm.

BBC News, 2010, "Pakistani agents 'funding and training Afghan Taliban'." June 13, viewed June 13, http://news.bbc.co.uk/2/hi/world/south_asia/10302946.stm.

Bearden, M., 2001, "Afghanistan Graveyard of Empires." *Foreign Affairs*, Volume 80, Number 6, pp. 17–30.

Beaty, J., and S. C. Gwynne, 1993, *The Outlaw Bank: A Wild Ride into the Secret Heart of BCCI*, reprinted in 2004, Beard Books, Washington, DC

Behn, S., 2005, "Retired general says drug money fueling Taliban, al Qaeda." *Washington Times*, October 1, p. A07.

Benjamin, D., and S. Simon, 2003, *The Age of Sacred Terror: Radical Islam's War Against America*, Random House, New York, NY.

Bennett, A., and C. Elman, 2007, "Case Study Methods in the International Relations Subfield." *Comparative Political Studies*, Volume 40, Number 2, pp. 170–195.

Bentz, V. M., and J. J. Shapiro, 1998, *Mindful Inquiry in Social Research*, Sage Publications, Thousand Oaks, CA.

Berdal, M., and M. Serrano, 2002, eds., *Transnational Organized Crime and International Security: Business as Usual?* Lynne Reinner Publishers, Boulder, CO.

Bergen, P., 2003, "The Dense Web of Al Qaeda." *Washington Post*, December 25, p. A29.

Bergen, P., 2007, "Afghanistan 2007: Problems, Opportunities and Possible Solutions." in *Afghanistan: Mission Impossible*, International Security Network (ISN),

Centre for European Policy Studies (CEPS), pp. 22–29 viewed January 3, 2008, http://www.isn.ethz.ch/pubs/ph/details.cfm?id=31075.

Bernstein, S., R. N. Lebow, J. G. Stein, and S. Weber, 2007, "Social science as case-based diagnostics." in *Theory and evidence in comparative politics and international relations*, eds., R. N. Lebow and M. I. Lichbach, Palgrave Macmillan, New York, NY, pp. 229–260.

Berridge, V., 1999, *Opium and the People*, Free Association Books, London, UK, p. xxii.

Bevir, M., 1994, "Objectivity in History." *History and Theory*, Volume 33, Number 3, pp. 328–344; or Postprint at: http://repositories.cdlib.org/cgi/viewcontent.cgi?article=3164&context=postprints.

Bhatia, M., J. Goodhand, H. Atmar, A. Pain, and M. Suleman, 2003, *Profits and poverty: Aid, livelihood and conflict in Afghanistan*, (HPG Background Paper), Overseas Development Institute, ODI, London, UK.

Bickman, L., and D. J. Rog, eds., 1998, *Handbook of Applied Social Research Methods*, Sage Publications, Thousand Oaks, CA, pp. 229–259.

Biden, J. R. 2003, (D-Delaware), *Narco-Terrorism: International Drug Trafficking and Terrorism—A Dangerous Mix*, statement during the hearing before the United States Senate, Committee on the Judiciary, Washington, DC, May 20, viewed transcript April 2, 2007, http://www.au.af.mil/au/awc/awcgate/congress/narco_terror_20may03.pdf.

Bin Laden, O., 1996, "Declaration of War against the Americans Occupying the Land of the Two Holy Places." from the Arabic-language daily *Al-Quds al-Arabi* (London), August 1996, reproduced in "Bin Laden's Fatwa." *Online News Hour with Jim Lehrer*, Public Broadcasting Service (PBS), viewed transcript July 5, 2007, http://www.pbs.org/newshour/terrorism/international/fatwa_1996.html.

Blackwell, T., 2007a, "Taliban, Drug Cartels Partners: RCMP." CanWest News Service, *Times Colonist* (Victoria, British Columbia), June 25, p. A3.

Blackwell, T., 2007b, "Hand in hand: Taliban and drug lords; Mountie tracks links in Afghanistan." CanWest News Service, *Gazette* (Montreal), June 25, p. A16.

Blackwell, T., 2007c, "Drug alliance propels terror attacks: RCMP; Narco-economy; Taliban, cartels have symbiotic relationship: officer." CanWest News Service, *National Post* (f/k/a Financial Post, Canada), June 25, p. A9.

Blair, D., 2010, "Annual Threat Assessment of the US Intelligence Community." testimony before the United States Senate Select Committee on Intelligence, Washington, DC, February 2, viewed June 16, 2010, http://www.dni.gov/testimonies/20100202_testimony.pdf.

Blanchard, C., 2004, *Afghanistan: Narcotics and U.S. Policy*, Congressional Research Service, Federal Research Division, The Library of Congress, CRS, Washington, DC, viewed March 20, 2007, https://www.policyarchive.org/bitstream/handle/10207/177/RL32686_20041207.pdf?sequence=1.

Blanchard, C., 2005, *Afghanistan: Narcotics and U.S. Policy*, updated May 26, 2005, Congressional Research Service, Federal Research Division, The Library of Congress, CRS, Washington, DC, viewed March 20, 2007, https://www.policyarchive.org/bitstream/handle/10207/177/RL32686_20050526.pdf?sequence=2.

Blanchard, C., 2006, *Afghanistan: Narcotics and U.S. Policy*, updated December 25, 2006, Congressional Research Service, Federal Research Division, The Library of Congress, CRS, Washington, DC, viewed March 20, 2007, https://www.policyarchive.org/bitstream/handle/10207/177/RL32686_20060125.pdf?sequence=3.

Blanchard, C., 2007a, *Afghanistan: Narcotics and U.S. Policy*, updated December 6, 2007, Congressional Research Service, Federal Research Division, The Library of Congress, CRS, Washington, DC, viewed January 5, 2008, http://www.fas.org/sgp/crs/row/RL32686.pdf.

Blanchard, C., 2007b, *Al Qaeda: Statements and Evolving Ideology*, Congressional Research Service, Federal Research Division, Library of Congress, CRS, Washington, DC, updated July 9, viewed October 10, 2007, http://www.fas.org/sgp/crs/terror/RL32759.pdf.

Blanchard, C., 2009, *Afghanistan: Narcotics and U.S. Policy*, updated August 12, 2009, Congressional Research Service, Federal Research Division, The Library of Congress, CRS, Washington, DC, p.4, viewed January 22, 2010, http://www.fas.org/sgp/crs/row/RL32686.pdf

Blank, S., 2001, "Narcoterrorism as a Threat to International Security." *World & I*, Volume 16, pp. 265–281.

Bliss, J., and T. Capaccio, 2010, "Al-Qaeda Turns to Extortion as Funds Cut, U.S. Says (Update1)." *Bloomberg Business Week*, April 7, viewed April 7, 2010, http://www.businessweek.com/news/2010-04-07/al-qaeda-turns-to-extortion-as-funds-cut-u-s-says-update1-.html.

Bonner, A., 1986, "Afghan Rebel's Victory Garden: Opium." *New York Times*, June 18, p. A1.

Booth, M., 1996, *Opium: A History*, St. Martin's Press, New York, NY.

Borum, R., and M. Gelles, 2005, "Al Qaeda's Operational Evolution: Behavioral and Organizational Perspectives." *Behavioral Sciences and the Law*, Volume 23, Issue 4, pp. 467–483.

Boston Globe, 2006, "5 Afghan officers die in opium area attacks." Globe Wire Services, March 12, viewed December 12, 2007, http://www.boston.com/news/world/asia/articles/2006/03/12/5_afghan_officers_die_in_opium_area_attacks/.

Brady, B., 2010, "Drugs and desertion: how the UK really rates Afghan police." *Independent*, March 28, viewed April 8, 2010, http://www.independent.co.uk/news/world/asia/drugs-and-desertion-how-the-uk-really-rates-afghan-police-1929508.html.

Braun, M. A., 2009, *U.S. Counternarcotics Strategy in Afghanistan*, statement before the U. S. Senate Caucus on International Narcotics Control, Washington, DC, October 21, viewed June 5, 2010, http://drugcaucus.senate.gov/Braun-Statement-10-21-09.pdf.

Brewster M., 2009, "Deadlier Taliban Network Surfaces." *Toronto Star*, February 9, viewed March 30, 2010, http://www.thestar.com/specialsections/article/584508.

Brimley, S., 2006, "Tentacles of Jihad: Targeting Transnational Support Networks." *Parameters*, Volume 36, Issue 2, pp. 30–46, viewed January 15, 2008, http://www.carlisle.army.mil/usawc/Parameters/06summer/brimley.pdf.

Brisard, J. C., 2003, CEO, JCB Consulting International, *Counterterror Initiatives in the Terror Finance Program*, statement before the United States Senate, Committee on Banking, Housing, and Urban Affairs, Washington, DC, October 22, viewed transcript December 17, 2007, http://frwebgate.access.gpo.gov/cgi-bin/getdoc.cgi?dbname=108_senate_hearings&docid=f:20396.pdf.

Brodzinsky, S., 2005, "Shining Path resurgence may be financed by cocaine money." *Guardian* (London), December 31, p. 13.

Brown, V., 2007, "Cracks in the Foundation: Leadership Schisms in al-Qa'ida from 1989–2006." (Harmony Project), Combating Terrorism Center at West Point, Military Academy, CTC, West Point, NY, viewed March 15, 2008, http://www.ctc.usma.edu/aq/aq3.asp.

Bruno, G., 2010, "Al-Qaeda's Financial Pressures." Council on Foreign Relations, February 1, viewed April 4, 2010, http://www.cfr.org/publication/21347/alqaedas_financial_pressures.html.

Buchanan, M., 2002, *Networks: Small Worlds and the Groundbreaking Science of Networks*, W.W. Norton & Company, Inc., New York, NY.

Buddenberg, D., and W. Byrd, eds., 2006, *Afghanistan's Drug Industry: Structure, Functioning, Dynamics, and Implications for Counter-Narcotics Policy*, United Nations Publications, New York, NY.

Burch, J., 2009, "Interview—Afghan govt members fuelling opium trade—minister." Reuters, December 27, viewed March 12, 2010, http://in.reuters.com/article/idINIndia-45004120091227.

Burch, J., 2010, "Report slams Pakistan for aiding Taliban." Reuters, 13 June, viewed 13 June, http://www.msnbc.msn.com/id/37665955/ns/world_news-south_and_central_asia/.

Burger, A. S., 1999, *Conundrum: Illicit Narcotics and Theoretical Approaches in International Politics*, paper prepared for the International Studies Association, February 16–20, Washington, DC, viewed November 12, 2007, http://www.uwmc.uwc.edu/political_science/Conundrum99.htm#_ednref19.

Burke, J., 1998a, "Bin Laden's Opium War: The U.S. Rained Missiles on the World's Top Terrorist. Now He's Using Drugs to Fund His Campaigns." *Observer*, November 29, p. 23.

Burke, J., 1998b, "Bin-Laden Said Buying Up Afghan Opium Crop." *Observer*, November 29.

Burke, J., 2003, *Al Qaeda: Casting a Shadow of Terror*, I.B. Tauris and Co. Ltd., London, UK, and New York, NY.

Burke, J., 2004, *Al Qaeda: The True Story of Radical Islam*, I.B. Tauris and Co. Ltd., London, UK, and New York, NY.

Burnett, V., 2004, "Crackdown on Afghanistan's Cash Crop Looms." *Boston Globe*, September 18, p. A10.

Burns, R., 2005a, "Afghan Progress is Cited." Associated Press, May 22.

Burns, R., 2005b, "Taliban still fighting, but U.S. commanders in Afghanistan say the opposition is waning." Associated Press, May 21.

Byman, D., B. Hoffman, W. Rosenau, and D. Brannan, 2001, *Trends in Outside Support for Insurgent Movements*, National Security Research Division, RAND Corporation, Santa Monica, CA, p. 4, viewed June 10, 2007, http://www.rand.org/pubs/monograph_reports/2007/MR1405.pdf.

Byrd, W., and C. Ward, 2004, "Drugs and Development in Afghanistan." paper number 18 of the World Bank series, *Social Development Papers; Conflict, Prevention and Reconstruction*, viewed December 10, 2007, http://www.gtz.de/en/dokumente/en-wb-drugs-development-afg.pdf.

Cable News Network (CNN), 2004, "Fear and Vigilance in the Skies; Probing Princess Diana's Death." *Anderson Cooper 360 DEGREES*, aired January 5, viewed transcript July 15, 2007, http://transcripts.cnn.com/TRANSCRIPTS/0401/06/acd.00.html.

Cable News Network (CNN), 2006, "Terror Summit; Shaky Alliance; Afghanistan: The Unfinished War." *Anderson Cooper 360 DEGREES*, aired September 27, viewed transcript July 15, 2007, http://transcripts.cnn.com/TRANSCRIPTS /0609/27/acd.02.html.

Callinan, R., 2004, "Taliban Back in Business of Drugs and Terror." *Australian*, May 31.

Calvani, S., 2008, UNICRI Director, "Illicit drugs are a main catalyst for conflicts." paper presented at the World Forum Against Drugs, Stockholm, Sweden, September 8, pp. 1–7, viewed October 3, 2008, http://www.unicri.it/wwa/staff/speeches/080909-a_dir.pdf.

Cameron, G., 1999, "Multi-track Microproliferation: Lessons from Aum Shinrikyo and Al Qaeda." *Studies in Conflict and Terrorism*, Volume 22, Number 4, pp. 277–309.

Campbell, D., 2001, "How the Plotters Slipped US Net." *Guardian* (London), September 27, p. 1.

Campbell, D., 2004, "Eleven Chinese workers shot dead in Afghanistan." *Guardian* (London) June 11, p. 17.

Carr, C., 2000, Series Editor, *The Book of War: Sun-Tzu, The Art of Warfare and Karl Von Clausewitz, On War*, Random House (Modern Library), New York, NY.

Caruso, J. T., 2001, Acting Assistant Director, Counterterrorism Division FBI, *al Qaeda International*, statement before the United States Senate, Committee on Foreign Relations, Subcommittee on International Operations and Terrorism, Washington, DC, December 18, viewed transcript May 20, 2007, http://www.fbi.gov/congress/congress01/caruso121801.htm.

Casteel, S. W., 2003, Assistant Administator for Intelligence, Drug Enforcement Administration, *Narco-Terrorism: International Drug Trafficking and Terrorism—A Dangerous Mix* statement and testimony before the United States Senate, Committee on the Judiciary, Washington, DC, May 20, pp. 7–10, 18–26, viewed transcript April 2, 2007, http://www.au.af.mil/au/awc/awcgate/congress/narco_terror_20may03.pdf; see also http://judiciary.senate.gov/testimony.cfm?id=764&wit_id=2111; and http://www.cip online.org/colombia/030513cast.htm.

Caulkins, J. P., M. A. R. Kleiman, and J. D. Kulick, 2010, *Drug Production and Trafficking, Counterdrug Policies, and Security and Governance in Afghanistan*, Center on International Cooperation, New York University, pp. 1–35, viewed June 26, 2010, http://www.cic.nyu.edu/Lead%20Page%20PDF/sherman_drug_trafficking.pdf.

CBS News, 2005, "U.N.: Iraq Key Drug Transit Point." May 12, viewed March 12, 2006, http://www.cbsnews.com/stories/2005/05/12/iraq/main694847.shtml?source=search_story.

Center for Geopolitical Drug Studies, 2001, *Charting Drug Territories: Axes of Afghan Drug Trade: Northern Itineraries*, Geopolitical Drug Newsletter, Number 3, viewed October 10, 2006, http://www.geodrugs.net/gb/minilettre.php3.

Center for Geopolitical Drug Studies, 2002a, *Charting Drug Territories: Axes of Afghan Drug Trade: Southern Routes through Pakistan*, Geopolitical Drug

Newsletter, Number 4, viewed October 10, 2006, http://www.geodrugs.net/gb/minilettre.php3.

Center for Geopolitical Drug Studies, 2002b, *Charting Drug Territories: Axes of Afghan Drug Trade: The Western Routes*, Geopolitical Drug Newsletter, Number 5, viewed October 10, 2006, http://www.geodrugs.net/gb/minilettre.php3.

Center for International Policy, Asia program: staff biography, viewed August 15, 2007, http://www.ciponline.org/asia/staff/asia.htm.

Center for the Study of the Presidency, 2008, *Afghanistan Study Group Report*, 2nd ed., Center for the Study of the Presidency, Washington, DC, January 30, viewed July 25, 2008, http://www.thepresidency.org/pubs/Afghan_Study_Group_final.pdf.

Central Asia-Caucasus Institute Analyst, 2005, "Russian Border Guards end Mission on Tajik-Afghan Border." *CACI Analyst*, September 1, viewed September 15, 2008, http://www.cacianalyst.org/?q=node/3383.

Central Intelligence Agency, 2007, "Terrorism FAQs." April 6, viewed June 10, 2007, https://www.cia.gov/news-information/cia-the-war-on-terrorism/terrorism-faqs.html.

Central Intelligence Agency, 2007, website viewed October 1, 2007, https://www.cia.gov/news-information/cia-the-war-on-terrorism/terrorism-faqs.html.

Central Intelligence Agency, n.d, *Guide to the Analysis of Insurgency*, Washington, DC: Central Intelligence Agency.

Century Foundation, 2004, "An Afghanistan Watch Interview with Dr. Pierre-Arnaud Chouvy." A Project of The Century Foundation, October 26, viewed July 25, 2007, http://www.afghanistanwatch.org/newsletterarchive/listserv10-26-04.htm.

Chalk, P. 2000, "Southeast Asia and the Golden Triangle's Heroin Trade: Threat and Response." *Studies in Conflict and Terrorism*, Volume 23, Number 2, pp. 89–106.

Chamberlain, W., 2003, Assistant Administrator, Bureau for Asia and the Near East, Agency for International Development, *The U.S. and South Asia: Challenges and Opportunities for American Policy*, testimony before the U.S. House of Representatives, Subcommittee on Asia and the Pacific of the Committee on International Relations, Washington, DC, March 20, pp. 28–29, 45–53, viewed April 20, 2007, http://commdocs.house.gov/committees/intlrel/hfa85841.000/hfa85841_0f.htm.

Chandra, V., 2006, "Warlords, Drugs and the War on Terror' in "Afghanistan: The Paradoxes." *Strategic Analysis*, January–March, pp. 64–92, viewed January 4, 2008, http://www.idsa.in/publications/strategic-analysis/2006/jan-mar06/VishalChandra.pdf.

Chang, A., 2002, "Splitting Profits." *ABC News*, September 19, viewed February 17, 2007, http://abcnews.go.com/sections/world/DailyNews/afghan020919_drugs.html.

Channel News Asia, 2004, "Afghanistan reconstruction challenged by drug-financed terrorism: US." April 2.

Charles, R. B., 2004a, Assistant Secretary for International Narcotics and Law Enforcement Affairs, *Afghanistan: Are the British Counternarcotics Efforts Going Wobbly*, statement before the U.S. House of Representatives Committee on Government Reform, Subcommittee on Criminal Justice, Drug Policy, and Human Resources, Washington, DC, April 1, pp. 14–18 viewed April 4, 2007, http://bulk.resource.org/gpo.gov/hearings/108h/96745.pdf.

Charles, R. B., 2004b, *Narcotics and Terrorism: Links, Logic and Looking Forward*, Chelsea House Publishers, New York, NY.

Chaudhry, M. S., 1999, "Fundamentals of Islamic Economic System." Chapter 3, *Prohibited Means of Production of Wealth*, Burhan Education and Welfare Trust, Lahore, Pakistan, viewed November 20, 2007, http://www.muslimtents.com/shaufi/b16/b16_3.htm.

Chaudhuri, P. P., 2007, "Confederation of Terror." *Washington Post*, Special to washingtonpost.com's Think Tank Town, September 15, viewed June 6, 2008, http://www.washingtonpost.com/wp-dyn/content/article/2007/09/14/AR2007091401980.html.

Chepesiuk, R., 1999, *Hard Target: The United States War Against International Drug Trafficking, 1982–1997*, McFarland & Company Inc., Jefferson, NC.

Chikhi, L., 2010, "Algeria says al Qaeda guards Sahara drug smugglers." Reuters, February 22.

China Daily, 2003, "UN: Afghan opium production spreading like cancer." October 30, viewed February 22, 2007, http://www.chinadaily.com.cn/en/doc/2003-10/30/content_276872.htm.

China Daily, 2010, "Xinjiang used by drug traffickers as point of entry to China." *Asia News Network*, viewed June 26, 2010, http://www.asiaone.com/News/AsiaOne+News/Crime/Story/A1Story20100626-224019.html.

Chossudovsky, M., 2006, *Who benefits from the Afghan Opium Trade?* Global Research, September 21, viewed November 20, 2007, http://www.globalresearch.ca/index.php?context=viewArticle&code=CHO20060921&articleId=3294.

Chouvy, P. A., 2002, "Drug Trade in Asia." in *Encyclopedia of Modern Asia* Volume 2, eds., D. Levinson & K. Christensen, Scribners, Chicago, Ill, viewed August 2, 2007, http://www.pa-chouvy.org/drugtradeinasia.html.

Chouvy, P. A., 2003, "Opium Smuggling Routes from Afghanistan to Europe and Asia." *Janes Intelligence Review*, March 1, viewed October 10, 2006, http://www.geopium.org/JIR3.htm.

Chouvy, P. A., 2004, "Narco-Terrorism in Afghanistan." *Terrorism Monitor*, Volume 2 Issue 6, March 25, pp. 7–9, viewed December 12, 2005, http://www.jamestown.org/terrorism/news/uploads/ter_002_006.pdf.

Cilluffo, F. J., 2000, Deputy Director, Global Organized Crime Program Director, Counterterrorism Task Force, Center for Strategic and International Studies, Washington, D. C., *The Threat Posed from the Convergence of Organized Crime, Drug Trafficking, and Terrorism*, statement before the U.S. House of Representatives, Committee on the Judiciary Subcommittee on Crime, Washington, DC, December 13, pp. 60–77, viewed April 20, 2007, http://commdocs.house.gov/committees/judiciary/hju68324.000/hju68324_0f.htm.

Clinton, W. J., President of the United States, 1999, Executive Order 13129 –"Blocking Property and Prohibiting Transactions with the Taliban." issued July 4, 1999, viewed June 15, 2007, http://www.fas.org/irp/offdocs/eo/eo-13129.htm.

Coghlan, T., 2005, "Violence stalls UK efforts to stamp out drug crop in Afghanistan." *Daily Telegraph* (London), April 21, p. O17.

Coleman, N. (R-Minnesota), 2003, *Terrorism Financing: Origination, Organization, and Prevention*, statement before the U.S. Senate Committee on Governmental Affairs, July 31, pp. 17–18, viewed March 15, 2008, http://frwebgate.access.gpo.gov/cgi-bin/getdoc.cgi?dbname=108_senate_hearings&docid=f:89039.pdf.

Coll, S., 2004, *Ghost Wars: The Secret History of the CIA, Afghanistan, and Bin Laden, From the Soviet Invasion to September 10, 2001*, Penguin Press, New York, NY.

Combating Terrorism Center, "Harmony and Disharmony: Exploiting al-Qa'ida's Organizational Vulnerabilities." Department of Social Sciences United States Military Academy, West Point, New York, NY: CTC, February 14, 2006, viewed March 20, 2008, http://merln.ndu.edu/merln/mipal/reports/harmony.pdf.

Comras, V., 2005, "Al Qaeda Finances and Funding to Affiliated Groups." *Strategic Insights*, Volume 4, Issue 1, pp. 1–16, viewed April 10, 2007, http://www.ccc.nps.navy.mil/si/2005/jan/comrasJan05.pdf.

Constable, P., 2006, "Pakistan Reaches Peace Accord With Pro-Taliban Militias; Deal Arouses Alarm in Afghanistan." Washington Post Foreign Service, *Washington Post*, September 6, p. A9.

Conyers, J., 1998, (D-Michigan), *Intelligence Authorization Act for Fiscal Year 1999*, statement during a hearing in the U.S. House of Representatives on the May 7, viewed April 20, 2007, http://www.pinknoiz.com/covert/MOU.html#anchor454177; see also, http://www.fas.org/irp/congress/1998_cr/980507-l.htm.

Cook, R., 2005 "The struggle against terrorism cannot be won by military means." *Guardian*, July 8, p. 24.

Cooley, J., 2002, *Unholy Wars: Afghanistan, America and International Terrorism*, 3rd ed., Pluto Press, London, UK and Sterling, VA.

Cooper, H. M., 1984, *The Integrative Research Review*, Sage Publications, Beverly Hills, CA.

Cooper, K. J., 1997, "Afghans Cultivate Islamic State but Ignore Illicit Harvest." *Washington Post*, May 11, p. A22.

Cornell, S. E., 2004, *"Narcotics, Radicalism and Security in Central Asia: The Islamic Movement of Uzbekistan."* Department of East European Studies, Uppsala University Working Papers No. 84, viewed April 12, 2008, http://www.diva-portal.org/diva/getDocument?urn_nbn_se_uu_diva-7385-2__fulltext.pdf.

Cornell, S. E., 2005a, "Narcotics, Radicalism, and Armed Conflict in Central Asia: The Islamic Movement of Uzbekistan." *Terrorism and Political Violence*, Volume 17, Issue 4, pp. 619–639.

Cornell, S. E., 2005b, "Stemming the Contagion: Regional Efforts to Curb Afghan Heroin's Impact." *Georgetown Journal of International Affairs*, Volume 6, Number 1, pp. 23–31.

Cornell, S. E., 2005c, "The Interaction of Narcotics and Conflict." *Journal of Peace Research*, Volume 42, Number 6, pp. 751–760.

Cornell, S. E., 2006a, "Taliban Afghanistan: A True Islamic State?" in *The Limits of Culture: Islam and Foreign Policy*, ed., B. Shaffer, MIT Press, Cambridge, MA, pp. 263–290.

Cornell, S. E., 2006b, "The Narcotics Threat in Greater Central Asia: From Crime-Terror Nexus to State Infiltration?" *China and Eurasia Forum Quarterly*, Volume

4, Number 1, pp. 37–67, viewed April 22, 2007, http://www.silkroadstudies.org/new/docs/CEF/Quarterly/February_2006/Svante_Cornell.pdf.

Cornell, S. E., 2007, "Narcotics and Armed Conflict: Interaction and Implications." *Studies in Conflict and Terrorism*, Volume 30, Number 3, pp. 207–227.

Cornell, S. E., and Londoño, M., 2001, "The 'Andean Syndrome'? Regional Implications of the Taliban Opium Eradication." *CACI Analyst*, June 6, viewed February 26, 2008, http://www.cacianalyst.org/?q=node/230.

Cornell, S. E., and Swanstrom, N. L. P., 2006, "The Eurasian Drug Trade: A Challenge to Regional Security." *Problems of Post Communism*, Volume 53, Number 4, pp. 10–28.

Council of Europe, 2001, "Organized Crime Situation Report 2000." PC-S-CO (2001), 13E (Provisional) Strasbourg, December 2001, viewed August 12, 2007, http://www.coe.int/t/dg1/legalcooperation/economiccrime/organisedcrime/Report2000E.pdf.

Council on Foreign Relations 2006, "Chechnya-based Terrorists (Russia, separatist)." Backgrounder, CFR, New York, NY, viewed August, 2007, http://www.cfr.org/publication/9181/.

Council on Hemispheric Affairs, 2004, "U.S. Southern Command (SouthCom) Struggles to Justify its Role in the War on Terror." viewed July 25, 2008, http://www.coha.org/2004/09/02/us-southern-command-southcom-struggles-to-justify-its-role-in-the-war-on-terror/.

Cousin, G., 2005, "Case Study Research." *Journal of Geography in Higher Education*, Volume 29, Number 3, pp. 421–427.

Crawley, J. W. "U.S. warships pinching Persian Gulf drug trade." *San Diego Union-Tribune*, February 9, p. B1.

Creswell, J. W., 2003, *Research Design: Qualitative, Quantitative, and Mixed Methods Approaches*, 2nd ed., Sage Publications, Thousand Oaks, CA.

Crossette, B., 2000, "Afghan Heroin Feeds Addiction in Region." U.N. Report Declares." *New York Times*, March 1, p. A6.

Cullen, K., 1987, "Soviet Soldiers in Afghanistan Using More Heroin, US Officials Say." *Boston Globe*. January 31, p. 1.

Cullison, A., 2004, "Inside Al-Qaeda's Hard Drive." *Atlantic Monthly*, Volume 294, Issue 2, pp. 55–70.

Cullison, A., and Higgins, A., 2002, "Strained Alliance: al Qaeda's Sour Days in Afghanistan--- Fighters Mocked the Place; Taliban, in Turn, Nearly Booted Out bin Laden—A Fateful U.S. Missile Strike." *Wall Street Journal*, August 2, p. A1.

Curtis, G., 2005, "Afghanistan's Opium Economy." *ADB Review*, Asian Development Bank, viewed August 15, 2006, http://www.adb.org/Documents/Periodicals/ADB_Review/2005/vol37-6/opium-economy.asp.

Curtis, G. E., 2002, *Involvement of Russian Organized Crime Syndicates, Criminal Elements in the Russian Military, and Regional Terrorist Groups in Narcotics Trafficking in Central Asia, the Caucasus, and Chechnya*, Federal Research Division, Library of Congress, Washington, DC, viewed November 15, 2005, http://www.loc.gov/rr/frd/pdf-files/RussianOrgCrime.pdf.

Curtis, G. E., and Karacan, T., 2002, *The Nexus Among Terrorists, Narcotics Traffickers, Weapons Proliferators, and Organized Crime Networks in Western Europe*, Federal Research Division, Library of Congress, Washington, DC, viewed November 15, 2005, http://www.loc.gov/rr/frd/pdf-files/West Europe_NEXUS.pdf.

Daily Times, 2007, "Taliban warns Kabul of more suicide attacks." (Pakistan), May 24, viewed June 15, 2007, http://www.dailytimes.com.pk/default.asp?page=2007%5C05%5C24%5Cstory_24-5-2007_pg7_22.

Davids, D. J., 2002, *Narco-Terrorism: A Unified Strategy to Fight a Growing Terrorist Menace*, Transnational Publishers, Ardsley, NY.

De Borchgrave, Arnaud, 2005, "Narco-state Conundrum." *The Washington Times*, June 2, p. A19.

Denzin, N. K., and Y. S. Lincoln, eds., 2005. *The SAGE Handbook of Qualitative Research*, 3rd ed. Thousand Oaks, CA: Sage Publications.

Deridder, W., 2002, *Interpol Asian Threat Assessment*, 17th Asian Regional Conference, Colombo, Sri Lanka, February 18–22, viewed May 20, 2007, http://www.interpol.int/Public/ICPO/speeches/20020218.asp.

De Young, K., 2006 "Bin Laden Tape Urges Insurgents to Forgo Talks." *Washington Post*, July 2, p. A23.

Diamond, J., 2006 "Captured al Qaeda documents show inner struggles, strategies." *USA Today*, February 16, p. 6A, viewed March 3, 2008, http://www.usatoday.com/news/washington/2006-02-16-al-qaeda-struggles_x.htm.

Dietz, J., 1980, "Drug Fight Faces Snarl." *Boston Globe*, June 11.

Dikaev, T., 2007, "Is Drug Trade on Tajik-Afghan Border Set to Expand?' *The Journal of Turkish Weekly*, May 5, viewed September 22, 2006, http://www.turkishweekly.net/comments.php?id=1029.

Dinmore, G., 2002, "Special Report Drugs Trade After the Taliban: General declares war on desert traffickers: The Iranian Trail." *Financial Times*, January 10, p. 10.

Dishman, C., 2003, "Terrorism, Crime, and Transformation," in *Terrorism in Perspective*, eds. Pamala L. Griset, and Sue Mahan, Sage Publications, Thousand Oaks, CA, pp. 59–72.

Dishman, C., 2001, "Terrorism, Crime, and Transformation." *Studies in Conflict and Terrorism*, Volume 24, Number 1, pp. 43–58.

Dollard, P., 2007, *Pakistan: Jihad Capital of the World*, September 10, viewed August 15, 2008, http://patdollard.com/2007/09/pakistan-jihad-capital-of-the-world/.

Dooley L. M., 2002, "Case Study Research and Theory Building." in *Advances in Developing Human Resources*, Volume 4, Number 3, pp. 335–354, viewed July 10, 2008, http://business.nmsu.edu/%7Emhyman/M610_Articles/Dooley%20Case%20Study%20Research%20&%20Theory%20Building%20 2002.pdf.

Dressler, J. and Forsberg, C., 2009, "The Quetta Shura Taliban in Southern Afghanistan: Organization, Operations, and Shadow Governance." *Institute for the Study of War*, December 21, viewed March 18, 2010, http://www.understandingwar.org/files/QuettaShuraTaliban_1.pdf

Drug War Chronicle, Web site, http://stopthedrugwar.org/chronicle.

Drug War Chronicle, 2001, "Drug Prohibition and Political Violence: Making the Connections." September 21, viewed August 10, 2007, http://stopthedrugwar.org/chronicle-old/203/politicalviolence.shtml.

Dunn, M. C., 1993, "On the Tajik-Afghan Border the Russians are Coming – Back." *Washington Report on Middle East Affairs*, p. 55, viewed August 15, 2008, http://www.wrmea.com/backissues/0993/9309055.htm.

Dupee, M., 2008, "The Haqqani Network: Reign of Terror." *The Long War Journal*, 2 August, viewed March 4, 2010, http://www.longwarjournal.org/archives/2008/08/the_haqqani_network.php.

Dupee, M. and Azizpour, H., 2006, "Interview: Dr. Seth Jones on Afghanistan." *Afgha.com*, December 19, viewed July 2, 2007, http://www.afgha.com/?q=node/1617.

Dupont, A., 1999, "Transnational Crime, Drugs, and Security in East Asia." *Asian Survey*, Volume 39, Number 3, pp. 433–455.

Dupree, Louis, 1980, *Afghanistan*, 3rd ed., Princeton University Press, Oxford, UK and New York, NY.

Dyer, G., 2003, "Creating democracy in Afghanistan was doomed from the start," *Salt Lake Tribune*, (Commentary), December 29, viewed September 15, 2007, http://www.ratical.org/ratville/CAH/Afghan1203.html.

Economic Cooperation Organization—Drug Control Coordination Unit, 2004, *Islamic Republic of Afghanistan, ECO DCCU Country Profile*, July 2, 2007, viewed November 12, 2007, http://www.ecodccu.org/English/coutry_profiles/AFGHANISTAN/AFGHANISTAN%202003.htm.

Economist, 2001, "Afghanistan's Opium Fiends." (U.S. ed.), February 22.

Eisenhardt, K. M., 1989, "Building Theories from Case Study Research." *The Academy of Management Review*, Volume 14, Number. 4, pp. 532–550.

Ellinger, A. D., and Marsick, V. J., 2005, "Case Study Research Methods." in *Research in Organizations: Foundations and Methods of Inquiry*, eds., R. A. Swanson and E. F. Holton III, Berrett-Koehler Publishers, San Francisco, CA, pp. 327–350.

Ehrenfeld, R., 1990, *Narco Terrorism*, Basic Books, New York, NY.

Ehrenfeld, R., 2003, *Funding Evil: How Terrorism Is Financed and How to Stop It*, Bonus Books, Chicago, IL.

Ehrlich, R., 1992, "Outsiders join 'jihad' in Kashmir." *Washington Times*, November 2, p. A10.

Eichenwald, K., 2001, "A Nation Challenged: The Money; Terror Money Hard to Block, Officials Find." *New York Times*, December 10, p. A1.

Eikenberry, K., 2006, Lt. Gen., Commander of the Combined Forces Command in Afghanistan, statement before the U.S. House of Representatives Armed Services Committee, Washington, DC, June 28, viewed July 2, 2007, http://www.globalsecurity.org/military/library/congress/2006_hr/060628-eikenberry.pdf.

Elias, B., 2007, ed., "Pakistan: The Taliban's Godfather?" National Security Archive, George Washington University, Electronic Briefing Book, No. 227, Documents 1–35, released through the Freedom of Information Act, posted August 14, viewed January 5, 2008, http://www.gwu.edu/~nsarchiv/NSAEBB/NSAEBB227/index.htm#7.

Embassy of India, n.d., *Global Terrorism: Attack on Democratic Societies*, A Note on Global Terrorism, viewed December 18, 2007, http://www.indianembassy.org/policy/Terorism/pak_terrorism.htm.

Erikson, M., 2002,"Bin Laden's terror wave 2." *Asia Times online*, October 29, viewed December 18, 2007, http://www.atimes.com/atimes/Central_Asia/DJ29Ag05.html.

Erwin, M., 2009,"The Insurgent-Narcotic Nexus in Helmand Province." *CTC Sentinel*, Volume 2, Issue 9, pp. 5–7.

Escobar, P., 2004,"Holdup at the ballot box." *Asia Times online*, February 20, viewed June 15, 2007, http://www.atimes.com/atimes/Central_Asia/FB20Ag01.html.

Esposito, J. L., 2002, *Unholy War, Terror in the Name of Islam*, Oxford University Press, Oxford, UK.

EUROPOL, 2005, *EU Organised Crime Report*, (public version), October 25, The Hague, Netherlands, viewed June 20, 2010, http://members.multimania.co.uk/ocnewsletter/reports/europol-OC2005-public.pdf.

EUROPOL, 2009, *Organized Crime Threat Assessment*, October 23, The Hague, Netherlands, pp. 13–35, viewed June 20, 2010, http://reportingproject.net/new/REPORTS/Organized_Crime_Threat_Assessment_2009.pdf.

Fair, C. C., 2007, *Suicide Attacks in Afghanistan (2001–2007)*, United Nations Assistance Mission in Afghanistan (UNAMA), September 1, viewed March 15, 2008, http://www.unama-afg.org/docs/_UN-Docs/ UNAMA%20-%20SUICIDE%20ATTACKS%20STUDY%20-%20SEPT%209th%202007.pdf.

Fair C., Malhotra, N, and Shapiro, J., 2009, *The Roots of Militancy: Explaining Support for Political Violence in Pakistan*, December 28, viewed February 4, 2010, http://iis-db.stanford.edu/evnts/5986/Shapiro_paper_2010_02_18.pdf.

Falco, M., 1980,"Opium: Deadly Harvest from Turmoil in Asia." *New York Times*, July 31, p. A19.

Farah, D., and Constable P., 1998,"Drug Business Flourishes in Afghanistan; Taliban Denies Involvement but Is Said to Reap Profit From Taxes, Transport." *Washington Post*, October 5, p. A15.

Farah, D., 2002,"Al Qaeda's Gold: Following Trail to Dubai." *Washington Post*, February 18, viewed September 15, 2008 http://www.globalpolicy.org/nations/corrupt/2002/0218gold.htm.

Farah, D., 2008, Senior Investigator, NEFA Foundation, Senior Fellow, International Assessment and Strategy Center, *Foreign Aid and the Fight Against Terrorism and Proliferation: Leveraging Foreign Aid to Achieve U.S. Policy Goals*, testimony before the United States House of Representatives, Committee on Foreign Affairs, Subcommittee on Terrorism, Nonproliferation and Trade, Washington, D.C., July 31, 2008, p. 97, viewed transcript April 2, 2010, http://www.nti.org/e_research/official_docs/congress/house080731.pdf.

Farmer, B., 2010,"Billions flown out of Kabul in suitcases." *Daily Telegraph*, June 29, viewed July 10, 2010, http://www.nationalpost.com/news/world/Billions+flown+Kabul+suitcases/3213440/story.html.

Favre, R., 2005,"Exploring the Roots of Opium and Illicit Economy in Afghanistan." *Aizon*, p. 21, Note 38, viewed August 15, 2007, http://www.aizon.org/Roots%20of%20Opium%20and%20Illicit%20Economy.pdf.

Fay, B., 1996, *Contemporary Philosophy of Social Science: A Multicultural Approach*, Blackwell Publishing, Oxford, UK.

Federation of American Scientists website, http://fas.org/irp/world/para/aymanh_bk.html; and http://www.fas.org/irp/news/2005/10/letter_in_english.pdf.

Federation of American Scientist Web site,"Terrorism in India: extracts from independent reports from the Western, Pakistani, and Indian Press." viewed August 15, 2007, http://www.fas.org/irp/news/1993/terrorism_press.html.

Felbab-Brown, V., 2005,"Afghanistan: When Counternarcotics Undermines Counterterrorism." *The Washington Quarterly*, Autumn, Volume 28, Number 4, pp. 55–72, viewed August 15, 2006, http://www.twq.com/05autumn/docs/05autumn_felbab.pdf.

Felbab-Brown, V., 2006a,"A Better Strategy Against Narcoterrorism." *Audit of the Conventional Wisdom*, MIT Center for International Studies, January 2006, viewed March 15, 2008, http://web.mit.edu/cis/pdf/Audit_01_06_Vanda.pdf.

Felbab-Brown, V., 2006b,"Hasty poppy eradication in Afghanistan can sow more problems; Peasant farmers left without new livelihoods are heeding the call to join the insurgency." *Christian Science Monitor*, March 23, p. 09.

Felbab-Brown, V., 2009, Statement to the U.S. Senate Caucus on International Narcotics Control, October 21, viewed March 15, 2010, http://drugcaucus.senate.gov/VANDA-FELBAB-BROWN-10-21-09.pdf.

Felbab-Brown, V., 2010,"The Drug-Conflict Nexus in South Asia: Beyond Taliban Profits and Afghanistan." In *The Afghanistan-Pakistan Theater: Militant Islam, Security & Stability*, eds. D. Gartenstein-Ross and C. D. May, Foundation for Defense of Democracies, Washington, DC, pp. 90–112.

Financial Times, 2003, "Drug Trafficking from Afghanistan Continues Toward Tajikistan, Central Asia." January 30.

Filkins, D., 2010, "Despite doubt, Karzai brother retains power." *New York Times*, March 31, p. A1.

Fisk, R., 1993,"Anti-Soviet warrior puts his army on the road to peace; The Saudi businessman who recruited mujahedin now uses them for large-scale building projects in Sudan. Robert Fisk met him in Almatig." *Independent* (London), December 6, p. 10.

Fisk, R., 1996, "Arab rebel leader warns the British: 'Get out of the Gulf'; Robert Fisk tracks Saudi Arabia's most wanted man to his lair in Afghanistan." *Independent* (London), July 10, p. 1.

Fisk, R., 2004, "Interviews with Osama bin Laden in 1996 by Robert Fisk." November 4, viewed March 3, 2008, http://everything2.com/index.pl?node_id=1682885.

Flyvbjerg, B., 2006,"Five Misunderstandings About Case Study Research." *Qualitative Inquiry*, Volume 12, Number 2, pp. 219–245.

Forbes.com, 2001, "Who is Osama bin Laden?'" viewed September 15, 2007, http://www.forbes.com/2001/09/14/0914whoisobl.html.

Franco, C., 2007, *A Taliban Resurgence: The Destabilization of Kabul*, The NEFA Foundation, November, p. 14, footnote 21, viewed July 25, 2008, http://www1.nefafoundation.org/miscellaneous/nefatalibankabul1107.pdf.

Franco, C., 2008, *Exclusive Interview with Taliban Spokesman Zahidullah Mujahid*, The NEFA Foundation, January 4, p. 1, viewed July 15, 2008, http://www1.nefafoundation.org/miscellaneous/nefatalibanintvu0108.pdf.

Freemantle, B., 1986, *The Fix: Inside the World Drug Trade*, Tom Doherty Associates, Inc., New York, NY.

Gaer, F., 2005, "Defining Terrorism: A Political Imperative?" United Nations Association of the United States of America and the Business Council for the United Nations, viewed October 26, 2006, http://www.unausa.org/site/pp.aspx?c=fvKRI8MPJpF&b=1351233&printmode=1.

Galeotti, M., 2006, "British Forces enter Opiumland." *Jane's Intelligence Review*, March 6.

Gall, C., 2004, "Taliban suspected in killing of 11 Chinese workers." *New York Times*, June 10, p. 13.

Gall, C., 2006a, "Afghan year of drug war, and the poppy crop flourishes." *New York Times*, February 17, p. 4.

Gall, C., 2006b, "Opium harvest at record level in Colombia." *New York Times*, September 3, p. 1.

Gall, C., 2006c, "Taliban Threat is Said to Grow in Afghan South." *New York Times*, May 3, p. A1.

Gall, C., 2008a, "Bush ex-official says corrupt Afghans and a hesitant military hinder drug fight." *New York Times*, July 24, p. 12.

Gall, C., 2008b, "Old-Line Taliban Commander Is Face of Rising Afghan Threat." *New York Times."* June 17, p. 1.

Gall, C., and French, H. W., 2004, "Taliban Suspected in Killing of 11 Chinese Workers." *New York Times*, June 11, p. A13.

Gall, C., and Khan, I., 2006, "Taliban and Allies Tighten Grip in North of Pakistan." *New York Times*, December 11, p. A1.

Gall, C., and Rohde, D., 2004, "Pakistan Lets Taliban Train, Prisoner Says." *New York Times*, August 4, p. A1.

Gannon, K., 2004, "Road Rage: Marauding Taliban and drug-dealing warlords on the road to Kandahar." *New Yorker*, March 22, pp. 40–48.

Gardner, D., 2001, "Terrorists get cash from drug trade: Trafficking prime source of funds for many groups." *Ottawa Citizen*, September 14, p. C3.

Gehriger, U., and Yousafzai, S., 2007, "'Ours is a Global Struggle': An Interview With Taliban Military Chief Mansoor Dadullah," *World Politics Review*, July 3, viewed June 15, 2007, http://www.worldpoliticsreview.com/article.aspx?id=899.

Geopolitical Drug Observatory, 2000, *The World Geopolitics of Drugs 1998/1999*, (Europe), Paris, France: OGD, pp. 77–126 at p. 112.

Gerring, J., 2004, "What is a Case Study and What is it Good for?" *The American Political Science Review*, Volume 98, Number 2, pp. 341–354.

Ghafour, H., 2006, "Escalating violence has roots beyond Taliban." *Globe and Mail* (Canada), January 17, p. A1.

Ghazi, J., 2002, "Arab Afghan Primer-Who Are The Ones That Got Away." *Pacific News Service*, March 28, viewed June 14, 2007, http://news.ncmonline.com/news/view_article.html?article_id=582.

Glantz, J., Rohde, D., and Gall, C., 2006, "Afghanistan: The Reach of War; U.S. Report Finds Dismal Training of Afghan Police." *New York Times*, December 4, p. 1.

GlobalSecurity.org, viewed April 5, 2008, http://www.globalsecurity.org/intell/library/congress/2006_rpt/al-qaeda_hpsci109-615-02.htm.

GlobalSecurity.org, viewed May 28, 2007, http://www.globalsecurity.org/military/world/para/hizbi-islami.htm.

GlobalSecurity.org, 2001, Text: "Taliban Profits from Drug Trade, State Department Says." October 4, viewed February 15, 2008, http://www.globalsecurity.org/military/library/news/2001/10/mil-011004-usia13.htm.

Godson, R., 1998, "International Crime Control Strategy." *Trends in Organized Crime*, Volume 4, Issue 1, pp. 1–3.

Godson, R., and Olson, W. J., 1995, "International Organized Crime." *Society*, Volume 32, Issue 2, pp. 18–29.

Gold Coast Bulletin, (Australia) 2001, "How 'the boss' works the network." October 20, p. 58.

Gold, D., 2005, "Economics of Terrorism." *New School University*, August 17, viewed October 15, 2007, http://www.ciaonet.org/casestudy/god01/god01.pdf.

Goldman, A. I., 1994, "Argumentation and Social Epistemology." *The Journal of Philosophy*, Volume 91, Number 1, pp. 27–49.

Goldman, A. I., 1999, *Knowledge in the Social World*, Oxford University Press, Oxford, UK.

Goldman, A. I., 2007, "Social Epistemology." *The Stanford Encyclopedia of Philosophy, Spring edition*, ed., Edward N. Zalta, viewed July 20, 2008, http://plato.stanford.edu/archives/spr2007/entries/epistemology-social/.

Goodhand, J., 2003, *Frontiers and Wars: a study of the opium economy in Afghanistan* (Draft), SOAS, University of London, London, UK.

Goodhand, J., n.d., *From war economy to peace economy*? (Draft), School of Oriental and African Studies, University of London, UK, p. 16, note 2, viewed October 10, 2005, http://unpan1.un.org/intradoc/groups/public/documents/APCITY/UNPAN015703.pdf.

Goodson, L. P., 2000, "Foreign Policy Gone Awry: the Kalashnikovization and Talibanization of Pakistan." In *Pakistan 2000*, eds., C. H. Kennedy and C. Baxter, Lexington Books, Lanham, MD, pp. 107–123.

Goodson, L. P., 2001, *Afghanistan's Endless War: State Failure, Regional Politics, and the Rise of the Taliban*, University of Washington Press, Seattle, WA.

Gopal, A., 2009, "The Most Deadly US Foe in Afghanistan." *Christian Science Monitor*, June 1, viewed online March 25, 2010, http://www.csmonitor.com/World/Asia-South-Central/2009/0601/p10s01-wosc.html.

Gordon, M. R., and Schmitt E., 2001, "Afghanistan Remains a Major Drug Trader Despite Taliban Ban on Poppy Growing." *New York Times*, September 26, p. B4.

Government of Afghanistan, 2006, *Afghan National Development Strategy: An Interim Strategy for Security, Governance, Economic Growth and Poverty Reduction*, Volume 1, pp. 56, 114, and 121, viewed June 14, 2007, http://www.ands.gov.af/admin/ands/ands_docs/upload/UploadFolder/I-ANDS%20by%20Chapters/chapter%204/chapter%204.pdf; http://www.ands.gov.af/admin/ands/ands_docs/upload/UploadFolder/I-ANDS%20by%20Chapters/Chapter%207/Chapter7.pdf; and http://www.nps.edu/programs/ccs/Docs/Pubs/unands_Jan.pdf.

Government of Australia, 2002, Listing of Terrorist Organizations: Jamiat ul-Ansar, November 14, 2002, re-listed November 5, 2004, and November 3, 2006, viewed June 22, 2007, http://www.nationalsecurity.gov.au/agd/www/nationalsecurity.nsf/AllDocs/FA20CAC87E771B95CA256FCD001CAD07?OpenDocument.

Grau, L. W., and Gress, M. A., 2002, eds., *The Soviet-Afghan War: How a Superpower Fought and Loss*, University Press of Kansas, Lawrence, KS.

Greenberg, M. R., Wechsler W. F., and Wolosky L. S., 2002, *Terrorist Financing*, report of an Independent Task Force sponsored by the Council on Foreign Relations, CFR, New York, NY, viewed April 15, 2007, http://www.cfr.org/content/publications/attachments/Terrorist_Financing_TF.pdf.

Greenberg, M. R., Factor, M., Wechsler, W. F., and Wolosky, L. S., 2004, *Update on the Global Campaign Against Terrorist Financing*; second report of an Independent

Task Force on Terrorist Financing, sponsored by the Council on Foreign Relations, CFR, New York, NY, viewed April 15, 2007, http://www.cfr.org/content/publications/attachments/Revised_Terrorist_Financing.pdf.

Griffin, M., 2003, *Reaping the Whirlwind: Afghanistan, al Qa'ida and the Holy War*, Pluto Press, Sterling, VA.

Grimes, W., 2007, "Afghan Struggle to Change Poppy Fields Into Roads." *New York Times*, November 7, p. E9.

Grono, N., and Nathan J., 2007,"Defeating Afghanistan's Drug Fix." *Christian Science Monitor*, May 31, p. 9.

Grusich, K., 2002, "Kirk takes steps to combat growing use of club drugs." *Chicago Daily Herald*, January 17, p. 4.

Guitta, O., 2006, "A Potential Specially Designated Global Terrorist Entity (SDGT) Working in Congress." *Counterterrorism Blog*, April 20.

Gunaratna, R., 2001, "The Lifeblood of Terrorist Organizations: Evolving Terrorist Financing Strategies." in *Countering Terrorism through International Cooperation*, ed. AP Schmid, ISPAC, Milan, pp. 182–185.

Gunaratna, R., 2002, *Inside al Qaeda: Global Network of Terror*, Columbia University Press, New York, NY.

Guthrie, J., 2002, "Police question al Qaeda suspects." *Financial Times*, January 21, p. 2.

Gutterman, S., 2005, "Outgoing Afghan interior minister: Government must be purged of drug traffickers." Associated Press, September 28.

Gwynne, R., 2001, "Al-Qacida and al-Qur'an: The 'Tafsir' of Usamah bin Ladin," September 18, viewed March 15, 2008, http://web.utk.edu/~warda/bin_ladin_and_quran.htm.

Habibzai, H., 2004, "Gunmen Kill 11 Chinese Workers in Afghanistan." *Washington Post*, June 11, p. A14.

Hall, W., 2000, "Output in Afghanistan Doubles." *Financial Times* (London), January 31, p. 2.

Hamilton, L., 2004, Vice Chairman, National Commission on Terrorist Attacks upon the United States, statement before the U.S. House of Representatives, the Committee on Financial Services, *The 9/11 Commission Report: Identifying and Preventing Terrorist Financing*, Washington, DC, August 23, pp. 5–10, viewed transcript April 3, 2007, http://www.access.gpo.gov/congress/house/pdf/108hrg/96943.pdf.

Hamm, M., 2005, *Crimes Committed by Terrorist Groups: Theory, Research and Prevention*, study conducted for the National Institute of Justice, Office of Justice Programs, U.S. Department of Justice, Document No. 211203, Award No. 2003-DT-CX-0002, June 1.

Haq, I., 1996, "Pak-Afghan Drug Trade in Historical Perspective." *Asian Survey*, Volume 36, Number 10, pp. 945–963.

Haq, I., 2005, "Fourth Anniversary of 911: Rise of Drug Trade and Terrorism." *Business Recorder*, September 9.

Harden, B., 2007, "South Koreans Held by Taliban Arrive in Seoul, Offer Apologies; Church Group Seen by Many at Home as Having Been Reckless." *Washington Post Foreign Service*, Suburban Edition, September 2, p. A17.

Harnden, T., 2006, "Drug trade reaches to Afghan cabinet." *Sunday Telegraph* (London), February 5, p. 25, viewed August 15, 2007, http://www.telegraph.co.uk/news/main.jhtml?xml=/news/2006/02/05/wafg05.xml.

Harrison, S. S., 1990, "Sparks of War in Kashmir." *Washington Post*, April 23, p. A11.

Harshe, R., 2003,"Cross-Border Terrorism: Road-Block to Peace Initiatives." *Economic and Political Weekly*, Volume 38, Number 35, pp. 3621–3625.

Haskell, T. L., 1998, *Objectivity is not Neutrality: Explanatory Schemes in History*, Johns Hopkins University Press, Baltimore, MD, pp. 145–173.

Hasnain, G., 2000, "The Taliban's Land of Milk and Honey." *TIME* (Asia), Volume 156, Number 21, May 29, viewed September 15, 2006, http://www.time.com/time/asia/magazine/2000/0529/afghanistan.herat.html.

Hedges, M., 2001, "Afghan opium benefits Taliban: Al-Qaida protects heroin smugglers, collects drug tax." *Houston Chronicle*, October 3, p. 1.

Herman, B., 2004, "Planned Tajik takeover of Afghan border from Russia worries international community." Associated Press, published in *The Agonist*, June 27, viewed September 15, 2008, http://agonist.org/20060303/planned_tajik_takeover_of_afghan_border_from_russia_worries_international_community.

Heron, J., and Reason P., 1997a, "Participative knowing and an extended epistemology." adapted from Heron, J., and Reason P., 1997a,"A Participative Inquiry Paradigm" *Qualitative Inquiry*, Volume 3, Number 3, pp. 274–294.

Hettena, S., 2004, "2 Plead Guilty in Terror Arms Sale Plot." Associated Press, March 3.

Hirschkorn, P., Gunaratna, R., Blanche, E., and Leader, S., 2001, "Blowback." *Jane's Intelligence Review*, Special Report, Volume 13, Number 8, August 1, pp. 42–45.

Hoffman, B., 1998, *Inside Terrorism*, Columbia University Press, New York, NY.

Holden-Rhodes, J. F., 1997, *Sharing the Secrets: Open Source Intelligence and the War on Drugs*, Praeger, Westport, CT.

Holloway, A., 2006, "Opium, corruption and the Taliban: the deadly alliance that our troops have to defeat." *Telegraph* (UK), April 23, p. 27.

Honwana, J., and Lamb G., 1998, *Small Arms Proliferation and Drug Trafficking in Southern Africa*, Centre for Conflict Resolution, University of Cape Town, South Africa, February, viewed February 15, 2008, http://ccrweb.ccr.uct.ac.za/archive/staff_papers/guy_small_arms_drugs.html.

Hopf, T., 2007,"The Limits of Interpreting Evidence." in *Theory and evidence in comparative politics and international relations*, eds., R. N. Lebow and M. I. Lichbach, Palgrave Macmillan, New York, NY, pp. 55–84.

Hsu, E., and Cole B., 2006, *Afghan Insurgency still a Potent Force*, (Briefing) United States Institute of Peace, viewed June 15, 2007. http://www.usip.org/pubs/usipeace_briefings/2006/0223_afghan.html.

Human Rights Watch, 2001, *Afghanistan, Crisis of Impunity: The Role of Pakistan, Russia, and Iran in Fueling the Civil War*, Volume 13, Number 3 (C), July 2001, viewed November 11, 2007, http://www.hrw.org/reports/2001/afghan2/Afghan0701.pdf.

Husain, M. Z., 2001,"The Politics of Islam in Pakistan." In *Religious Fundamentalism in Developing Countries*, eds., SC. Soha and TK Carr, Greenwood Publishing Group, Westport, CT, pp. 9–48.

Hussain, N., 1999, *Proliferation of Small Arms and Politics in South Asia: The Case of Bangladesh*, Regional Centre for Strategic Studies, RCSS Policy Studies 7, Chapter 2, pp. 1–8, viewed November 11, 2007, http://www.rcss.org/policy_studies/ps_7_2.html.

Hussain, R., 2005, *Pakistan and the Emergence of Islamic Militancy in Afghanistan*, Ashgate Publishing Ltd, Aldershot, Hampshire, UK.

Hussein, A., 2005, "Fears of Iraq becoming drug haven." *The Age*, September 5.

Hutchinson, A., (Administrator), Drug Enforcement Administration, U.S. Department Of Justice 2001, *Drug Trade and the Terror Network*, statement before the U.S. House of Representatives, Committee on Government Reform, Subcommittee on Criminal Justice, Drug Policy and Human Resources, Washington, DC, October 3, 2001, pp. 16–24, viewed March 15, 2007, http://frwebgate.access.gpo.gov/cgi-bin/getdoc.cgi?dbname=107_house_hearings&docid=f:81496.pdf.

Hutchinson, A., (Administrator), Drug Enforcement Administration, U.S. Department Of Justice 2002a, *Narco-Terror: The International Connection between Drugs and Terror*, speech given at the Heritage Foundation Institute for International Studies, Washington, DC, April 2, 2002, viewed March 15, 2007, http://www.usdoj.gov/dea/speeches/s040202p.html.

Hutchinson, A., (Administrator), Drug Enforcement Administration, U.S. Department Of Justice 2002b, *Narco-Terror: The Worldwide Connection Between Drugs and Terrorism*, statement before the U.S. Senate, Committee on the Judiciary, Subcommittee on Technology, Terrorism, and Government Information, Washington, DC. March 13, 2002, pp. 9–15, viewed March 15, 2007, http://www.au.af.mil/au/awc/awcgate/congress/narco_terror_13mar02.pdf.

Ibrahimi, S. Y., 2005, "Afghanistan Harvests Another Bumper Opium Crop." *Environment News Service*, May 31, published in cooperation with the *Institute for War and Peace Reporting*, viewed November 29, 2007, http://www.ens-newswire.com/ens/may2005/2005-05-31-03.asp.

Ibrahimi, S. Y., 2008, "Turning Afghan Heroin in Kalashnikovs." June 30, *Institute for War and Peace Reporting*, published in cooperation with *Ground Report*, viewed March 2, 2010, http://www.groundreport.com/World/Turning-Afghan-Heroin-in-Kalashnikovs/2864120.

Inciyan, E., 2001, (Untitled) *Le Monde*, October 21, viewed November 27, 2007, http://debug.sandersresearch.com/index.php?option=com_content&task= view&id=856&Itemid=99999999.

Indo-Asian News Service, 2005, "Links between Dawood, Al Qaeda: US magazine." November 28.

Institute for Policy Studies. *A Tangled Web: A History of CIA Complicity in Drug International Trafficking*, inserted into the Congressional Record by Congressman John Conyers (D-Michigan), May 7, 1998, p H2956, viewed March 10, 2007, http://www.csun.edu/coms/ben/news/cia/7May98/ips.html; see also, http://www.pinknoiz.com/covert/MOU.html#anchor454177.

Integrated Regional Information Networks (IRIN), 2004, *Bitter-Sweet Harvest: Afghanistan's New War*. IRIN Web Special on the Threat of Opium to Afghanistan and the Region (Documentary), UN Office for the Coordination of Humanitarian Affairs, Nairobi, Kenya, July.

International Crisis Group, 2001, *Central Asia: Drugs and Conflict*, ICG Asia Report No. 25, Osh/Brussels, November 26, viewed January 13, 2007, http://www.who.int/disasters/repo/7456.pdf.

International Crisis Group, 2002, *The IMU and the Hizb-Ut-Tahrir: Implications of the Afghanistan campaign*, Asia Briefing, Number 11, Overview, viewed September 15, 2007, http://www.crisisgroup.org/home/index.cfm?id=1760&l=1.

International Monetary Fund, 2003,"Islamic State of Afghanistan: Rebuilding a Macroeconomic Framework for Reconstruction and Growth." IMF Country Report Number 03/299, IMF Publication Services, Washington, DC, viewed February 15, 2008, http://www.imf.org/external/pubs/ft/scr/2003/cr03 299.pdf.

INTERPOL, 2005, *Heroin*, Last updated December 8, 2005, viewed January 10, 2007, http://www.interpol.com/Public/Drugs/heroin/default.asp.

Investigative Project on Terrorism (court cases), Washington, DC, viewed April 22, 2010, http://www.investigativeproject.org/cases.php#281.

IRIN News Service, 2004, "Afghanistan: Interview with Mirwais Yasini, head of the Counter Narcotics Directorate (CND)." October 19, viewed transcript October 25, 2007, http://www.irinnews.org/report.aspx?reportid=25853.

IRIN NEWS SERVICE, 2005, "Afghanistan: Interview with counter-narcotics minister." United Nations Office for the Coordination of Humanitarian Affairs, January 26, viewed transcript October 25, 2007, http://www.irinnews.org/Report.aspx?ReportId=28039.

Iselin, B., 2004,"The Afghan-rim's Heroin Economy," paper presented to the Working Group for the 2nd Ministerial Conference on Transport and Trade in Central and South Asia March 4–5, Dubai, United Arab Emirates, viewed September 20, 2007, http://www.iselinconsulting.com/AFGHAN.pdf.

Ismail, J., 1999, "I Am Not Afraid of Death." *Newsweek*, Volume 133, Issue 2, January 11, pp. 36–37.

Ispahani, M., 1987, "Pakistan—A Country in Crisis." *San Francisco Chronicle*, March 18, p. A1.

Jacobson, M., and Levitt, M., 2010,"Tracking Narco-Terrorist Networks: The Money Trail." *The Fletcher Forum of World Affairs*, Volume 34, Number 1, Winter, Washington Institute, pp. 117–124, viewed April 12, 2010, http://fletcher.tufts.edu/forum/archives/pdfs/34-1pdfs/ForumTOC_rev1-1.pdf.

Jalali, A. A., 2001, "Afghanistan: The Anatomy of an Ongoing Conflict." *Parameters*, Volume 31, Number 1, pp. 85–98, viewed June 20, 2007, http://www.carlisle.army.mil/usawc/Parameters/01spring/jalali.htm.

Jelsma M., and Kramer T., 2009, *Redefining Targets: Towards a Realistic Afghan Drug Control Strategy*, Transnational Institute, Drug Policy Briefing Number 30, viewed January 28, 2010, http://www.idpc.net/publications/tni-briefing-redefining-targets-afghanistan

Jick, T. D., 1979, "Mixing Qualitative and Quantitative Methods: Triangulation in Action." *Administrative Science Quarterly*, Volume 24, Number 4, pp. 602–611.

Johnson, C., and Leslie, J., 2004, *Afghanistan: The mirage of peace*, Zed Books, London, UK, and New York, NY.

Johnson, E., 2007, "Most Afghanistan Suicide Bombers Trained in Pakistan." (Update 1), *Bloomberg.com*, September 9, viewed June 20, 2007, http://www.bloomberg.com/apps/news?pid=20601087&sid=ap5SFbB0UT6c&refer=home.

Johnson, E., 2008, "Afghan Drug Lords Hire Chemists to Make Purer Heroin" (Update 1), *Bloomberg.com*, July 29, viewed June 9, 2010, http://www.bloomberg.com/apps/news?pid=20601103&sid=aDElWyeerTaA.

Johnson, L. K., 2000, *Bombs, Bugs, Drugs and Thugs: Intelligence and America's Quest for Security*, New York University Press, New York, NY.

Jones, S. G., 2007,"Pakistan's Dangerous Game." *Survival*, Volume 49, Issue 1, pp. 15–22.

Jones, S. G., 2008, *Counterinsurgency in Afghanistan*, RAND Counterinsurgency Study, Vol. 4, prepared for the Office of the Secretary of Defense, RAND Corporation, Santa Monica, CA, pp. 37–66, viewed August 25, 2008, http://www.rand.org/pubs/monographs/2008/RAND_MG595.pdf.

Josselin, D., and Wallace, W., 2001, "Non-State Actors in World Politics: A Framework." in *Non-State Actors in World Politics*, eds., D. Josselin and W. Wallace, Palgrave Press, New York, NY, pp. 1–20.

Jun, J., 2006, "Afghanistan: Poppy Eradication Failing and Taliban Benefitting." *RFE/RL*, June 7, viewed January 15, 2008, http://www.rferl.org/content/article/1068980.html.

Kabul Afghan Radio Kelid 2004, "Narcotics seized in Central Afghan Province of Oruzgan." Trans. Foreign Broadcast Information Service, April 3.

Kalic, S. N., 2005, *Combating a Modern Hydra: Al Qaeda and the Global War on Terrorism*, Global War on Terrorism, Occasional Paper 8, Fort Leavenworth, Kansas: Combat Studies Institute Press, viewed April 20, 2008, http://www-cgsc.army.mil/carl/download/csipubs/kalic.pdf.

Kamm, H., 1988, "Afghan Opium Yield up as Pakistan Curbs Crop." *New York Times*, April 14, p. A16.

Kaplan, B., and Duchon, D., 1988, "Combining Qualitative and Quantitative Methods in Information Systems Research: A Case Study." *MIS Quarterly*, Volume 12, Number 4, pp. 571–586.

Kaplan, D., Fang, B., and Sangwan, S., 2005, "Paying for Terror." *U.S. News & World Report*, Volume 139, Issue 21, December 5, pp. 40–54.

Kaplan, R. D., 2000, "The Lawless Frontier." *Atlantic Monthly*, Volume 286, Number 3, pp. 66–80.

Kavkaz-Center News Agency 2004, "Report about bin Laden's ties to Chechnya: pack of lies." viewed November 10, 2007, http://www.kavkazcenter.com/eng/content/2004/11/20/3306.shtml.

Katzman, K., 2010, "*Afghanistan: Post-Taliban Governance, Security, and U.S. Policy.*" Congressional Research Service, Federal Research Division, The Library of Congress, CRS, Washington, DC, viewed June 14, 2010, http://www.fas.org/sgp/crs/row/RL30588.pdf.

Kearney, C., Nichols, M., and Eastham, T., 2009, "Afghan charged in New York with financing Taliban." Reuters, 21 April, viewed 22 April 2010, http://www.reuters.com/article/idUSTRE53K6IX20090421.

Keegan, J., 1985, "The Ordeal of Afghanistan." *Atlantic Monthly*, Volume 256, pp. 94–105.

Kellerhals, M. D., Jr., 2004, "Foreign Terrorist List Vital in Global War on Terrorism." *USINFO*, January 5, viewed June 29, 2007, http://usinfo.state.gov/dhr/Archive/2004/Jan/06-111724.html.

Kerry, J. F., et al., 2009, *Afghanistan's Narco War: Breaking the Link Between Drug Traffickers and Insurgents*: a report to the Committee on Foreign Relations, United States Senate, One Hundred Eleventh Congress, first session, August 10, U.S. Government Printing Office, Washington, DC, viewed November 15, 2009, http://www.newsweek.com/media/5/Afghan-Narco-War.pdf.

Khalilova, K., 2002, "Chechen Fighter's Death Reveals Conflicted Feelings in Azerbaijan." *Eurasia Insight*, May 14, viewed December 20, 2008, http://www.eurasianet.org/departments/insight/articles/eav051402_pr.shtml.

Khan, N., 2004, "Afghan Village Stormed After Pilot Killed." Associated Press, February 23.

Khan, N., 2007, "Taliban Collected Taxes, Ran Heroin Labs." Associated Press, December 12.

Kilcullen, D., 2004, "Countering Global Insurgency (version 2.2), November 30, pp. 1–72, viewed March 15, 2008, http://smallwarsjournal.com/documents/kilcullen.pdf; and http://www.smallwars.quantico.usmc.mil/search/Articles/CounteringGlobalInsurgency.pdf

Kilcullen, D., 2005, "Countering Global Insurgency." *Journal of Strategic Studies*, Volume 28, Number 4, pp. 597–617.

Kimmage, D., 2004, "The growth of radical Islam in Central Asia." *Asia Times online*, March 31, viewed November 20, 2007, http://www.atimes.com/atimes/Central_Asia/FC31Ag02.html.

King, G., Keohane, R. O., and Verba, S., 1995, "The Importance of Research Design in Political Science." *The American Political Science Review*, Volume 89, Number 2, pp. 475–481.

Kirk, M. S. (R-Illinois), 2004a, *Afghanistan: Drugs and Terrorism and U.S. Security Policy*, statement before the U.S. House of Representatives Committee on International Relations, Washington, DC, February 12, pp. 11–12, viewed transcript April 10, 2007, http://www.ahrn.net/library_upload/uploadfile /file2217.pdf.

Kirk, M. S. (R-Illinois), 2004b, *Al Qaeda Deals Heroin to Fund Terrorism Operations*, statement before the U.S. House of Representatives, Washington, D.C., January 21, pp. H62-H63, viewed transcript April 10, 2007, http://thomas.loc.gov/cgi-bin/query/D?r108:40:./temp/~r1081ALAYL::; see also http://www.govtrack.us/congress/record.xpd?id=108-h20040121-40.

Kirk, M. S. (R-Illinois), Web site, http://www.house.gov/kirk/district.shtml

Kleiman, M. A. R., 2004, *Illicit Drugs and the Terrorist Threat: Causal Links and Implications for Domestic Drug Control Policy*, Congressional Research Service, Federal Research Division, Library of Congress, viewed April 20, 2007, http://www.au.af.mil/au/awc/awcgate/crs/rl32334.pdf.

Knickmeyer, E., and Finer, J., 2006, "Insurgent Leader Al-Zarqawi Killed in Iraq." Washington Post Foreign Service, *Washington Post*, June 8, viewed April 7, 2010, http://www.washingtonpost.com/wp-dyn/content/article/2006/06/08/AR2006060800114.html.

Kohlmann, E. F., 2004, *Al Qaeda's Jihad in Europe*, BERG, Oxford, UK and New York, NY.

Kohlmann, E. F., 2007, "Transcript: Weltwoche Interview with Taliban Commander Mansoor Dadullah." April 7, viewed transcript July 10, 2007, http://www.afgha.com/?q=node/3448.

Korgun, V., 2003, "Afghanistan's Resurgent Taliban." *Terrorism Monitor*, Volume 1, Issue 4, Jamestown Foundation, October 24, pp. 5–7, viewed May 20, 2007, http://www.jamestown.org/terrorism/news/uploads/ter_001_004.pdf.

Kranti, V., 1997, "ISI Turning Afghanistan into drug laboratory." *Observer*, June 14.

Kratochwil, F. V., 2007, "Evidence, inference, and truth as problems of theory building in the social sciences." In *Theory and evidence in comparative politics and international relations*, eds., R. N. Lebow and M. I. Lichbach, Palgrave Macmillan, New York, NY., pp. 25–54.

Krauss, C., 1992, "U.S. Will Assist Peru's Army in Fighting Cocaine and Rebels; The military is now beginning to embrace the war on Drugs, *New York Times*, January 25, p. 4.

Kronstadt, A. K., 2006, *Pakistan-U.S. Relations*, Congressional Research Service, Federal Research Division, Library of Congress, updated March 6, 2006.

Kuala Lumpur Declaration on International Terrorism. 2002, adopted at the Extraordinary Session of the Islamic Conference of Foreign Ministers on Terrorism, April 1–3, viewed September 5, 2008, http://domino.un.org/unispal.nsf/fd807e46661e3689852570d00069e918/55625226ccc4c7fa85256ba40049e3cf!OpenDocument.

Kyl, J. (R-Arizona), 2002, statement before the Subcommittee on Technology, Terrorism, and Government Information of the Committee on the Judiciary, *Narco–Terror: The Worldwide Connection Between Drugs And Terrorism*, Washington, DC., March 13, pp. 5–6, viewed transcript March 15, 2007, http://www.au.af.mil/au/awc/awcgate/congress/narco_terror_13mar02.pdf.

Kyl, J. (R-Arizona), 2003, *Narco-Terrorism: International Drug Trafficking and Terrorism—A Dangerous Mix*, statement before the United States Senate, Committee on the Judiciary, Washington, DC, May 20, pp. 6–7, viewed transcript April 2, 2007, http://www.au.af.mil/au/awc/awcgate/congress/narco_terror_20may03.pdf.

Labrousse, A., 1999, "Conflict, Drugs and Mafia Activities." contribution to the *Preparatory Work for the Hague Peace Conference*, May 11–16; paper also presented to Canada's Senate Special Committee on Illegal Drugs, May 28, 2001, viewed September 1, 2006, http://www.parl.gc.ca/37/1/parlbus/commbus/senate/com-e/ille-e/presentation-e/labrousse2-e.htm.

Lal, R., 2005, "South Asian Organized Crime and Terrorists Networks." *Orbis*, Volume 49, Issue 2, pp. 293–304.

Lamb, C., 2006, "British enlisted to smash Afghan opium capital." *Australian*, February 6, p. 13.

Lamb, C., 2008a, "Mission Impossible." *Sunday Times* (London), October 12, p. 1.

Lamb, C., 2008b, "Taliban leader killed by SAS was Pakistan officer." *Sunday Times* (London), October 12, p. 4.

Lamour, C., and Lamberti, M. R., 1974, *The International Connection: Opium From Growers to Pushers*, Pantheon Books, New York, NY.

Land, T., 1996, "Middle East Drug Traffic Set to Rise." *Middle East*, Number 258, July-August, pp. 20–22.

Laqueur, W., 2005, "The Danger That Lies in Our Midst." *Wall Street Journal*, July 12, p. A16.

Lederer, E. M., 2001, "UN Panel Accuses Taliban on Drugs." Associated Press, May 25, viewed July 30, 2007, http://www.globalpolicy.org/security/sanction/afgnstan/2001/0525moni.htm.

Lee, G. D., 2004, *Global Drug Enforcement: Practical Investigative Techniques*, CRC Press, Boca Raton, FL.

Lee, R. W., 2002b, *Terrorist Financing: The U.S. and International Response*, Congressional Research Service, Federal Research Division, Library of Congress, December

6, viewed October 22, 2007, http://www.law.umaryland.edu/marshall/crsreports/crsdocuments/RL31658_12062002.pdf

Lee, R. W., 2003, president of Global Advisory Services, Alexandria, Virginia, *Narco-Terrorism: International Drug Trafficking and Terrorism—A Dangerous Mix* statement and testimony before the United States Senate, Committee on the Judiciary, Washington, DC, May 20, 2003, pp. 30–32 viewed transcript April 2, 2007, http://www.au.af.mil/au/awc/awcgate/congress/narco_terror_20may03.pdf.

Levin, C. (D-Michigan), 2003, *Terrorism Financing: Origination, Organization, and Prevention*, statement before the United States Senate, Committee on Governmental Affairs, Washington, DC, July 31, pp. 19–22, viewed March 15, 2007, http://hsgac.senate.gov/public/_files/sprt108245terror_finance.pdf.

Levitt, M. A., 2002, senior fellow, Washington Institute for Near East Policy, *The Role of Charities and NGOs in the Financing of Terrorist Activities*, statement before the U.S. Senate, Committee on Banking, Housing, and Urban Affairs, Subcommittee on International Trade and Finance, Washington, DC, August 1, viewed December 20, 2007, http://banking.senate.gov/02_08hrg/080102/levitt.htm.

Levitt, M. A., 2005, Senior Fellow and Director of Terrorism Studies, Washington Institute for Near East Policy, *Hezbollah: Financing Terror through Criminal Enterprise*, testimony before the United States Senate, Committee on Homeland Security and Governmental Affairs, Washington, DC, May 25, p. 11, viewed December 20, 2007, http://hsgac.senate.gov/_files/LevittTestimony.pdf.

Levy, C. J., 2009, "Central Asia Sounds Alarm Over Islamic Radicalism." *New York Times*, August 18, p. A4.

Lewis, B., 1998, "License To Kill: Usama bin Ladin's Declaration of Jihad." *Foreign Affairs*, Volume 77, Number 6, pp. 14–19.

Lichbach, M. I., 2007, "Theory and Evidence." In *Theory and evidence in comparative politics and international relations*, eds., R. N. Lebow and M. I. Lichbach, Palgrave Macmillan, New York, NY, pp. 261–284.

Lifschultz, L., 1988, "Bush, Drugs and Pakistan: Inside the Kingdom of Heroin." *The Nation*, Volume 247, Issue 14, pp. 477–496.

Little, D., 1995, "Objectivity, Truth, and Method: A Philosopher's Perspective on the Social Sciences." *Anthropology Newsletter*, [Commentary], Colgate University, viewed May 13, 2008, http://www-personal.umd.umich.edu/~delittle/anthnew3.pdf.

Lormel, D. M., 2001, chief, Financial Crimes Section, FBI, *Cutting off the Financial Lifeblood of the Terrorists*, testimony before the U.S. House of Representatives, Committee on Financial Services, October 3, viewed March 10, 2007, http: //www.fbi.gov/congress/congress01/lormel100301.htm; see also http://www.investigativeproject.org/documents/testimony/236.pdf. Lormel, D. M., 2002, chief, Terrorist Financial Review Group, FBI, *The Identity Theft Penalty Enhancement Act*, testimony before the U.S. Senate, Judiciary Committee, Subcommittee on Technology, Terrorism and Government Information, Washington, D.C., July 9, viewed March 10, 2007, http://www.fbi.gov/congress/congress02/idtheft.htm.

Loyd, A., 2006, "Who are the Taleban? The question that is snaring Nato in tribal Wars." *Times* (London), October 21, p. 43.

Loyd, A., 2007, "Corruption, bribes and trafficking: a cancer that is engulfing Afghanistan." *Times* (London), November 24, viewed May 2, 2010, http://www.timesonline.co.uk/tol/news/world/asia/article2933472.ece.

Loyd, A., 2010, "Terror link alleged as Saudi millions flow into Afghanistan war zone." *Times* (London), May 31, viewed June 30, 2010, http://www.timesonline.co.uk/tol/news/world/afghanistan/article7140745.ece.

Lubin, N., 2001, "Drug Trafficking in Central Asia: A Matter of Survival for Some." *Eurasia Insight*, May 9, Part 1, viewed December 20, 2006, http://www.eurasianet.org/departments/insight/articles/eav050901.shtml.

Lubin, N., 2001, "International Drug Programs in Central Asia Clouded in Controversy." *Eurasia Insight*, May 10, Part 2, viewed, December 20, 2006, http://www.eurasianet.org/departments/insight/articles/eav051001.shtml.

Lubin, N., 2001, "Central Asia's War on Drug[s] Takes a High Human Toll." *Eurasia Insight*, May 14, Part 3, viewed December 20, 2006, http://www.eurasianet.org/departments/insight/articles/eav051401.shtml.

Ludlow, L., 2001, "Osama speaks: Inside the mind of a terrorist." *San Francisco Chronicle*, October 7, p. D1.

Lycos Retriever, 2008, Ahmed Shah Massoud: Northern Alliance, viewed July 15, 2008, http://www.lycos.com/info/ahmed-shah-massoud--northern-alliance.html.

Mabrey, D. J., 2003, *Fact or Fiction: The Nexus Between Terrorism and Organized Crime*, presented November 21, 2003, at the American Society of Criminology Meeting, Denver, CO.

MacDonald, D., 2005, "Blooming flowers and false profits: the dynamics of opium cultivation and production in Afghanistan under the Taliban." *International Journal of Drug Policy*, Volume 16, Issue 2, pp. 93–97.

MacDonald, K., and Tipton, C., 1993, "Using Documents." In *Researching Social Life*, ed., G. Nigel, Sage Publications, London, UK.

MacFarquhar, N., 2001, "Bin Laden and His Followers Adhere To an Austere, Stringent Form of Islam." *New York Times*, October 7, 1B.7.

Mack, J., 2001, Deputy Assistant Secretary of State for International Narcotics and Law Enforcement Affairs, U.S. Department of State, *The Western Hemisphere's Response to the September 11, 2001 Terrorist Attack on the United States*, statement before the U. S. House of Representatives, Committee on International Relations Subcommittee on the Western Hemisphere, October 10, pp. 33–39, viewed April 25, 2007, http://commdocs.house.gov/committees/intlrel/hfa75633.000/hfa75633_0f.htm.

Maclean, W., 2009, "alQaeda struggling with slump in donations." Reuters, June 12, viewed April 4, 2010, http://www.reuters.com/article/idUS TRE55B3D Z20090612.

Magnus, R., and Naby E., 2002, *Afghanistan: Mullah, Marx and Mujahid*, Westview Press, Cambridge, MA.

Maitra, R., 2005, "Follow the drugs: US shown the way." *Asia Times online*, October 27, viewed August 13, 2006, http://www.atimes.com/atimes/Central_Asia/GJ27Ag02.html.

Makarenko, T., 2000, "Terrorism and Drug Trafficking Threaten Stability in Central Asia." *Jane's Intelligence Review*, Volume 12, Number 11, pp. 28–31.

Makarenko, T., 2002a, "Bumper Afghan narcotics crop indicates resilience of networks." *Jane's Intelligence Review*, Volume 14, Issue 5, pp. 28–31.

Makarenko, T., 2002b "Central Asia's Opium Terrorists." PBS, *[wideangle] Briefing*, Educational Broadcasting Corporation August 22, viewed November 11, 2005, http://www.pbs.org/wnet/wideangle/printable/centralasia_briefing_print.html.

Makarenko, T., 2002c, "Compromised from the start: The Afghan Interim Administration and the drugs trade." Central-Asia Caucasus Institute Analyst, August 2, viewed November 11, 2005, http://www.e-ariana.com/ariana/eariana.nsf/allDocsArticles/D1D46F63A16253CF87256C09005F6218?OpenDocument.

Makarenko, T., 2002d, "Crime, Terror and the Central Asian Drug Trade." *Harvard Asia Quarterly*, Volume 6, Number 3, viewed November 11, 2005, http://www.cornellcaspian.com/publications/pdf/25_0207CA_Drugs.pdf; and http://www.asiaquarterly.com/content/view/121/40/.

Makarenko, T., 2004, "The Crime-Terror Continuum: Tracing the Interplay between Transnational Organized Crime and Terrorism." *Global Crime*, Volume 6, Number 1, pp. 129–145.

Makarenko, T., 2005, "Terrorism and Transnational Organized Crime: Tracing the Crime-Terror Nexus in Southeast Asia." In *Terrorism and Violence in Southeast Asia: Traditional Challenges to States and Regional Stability*, ed., P. J. Smith, M. E. Sharpe, Armonk, NY, pp. 169–187.

Makgabo, T., and Feyerick, D., 2001, "International Terrorism: How Can It Be Stopped?" CNN International *Q&A*, transcript # 020800cb.k18, February 8.

Maley, W., 2000, *The Foreign Policy of the Taliban*, Council on Foreign Relations Press New York, NY, viewed January 15, 2008, http://www.cfr.org/content/publications/attachments/ForeignPolicy_Taliban_Paper.pdf

Malik, S. K., 1979, *The Quranic Concept of War*, Wajidalis, Lahore, India.

Manayev, K., 2000, "Central Asia: Narcotic flood threatens to wash away Central Asian stability." *Times of Central Asia*, 29 December, viewed January 4, 2008, http://www.eurasia.org.ru/archive//2000/press_en/12_29_Narcoticflood_eng.htm.

Manayev, K., 2001, "Drug-Fuelled Crime in Central Asia." *Times of Central Asia*, January 4.

Manchester Evening News 2000, "Terror Crackdown." December 20, p. 6.

Mandel, R., 1999, *Deadly Transfers and the Global Playground: Transnational Security Threats in a Disorderly World*, Praeger, Westport, CT.

Manwaring, M. G., 1993, ed., *Gray Area Phenomenon: Confronting the New World Disorder*, Westview Press, Boulder, CO.

Maples, M. D., 2007a, U.S. Army Director, Defense Intelligence Agency, *Current and Projected National Security Threats to the United States*, statement for the record, Senate Select Committee on Intelligence, January 11, viewed August 10, 2008, http://www.dia.mil/publicaffairs/Testimonies/statement26.html.

Maples, M. D., 2007b, U.S. Army Director, Defense Intelligence Agency, *Current and Projected National Security Threats to the United States*, statement before the U.S. House of Representatives, Permanent Select Committee on Intelligence, Washington, DC, January 18, viewed August 10, 2008, http://www.dia.mil/publicaffairs/Testimonies/statement_027.pdf.

Marks, S., Meer, T., and Nilson, M., 2005, *Manhunting: a methodology for finding Persons of national interest*, MSc thesis, Naval Postgraduate School, Monterey, CA,

June 2005, viewed March 15, 2008, http://www.au.af.mil/au/awc/awcgate/nps/manhunting_marks_jun05.pdf.

Marquand, R., 2001, "The Tenets of Terror: A Special Report on the Ideology of Jihad and the Rise of Islamic Militancy." *Christian Science Monitor*, October 18, p. 1.

Marsden, P., 1998, *The Taliban: War, Religion and the New Order in Afghanistan*, Zed Books, London, UK.

Marshall, J., 1991, *Drug Wars: Corruption, Counterinsurgency and Covert Operations in the Third World*, Cohan & Cohen Publishers, Forestville, CA.

Marzban, O., 2006a, "Gulbuddin Hekmatyar: From Holy Warrior to Wanted Terrorist." *Terrorism Monitor*, Volume 4, Issue 18, pp. 7–9, viewed November 11, 2007, http://www.jamestown.org/terrorism/news/uploads/TM_004_018.pdf.

Marzban, O., 2006b, "Mullah Dadullah: The Military Mastermind of the Taliban Insurgency." *Terrorism Focus*, Volume 3, Issue 11, pp. 3–4, viewed June 15, 2007, http://www.jamestown.org/terrorism/news/uploads/tf_003_011.pdf.

Marzban, O., 2006c, "Taliban Shift Tactics in Afghanistan." *Terrorism Focus*, Volume 3, Issue 15, pp. 2–3, viewed July 28, 2008, http://www.jamestown.org/ terrorism/news/uploads/tf_003_015.pdf.

Maskaliunaite, A., 2002, "Defining Terrorism in the Political and Academic Discourse." *Baltic Defense Review* # 8, Volume 2, August 8, viewed December 15, 2005, http://www.bdcol.ee/fileadmin/docs/bdreview/bdr-2002-8-04.pdf.

Mazzetti, M., Perlez, J., Schmitt, E., and Lehren A. W., 2010, "Pakistan Aids Insurgency in Afghanistan, Reports Assert." *New York Times*, July 26, p. A1.

Mazzetti, M., and Schmitt, E., 2008, "C.I.A. Outlines Pakistan Links with Militants." *New York Times*, July 30, p. 1.

Mazzetti, M. and Smucker, P., 2002, "On the Ground." *U.S. News & World Report*, Volume 132, Number 6, pp. 12–17.

McCaffrey, B. R., 1999, Director, Office of National Drug Control Policy. *The Department of Defense's Role in U.S. Drug Control Policy*, testimony before the U.S. Senate Committee on Armed Services, Subcommittee on Emerging Threats and Capabilities, Washington, DC, April 27, pp. 1–40, viewed October 25, 2007, http://armed-services.senate.gov/statemnt/1999/990427bm.pdf.

McCarthy, D., 2003, Deputy Assistant Secretary, International Narcotics and Law Enforcement Affairs, Department Of State, statement before the United States Senate, Committee on the Judiciary, *Narco–Terrorism: International Drug Trafficking and Terrorism—A Dangerous Mix*, Washington, D.C., May 20, p. 13, viewed transcript April 2, 2007, http://www.au.af.mil/au/awc/awcgate/congress/narco_terror_20may03.pdf.

McChrystal, S., 2009, "Commander's Initial Assessment." (Unclassified) NATO International Security Assistance Force, Kabul, Afghanistan, August 30, viewed October 10, 2009, http://media.washingtonpost.com/wp-srv/politics/documents/Assessment_Redacted_092109.pdf

McCloud, K., and Osborne, M., 2001, "WMD terrorism and Usama bin Laden." Center for Nonproliferation Studies, Monterey Institute of International

Studies, March 7; updated November 20, 2001, viewed June 10, 2007, http://cns.miis.edu/pubs/reports/binladen.htm.

McCoy, A. W., n.d., *Opium History Up To 1858* AD, BLTC Research, viewed August 25, 2006, http://opioids.com/opium/history/index.html.

McCoy, A. W., 2003, *The Politics of Heroin—CIA Complicity in the Global Drug Trade*, Lawrence Hill Books, New York, NY.

McCraw, S. C., 2003, Assistant Director, Office of Intelligence, Federal Bureau of Investigation (FBI), *Narco-Terrorism: International Drug Trafficking and Terrorism—A Dangerous Mix*, statement before the United States Senate, Committee on the Judiciary, Washington, DC, May 20, pp. 10–12 and 103–106, viewed transcript April 2, 2007, http://www.au.af.mil/au/awc/awcgate/congress/narco_terror_20may03.pdf.

McDonald, M., 2004a, "As Heroin Flourishes, So Could Terror." *Philadelphia Inquirer*, May 10, p. A01.

McDonald, M., 2004b, "Heroin boom in Afghanistan overwhelms border nations." Knight Ridder (Washington Bureau), May 5.

McDonald, M., 2004c, "Tajikistan at the Crossroads of the Drug Trade." *Free Press*, May 4.

McGeary, J., 2001, "A Traitor's Tale." *TIME*, February 11, viewed June 12, 2007, http://www.time.com/time/magazine/article/0,9171,98939,00.html.

McGirk, T., 2003, "Drugs? What Drugs?' *TIME*, Volume 162, Issue 7, August 18, p. 18.

McGirk, T., 2004, "Terrorisms' Harvest." *TIME*, Volume 164, Issue 6, August 9, p. 41.

McGirk, T., and Ware, M., 2004, "Remember Afghanistan?' *TIME*, Volume 163, Issue 10, March 8, pp. 46–61.

McGregor, A., 2005, "Beyond the Myth: A Review of the Wolves of Islam." *Chechnya Weekly*, Jamestown Foundation, Volume 6, Issue 12, viewed, August 15, 2007, http://www.jamestown.org/publications_details.php?volume_id=409&issue_id=3273&article_id=2369469.

McMahon, R., 2000, "UN: Balkan instability feeds rise in crime." *Radio Free Europe / Radio Liberty*, June 23, viewed July 22, 2007, http://www.rferl.org/features/2000/06/f.ru.000623125252.asp.

Medler, J. D., 2005, "Afghan Heroin: Terrain, Tradition and Turmoil." *Orbis*, Volume 49, Issue 2, pp. 275–291.

Meier, A., 1997, "Afghanistan's Drug Trade." *Muslim Politics Report*, Number 11, January-February, p. 4.

Meo, N., and Crichton, T., 2004, "The Spoils of War: hate & heroin; Afghanistan: We were told war would stem the flood of heroin into the West. Instead it's worse than ever. Why? Eyewitness." *Sunday Herald* (Scotland) November 21, p. 18.

Merriam-Webster's Collegiate Dictionary, 10th ed. 2001.

Mickolus, E. F., 1980, *Transnational Terrorism: A Chronology of Events, 1968–1979*, Greenwood Press, Westport, CT.

Memorial Institute for the Prevention of Terrorism, 2005a, Terrorism Knowledge Base, incident analysis wizard, *Domestic and International Terrorist Incidents in Afghanistan 1968 through 2006*, viewed May 30–June 5, 2007, http://www.tkb.org/chwiz4.jsp.

Memorial Institute for the Prevention of Terrorism, 2005b, Terrorism Knowledge Base Web site, http://www.tkb.org/; http://www.tkb.org/Group Comparison

Report.jsp; http://www.tkb.org/Group.jsp?groupID=4405; http://www.tkb.org/Group.jsp?groupID=3956; and http://www.tkb.org/OtherTerr.jsp.

Memorial Institute for the Prevention of Terrorism, 2005c, Terrorism Knowledge Base, MIPT-RAND Incident Analysis Wizard, viewed May 30-June 5, 2007, http://www.tkb.org/chwiz1.jsp.

Memorial Institute for the Prevention of Terrorism, 2005d, Terrorism Knowledge Base, MIPT-RAND Terrorism Incident database (1998-Present), viewed May 30–June 5, 2007, http://www.tkb.org/RandSummary.jsp?page=method.

Memorial Institute for the Prevention of Terrorism, 2005e, Terrorism Knowledge Base, MIPT/RAND terrorist incident reports (incidents by groups), viewed May 30–June 5, 2007, http//www.tkb.org/incidentgroupmodule.jsp.

Metz, H. C., 1991, ed., Sudan: A Country Study, [Chapter 4, Government] Library of Congress, GPO, Washington, D.C., viewed February 12, 2008, http://countrystudies.us/sudan/.

Michaels, J., 2010, "U.S. General: Taliban Beaten in Helmand Province." *USA Today*, January 12, viewed March 31, 2010, http://www.usatoday.com/news/military/2010-01-11-Helmand-Taliban_N.htm.

Miller, J. L., 2003, "The Narco-Insurgent Nexus in Central Asia and Afghanistan." *In The National Interest*, Volume 2, Issue 18, May 7, viewed January 10, 2008, http://www.inthenationalinterest.com/Articles/Vol2Issue18/vol2issue18Miller.html.

Mintz, J., 1998, "Bin Laden's Finances Are a Moving Target; Penetrating Empire Could Take Years." *Washington Post*, August 28, p. A01.

Mir, A., n.d., "The Pakistanis Training in Al Qaeda Camps." *Cobrapost News Features*, viewed June 28, 2007, http://www.cobrapost.com/documents/Training AlQaeda.htm.

Mir, A., 2005, "The jihad lives on." *Asia Times online*, March 11, viewed August 20, 2007, http://www.atimes.com/atimes/South_Asia/GC11Df07.html.

Mishra, B., 2000, "Heroin is New Weapon of Militancy in J-K." *Times of India*, May 23.

Montero, D., 2006, "Corruption Eroding Afghan Security; Violence is spreading beyond the restive south, fueled in large part by poor governance, say analysts." *Christian Science Monitor*, April 28, p. 7.

Moran, N., 2007, "Defining Organized Crime: Economic, Legal and Social Factors." in *Organized Crime: From Trafficking to Terrorism*, eds., F. Shanty and P. Mishra, ABC-CLIO, Santa Barbara, CA, pp. 43–47.

Morarjee, R., 2006, "War on drugs strengthens Afghan mafia." *Financial Times* (London), November 27, viewed September 12, 2007, http://www.ft.com/cms/s/0/d4a8046a-7e3b-11db-84bb-0000779e2340.html.

Moreau, R., and Yousafzai, S., 2006, "A Harvest of Treachery." *Newsweek*, Volume 147, Issue 2, January 9, pp. 32–35.

Morgan, A., 2008, "The Looming Threat of Islamist Terror in Pakistan." *Family Security Matters*, January 9, viewed March 15, 2008, http://www.familysecuritymatters.org/terrorism.php?id=1386093#.

Motlagh, J., 2006, "Taliban part of 'global jihad'; Specialists says al Qaeda training suicide bombers to hit Afghanistan." *Washington Times*, September 30, p. A07.

MSN Encarta World English Dictionary [North American Edition], 2007, viewed April 20, 2008, http://encarta.msn.com/dictionary_/anecdote.html.

Muhlberger, S., 1999, *Consequences of the Iranian Revolution*, Nipissing University, viewed February 22, 2007, http://www.nipissingu.ca/department/history/muhlberger/2805/postiran.htm.

Murray, J., and Ward, R. H., 1996, eds., *Extremist Groups: An International Compilation of Terrorist Organizations, Violent Political Groups, and Issue-Oriented Militia Movements*, Office of International Criminal Justice, Chicago, IL.

Mutschke, R., 2000, Assistant Director Criminal Intelligence Directorate International Criminal Police Organization—Interpol General Secretariat, *The Threat Posed by the Convergence of Organized Crime, Drugs Trafficking and Terrorism*, statement before the U.S. House of Representatives, Committee on the Judiciary, Subcommittee on Crime, December 13, pp. 85–120, viewed transcript May 28, 2007, http://commdocs.house.gov/committees/judiciary/hju68324.000/hju68324_0.HTM#121.

Najm, S., 1999 "Usamah Bin-Ladin, the Destruction of the Base." interview with Usamah Bin-Ladin, conducted by Jamal Isma'il in an unspecified location in Afghanistan in December 1998; aired on *al Jazeera* on June 10, 1999, viewed transcript October 15, 2007, http://web.archive.org/web/20021113111503/http://www.terrorism.com/terrorism/BinLadinTranscript.shtml.

Napoleoni, L., 2003, *Modern Jihad: Tracing the Dollars Behind the Terror Networks*, Pluto Press, London, UK and Sterling, VA.

Napoleoni, L., and Carish, R., 2005, "Confronting Terrorism: The Club de Madrid Series on Democracy and Terrorism." *International Summit on Democracy, Terrorism and Security*, Volume 2, March 8–11, pp. 27–31, viewed November 6, 2007, http://media.clubmadrid.org/docs/CdM-Series-on-Terrorism-Vol-2.pdf.

Napoli, A. M., 1992, *Human Knowledge, Reliability and Fallibilism*, Sciences School and Ecclesiastical School of Philosophy; University of Navarra, viewed May 10, 2008, http://www.unav.es/cryf/english/conocimientofiablidadyfalibilismo.html.

Nasir, S. A., 2006, "Al Qaeda's Operational Corridor on the NWFP." *Terrorism Monitor*, Volume 4, Issue 6, pp. 5–7, viewed June 18, 2007 http://www.jamestown.org/terrorism/news/article.php?articleid=2369938.

National Commission on Terrorist Attacks upon the United States, 2004, *The 9/11 Commission Report*, July 22, 2004, viewed March 13, 2007, http://www.9-11commission.gov/report/911Report.pdf; see also http://www.9-11commission.gov/staff_statements/911_TerrFin_Ch2.pdf; and http://www.9-11commission.gov/report/911Report_Ch5.htm.

National Defense University, Institute for National Strategic Studies: staff bios, viewed December 12, 2008, http://www.ndu.edu/inss/Staff/Staff_Bios_2005/Jalali_Narrative_05.pdf.

National Public Radio, 2009, "Hard Choices in Afghanistan: What's Next?" November 5, viewed March 5, 2010, http://www.npr.org/templates/story/story.php?storyId=120059417

NATO/ISAF Web site http://www.jfcbs.nato.int/htm/operations/isaf.htm.

NATO Public Diplomacy Division, 2008, "Progress in Afghanistan: Bucharest Summit, April 2–4, 2008." Brussels, Belgium, p.20, viewed July 25, 2008, http://www.nato.int/ISAF/docu/epub/pdf/progress_afghanistan.pdf

Naylor, R. T., 2002, *Wages of Crime: Black Markets, Illegal Finance, and the Underworld Economy*, Cornell University Press, Ithaca, NY.

Negroponte, J. D., 2006, Director of National Intelligence, *Threats, Challenges, and Opportunities for the United States*, statement before the United States Senate Armed Services Committee, Annual Threat Assessment, Washington, DC, February 28, pp. 1–25, viewed July 1, 2007, http://armed-services.senate.gov/statemnt/2006/February/Negroponte%2002-28-06.pdf; see also, http://www.state.gov/s/inr/rls/62787.htm.

Neighbour, S., 2010, "Taliban's Heroin Inc." *The Australian*, May 21, p. 013.

New York Times, 2003, "Taliban Blamed for 4 Aid Workers' Deaths," September 11, p. A4.

Norchi, C., 1994, "Whose war is it now?' [Op-Ed] *New York Times*, March 21, p. A17.

Norell, M., 2007, "The Taliban and the Muttahida Majlis-e-Amal (MMA)." *The China and Eurasia Forum Quarterly*, Volume 5, Number 3, pp. 61–82.

Nyrop, R. F., and Seekins, D. M., 1986, eds., *Afghanistan: A Country Study*, Foreign Area Studies, American University, U.S. Government Printing Office, Washington, DC.

O'Connell, T. W., 2004, Assistant Secretary Of Defense for Special Operations and Low–Intensity Conflict, U.S. Department of Defense, *Afghanistan: Drugs and Terrorism and U.S. Security Policy*, statement before the Committee on International Relations U.S. House of Representatives, Washington, DC, February 12, pp. 22–25, viewed April 10, 2007, http://www.ahrn.net/library_upload/uploadfile/file2217.pdf.

O'Harrow, R., Jr., Hilzenrath, D. S., and DeYoung, K., 2001, "Bin Laden's Money Takes Hidden Paths To Agents of Terror: Records Hint at Complex Financial Web." *Washington Post*, September 21, p. A13.

O'Malley, P., and Hutchinson, S., 2006, *Actual and Potential Links between Terrorism and Criminality*, Canadian Centre for Intelligence and Security Studies (CSIS), Trends in Terrorism Series, Volume 2006–5, viewed November 10, 2007, http://www.carleton.ca/cciss/res_docs/itac/omalley_e.pdf.

O'Neill, B. E., 2005, *Insurgency and Terrorism: From Revolution to Apocalypse*, 2nd ed., Potomac Books, Dulles, VA.

Olcott, M. B., 2002, Senior Associate, Carnegie Endowment for International Peace, *Drugs, Terrorism and Regional Security*, testimony before the U.S. Senate Judiciary Committee, Subcommittee of Technology, Terrorism and Government Operations. Washington, DC, March 13, viewed April 10, 2007, http://www.carnegieendowment.org/publications/index.cfm?fa = view&id=936&prog=zru.

Olcott, M. B., 2003, Senior Associate, Carnegie Endowment for International Peace, *Central Asia: Terrorism, Religious Extremism, And Regional Stability*, statement before the U.S. House of Representatives, Committee on International Relations, Subcommittee on the Middle East and Central Asia, Washington, DC, October 29, viewed June 22, 2007, http://www.foreignaffairs.house.gov/archives/108/90361.pdf.

Olcott, M. B., and Udalova, N., 2000, *Drug Trafficking on the Great Silk Road: The Security Environment in Central Asia*, Carnegie Endowment for International Peace, Working Papers, No. 11, Russian and Eurasian Program.

Oppel, R., 2009, "Corruption Undercuts U.S. Hopes for Afghan Police." *New York Times*, April 9, p. 1.

Oscapella, E., 1998. *The Relationship between Illegal Drugs and Firearms*, Department of Justice Canada: Literature Review, viewed September 18, 2008, http://www.cfc-cafc.gc.ca/pol-leg/res-eval/publications/1998/pdfs/dg_en.pdf.

Osler, D., 2001, "Investigators closing in on bin Laden vessels." *Lloyd's List*, December 12, p. 1.

Otis, J., 2004, "Afghanistan: The Other War." *Houston Chronicle*, June 20, p. 1.

O'Toole, P., 2006, "Who are the militants in Afghanistan?" BBC News, August 18, viewed May 15, 2007, http://news.bbc.co.uk/2/hi/south_asia/4801303.stm.

Oziewicz, E., 2003, "Hashish Bust Links al Qaeda to Drug Trade." *Canadian Globe and Mail*, December 20, p. A21, viewed February 26, 2007, http://www.mapinc.org/drugnews/v03.n1961.a10.html.

Packer, G., 2006, "Knowing the Enemy." *New Yorker*, December 18, pp. 60–69, viewed August 15, 2008, http://www4.ncsu.edu/~twallace/ANT412%20New%20Yorker%20aticle%20on%20Human%20Terrain%20System.pdf.

Pajhwok News Agency, 2007, "More Forces in South to Tackle Poppy Problem." August 30.

Pakistan Newswire, "Afghanistan (Taliban involved in drug trade: US State Dept.)" Pakistan Press International, October 5, 2001.

Pakistan Planning and Development Ministry, viewed November 22, 2007, http://www.pakistan.gov.pk/ministries/planninganddevelopment-ministry/organization/sections/nlc.pdf.

Pant, H. V., 2006, "The Resurgence of the Taliban in Afghanistan." *The Power and Interest News Report*, September 25, viewed June 22, 2007, http://www.pinr.com/report.php?ac=view_report&report_id=559&language_id=1.

Pape, R. A., 2003, "The Strategic Logic of Suicide Terrorism." *American Political Science Review*, Volume 97, Number 3, pp. 1–19.

Parthasarathy, G., 2003, "Fundamentalism, Narcotics and ISI: Linkage is clear and menacing," *Tribune*, March 27, viewed August 12, 2007, http://meaindia.nic.in/opinion/2003/03/27o04.htm.

Paz, R., 2003, *The Endless Global Jihad: Are They Looking for the Post Bin-Laden Era?* Project for Research of Islamist Movements (PRISM), March 17, viewed January 7, 2008, http://www.terrorism-info.org.il/malam_multimedia/html/final/eng/g_j/rp_c_11_03.htm.

Pennington, M., 2005, "Afghan Minister Quits after 'Drug War Rift' with Karzai." *Scotsman*, September 28, viewed November 22, 2007, http://news.scotsman.com/viewarticle.aspx?articleid=2665047.

Perl, R. F., 2001, *Taliban and the Drug Trade*, Congressional Research Service, Federal Research Division, Library of Congress, October 5, viewed April 25, 2007, http://fpc.state.gov/documents/organization/6210.pd

Perlez, J., 2009, "Pakistan rebuffs U.S. demands on Taliban." *New York Times*, December 15, p. A1.

Peters, G., 2006a, "Opium Bumper Crop Seen to Benefit Taliban." ABC News, September 3, viewed December 18, 2007, http://abcnews.go.com/International/story?id=2390033&page=1.

Peters, G., 2006b, "Taliban drug trade: Echoes of Colombia." *Christian Science Monitor*, November 21, p.O4.

Peters, G., 2009, *Seeds of Terror: How Heroin is Bankrolling the Taliban and al Qaeda*, St. Martin's Press, New York, NY.

Peter, T. A., 2010, "Pakistani Taliban designated a terrorist group by US." *Christian Science Monitor*, September 2, viewed September 3, 2010, http://www.csmonitor.com/World/terrorism-security/2010/0902/Pakistani-Taliban-designated-a-terrorist-group-by-US.

Peuch, J. C., 2001, "Central Asia: Charges link Russian military to drug trade." *RFE/RL*, June 8, viewed September 14, 2008, http://www.rferl.org/content/Article/1096646.html.

Pistole, J., 2003, Acting Assistant Director for Counterterrorism, Federal Bureau of Investigation, *Terrorism Financing: Origination, Organization, and Prevention*, statement and testimony before the United States Senate, Committee on Governmental Affairs, July 31, pp. 4–7 and 13–33, viewed March 15, 2008, http://hsgac.senate.gov/_files/sprt108245terror_finance.pdf.

Poole, J. H., 2005, *Militant Tricks: Battlefield Ruses of the Islamic Insurgent*, Posterity Press, Emerald Isle, NC.

Pope, H., Pearl, D., and Trofimov, Y., 2001, "Line in the Sand: Saudi Role in Alliance Fuels Religious Tension in Oil Rich Kingdom—Crucial to American Strategy Against bin Laden, Royals are Caught in the Middle—Signs of Pent-Up Resentment,' *Wall Street Journal* (Europe), October 4, p. A1.

Porter, C., 2001, "Drug Trade Is Primary Income Source for Taliban, DEA Says." *Washington File*, October 3, viewed March 12, 2008, http://www.globalsecurity.org/military/library/news/2001/10/mil-011003-usia13a.htm.

Pound, E. T., Ragavan, C., Witken, G., and Dimmler, E. E., 2001. "Opium Den: In the Afghan badlands, add drugs to a devil's brew." *U.S. News & World Report*, Volume 131, Number 15, October 5, p. 20.

Pound, E. T., and Ragavan, C., and Robinson, L., 2001, "Tears of Allah' Another Weapon in Osama bin Laden's War Against the West." *U.S. News & World Report*, October 4, viewed May 15, 2007, http://www.usnews.com/usnews/news/terror/heroin.htm.

Powell, B., 2007, "The Strange Case of Haji Bashar Noorzai (Warlord or Drug-lord?)." *TIME*, February 19, viewed April 18, 2007, http://www.time.com/time/magazine/article/0,9171,1587252-6,00.html.

Prabha, K., 2001, "Narco-Terrorism and India's Security." *Strategic Analysis*, Volume 24, Number 10, viewed October 12, 2007, http://www.ciaonet.org/olj/sa/sa_jan01prk01.html.

Press Trust of India, 2001, "Pakistan using drug trafficking to finance Kashmiri militants." Nationwide International News, May 14.

Press Trust of India, 2003, "US brands Dawood as Global Terrorist." Nationwide International News, October 17.

Press TV, 2009, "Pakistan govt. admits Quetta Shura on country's soil." December 11, viewed April 7, 2010, http://www.presstv.com/detail.aspx?id=113493&sectionid=351020401

Raab, J., and Milward, H. B., 2003, "Dark Networks as Problems." *Journal of Public Administration Research and Theory*, Volume 13, Issue 4, pp. 413–439.

Rabasa, A., and Chalk, P., 2001, *Colombian Labyrinth: The Synergy of Drugs and Insurgency and its Implications for Regional Stability*, RAND Corporation, Santa Monica, CA.

Rabasa, A., Chalk, P., Cragin, K., Daly, S. A., Gregg, H. S., Karasik, T. W., O'Brien, K. A., and Rosenau, W., 2006a, *Beyond al Qaeda:* Part 1, RAND Corporation,

Santa Monica, CA, pp. 1–228, viewed June 15–16, 2007, http://www.rand.org/pubs/monographs/2006/RAND_MG429.pdf.

Rabasa, A., Chalk, P., Cragin, K., Daly, S. A., Gregg, H. S., Karasik, T. W., O'Brien, K. A. and Rosenau, W., 2006b, *Beyond al Qaeda:* Part 2, RAND Corporation, Santa Monica, CA, pp. 1–216, viewed June 15–16, 2007, http://www.rand.org/pubs/monographs/2006/RAND_MG430.pdf.

Radhakrishnan, R., 2003, "Drug Trafficking in Central Asia." *Institute of Peace and Conflict Studies*, Article Number 1215, November 28, viewed October 20, 2006, http://www.ipcs.org/printArticle.jsp?kValue=1215.

Raghavan, T., 2005, "The Narcotics Trade in Southwest Asia: Geography and Production." *Security Research Review*, Volume 1, Number 4, viewed July 6, 2007, http://www.bharat-rakshak.com/SRR/Volume14/raghavan.html

Rahman, T., 2004, "The Madrassa and the State of Pakistan: Religion, Poverty and the Potential for Violence in Pakistan." *HIMAL South Asian*, viewed February 11, 2007, http://www.himalmag.com/2004/february/essay.htm

Rahmani, W., 2006, "Combating the Ideology of Suicide Terrorism in Afghanistan." *Terrorism Monitor*, Volume 4, Issue 21, pp. 7–9, viewed April 6, 2008, http://www.jamestown.org/terrorism/news/article.php?articleid=2370192.

Rais, R. B., 1994, *War Without Winners: Afghanistan's Uncertain Transition After the Cold War*, Oxford University Press, Oxford, UK.

Ramachandran, S., 2006, "India awakens to al-Qaeda threat." *Asia Times online*, August 22, viewed September 10, 2007, http://www.atimes.com/atimes/South_Asia/HH22Df02.html.

Raman, B., 2002, "Smoking al Qaeda out of Karachi." *Asia Times online*, September 17, viewed February 15, 2008, http://www.atimes.com/atimes/South_Asia/DI17Df04.html.

Raman, B., 2003, "The fall and rise of the Taliban." *Asia Times online*, October 23, viewed June 22, 2007, http://www.atimes.com/atimes/Central_Asia/EJ23Ag02.html.

Raman, B., 2004, *Terrorism in Afghanistan and Central Asia*, South Asia Analysis Group, November 24, viewed April 5, 2010, http://www.southasiaanalysis.org/papers12/paper1172.html.

Randal, J. C., 1978, "Afghanistan's Promised War on Opium; New Rulers Said to be Deterred by Poppy Crop's Importance." Washington Post Foreign Service, *Washington Post*, November 2, p. A30.

Raphaeli, N., 2003, "Financing of Terrorism: Sources, Methods, and Channels." *Terrorism and Political Violence*, Volume 15, Number 4, pp. 59–82.

Rashid, A., 1995, "Nothing to Declare: The political void in Afghanistan has spawned a vast smugglers' market that is crippling Pakistan's economy and threatens those of other nations in the region." *Far Eastern Economic Review*, May 11.

Rashid, A., 1999a, "Les Talibans Au Coeur De La Destabilisation Regionale," *Le Monde Diplomatique* [English translation], pp. 4–5.

Rashid, A,. 1999b, "The Taliban: Exporting Extremism." *Foreign Affairs*, Volume 78, Number 6, pp. 22–35.

Rashid, A., 2000, "Asking for Holy War: For 10 years the region's leaders have ruled out democracy; The result: an increasingly militant underground Islamic opposition." *Far Eastern Economic Review*, November 9, viewed November 20,

2006, http://www.geocities.com/tula_hidalgo/islam/rashid_afghan_ pak .html.

Rashid, A., 2001a, "A Long, Hot Summer Ahead." *Far Eastern Economic Review*, April 19, viewed June 22, 2007, http://www.geocities.com/tula_hidalgo/islam/rashid_afghan_pak.html.

Rashid, A., 2001b, "First, the War: A new Bush policy aims at the Taliban, though the final target is still Osama bin Laden." *Far Eastern Economic Review*, August 2, viewed June 22, 2007, http://www.geocities.com/tula_hidalgo/islam/rashid_afghan_pak.html; see also, http://www.afghanistannews-center.com/news/2001/july/jul262001.html.

Rashid, A., 2001c, "Inside the Taliban." *Frontline*, Volume 18, Issue 22, October 27–November 9, viewed June 22, 2007, http://flonnet.com/fl1822/18220210.htm; http://www.geocities.com/tula_hidalgo/islam/rashid_afghan_pak.html; and http://www.afghanistannewscenter.com/news/2001/october/oct14u2001.html.

Rashid, A., 2001d, "Mountain Launchpad." *Far Eastern Economic Review*, April 19, viewed June 22, 2007, http://www.geocities.com/tula_hidalgo/islam/rashid_afghan_pak.html.

Rashid, A., 2001e, "Mysterious Mullah." *Far Eastern Economic Review*, October 4, viewed June 44, 2007, http://www.geocities.com/tula_hidalgo/islam/rashid_afghan_pak.html.

Rashid, A., 2001f, *Taliban: Militant Islam, Oil and Fundamentalism in Central Asia*, Yale University Press, New Haven, CT and London, UK.

Rashid, A., 2001g, "Al Qaeda Has Network Of Sleepers Across North America Hundreds Of Hidden Terrorists Loyal To Osama Bin Laden Are Simply Awaiting The Call To Strike Again." *Daily Telegraph* (London), September 15, p. 09; see also, http://www.afghanistannewscenter.com/news/2001/september/sep12j2001.html

Rashid, A., 2002 "They're Only Sleeping." *The New Yorker*, January 14, Volume 77, pp. 34–42.

Rashid, A., 2003, *Jihad: The Rise of Militant Islam in Central Asia*, Penguin Books, New York, NY.

Rashid, A., 2006a, "British General Pushes for Action on Taliban Sanctuaries." *Daily Telegraph*, (London), October 10, p. 14, viewed June 22, 2007, http://www.telegraph.co.uk/news/worldnews/1531074/british-general-pushes-for-action-on-taliban-sanctuaries.html.

Rashid, A., 2006b, "He's Welcome in Pakistan." *Washington Post*, February 26, p. B01.

Rashid, A., 2006c, "Nato's top brass accuse Pakistan over Taliban aid." *Daily Telegraph* (London), October 6, p. 16.

Rashid, A., 2009, *Descent into Chaos*, Penguin Books, New York, NY, and London, UK.

Redo, S., 2004, *Organized Crime and its Control in Central Asia*, Office of International Criminal Justice, OICJ, Huntsville, TX.

Reeves, S., 1999, *The New Jackals: Ramzi Youssef, Osama bin Laden and the Future of Terrorism*, Northeastern University Press, Boston, MA.

Reuter, P., and Petrie, C., 1999, eds., *Transnational Organized Crime: Summary of a Workshop*, National Research Council, Washington, DC.

Reuter, P., and Truman, E. M., 2005, "Money Laundering Controls and Terrorist Finance." *Financial Regulator*, Volume 10, Number 2, pp. 35–37.

Reuters, 1985, "Tribes Fight for Their Wrongs: Pakistan Rebels Act to Keep Drugs, Arms Trade." Published in the *Chicago Tribune*, May 3, p. 10.

Reuters, 2003, "UN: Afghan Opium Production Spreading Like Cancer." October 29, viewed February 22, 2007, http://www.yirmeyahureview.com/archive/afghanistan/collection_opium.htm.

Reuters, 2006, "Iran, Neighbors should share drug trade info—UN." November 10, viewed March 3, 2007, http://www.alertnet.org/the news/newsdesk/L10827722.htm.

Reynolds, P., 2007, "Afghanistan: Winning or Losing?' BBC News, February 14.

RFE/RL, 2007, "Afghanistan: Government Pledges End to Hostage Deals." April 16.

Richani, N., 1997, "The Political Economy of Violence: The War System in Colombia." *Journal of Interamerican Studies and World Affairs*, Volume 39, Issue 2, pp. 37–81.

Risen, J., 1998, "Russians Are Back in Afghanistan Aiding Rebels." *New York Times*, July 27, p. A1.

Risen, J., 2007, "An Afghan's Path from Ally of U.S. to Drug Suspect." *New York Times*, February 2, p. A1.

Risen, J., 2008. "Reports link Karzai's brother to Afghanistan heroin trade." *New York Times*, October 5, p. A1.

Risen J., and Miller J., 2001, "A Nation Challenged: The Spies; Pakistan intelligence had links to al Qaeda." *New York Times*, October 29, p. 1.

Robichaud, C., 2006, *Afghanistan Watch: Portraits of an Insurgency*, Century Foundation, August 29, viewed May 20, 2007, http://www.afghanistan-watch.org/2006/08/snapshot_of_an_.html.

Robinson, C. S., Tomisek, S. J., Kligge, K., 2009, *Perspectives from Fragile Crescent: A South Asia Crisis Simulation*, Institute for National Strategic Studies, February 24, pp. 3–4, viewed June 15, 2010, http://www.ndu.edu/inss/docUploaded/INSSproceedings2.pdf.

Robinson, J., 2004, "The Money Trail: How Petty Crime Funds Terror." *International Herald Tribune*, August 13, viewed November 22, 2007, http://www.iht.com/articles/2004/08/13/edrobin_ed3_.php.

Roggio, B., 2007, "Taliban dismisses senior Afghan commander [Updated]." *The Long War Journal*, December 29, viewed March 30, 2010, http://www.longwarjournal.org/archives/2007/12/taliban_dismisses_se.php.

Roggio, B., 2008a, "Former Taliban commander Mansoor Dadullah captured in Pakistan." *The Long War Journal*, February 11, viewed March 30, 2010 http://www.longwarjournal.org/archives/2008/02/former_taliban_comma.php

Roggio, B., 2008b, "Haqqani Network behind Kabul hotel attack." *The Long War Journal*, January 15, viewed April 1, 2010, http://www.longwarjournal.org/archives/2010/04/taliban_cooperation.php.

Roggio, B., 2010, "Taliban cooperation with al Qaeda 'is at the highest limits'—Siraj Haqqani." *The Long War Journal*, April 15, viewed June 1, 2010, http://www.longwarjournal.org/archives/2008/01/haqqani_network_behi.php.

Rohani, A. S., 2005, "Helmand farmers in limbo over poppy cultivation." *Pajhwok News Agency*, October 30.

Rosenau, W., 2007, *Subversion and Insurgency*, RAND Corporation, Santa Monica, CA.

Roston, A., 2002, "Central Asia's Heroin Problem." *The Nation*, Volume 274, Issue 11, March 25, pp. 23–26.

Roston, A., 2009, "How the US Funds the Taliban." *The Nation*, Volume 289, Issue 18, November 30, pp. 12–16.

Rotar, I., 2007, "Ferghana Valley: Return of the Jihad." *Eurasia Insight*, August 28, viewed June 2007, http://www.eurasianet.org/departments/insight/articles/eav082807.shtml.

Roth, J., Greenburg, D., and Wille, S., 2004, *Monograph on Terrorist Financing: Staff Report to the Commission*, National Commission on Terrorist Attacks upon the United States, Washington, DC, pp. 1–155, viewed March 30, 2007, http://www.9-11commission.gov/staff_statements/911_TerrFin_Monograph.pdf.

Rovella, D. E., and Weidlich, T., 2005, "U.S. Arrests Accused Afghan Drug Lord Tied to Taliban (Update3)." *Bloomberg.com*, April 25, viewed April 15, 2007, http://www.bloomberg.com/apps/news?pid=10000103&sid=akst8l2VlHEI&refer=us#.

Roy, L. S., 2004, "The Establishment Clause and the Concept of Inclusion." *Oregon Law Review*, Volume 83, Number 1, pp. 001–047.

Roy, O., 1990, *Islam and Resistance in Afghanistan*, 2nd ed., Cambridge University Press, Cambridge, MA.

Roy, O., 1995, *Afghanistan: From Holy War to Civil War*, Darwin Press, Princeton, NJ.

Rubin, B. R., 1995, *The Search for Peace in Afghanistan: From Buffer State to Failed State*, Yale University Press, New Haven, CT, and London, UK.

Rubin, B. R., 1998, *Situation in Afghanistan: Recent Events and Political Actors*, testimony before the United States Senate, Committee on Foreign Relations, October 8, viewed October 14, 2007, http://www.cfr.org/publication/3088/testimony_on_the_situation_in_afghanistan_before_the_united_states_senate_committee_on_foreign_relations.html?breadcrumb=%2Fbios%2F115%2Fdr_barnett_r_rubin; and http://www.ciaonet.org/conf/rub02.

Rubin, B. R., 2000, "The Political Economy of War and Peace in Afghanistan." *World Development*, Volume 28, Issue 10, pp. 1789–1803.

Rubin, B. R., 2002, *The Fragmentation of Afghanistan: State Formation and Collapse in the International System*, 2nd ed., Yale University Press, New Haven, CT, and London, UK.

Rubin, B. R., 2004a, *Road to Ruin: Afghanistan's Booming Opium Industry*, Center for American Progress, Center on International Cooperation, NY: New York University, October 7, viewed October 16, 2007, http://www.cic.nyu.edu/archive/pdf/RoadtoRuin.pdf.

Rubin, B. R., 2004b, "U.S. must confront warlords, deal with Taliban." Council on Foreign Relations, interview on July 14, viewed transcript October 16, 2007, http://www.cfr.org/publication/7191/rubin.html?breadcrumb=%2Fbios%2F115%2Fdr_barnett_r_rubin.

Rubin, B. R., 2006, "Afghanistan at Dangerous Tipping Point." *Council on Foreign Relations*, interview with consulting editor Bernard Gwertzman, October 6, viewed transcript October 1, 2007, http://www.cfr.org/publication/11620/rubin.html?breadcrumb=%2Fissue%2Fpublication_list%3Fid%3D135%26page%3D4.

Rubin, B. R., 2007, "Saving Afghanistan." *Foreign Affairs*, Volume 86, Issue 1, pp, 57–78.

Rubin, B. R., and Sherman J., 2008, *Counter-Narcotics to Stabilize Afghanistan: The False Promise of Crop Eradication*, Center on International Cooperation, July 15, 2008, viewed April 5, 2008, http://www.cic.nyu.edu/afghanistan/docs/counternarcoticsfinal.pdf.

Rubin, E., 2006, "In the Land of the Taliban." *New York Times Magazine*, October 22, pp. 86–97 and 172–174.

Rubin, M., 2002a, "When Pushtun Came To Shove: Who is really responsible for the Taliban?' *The Review*, Australia/Israel and Jewish Affairs Council, viewed June 12, 2007, http://www.aijac.org.au/review/2002/274/essay274.html.

Rubin, M., 2002b, "Who is Responsible for the Taliban?' *Middle East Review of International Affairs* (MERIA), Volume 6, Number 1, pp. 1–16, viewed January 17, 2007, http://meria.idc.ac.il/journal/2002/issue1/jv6n1a1.html.

Rupert, J., and Coll, S., 1990, "U.S. Declines to Probe Afghan Drug Trade; Rebels, Pakistani Officers Implicated." *Washington Post*, May 13, p. A01

Sageman, M., 2004, *Understanding Terror Networks*, University of Pennsylvania Press, Philadelphia, PA.

Saidazimova, G., 2006, "Central Asia: 'Is Islamic Movement of Uzbekistan Really Back?' *RFE/RL*, February 2, viewed November 17, 2007, http://www.freerepublic.com/focus/f-news/1570685/posts.

Sanger, D. E., 2010, "Overseas, an Enemy That May Mutate and Grow." *New York Times*, May 7, p. WK1.

Sarantakos, S., 1993, *Social Research*, MacMillan Education Australia PTY LTD., South Melbourne, Australia.

Savage, D. G., 2009, "Saudi Arabia-based charities still funding terrorists, GAO says." Los Angeles Times, September 30, viewed April 6, 2010, http://articles.latimes.com/2009/sep/30/nation/na-terror-funding30.

Scarborough, R., 2004a, "Heroin Traffic Finances bin Laden." *Washington Times*, December 6, p. A01.

Scarborough, R., 2004b, "Osama bin Laden a 'narco-terrorists'; Legislator cites heroin trade link." *Washington Times*, January 22, p. A07.

Scarborough, R., 2004c, "Terrorists said to tap into illicit-drug trade." *The Washington Times*, September 13, p. A11.

Schetter, C., 2004, *The "Bazaar Economy" of Afghanistan: A Comprehensive Approach*, Sudasien-Informationen, No. 3, pp. 1–18, viewed October 22, 2006, http://archiv.ub.uni-heidelberg.de/savifadok/volltexte/2007/68/pdf/nr3_bazaar.pdf.

Scheuer, M., 2006a, "Central Asia in Al-Qaeda's Vision of the Anti-American Jihad, 1979–2006." *China and Eurasia Forum Quarterly*, Volume 4, Number 1, pp. 5–10.

Scheuer, M., 2006b, *Through Our Enemies Eyes: Osama bin Laden, Radical Islam, and the Future of America*, Potomac Books, Washington, DC.

Schmid, A. P., 1996, "The Links between Transnational Organized Crime and Terrorist Crimes." *Transnational Organized Crime*, Volume 2, Number 4, pp. 40–82.

Schmid, A. P., 2001, *The Nexus between Terrorism, Poverty, Illicit Drugs and Organized Crime*, presented at Bishkek, Kyrgyz Republic, December 2001, p. 126, viewed November 12, 2008, http://www.osce.org/documents//2001/12/4130_en.pdf.

Schmid, A. P., 2003, "Links between Terrorist and Organized Crime Networks: Emerging Patterns and Trends." *Seminar: Terrorism in Southern Africa*, paper prepared for the Institute for Security Studies, September 18–19.

Schmid, A. P., 2004, "Links between Terrorism and Other Forms of Crime: The Case of Narcoterrorism." *Turkish Policy Quarterly*, Volume 3, Number 2, pp. 43–56.

Schmid, A. P., and Jongman, A. J., 1988, *Political Terrorism: A New Guide to Actors, Concepts, Data Bases, Theories and Literature*, revised, expanded and updated edition, Transaction Books, Amsterdam, Oxford, UK and New York, NY.

Schmitt, E., 2009, "Many Sources Feed Taliban's War Chest." *New York Times*, October 19, p. A1.

Schmitt, E., and Mazzetti, M., 2009, "Taliban Widen Afghan Attacks From Base in Pakistan." *New York Times*, September 24, viewed April 1, 2010, http://www.nytimes.com/2009/09/24/world/asia/24military.html?_r=1&hp.

Schneider, M. L., 2004, *Afghanistan—Continuing Challenges*, testimony before the U.S. Senate Foreign Relations Committee, Washington, D.C., May 12, viewed May 18, 2007, http://www.crisisgroup.org/home/index.cfm?id=2751&l=1.

Schultz, F., 2004, "Breaking the Cycle: Empirical Research and Postgraduate Studies on Terrorism." In *Research on Terrorism: Trends, Achievements and Failures*, ed., A. Silke, Frank Cass, Portland, Oregon and London, UK, pp. 161–185.

Schwartz, S., 2006, "The Origins of British Jihad." *Weekly Standard*, August 31, viewed May 25, 2007, http://www.weeklystandard.com/Content/Public/Articles/000/000/012/605jegwd.asp.

Schweich, T., 2008, "Is Afghanistan a Narco-State?' *New York Times*, July 27, p. MM45.

Sciutto, J., and Perez, C., 2010, "DEA Cracks Down on Taliban Heroin Trade." May 2, viewed May 30, 2010, http://abcnews.go.com/WN/dea-cracks-taliban-heroin-trade/story?id=10535302.

Senlis Council, 2006a, *Afghanistan Five Years Later: The Return of the Taliban; Conclusions and Recommendations*, viewed November 15, 2007, http://www.senliscouncil.net/modules/publications/Afghanistan_Five_Years_Later/modules/publications/Afghanistan_Five_Years_Later/con_rec.

Senlis Council, 2006b, *Helmand at War: The Changing Nature of Insurgency in Southern Afghanistan and its Effects on the Future of the Country*, viewed November 15, 2007, http://www.senliscouncil.net/documents/Helmand_Report_June_2006.

Senlis Council, 2006c, *The Taliban's Successful Hearts and Minds Propaganda Damning the West*, viewed November 15, 2007, http://drug-policy.org/modules/publications/Hearts_and_Minds_Campaign/The_Report/documents/HM_c6

Seper. J, 2006, "DEA says Afghanistan's heroin begets violence." *Washington Times*, June 29, p. A03.

Sevunts, L., 1999, "Who's calling the shots?: Chechen conflict finds Islamic roots in Afghanistan and Pakistan." *Gazette* (Montreal, Quebec), October 26, p. B1.

Shafiq, M., Shah, Z., Saleem, A., Siddiqi, M. T., Shaikh, K. S., Salahuddin, F. F., Siwani, R., and Naqvi, H., 2006, "Perceptions of Pakistani medical students about drugs and alcohol: a questionnaire-based survey." *Substance Abuse Treatment, Prevention, and Policy*, Volume 1, Article 31, October 25, pp. 93–97, viewed November 15, 2007, http://www.substanceabusepolicy.com/content/pdf/1747-597X-1-31.pdf.

Shahzad, S. S., 2001, "Osama bin Laden: The thorn in Pakistan's flesh." *Asia Times online*, August 22, viewed June 12, 2007, http://www.atimes.com/ind-pak/CH22Df02.html.

Shalizi, H., 2008, "Suicide attack on Afghan luxury hotel kills seven." Reuters, January 15, viewed March 17, 2008, http://in.reuters.com/article/worldNews/idINIndia-31392920080114.

Shanker, T., 2003, "Navy Seizes Hashish; Sees Ties to al Qaeda." *New York Times*, December 20, p. A3.

Shanker, T., and Schmitt, E., 2010, "U.S. Intelligence Puts New Focus on Afghan Graft." June 12, p. A1.

Shannon, E., 2002, "The New War on Afghan Heroin." *TIME*, Volume 160, Number 22, November 25, p. 23.

Shanty, F., 2003, "Directory of Terrorist Groups and Organizations." In *Encyclopedia of World Terrorism*, eds., F. Shanty, R. Picquet and J. Lalla, M. E. Sharpe, Armonk, NY, pp. 599–608.

Shanty, F., 2007a, "Has al Qaeda Acquired Nuclear Weapons? The State of Existing Knowledge." In *Organized Crime: From Trafficking to Terrorism*, eds., F. Shanty and P. Mishra, ABC-CLIO, Santa Barbara, CA, pp. 350–357.

Shanty, F., 2007b, "The Taliban, al Qaeda, the Global Drug Trade, and Afghanistan as a Dominant Opium Source," *Professional Issues in Criminal Justice: A Professional Journal*, Volume 2, Number 1, January, pp. 81–90.

Shanty, F., 2009a, "Cartel Alliances: International Drug Trade." in *Mafia: The Necessary Reference to Organized Crime*, eds., C. Edwards, H. Jackson, and C. Jacobson, Millennium House PTY LTD, NSW, 2101, Australia, pp. 252–257.

Shanty, F., 2009b, "Drug Cartels: South America," in *Mafia: The Necessary Reference to Organized Crime*, eds., C. Edwards, H. Jackson, and C. Jacobson, Millennium House PTY LTD, NSW, 2101, Australia, pp. 180–189.

Shanty, F., 2009c, "Drug Cartels: The Business of Illegal Drug Trafficking." in *Mafia: The Necessary Reference to Organized Crime*, eds., C. Edwards, H. Jackson, and C. Jacobson, Millennium House PTY LTD, NSW, 2101, Australia, pp. 92–101.

Shanty, F., and Mishra, P., 2007, eds., *Organized Crime: From Trafficking to Terrorism*, Volume 1 and 2, ABC-CLIO, Santa Barbara, CA.

Shanty, F. and Picquet R., 2000, *International Terrorism: An Annual "Event Data" Report, 1998*, DIANE Publishing, Collingdale, PA.

Shanty, F., and Picquet R., 2004, *International Terrorism: An Annual "Event Data" Report, 1999*, DIANE Publishing, Collingdale, PA.

Shanty, F., Picquet, R., and Lalla, J., 2003, eds., *Encyclopedia of World Terrorism, 1996–2002*, M. E. Sharpe, Inc., Armonk, NY:

Shaw, M., 2006, "Drug Trafficking and the Development of Organized Crime in Post-Taliban Afghanistan." in *Afghanistan's Drug Industry: Structure, Functioning, Dynamics, and Implications for Counter-Narcotics Policy*, eds., D. Buddenberg and W. Byrd, United Nations Publications, New York, NY, pp. 189–214, viewed July 15, 2007, http://www.unodc.org/pdf/Afgh_drugindustry_Nov06.pdf.

Sheehan, M., 2000, Coordinator for Counterterrorism, U.S. Department of State, *Threat Posed by the Convergence of Organized Crime, Drug Trafficking*, statement and testimony before the U.S. House of Representatives Judiciary Committee, Subcommittee on Crime, Washington, DC, December 13, pp. 33–45 and 45–58, viewed April 12, 2008, http://commdocs.house.gov/committees/

judiciary/hju68324.000/hju68324_0f.htm; see also http://www.milnet.com/state/sheehan-121300.htm.

Shelley, L., n.d., "Identifying, Counting and Characterizing Transnational Criminal Organizations." Conference paper.

Shelley, L., 1995, "Transnational organized crime: An imminent threat to the nation-state?" *Journal for International Affairs*, Volume 48, Number 2, pp. 463–489.

Shelley, L., 1999, "Transnational Organized Crime: The New Authoritarianism." In *The Illicit Global Economy and State Power*, eds., H. R. Freeman and P. Andreas, Rowman & Littlefield Publishers, Inc., New York, NY, pp. 25–51.

Shelley, L. I., and Picarelli J. T., 2002, "Methods not Motives: Implications of the Convergence of International Organized Crime and Terrorism." *Police Practice and Research*, Volume 3, Number 4, pp. 305–318.

Shelley, L. I., and Picarelli J. T., Irby, A., Hart, D. M., Craig-Hart P. A., Williams, P., Simon, S., Abdullaev, N., Stanislawski, B., and Covill, L., 2005, *Methods not Motives: Exploring the Links between Transnational Organized Crime & International Terrorism*, National Institute of Justice, Office of Justice Programs, U.S. Department of Justice, Washington, DC, June 23.

Sidikov, A., 2008, "Pakistan Blames IMU Militants For Afghan Border Unrest." RFE/RL, July 2, viewed June 1, 2010, http://www.rferl.org/content/Pakistan_IMU_Militants_Afghan_Border_Unrest/1181286.html.

Silke, A., 2004, ed., *Research on Terrorism: Trends, Achievements and Failures*, Frank Cass, Portland, Oregon and London, UK.

Simpson, G.R., 2004, "Terror-Fund Countermeasures Ripped." *Wall Street Journal*, August 23, p. B2.

SITE Institute, 2004, Background on Terrorist Groups: Harakat ul Mujahidin (HUM), viewed June 15, 2007, http://www.siteinstitute.org/bin/display_groupbackground.cgi?Category=Groups&ID=12.

Smith, G., 2008, "Karzai's brother angrily denies drug connections; Provincial chairman summons journalists to his home to denounce allegations in U.S. paper from 'politically motivated' sources." *Globe and Mail* (Canada), October 7, p. A11.

Smith, G., 2009, "Corrupt politicians are safeguarding traffickers who then help the Taliban, Globe Investigation finds." *Toronto Globe and Mail*, March 21, viewed April 15, 2010, http://www.afghanistannewscenter.com/news/2009/march/mar212009.html#10.

Smith, P. J., 2002, "Transnational Terrorism and the al Qaeda Model: Confronting New Realities." *Parameters*, Volume 32, Issue 2, pp. 33–46.

Smith, S., 2004, "Singing Our World into Existence: International Relations Theory and September 11." *International Studies Quarterly*, Volume 48, Number 3, pp. 499–515.

Sommerville, Q., 2010, "Afghan corruption has doubled since 2007, survey says." BBC News, July 8, viewed July 12, 2010, http://www.bbc.co.uk/news/10549258.

Souder, M. (R. Indiana), Web Site, http://souder.house.gov/index.cfm? Fuse Action=AboutMarkSouder.Biography.

Souder, M. (R-Indiana), 2001, *Drug Trade and the Terror Network*, statement before the U.S. House of Representatives, Subcommittee on Criminal Justice, Drug Policy and Human Resources of the Committee on Government Reform, Washington, D.C., October 3, pp. 3–5, viewed March 15, 2007, http://

frwebgate.access.gpo.gov/cgi-bin/getdoc.cgi?dbname=107_house_hearings&docid=f:81496.pdf.

Souder, M. (R-Indiana), 2004, *Heroin Growth in Afghanistan*, statement before the U.S. House of Representatives, Congressional Record, Washington, DC, March 2, pp. H729–H730, viewed March 15, 2007, http://bulk.resource.org/gpo.gov/record/2004/2004_H00729.pdf.

Souder, M. (R-Indiana), 2006, *Narcotics Problem in Afghanistan*, statement before the House of Representatives as it appeared in the Congressional Record, September 13, pp. H6511–H6513, viewed March 15, 2007, http://frwebgate.access.gpo.gov/cgi-bin/getpage.cgi?position=all&page=H6511&dbname=2006_record; http://thomas.loc.gov/cgi-bin/query/D?r108:27:./temp/~r108h12SEI.

South Asia Terrorism Portal (SATP), viewed November 22, 2007, http://www.satp.org/.

Stares, P. B., 1996, *The Global Habit: The Drug Problem In A Borderless World*, Brookings Institution, Washington, DC.

Starr, B., and Courson, P., 2003, "U.S. links al Qaeda to Persian Gulf drug boat." CNN, December 19, viewed March 12, 2007, http://www.cnn.com/2003/WORLD/meast/12/19/alqaeda.drugbust/index.html.

Stepanova, E., 2002, "Illicit Drug Trafficking in Afghanistan and Central Asia in the Context of the Anti-Terrorism Campaign." *Yadernyy Kontrol*, trans. Foreign Broadcast Information Service, September 18, pp. 36–48.

Stepanova, E., 2004, "Illicit Drug Trafficking and Islamic Terrorism as Threats to Russian Security: The Limits of the Linkage." *Institute for World Economy and International Relations*, PONARS Policy Memo, Number 393, viewed December 15, 2007, http://www.csis.org/media/csis/pubs/pm_0393.pdf.

Stern, J., 2000, "Pakistan's Jihad Culture." *Foreign Affairs*, Volume 79, Number 6, pp. 115–126.

Stern, J., 2003, "The Protean Enemy." *Foreign Affairs*, Volume 82, Number 4, pp. 27–40.

Sumii, R., Asano, E., Sakurai E., and Sakurai N., 2005, "Investigation: Iranian Crimes; (3) Deepening Suspicion of Drug Money as 'Terrorist Funds,'" *Sankei Shimbun*, October 27.

Suri, K., 2000, "Money Keeps J & K Insurgency Going." *Statesman* (India), June 10.

Suri, S., 2006, "Afghanistan: 'Taliban Taking Over." *Inter Press Service News Agency*, September 5, viewed April 2, 2008, http://ipsnews.net/news.asp?idnews=34595.

Susnjara, B., 2005, "Heroin fight taking Kirk to Afghanistan." *Chicago Daily Herald* (Cook Edition), January 8, p. 4.

Suyono, S. J., and Zuhaid, E. Q., 2001, "After the Taliban, Old Dangers Resurface: The Rise of Warlords." *Tempo* (independent), Jakarta, Indonesia, December 2.

Swanstrom, N., n.d., *Drug Trade a Threat to Security: the Cases of Central Asia and the Caucasus*, Silk Road Studies Program, Uppsala University (draft version), viewed November 25, 2006, http://www.silkroadstudies.org/presentation.pdf.

Swanstrom, N., 2003, "Central Asia as a transit region for drugs." *Asia Times online*, August 28.

Swanstrom, N., 2007, "The Narcotics Trade: A Threat to Security? National and Transnational Implications." *Global Crime*, Volume 8, Number 1, pp. 1–25.

Synovitz, R., 2005, "Afghanistan: Alleged Taliban-Linked Drug Lord Extradited To United States." *Radio Free Europe/Radio Liberty*, October 25, viewed March 15, 2008, http://www.rferl.org/featuresarticle/2005/10/4D91B714-1D11-4458-9867-E50EC5C89945.html.

Tandy, K. P., 2004a, Administrator, U.S. Drug Enforcement Administration, *Afghanistan: Drugs and Terrorism and U.S. Security Policy*, statement before the Committee on International Relations U.S. House of Representatives, Washington, DC, February 12, pp. 17–21, viewed April 10, 2007, http://www.ahrn.net/library_upload/uploadfile/file2217.pdf.

Tandy, K. P., 2004b, Administrator, U.S. Drug Enforcement Administration, *Afghanistan: Law Enforcement Interdiction Efforts in Transshipment Countries to Stem the Flow of Heroin*, statement before the U.S. House of Representatives, Committee on Government Reform, Subcommittee on Criminal Justice, Drug Policy and Human Resources, February 26, viewed April 10, 2007, http://www.dea.gov/pubs/cngrtest/ct022604.htm.

Tanner, S., 2002, *Afghanistan: A Military History from Alexander the Great to the Fall of the Taliban*, Da Capo Press, Cambridge, MA.

Tarzi, A., 2005a, "Afghanistan: Is Reconciliation with the Neo-Taliban Working?' *Radio Free Europe/Radio Liberty*, June 2, viewed March 10, 2008, http://www.rferl.org/featuresarticle/2005/06/514ec97a-7727-4327-91db99894c9e0505.html.

Tarzi, A., 2005b, "Afghanistan: Who Exactly is the Enemy?" *Radio Free Europe/Radio Liberty*, November 23, viewed March 10, 2008, http://www.rferl.org/featuresarticle/2005/11/28bc5611-dcc7-4059-bb24-8f17547aa960.html.

Taylor, F. X., 2002, Ambassador–At–Large for Counterterrorism, Department Of State, *Narco–Terror: The Worldwide Connection between Drugs and Terrorism*, statement before the United States Senate, Subcommittee on Technology, Terrorism, and Government Information of the Committee on The Judiciary, Washington, DC, March 13, pp. 23, 25, viewed March 15, 2007, http://www.au.af.mil/au/awc/awcgate/congress/narco_terror_13mar02.pdf.

Taylor, G., 2004, "Heroin money fuels terrorists; Three groups linked to Afghanistan trafficking." *Washington Times*, February 13, p. A03.

Taylor, L., 2006, *The Nexus of Terrorism and Drug Trafficking in the Golden Crescent: Afghanistan*, U.S. Army War College, Strategy Research Project, Carlisle Barracks, PA, March 15, viewed July 25, 2007, http://www.strategicstudiesinstitute.army.mil/pdffiles/ksil514.pdf.

Tenet, G. J., 2000, *The Worldwide Threat in 2000: Global Realities of Our National Security*, statement before the U.S. Senate Select Committee on Intelligence, Washington, DC, February 2, viewed August 2, 2007, http://www.loyola.edu/dept/politics/intel/SSCI-Tenet-2Feb2000.html.

Thomas, E., and Thomas L., 2004, *U.S. Southern Command (SouthCom) Struggles to Justify its Role in the War on Terror*, Council on Hemispheric Affairs, Washington, DC, September 2, viewed May 6, 2007, http://www.coha.org/2004/09/us-southern-command-southcom-struggles-to-justify-its-role-in-the-war-on-terror/.

Thornton, M., 1982, "Hosts Could Not Insure Attorney General's Safety." *Washington Post*, November 26, p. A3.

Tohid, O., 2003, "Bumper year for Afghan poppies; Money from the opium trade may diminish US influence over the warlords, and aid Taliban." *Christian Science Monitor*, July 24, p. O6.

Townsend, J., 2005, "China and Afghan Opiates: Assessing the Risk." *Central Asia-Caucasus Institute*, Silk Road Studies Program, Johns Hopkins University-SAIS, viewed November 20, 2006, http://www.silkroadstudies.org/Town send.htm.

Toosi, N., 2008, "UN: Smuggled chemicals let Afghans process opium." Associated Press, July 28.

Townsend, J., 2006, "The Logistics of Opiate Trafficking in Tajikistan, Kyrgyzstan and Kazakhstan." *China and Eurasia Forum Quarterly*, Volume 4, Number 1, pp. 69–91, viewed February 2, 2007, http://www.silkroadstudies.org/new/docs/CEF/Quarterly/February_2006/Jacob_Townsend.pdf.

Tran, T., 2006, "Taliban Following Lead of Militant Iraqis." Associated Press */Fox News*, June 30, viewed August 15, 2008, http://origin.foxnews.com/wires/2006Jun30/0,4670,AfghanMimickingIraqLH1,00.html.

Transnational Institute, 2005, "Drug Policy Briefing." Number 10, January 2005, viewed July 27, 2007, http://www.tni.org/policybriefings/brief10.pdf.

Trujillo, S..G., 1992, "Peru's Maoist Drug Dealers." *New York Times*, April 8, p. A25.

Tumelty, P., 2006, "The Rise and Fall of Foreign Fighters in Chechnya." *Terrorism Monitor*, Volume 4, Issue 2, pp. 8–10, viewed September 15, 2007, http://www.jamestown.org/terrorism/news/article.php?articleid=2369881.

Tynan, D., 2009, "Central Asia: The Islamic Movement of Uzbekistan Undergoing Dangerous Transformation." October 19, viewed June 1, 2010, http://www.eurasianet.org/departments/insightb/articles/eav102009b.shtml.

United Nations, 2002, "Report of the International Narcotics Control Board for 2001." International Narcotics Control Board, Section III: Asia; Items 443 and 446, p. 67, United Nations, New York, NY, viewed June 25, 2006, http://www.incb.org/pdf/e/ar/2001/incb_report_2001_3_asia.pdf.

United Nations, 2005, "Report of the International Narcotics Control Board for 2005." International Narcotics Control Board, United Nations, New York, NY, viewed February 2, 2007, http://www.incb.org/pdf/e/ar/2005/incb_report_2005_full.pdf.

United Nations, 2007, *List of Precursors and Chemicals Frequently Used in the Illicit Manufacture of Narcotic Drugs and Psychotropic Substances Under International Control*, International Narcotics Control Board, United Nations, Vienna, Austria, viewed September 5, 2008, http://www.incb.org/pdf/e/list/red.pdf.

United Nations Assistance Mission to Afghanistan, 2007, "Suicide Attacks in Afghanistan (2001–2007)." September 1, viewed January 15, 2008, http://www.unama-afg.org/docs/_UN-Docs/UNAMA%20-%20SUICIDE%20ATTACKS%20STUDY%20-%20SEPT%209th%202007.pdf.

United Nations Center for International Crime Prevention, n.d., *Assessing Transnational Organized Crime Groups: Dangerousness and Trends*, Center for International Crime Prevention, Office for Drug Control and Crime Prevention, United Nations, Vienna, Austria.

United Nations Convention Against Illicit Traffic in Narcotics Drugs and Psychotropic Substances, 1988, United Nations, New York, NY, viewed February 2, 2007, http://www.unodc.org/pdf/convention_1988_en.pdf.

United Nations Convention Against Transnational Organized Crime, 2000, United Nations, New York, NY, viewed June 20, 2006, http://www.uncjin.org/Documents/Conventions/dcatoc/final_documents_2/convention_eng.pdf.

United Nations Drug Control Program, 2001, *Afghanistan Annual Opium Poppy Survey 2001*, UNDCP, Islamabad, Pakistan, viewed December 15, 2006, http://www.unodc.org/pdf/afg/report_2001-10-16_1.pdf.

United Nations General Assembly Report, 2006, "The Situation in Afghanistan and its Implications for Peace and Security." (A/61/326–S/2006/727), September 11, viewed January 15, 2008, http://www.reliefweb.int/library/documents/2006/unga-afg-11sep.pdf.

United Nations Office for Drug Control and Crime Prevention, 2000, *World Drug Report 2000*, Oxford University Press, Oxford, UK, viewed June 22, 2006, http://www.unodc.org/pdf/world_drug_report_2000/report _2001-01-22_1.pdf.

United Nations Office for Drug Control and Crime Prevention, 2001, *Global Illicit Drug Trends 2001*, United Nations, New York, NY, viewed June 5, 2006, http://www.unodc.org/unodc/en/data-and-analysis/global_illicit_drug_drug_trends.html.

United Nations Office for Drug Control and Crime Prevention, 2002a, *Illicit Drugs Situation in the Regions Neighbouring Afghanistan and the Response of ODCCP*, United Nations, Vienna, Austria, viewed June 18, 2006, http://www.unodc.org/pdf/afg/afg_drug-situation_2002-10-01_1.pdf

United Nations Office for Drug Control and Crime Prevention, 2002b, *Afghanistan Opium Survey 2002*, United Nations, Vienna, Austria, viewed September 28, 2006, http://www.unodc.org/pdf/afg/afg_opium_survey_2002.pdf

United Nations Office on Drugs and Crime, 2003a, *The Opium Economy in Afghanistan: An International Problem*, United Nations, Vienna, Austria, viewed June 20, 2006, http://www.unodc.org/pdf/publications/afg_opium_economy_www.pdf.

United Nations Office on Drugs and Crime, 2003b, *Afghanistan Opium Survey 2003*, United Nations, Vienna, Austria, viewed September 28, 2006, http://www.unodc.org/pdf/afg/afghanistan_opium_survey_2003.pdf.

United Nations Office on Drugs and Crime, 2003c, *Global Illicit Drug Trends 2003*, United Nations, Vienna, Austria, viewed September 30, 2006, http://www.unodc.org/unodc/en/data-and-analysis/global_illicit_drug_drug_trends.html.

United Nations Office on Drugs and Crime, 2004, "International Counter Narcotics Conference on Afghanistan." Held in Kabul, Afghanistan, February 8–9, viewed July 15, 2006, http://www.unodc.org/pdf/afg/afg_intl_counter_narcotics_conf_2004.pdf.

United Nations Office on Drugs and Crime, 2004a, *Afghanistan Opium Survey 2004*, United Nations, Vienna, Austria, viewed June 20, 2006, http://www.unodc.org/pdf/afg/afghanistan_opium_survey_2004.pdf.

United Nations Office on Drugs and Crime, 2004b, *Afghanistan Farmers' Intentions Survey 2003/2004*, United Nations, Vienna, Austria, viewed September 28, 2006, http://www.unodc.org/pdf/afg/afg_fis_report_2003-2004.pdf.

United Nations Office on Drugs and Crime, 2004c, *World Drug Report 2004*, United Nations, New York, NY, viewed June 23, 2006, http://www.unodc.org/unodc/en/data-and-analysis/WDR.html.

United Nations Office on Drugs and Crime, 2005a, *Afghanistan Opium Survey 2005*,
United Nations, Vienna, Austria, viewed June 20, 2006, http://www.unodc.org/pdf/afg/afg_survey_2005.pdf.

United Nations Office on Drugs and Crime, 2005b, *Summary Findings of Opium Trends in Afghanistan, 2005*, United Nations, Vienna, Austria, viewed August 20, 2007, http://www.unodc.org/pdf/afg/2005SummaryFindingsOfOpiumTrendsAfghanistan.pdf.

United Nations Office on Drugs and Crime, 2005c, *World Drug Report 2005*, United Nations, New York, NY, viewed June 23, 2006, http://www.unodc.org/unodc/en/data-and-analysis/WDR-2005.html.

United Nations Office on Drugs and Crime, 2006, *World Drug Report 2006*, United Nations, New York, NY, viewed January 10, 2007, http://www.unodc.org/pdf/WDR_2006/wdr2006_volume1.pdf.

United Nations Office on Drugs and Crime, 2007a, *Afghanistan Opium Survey 2007*, United Nations, Vienna, Austria, viewed March 24, 2010, http://www.unodc.org/documents/crop-monitoring/Afghanistan-Opium-Survey-2007.pdf.

United Nations Office on Drugs and Crime, 2007b, *Monitoring of Drug Flow in Afghanistan*, Illicit Crop Monitoring Program, United Nations, Kabul, Afghanistan, viewed April 24, 2010, http://www.unodc.org/documents/afghanistan//Counter_Narcotics/Drug_flow_final_report_SR.pdf.

United Nations Office on Drugs and Crime, 2007c, *World Drug Report 2007*, United Nations, New York, NY, viewed September 2, 2008, http://www.unodc.org/unodc/en/data-and-analysis/WDR-2007.html.

United Nations Office on Drugs and Crime, 2008, *Afghanistan Opium Survey 2008*, Executive Summary, United Nations, Vienna, Austria, viewed April 23, 2010, http://www.humansecuritygateway.com/documents/UNODC_Afghanistan_Opium_Survey_2008.pdf.

United Nations Office on Drugs and Crime, 2009a, *Addiction, Crime, and Insurgency: The Transnational Threat of Afghan Opium*, United Nations, Vienna, Austria, viewed February 5, 2010, http://www.unodc.org/documents/data-and-analysis/Afghanistan/Afghan_Opium_Trade_2009_web.pdf.

United Nations Office on Drugs and Crime, 2009b, *Afghanistan Opium Survey 2009, Summary Findings*, United Nations, Kabul, Afghanistan, viewed April 13, 2010, http://www.unodc.org/documents/crop-monitoring/Afghanistan/Afghanistan_opium_survey_2009_summary.pdf.

United Nations Office on Drugs and Crime, 2009c, *World Drug Report 2009*, United Nations, New York, NY, viewed May 2, 2010, http://www.unodc.org/documents/wdr/WDR_2009/Seizures_Tables.pdf.

United Nations Office on Drugs and Crime, 2010a, *Afghanistan Opium Survey 2010, Winter Rapid Assessment*, United Nations, Kabul, Afghanistan, viewed April 3, 2010, http://www.unodc.org/documents/research/Afghanistan_Opium_Survey_2010_Winter_Rapid_Assessment.pdf.

United Nations Office on Drugs and Crime, 2010b, *Corruption in Afghanistan*, United Nations, New York, NY, viewed March 3, 2010, http://www.unodc.org/documents/data-and-analysis/Afghanistan/Afghanistan-corruption-survey2010-Eng.pdf.

United Nations Office on Drugs and Crime, 2010c, *Promoting Health, Security and Justice*, United Nations, New York, NY, viewed April 8, 2010, http://www.unodc.org/documents/frontpage/UNODC_Annual_Report_2010_LowRes.pdf.

United Nations Office on Drugs and Crime, 2010d, *The Globalization of Crime: A Transnational Organized Crime Threat Assessment*, United Nations, Vienna, Austria, pp. 109–126; 243–256, viewed June 18, 2010, http://www.unodc.org/documents/data-and-analysis/tocta/TOCTA_Report_2010_low_res.pdf.

United Nations Office on Drugs and Crime, 2010e, *World Drug Report 2010*, United Nations, Vienna, Austria, viewed June 23, 2010, http://www.unodc.org/documents/wdr/WDR_2010/World_Drug_Report_2010_lo-res.pdf.

United Nations Security Council Resolution 1267, dated October 15, 1999, and UN Security Council Resolution 1333, dated December 18, 2000, viewed June 15, 2007, http://www.un.org/sc/committees/1267/index.shtml

United Nations Security Council Resolution 1267, dated October 15, 1999, "Monitoring Group Reports pursuant to Resolution 1267 concerning Al-Qaida and the Taliban and associated individuals and entities." January 15, 2002–May 14, 2008.

United Nations Security Council Resolution 1456, adopted by the Security Council at its 4688th meeting on January 20, 2003, viewed 15 June 2007, http://www.unhchr.ch/Huridocda/Huridoca.nsf/(Symbol)/S.RES.1456+(2003).En?Opendocument.

United Nations Security Council, Second Report of the Monitoring Group established pursuant to resolution 1363 (2001) and extended by resolutions 1390 (2002) and 1455 (2003), on sanctions against Al-Qaida, the Taliban and individuals and entities associated with them, viewed June 20, 2007, http://daccessdds.un.org/doc/UNDOC/GEN/N03/600/46/PDF/N0360046.pdf?OpenElement.

United States Attorney, Southern District of New York, 2005, "U.S. Arrests Afghan Drug Kingpin Aligned with the Taliban and Charges Him with Importing over $50 Million in Heroin." (Press Release), April 25, viewed June 28, 2005, http://www.usdoj.gov/usao/nys/pressreleases/April05/noorzaiindictmentpr.pdf.

United States Code, Title 22 of the Section 2656f (d)

United States Defense Intelligence Agency, 1983, *The Economic Impact of Soviet Involvement in Afghanistan*, report prepared by the Resources Division, Directorate for Research, Defense Intelligence Agency, Washington, DC.

United States Defense Intelligence Agency, 1998, "Osama bin Laden's Current and Historical Activities." Intelligence Information Report [declassified], released to *Judicial Watch, Inc.*, Washington, DC, October 30, 2004; posted November 16, 2004, viewed August 15, 2007, http://www.judicialwatch.org/cases/102/dia.pdf.

United States Department of Defense, 2001, *Department of Defense Dictionary of Military and Associated Terms*, Joint Publication 1–02 amended through June 9, 2004, p. 355.

U.S. Department of Homeland Security, 2009, *Global Terrorism Database*, National Consortium for the Study of Terrorism and Responses to Terrorism, University of Maryland, College Park, MD, available online at http://www.start.umd.edu/gtd/

United States Department of Justice, 2008, *The U.S. Department of Justice Announces Indictments of Members of FARC Drug Cartel*, (Press Release), issued March 22, viewed May 12, 2008, http://justice.gov/archive/ag/speeches/2006/ag_speech_0603221.html.

United States Department of State, 1994, *Patterns of Global Terrorism 1993*, U.S. Department of State, Washington, DC, p. 5, issued April 1, viewed August 22, 2007, http://www.fas.org/irp/threat/terror_93/index.html.

United States Department of State, 1995, *International Narcotics Control Strategy Report 1994*, (Southwest Asia; Afghanistan), released by the Bureau of International Narcotics Matters, U.S. Department of State, Washington, DC, viewed June 5, 2007, http://dosfan.lib.uic.edu/ERC/law/INC/1994/06.html.

United States Department of State, 1999, *Patterns of Global Terrorism 1998*, Office of the Coordinator for Counterterrorism, U.S. Department of State, Washington, DC, issued April 1, viewed January 6, 2006, http://www.state.gov/www/global/terrorism/1998Report/1998index.html.

United States Department of State, 2000, *Patterns of Global Terrorism 1999*, Office of the Coordinator for Counterterrorism, U.S. Department of State, Washington, DC, issued April 1, viewed January 5, 2006, http://www.loyola.edu/dept/politics/intel/terrorism/patterns1999.pdf.

United States Department of State, 2001a, *International Narcotics Control Strategy Report 2000*, (Southwest Asia; Afghanistan), Bureau for International Narcotics and Law Enforcement Affairs, U.S. Department of State, Washington, DC, issued March 1, viewed October 20, 2006, http://www.state.gov/p/inl/rls/nrcrpt/2000/940.htm.

United States Department of State, 2001b, *Patterns of Global Terrorism 2000*, Office of the Coordinator for Counterterrorism, U.S. Department of State, Washington, DC, issued April 1, viewed January 10, 2006, http://www.state.gov/s/ct/rls/crt/2000/; see also http://www.mipt.org/pdf/2000pogt.pdf.

United States Department of State, 2002a, "Executive Order 13224." Office of the Coordinator for Counterterrorism, U.S. Department of State, Washington, DC (Fact Sheet), December 20, viewed June 20, 2007, http://www.state.gov/s/ct/rls/fs/2002/16181.htm.

United States Department of State, 2002b, *International Narcotics Control Strategy Report 2001*, Bureau for International Narcotics and Law Enforcement Affairs, U.S. Department of State, Washington, DC, issued March 1.

United States Department of State, 2002c, *The Nexus Between Drug Trafficking and Terrorism*, Bureau for International Narcotics and Law Enforcement Affairs, U.S. Department of State, Washington, DC (Fact Sheet), issued April 10, 2002, viewed October 26, 2006, http://www.state.gov/p/inl/rls/fs/9242.htm.

United States Department of State, 2003a, "Chechen Terrorist Organizations: Statement of the Case." U.S. Department of State, Washington, DC, February 28, viewed August 16, 2007, http://www.peaceinthecaucasus.org/reports/paper_statedepartment.htm.

United States Department of State, 2003b, "Designation of Gulbuddin Hekmatyar as a Terrorist." Washington, DC, press release issued on February 19, viewed May 25, 2007, http://www.state.gov/r/pa/prs/ps/2003/17799.htm.

United States Department of State, 2003c, *Foreign Terrorist Organizations*, Office of the Coordinator for Counterterrorism, U.S. Department of State, Washington, DC,

(Fact Sheet), January 30, viewed May 25, 2007, http://www.state.gov/s/ct/rls/fs/2003/17067.htm.

United States Department of State, 2003d, *Patterns of Global Terrorism 2002*, Office of the Coordinator for Counterterrorism, U.S. Department of State, Washington, DC, issued April 2003, viewed January 12, 2006, http://www.state.gov/s/ct/rls/crt/2002/pdf/.

United States Department of State, 2004a, *International Narcotics Control Strategy Report 2003*, Bureau for International Narcotics and Law Enforcement Affairs, U.S. Department of State, Washington, DC, issued March 1, viewed October 20, 2006, http://www.state.gov/p/inl/rls/nrcrpt/2003/.

United States Department of State, 2004b, *International Narcotics Control Strategy Report 2003*, (Southwest Asia-Pakistan), Bureau for International Narcotics and Law Enforcement Affairs, U.S. Department of State, Washington, DC, issued March 1, viewed October 20, 2006, http://www.state.gov/p/inl/rls/nrcrpt/2003/vol1/html/29836.htm.

United States Department of State, 2004c, *Patterns of Global Terrorism 2003*, Office of the Coordinator for Counterterrorism, U.S. Department of State, Washington, DC, issued April 1, viewed January 5, 2006, http://www.state.gov/s/ct/rls/crt/2003/c12153.htm.

United States Department of State, 2004d, *Terrorism Exclusion List*, Office of the Coordinator for Counterterrorism, U.S. Department of State, Washington, DC, (Fact Sheet), December 29, viewed May 25, 2007, http://www.state.gov/s/ct/rls/fs/2004/32678.htm.

United States Department of State, 2005a, *Country Reports on Terrorism 2004*, Office of the Coordinator for Counterterrorism, U.S. Department of State, Washington DC, issued April 27, viewed January 12, 2006, http://www.state.gov/s/ct/rls/crt/c14813.htm.

United States Department of State, 2005b, *International Narcotics Control Strategy Report 2005*, (Southwest Asia-Pakistan), released by the Bureau for International Narcotics and Law Enforcement Affairs, U.S. Department of State, Washington, DC, issued March 1, viewed August 10, 2007, http://www.shaps.hawaii.edu/drugs/incsr2005/incsr_2005_pakistan.html.

United States Department of State, 2005c, *International Narcotics Control Strategy Report 2005, Volume 1: Drug and Chemical Control*, released by the Bureau for International Narcotics and Law Enforcement Affairs, U.S. Department of State, Washington, DC, issued March 1, viewed August 10, 2007, http://www.state.gov/p/inl/rls/nrcrpt/2005/.

United States Department of State, 2005d, *International Narcotics Control Strategy Report 2005, International Narcotics Control Strategy Report Vol. II: Money Laundering and Financial Crimes*, released by the Bureau for International Narcotics and Law Enforcement Affairs, U.S. Department of State, Washington, DC, issued March 1, viewed August 10, 2007, http://www.state.gov/documents/organization/42882.pdf.

United States Department of State, 2006a, *Country Reports on Terrorism 2005*, Office of the Coordinator for Counterterrorism, U.S. Department of State, Washington, DC issued in April, viewed June 15, 2006, http://www.state.gov/documents/organization/65462.pdf.

United States Department of State, 2006b, *Country Reports on Terrorism 2005*, "Foreign Terrorist Organizations." (Chapter 8), Office of the Coordinator for Counterterrorism, U.S. Department of State, Washington, DC, issued in April, viewed June 15, 2006, http://www.state.gov/s/ct/rls/crt/2005/65275.htm.

United States Department of State, 2006c, *Information for Travelers, Warden Message*, Embassy of the United States: Kabul, Afghanistan, issued January 9, viewed June 22, 2007, http://kabul.usembassy.gov/jan._9_2006.

United States Department of State, 2009a, *Country Reports on Terrorism 2008*, "Foreign Terrorist Organizations." (Chapter 6), Office of the Coordinator for Counterterrorism, U.S. Department of State, Washington, DC, issued in April, viewed April 6, 2010, http://www.state.gov/documents/organization/122599.pdf.

United States Department of State, 2009b, *International Narcotics Control Strategy Report 2008*, (Afghanistan), released by the Bureau of International Narcotics and Law Enforcement Affairs, U.S. Department of State, Washington, DC, issued February 27, viewed April 3, 2010, http://www.state.gov/p/inl/rls/nrcrpt/2009/.

United States Department of State, 2010a, *International Narcotics Control Strategy Report 2009*, (Afghanistan), released by the Bureau of International Narcotics and Law Enforcement Affairs, U.S. Department of State, Washington, DC, issued March 1, viewed June 6, 2010, http://www.state.gov/p/inl/rls/nrcrpt/2010/index.htm.

United States Department of State, 2010b, *Designations of Tehrik-e Taliban Pakistan and Two Senior Leaders*, released by the Bureau of Public Affairs, U.S. Department of State, Washington, DC, issued September 1, viewed September 3, 2010, http://www.state.gov/r/pa/prs/ps/2010/09/146545.htm.

United States Department of the Treasury, 2001a, *Specially Designated Global Terrorist (SDGT)* list, pp. 53, 73, and 100, viewed July 1, 2007, http://www.treas gov/offices/enforcement/ofac/sdn/t11sdn.pdf.

United States Department of the Treasury, 2001b, *What You Need To Know About U.S. Sanctions*, Office of Foreign Assets Control, U.S. Department of the Treasury, Washington, DC, September 23, viewed July 1, 2007, http://www.treas .gov/offices/enforcement/ofac/programs/terror/terror.pdf.

United States Department of the Treasury, 2002, *Recent OFAC Actions*, Office of Foreign Assets Control, U.S. Department of the Treasury, Washington, DC, July 3, viewed July 1, 2007, http://www.treas.gov/offices/enforcement/ofac/actions/20020703.shtml.

United States Department of the Treasury, 2003, "U.S. Designates Dawood Ibrahim as Terrorist Supporter." Press Release, October 16, viewed December 5, 2007, http://www.ustreas.gov/press/releases/js909.htm.

United States Department of the Treasury, 2006, *Terrorist Assets Report*, Office of Foreign Assets Control: Assets in the United States of Terrorist Countries and International Terrorism Program Designees (Fifteenth Annual Report to Congress), Washington, DC: U.S. Department of the Treasury, p. 6, footnote 8, viewed July 1, 2007, http://www.treasury.gov/offices/enforcement/ofac/reports/tar2006.pdf.

United States District Court, Eastern District of Virginia (Alexandria Division), 2002, TEXT: US GRAND JURY INDICTMENT AGAINST JOHN PHILLIP WALKER LINDH, a/k/a "Suleyman al-Faris," a/k/a "Abdul Hamid,"

February 5, Criminal No. 02–37A, Item 2, p. 3, viewed September 22, 2007, http://fl1.findlaw.com/news.findlaw.com/hdocs/docs/lindh/uswlindh-020502cmp.pdf.

United States District Court, Southern District of New York, 1998. November 6, viewed June 6, 2007, http://www.fas.org/irp/news/1998/11/indict1.pdf.

United States District Court, Southern District of New York, 2001a, *United States of America v. Usama bin Laden, et al.* Indictment 98 Cr., Day 2 (February 7, 2001); Jamal Ahmed Mohamed Al-Fadl-direct. pp. 348–411; see also Al-Fadl's testimony from day's 1, February 6, pp. 158–346 and 3, February 13, pp. 411–535, viewed 6 June 2007, http://cns.miis.edu/pubs/reports/pdfs/binladen/060201.pdf; http://cns.miis.edu/pubs/reports/pdfs/binladen/070201.pdf; http://cns.miis.edu/pubs/ reports/Âpdfs/binladen/130201.pdf.

United States District Court, Southern District of New York, 2001b, *United States of America vs. Usama bin Laden*, Indictment 98 Cr., Day 7, Jamal Ahmed Mohamed Al-Fadl under cross-examination, February 20, p. 1041; see also Al-Fadl's testimony from days 3, February 7, p. 357 and 4, February 13, p. 528, viewed June 6, 2007, http://cryptome.org/usa-v-ubl-dt.htm.

United States District Court, Southern District of New York, 2004, *World Trade Center Properties et al v. Al Baraka Investment and Development Corporation et al.*; Civil Action: Complaint No. 04–7280 (RCC) September 10, pp. 229–236, viewed June 8, 2007, http://fl1.findlaw.com/news.findlaw.com/hdocs/docs/terrorism/burnettba81502cmp.pdf.

United States District Court, Southern District of New York, 2005a, *United States of America v. Noorzai*, 05-CR-19, April 25, viewed April 15, 2007, http://www.house.gov/kirk/pdf/NorzaiIndictment.pdf.

United States District Court, Southern District of New York, 2005b, TEXT: US GRAND JURY INDICTMENT AGAINST Bashir Noorzai, a/k/a "Haji Bashir Noorzai," April 25, Sl 05 Cr. 19, Count 1, Item 4c, p. 3, viewed April 15, 2007, http://www.house.gov/kirk/pdf/NorzaiIndictment.pdf.

United States District Court Southern District of New York, 2005c, TEXT: US GRAND JURY INDICTMENT AGAINST Bashir Noorzai, a/k/a "Haji Bashir Noorzai," April 25, Sl 05 Cr. 19, Count 1, Item 5c, p.4, viewed April 15, 2007, http://www.house.gov/kirk/pdf/NorzaiIndictment.pdf.

United States District Court, Southern District of New York, 2005d; TEXT: US GRAND JURY INDICTMENT AGAINST Baz Mohammad, a/k/a "Haji Baz Mohammad," and Bashir Ahmad Rahmany, October 24, S14 03 Cr. 486 (DC), viewed March 17, 2008, http://www.investigativeproject.org/documents/case_docs/101.pdf.

United States District Court, Southern District of New York, 2005e, TEXT: US GRAND JURY INDICTMENT AGAINST Baz Mohammad, a/k/a "Haji Baz Mohammad," and Bashir Ahmad Rahmany, October 24, S14 03 Cr. 486 (DC), Count 1, Item 4c, p. 3, viewed March 17, 2008, http://www.investigative-project.org/documents/case_docs/101.pdf.

United States District Court, Southern District of New York, 2005f, TEXT: US GRAND JURY INDICTMENT AGAINST Baz Mohammad, a/k/a "Haji Baz Mohammad," and Bashir Ahmad Rahmany, October 24, S14 03 Cr. 486 (DC), Count 1, Item 5r, p. 7–8, viewed March 17, 2008, http://www.investigativeproject.org/documents/case_docs/101.pdf.

United States District Court, Southern District of New York, 2008, *United States of America v. Haji Juma Khan*, S1 08 Cr. 621, October 24, viewed April 15, 2010, http://www.justice.gov/usao/nys/pressreleases/October08/usvkhan-signedindictment.pdf.

United States Drug Enforcement Administration, 2001, *Afghanistan Country Brief-Drug Situation Report*, September 2001, viewed July 25, 2007, http://www.shaps.hawaii.edu/drugs/dea0901/dea0901.html.

United States Drug Enforcement Administration, 2005, *U.S. Extradites Taliban-Linked Narco-Terrorist*, (News Release) DEA Public Affairs, October 24, viewed February 22, 2008, http://www.dea.gov/pubs/pressrel/pr102405.html.

United States Drug Enforcement Administration, 2008, "Afghan Drug Kingpin Charged with Financing Taliban Terrorist Insurgency," press release, October 24, viewed November 15, 2009, http://www.justice.gov/usao/nys/pressreleases/October08/khanjumaindictmentpr.pdf.

United States Government Accountability Office, 1990, *Case Study Evaluations*, Program Evaluation and Methodology Division, GAO, Washington, DC, viewed June 13,2005, http://www.gao.gov/special.pubs/10_1_9.pdf.

United States Government Accountability Office, 2000, *Southwest Asia* (Afghanistan), *Heroin Production Estimates*, briefing paper prepared for the Senate Caucus on International Narcotics Control, GAO, Washington, DC, June 21, viewed October 28, 2006, http://www.gao.gov/archive/2000/os00012r.pdf.

United States Government Accountability Office, 2003, *U.S. Agencies Should Systematically Assess Terrorists' Use of Alternative Financing Mechanisms*, GAO-04-163, Report to Congressional Requesters, GAO, Washington, DC.

United States Government Accountability Office, 2006, *Afghanistan Drug Control: Despite Improved Efforts, Deteriorating Security Threatens Success of U.S. Goals*, GAO-07-78, Report to Congressional Committees, GAO, Washington, DC, viewed November 20, 2007, http://www.gao.gov/new.items/d0778.pdf.

United States Government Accountability Office, 2009, *Combating Terrorism: "U.S. Agencies Report Progress Countering Terrorism and Its Financing in Saudi Arabia, but Continued Focus on Counter Terrorism Financing Efforts Needed*, GAO-09-883, Report to Congressional Requesters, GAO, Washington, DC, September 30, pp. 33 and 40, viewed February 7, 2010, http://www.gao.gov/new.items/d09883.pdf.

United States Government Interagency Working Group, 2000, *International Crime Threat Assessment 2000*, Chapter 1, viewed November 12, 2006, http://clinton4.nara.gov/WH/EOP/NSC/html/documents/pub45270/pub45270chap1.html#1

United States Government Interagency Working Group, 2000, *International Crime Threat Assessment*, Chapter 3, viewed November 12, 2006, http://clinton4.nara.gov/WH/EOP/NSC/html/documents/pub45270/pub45270chap3.html.

United States House of Representatives, Committee on the Judiciary, Subcommittee on Crime, 2000, *Threat Posed by the Convergence of Organized Crime, Drug Trafficking, and Terrorism*, Washington, DC, December 13, viewed May 28, 2007, http://commdocs.house.gov/committees/judiciary/hju68324.000/hju68324_0f.htm.

United States House of Representatives, Committee on Financial Services, 2004, *The 9/11 Commission Report: Identifying and Preventing Terrorist Financing,*

Washington, DC, August 23, viewed transcript March 8, 2007, http://www.access.gpo.gov/congress/house/pdf/108hrg/96943.pdf.

United States House of Representatives, 2006, *Al-Qaeda: The Many Faces of an Islamist Extremist Threat*, report of the U.S. House Permanent Select Committee on Intelligence, viewed April 5, 2008, http://www.fas.org/irp/congress/2006_rpt/hrpt109-615.pdf.

United States Senate, Committee on Appropriations, Subcommittee on Foreign Operations, Export Financing and Related Programs, 1996, *International Crime, Terrorism, and Narcotics*, One Hundred Fourth Congress, Second Session: Special Hearing, U.S. Government Printing Office, Washington, DC.

United States Senate, Committee on Foreign Relations, 2009, *Afghanistan's Narco War: Breaking the Link Between Drug Traffickers and Insurgents*, A Report to the Committee on Foreign Relations, One Hundred Eleventh Congress, First Session, U.S. Government Printing Office, Washington, DC, August 10, viewed December 15, 2009, http://www.newsweek.com/media/5/Afghan-Narco-War.pdf

United States Senate, Committee on the Judiciary, 2003, *Narco-Terrorism: International Drug Trafficking and Terrorism—A Dangerous* Mix, One Hundred Eighth Congress, First Session, Washington, DC, May 20, viewed transcript April 2, 2007, http://www.au.af.mil/au/awc/awcgate/congress/narco_terror_20may03.pdf.

Uppsala University, 2003, Conflict Database (Kashmir Insurgency), Uppsala Conflict Data Program, Department of Peace and Conflict Research, viewed August 15, 2007, http://www.pcr.uu.se/database/.

Urban, M., 1990, *War in Afghanistan*, 2nd ed., St Martin's Press, New York, NY.

USA Today, 2007, "Bin Laden Tape Urges Pakistanis to Rebel." September 20, viewed November 17, 2007, http://www.usatoday.com/news/world/2007-09-20-al-qaeda-video_N.htm.

U.S. Legal, n.d., "Definitions and Legal Terms Defined," viewed September 9, 2006, and May 10, 2008, http://definitions.uslegal.com/.

U.S. News & World Report, 2005, "A Godfather's Lethal Mix of Business and Politics." November 27, viewed November 15, 2007, http://www.usnews.com/usnews/news/articles/051205/5terror.b.htm.

Vinocur, J., 1984, "Heroin Trade: Third World Cuts Out Marseilles." *New York Times*, March 22, p. A2.

Von Lampe, K., n.d., "Definitions of Organized Crime," viewed January 12, 2006, http://www.organized-crime.de/OCDEF1.htm.

Vora, B., 1994, "CIA Report Bares Drugs-Politics Nexus In Pak." *News India-Times*, Volume 24, Issue 6, February 11, p. 48.

Waldman, A., 2004, "Afghan Route to Prosperity: Grow Poppies," *New York Times*, April 10, p. A1.

Waldman, M., 2010, *The Sun in the Sky: The Relationship between Pakistan's ISI and Afghan Insurgents*, Crisis States Research Centre, DESTIN, LSE, London, UK, June 10, viewed July 7, 2010, http://www.crisisstates.com/download/dp/DP%2018.pdf.

Walia, V., 2006, "Opium trade transcends borders." *Tribune* (India), August 17, viewed December 12, 2006, http://www.tribuneindia.com/2006/20060817/aplus.htm.

Walsh, D., 2005, "In Afghanistan, Taliban Turning To The Drug Trade." *Boston Globe*, December 18, p. A42.

Walsh, D., 2008, "Flower power." *The Guardian*, August 16, viewed April 22, 2010, http://www.guardian.co.uk/lifeandstyle/2008/aug/16/drugstrade.afghanistan.

Walsh, D., 2010, "Taliban's leadership council runs Afghan war from Pakistan." *Guardian*, January 29, 2010, viewed April 1, 2010, http://www.guardian.co.uk/world/2010/jan/29/taliban-quetta-shura.

Ward, C., and Byrd, W., 2004, *Afghanistan's Opium Drug Economy*, World Bank (South Asia Poverty Reduction and Economic Management), Washington, DC, viewed January 10, 2006,. http://www-wds.worldbank.org/external/default/WDSContentServer/WDSP/IB/2005/01/06/000012009_20050106091108/Rendered/PDF/311490PAPER0AF100SASPR0no051Dec0171.pdf

Ward, D., 1995, "Gray Area Phenomena: The Changing Nature of Organized Crime and Terrorism." *Criminal Justice International*, Volume 11, Issue 2, pp. 16–21.

Washington Post, 2003, "Washington in Brief." compiled from reports by the Associated Press, December 30, p. A04.

Watson, P., 2005a, "World; Afghan Minister Who Denounced Corruption Quits." *Los Angeles Times*, September 28, p. A3.

Watson, P., 2005b, "Afghanistan: A Harvest of Despair; The Lure of Opium Wealth is a Potent Force in Afghanistan; Western Officials Warn of a Nascent Narco-state as Drug Traffickers act with Impunity, some Allegedly with the Support of Top Officials." *Los Angeles Times*, May 28, p. A1.

Weaver, M. A., 2002, *Pakistan: In the Shadow of Jihad and Afghanistan*, Farrar, Straus and Giroux, Union Square, West, NY.

Weekly Standard, 2005, "Ayman al-Zawahiri's letter to Abu Musab al-Zarqawi' (English translation), October 12, viewed June 15, 2007, http://www.weeklystandard.com/Content/Public/Articles/000/000/006/203gpuul.asp.

Weinberg, L., and Eubank, W., 2000, "Terrorism and the Shape of Things to Come." in *The Future of Terrorism*, eds. M. Taylor and J. Horgan, Routledge, New York, NY, pp. 94–105.

Weinberger, S., 2009, "Deaths Shine Light on DEA's Hidden War in Afghanistan." AOL News, November 4, viewed June 5, 2010, http://www.aolnews.com/article/deaths-shine-light-on-deas-hidden-war-in-afghanistan/19260578.

Weiser, B., 2001, "Witness Describes Break with Group Led by Bin Laden." *New York Times*, February 8, p. A1.

Weiser, B., 2008, "Manhattan jury convicts man linked to Taliban leader in drug smuggling case." *New York Times*, September 24, p. B4.

Weiser, B., 2009, "Afghan Linked to Taliban Sentenced to Life in Drug Trafficking Case." *New York Times*, May 1, p. A10.

Weldon, C. (R-Pennsylvania), 1999, U.S. House of Representatives Floor Speech, October 28.

White, J., 2006, "Rumsfeld arrives in Kabul after talks in Tajikistan." *Washington Post*, July 11, p. A14.

Whitlock, C., 2007, "The new al Qaeda central; far from declining, the network has rebuilt, with fresh faces and a vigorous media arm." *Washington Post*, September 9, p. A1.

Whitlock, C., 2009, "Diverse Sources Fund Insurgency in Afghanistan." *Washington Post*, September 27, p. A1.

Whitmore, B., 2001, "A new drug route is traced to the old Balkans anarchy." *Boston Globe*, June 3, p.14.

Wilder, A., 2007, *Cops or Robbers? The Struggle to Reform the Afghàn National Police*, Afghanistan Research and Evaluation Unit, issue paper series, viewed January 7, 2008, http://www.areu.org.af/.

Wilke, B., 2004, "State-Building in Afghanistan." German Institute for International and Security Affairs, SWP Research Paper, S 30, (English version), viewed May 29, 2007, http://www.swp-berlin.org/common/get_document.php?asset_id=1800.

Williams, B. G., 2007, "The Taliban Fedayeen: The World's Worst Suicide Bombers?' *Terrorism Monitor*, Volume 5, Issue 14, pp. 1–4, viewed June 22, 2007, http://www.jamestown.org/terrorism/news/uploads/TM_005_014.pdf.

Williams, P., 2002, "Strategy for a New World: Combating Terrorism and Transnational Organized Crime." in *Strategy in the Contemporary World: An Introduction to Strategic Studies*, 2nd ed., eds., J. Baylis, J. J. Wirtz, E. Cohen, and C. Gray, Oxford University Press, Oxford, UK., pp. 192–208, viewed chapter April 4, 2008, http://www.oup.com/uk/orc/bin/9780199289783/baylis_chap09.pdf.

Williams, P., 2003, "Criminalization and Stability in Central Asia and South Caucasus." In *Faultlines of Conflict in Central Asia and the South Caucasus*, eds., O. Oliker, and T. Szayna, RAND Corporation, Santa Monica, CA, pp. 71–107.

Williamson, H., and Burnett, V. 2004, "Terror link to booming Afghan drugs trade." *Financial Times* (London), April 3, p. 7.

Winchell, S. P., 2003, "Pakistan's ISI: The Invisible Government." *International Journal of Intelligence and CounterIntelligence*, Volume 16, Number 3, pp. 374–388.

Winer, J., 2003, Alston & Bird LLP 2003, *Terrorism Financing: Origination, Organization, and Prevention*, statement before the United States Senate Committee on Governmental Affairs, July 31, pp. 28–31, 110–130, viewed March 15, 2007, http://www.globalsecurity.org/security/library/congress/2003_h/030731-winer.htm.

Wiseman, P., 2006, "Revived Taliban waging full-blown insurgency." *USA Today*, June 20, viewed June 12, 2007, http://www.usatoday.com/news/world/2006-06-19-taliban-afghanistan-cover_x.htm.

Wolfe, A., 2004, "China's Xinjiang Region: An Area of Strategic Interest,'" *Power and Interest News Report*, September 16, viewed June 12, 2007, http://www.pinr.com/report.php?ac=view_printable&report_id=209&language_id=1.

Wong, M., 2002, "Three Wanted by U.S. Appear in Court." Associated Press, November 26.

Woodward, B., 2009, "McChrystal: More Forces or 'Mission Failure'." *Washington Post*, September 21, p. A1.

World Bank, 2004, *Afghanistan: State Building, Sustaining Growth, and Reducing Poverty* (A Country Economic Report No. 29551-AF). Washington, DC: World Bank, viewed June 10, 2007, http://www.cmi.no/pdf/?file=/afghanistan/doc/AfghanistanEconomicReportfinalversion909.pdf.

World Tribune, 2009, "GAO report: Saudis are top financiers of Taliban." October 5, viewed April 5, 2010, http://www.worldtribune.com/worldtribune/WTARC/2009/me_terror0777_10_05.asp.

WorldViews, 1997, *Struggles Unknown: Sudan and Western Sahara*, AFRICA: Africa World Press Guide, viewed December 2, 2007, http://worldviews.igc.org/awpguide/strugtwo.html

Worth, R., 2001, "The Deep Intellectual Roots of Islamic Terror." *New York Times*, October 13, p. A13.

Wright, J., 2006, "The changing structure of the Afghan opium trade." *Jane's Intelligence Review*, Volume 18, Number 9, pp. 6–14, viewed March 22, 2008, http://www.unodc.org/pdf/brazil/word_midia/JIR_09_p06_14_FOCUS_Afghan.pdf.

Yates, R. E., 1987, "Afghanistan Invasion Propels Pakistan to Top in Opium Trade." *Chicago Tribune*, February 12, p. 32.

Yegorov, Y., 2004, "IMU Regrouping Into New Movement." *Eurasia Daily Monitor*, Volume 1, Issue 19, May 27, viewed October 22, 2007, http://www.jamestown.org/publications_details php?volumc_id =40 1&issue_id =2966 & article_id=236776.

Yin, R. K., 1998, "The Abridged Version of Case Study Research: Design and Methods." in *Handbook of Applied Social Research Methods*, eds. L. Bickman and D. J. Rog, Sage Publications, Thousand Oaks, CA, pp. 229–259.

Yin, R. K., 2003, *Case Study Research: Design and Methods*, 3rd ed., Sage Publications, Thousand Oaks, CA.

Yin, R. K., 2004, "Case Study Methods." COSMOS Corporation, revised draft, October 1.

Yousaf, M. and Adkin, M., 2001, *Afghanistan: The Bear Trap*, 2nd ed., CASEMATE. Havertown, PA.

Zabriskie, P., 2003, "That Other War." *TIME*, August 31, viewed May 26, 2007, http://www.time.com/time/magazine/article/0,9171,1101030908-480227,00.html

Zakaria, F.,2004, "Warlords, Drugs and Votes." *Newsweek*, Volume 144, Issue 6, August 9, p. 39.

Zaqvi, Z. F., 1999, *Afghanistan-Pakistan Trade Relations*, World Bank, Islamabad.

Index

About the Author

FRANK SHANTY, Ph.D. is co-founder and Director of Research for the Cobra Institute, a terrorism and counterterrorism research firm in Abingdon, Maryland, USA. Dr. Shanty has co-authored two published studies on terrorism and has served as General Editor and contributing author on *Encyclopedia of World Terrorism*, Vol. 4 (M.E. Sharpe Publishers, Armonk, N.Y.) and *Organized Crime: From Trafficking to Terrorism* (ABC-CLIO Publishers, Santa Barbara, CA). Dr. Shanty has served as chief consultant and contributing author for *Mafia*, published by Millennium House Publishers in 2009.